# The Book of
# Minor Perverts

# The Book of Minor Perverts

*Sexology, Etiology, and
the Emergences of Sexuality*

BENJAMIN KAHAN

The University of Chicago Press   Chicago and London

The University of Chicago Press, Chicago 60637
The University of Chicago Press, Ltd., London
© 2019 by The University of Chicago
Published 2019
Printed in the United States of America

28  27  26  25  24  23  22  21  20      2  3  4  5

ISBN-13: 978-0-226-60781-8 (cloth)
ISBN-13: 978-0-226-60795-5 (paper)
ISBN-13: 978-0-226-60800-6 (e-book)
DOI: https://doi.org/10.7208/chicago/9780226608006.001.0001

Library of Congress Cataloging-in-Publication Data

Names: Kahan, Benjamin, author.
Title: The book of minor perverts : sexology, etiology, and the
    emergence of sexuality / Benjamin Kahan.
Description: Chicago : The University of Chicago Press, 2019. |
    Includes bibliographical references and index.
Identifiers: LCCN 2018033471 | ISBN 9780226607818 (cloth :
    alk. paper) | ISBN 9780226607955 (pbk. : alk. paper) |
    ISBN 9780226608006 (ebook)
Subjects: LCSH: Paraphilia. | Sexology.
Classification: LCC HQ71.K34 2019 | DDC 306.7—dc23
LC record available at https://lccn.loc.gov/2018033471

*For Madoka, my always*

# Contents

# Acknowledgments

Fittingly for a book about a multiplicity of origins, this project's beginnings are difficult to locate. It likely began in earnest when the incomparable Heather Love suggested that I read *Down and Out in Paris and London* and I found myself buoyed up and inspired in Philadelphia, enamored by Orwell's account of acquired sexuality and Heather's unfailing knack for pointing me in the right direction. Or perhaps it began much earlier when Julia Stern sensitized me to the language of etiology when she outlawed the use of the word "lifestyle" in her undergraduate classes (the significance of which I didn't fully understand). The happiness of these ever-proliferating beginnings has been sustained and amplified by the unending conversation, rambunctious laughter, and foodlust of many friends.

At LSU, I have been blessed with an uncommonly tranquil atmosphere for writing and thinking made possible by the warmest of colleagues: Dana Berkowitz, Elena Castro, Brannon Costello, Lara Glenum, Phil Maciak, Eric Mayer-Garcia, Rick Moreland, Pallavi Rastogi, Chris Rovee, Sharon Weltman, Sunny Yang, and Michelle Zerba. Ann Whitmer's omniscient institutional savvy has navigated me smoothly through many rough waters. My sheer glee at having an office next to Soli Otero no doubt echoes down the hallway and daily enriches my life on campus. Elsie Michie's generous spirit and theoretical acuity imbue many of these pages; I could not have a better senior colleague. Michael Bibler and Chris Barrett make my department feel like a home. My life would certainly be diminished if it were not for Michael's bigheartedness, humor, passion for gooey butter cake, and willingness to chat about queer theory. He is the quintessence of collegiality. Chris's room-illuminating smile, gusto, and intellectual panache have so often stirred me to reconnect with this project. Anyone who has been the recipient of her prodigious gifts of friendship—which is to say anyone who has met her—understands that there is no way to ever repay her. We all miss Lisi Oliver's zaniness and zest for living, which makes her passing all the more sorrowful.

An Early Career Fellowship at the University of Pittsburgh's Humanities Center afforded the opportunity for some of this project's earliest chapters to take shape. The intellectual frisson of meeting Julie Beaulieu, Randall Halle, Dan Morgan, and Todd Reeser provided a much-needed initial spark for writing. Jonathan Arac's gracious hospitality, mentorship, and infectious love of literature have touched many parts of this project. Gayle Rogers's zeal for modernism and interest in all things Havelock Ellis have made us friends for life and the happiest of interlocutors.

Most of this book was written at The United States Studies Centre at the University of Sydney on a Visiting Fellowship. There I was welcomed with open arms by Thomas Adams, Ivan Crozier, John Frow, Paul Giles, Michael Griffiths, Elizabeth Ingleson, Malcolm Jorgensen, Heather Murray, Aaron Nyerges, Matthew Sussman, Lee Wallace, and Matthew Wittman. Arriving on a continent where I didn't know anyone, Rodney Taveira and Sarah Gleeson-White made me feel that I was in the company of old friends. Annamarie Jagose introduced me to orange wine and improved my manuscript with her incisive comments and deep engagement. Melissa Hardie's and Kate Lilley's rollicking conversation and intellectual camaraderie have inspired this project many times over. Perhaps the best part of being in Australia was meeting Guy Davidson, whose steadfast friendship and brilliance made my life and this project much better.

I completed the initial draft of this book at the National Humanities Center with the support of the Delta Delta Delta Fellowship. The intellectual paradise of the Center—to say nothing of Tom Reed's positively divine peanut butter cookies—brought me many new friendships and serendipitous discoveries. I am especially grateful to have met Marlene Daut, Florence Dore, Laurent Dubois, Mary Floyd-Wilson, Kim Hall, Richard Mizelle, and Luise White. The most unanticipated pleasure, however, was sharing my time at the Center with my writing partner extraordinaire and previous fellowship-sharer, James Mulholland. James has been thinking and talking with me about this project for nearly a decade now, and its every sentence, paragraph, and chapter have been improved by the force of his intelligence, joviality, happy contrariness, and generosity. I cannot say how much I've benefited from both the extensiveness and intensiveness of his engagement. Finally, I am grateful to Robert Newman for his stewardship of the Center and to all of its staff, but particularly the world's best librarians: Brooke Andrade, Sarah Harris, and Joe Milillo.

I have never once lost interest in this project, and that is in large part due to the profound engagement and inspiration of a diffuse network of interlocutors and friends: GerShun Avilez, Tiffany Ball, Robert Caserio, Matt Cohen, Pete Coviello, Lee Edelman, Jonathan Flatley, Jennifer Fleissner, Julian Gill-Peterson, Jonathan Goldberg, Andrew Gustafson, Eric Hayot, Peter Jaros, Jonathan Ned Katz, Michael LeMahieu, Bill Maxwell, Melanie Micir, Michael Moon, Vivian Pollack, Gayle Rubin, Chris Tiffin, Shane Vogel, Kyle Wagner, Rebecca Walkowitz, Lynn Wardley, and Robyn Wiegman. Jeff Masten's boundless generosity and scholarly example have so thoroughly shaped my lexicon of scholarly possibility that I'd hardly know how to gloss a text without him. J. B. Capino introduced me to queer theory when I was an undergrad and his enduring mentorship continues to guide me. The keen advice and quick wit of Crystal Lake have provided both unwavering support for this project and frequent happy respites from it. Henry Abelove is easily the most charming man in New York City and embodies friendship as a way of life. He has given and given to this project, unsparingly offering his stunning intellect and his beneficence. Andy Gaedtke is a friend for all seasons, helping me think through perplexing theoretical quandaries when I was feeling most winter bound, ready with a quick smile and a joke, and always chilling the champagne in time for a celebration. There is not a better friend to be had in this world. The expansiveness and range of Josh Schuster's interests, his insatiable curiosity, and his love of shoptalk have provided hours of necessary, enthralling conversation. Rebecca Sheehan is a fireball of fun, making me roar with laughter, all the while furnishing this project with blinding insights. Joe Drury has a rare elective affinity (a high compliment in the vocabulary of this book) for my writing, able to attune himself and help me find articulacy better than anyone else. But even more than his uncommon editorial prowess, his inexhaustible kindness and exciting phone chat nurtures and sustains me on a near daily basis. Greta LaFleur is my co-conspirator in the natural and unnatural history of sexuality and her spirit of mischief and mirth has made many aspects of my life and this project better. Jane Funke selflessly lent me her synoptic knowledge of sexology, strengthening the entire manuscript in its final stages. The unmatched kindness of Paul Saint-Amour, his sheer goodness and brilliance, have cast their golden rays on many parts of this project, but especially its last chapter, which was prompted by his characteristically generous invitation to write about weak theory. Beth Freeman has been one of my most enthusiastic boosters and her rich engagement with this project in many forms over many years has been of inestimable assistance. Valerie Traub has seen this project with the farsightedness of binoculars, helping me to approach its most ambitious goals. Her thoughtfulness, thoroughness, attention to detail, and encyclopedic command of the field set a new standard of excellence that we should all aspire to.

This work has benefited enormously from the feedback, questions, consideration, and engagement of many audiences. I am grateful for the hospitality and kindness of Dan Novak, Dan Stout, Cristin Ellis, and Ari Friedlander at the University of Mississippi, which has become something of a second departmental home; Priscilla Wald at Duke; Michael Warner, Ian Cornelius, Cathy Nicholson, Caleb Smith, and Katie Trumpener at Yale; Stuart Christie and John Ernie at Hong Kong Baptist University; Sara Crangle and Natalia Cecire at the University of Sussex; Deak Nabers and especially Rick Rambuss and Chuck O'Boyle for welcoming me and hosting me with such style at Brown; Libby Otto, Jonathan David Katz, and Cristanne Miller at Buffalo; Monique Rooney at Australian National University; Simon Stern, Dana Seitler, and the people at the University of Toronto, Critical Analysis of Law Workshop; Katy Chiles, Gerard Cohen-Vrignaud, Patrick Grzanka, Ben Lee, and especially Lisi Schoenbach for making my visit to the University of Tennessee so dazzlingly fun; Matt Hart and Sarah Cole at Columbia University; Sean Pryor and the Centre for Modernism Studies in Australia at the University of New South Wales; John Lowe at the University of Georgia; and Lenny Cassuto and Jordan Stein for hosting me at Fordham on several occasions. I am particularly grateful to Masaaki and Iku Takeda for welcoming me at the University of Tokyo and for weaving me so heartfeltedly and ebulliently into the rhythm of their lives. I am indebted to Ali Behdad for inviting me to present at the Penny and Edward Kanner Forum on Literary and Cultural Studies at UCLA and to Michael Cohen, Carrie Hyde, and especially Chris Looby for enabling me to share my work with the famed Americanist Research Colloquium. Chris has been one of this project's most stalwart champions, and his fathomless generosity, love of archives, intellectual provocations, and sartorial flair have improved this project immeasurably. I feel fortunate to have gotten to know Debra Rae Cohen, Cat Keyser, Ed Madden, and Brian Glavey. Brian is the colleague that I always dreamed of meeting when I went into this profession: the one who inspires you, with whom you enthusiastically trade work and hurriedly share the latest discovery. Scott Herring not only inducted me into the secrets of the Kinsey Institute but has also been my consummate companion on three continents, gently and carefully guiding this project into its current form. He is, in short, the very soul of mentorship. Of the many gifts that he has bestowed, introducing me to Doug Mitchell—paragon of editors and prince of bon vivants—is undoubtedly the greatest. Doug has imagined this project with me in its boldest colors and added his pigments with the verve of a master painter. Having him as a fellow traveler and fellow dreamer has been an unspeakable blessing.

This book would not be possible without the effusive, effortless love of my parents. My dad's inveterate happiness and bottomless munificence have taught me to find joy in everything that I do and to give unstintingly to others, and I only hope to live up to his example. My mom's passion for words, puns, and other linguistic pleasures has passed on to me a love of writing, and her unflinching determination has given me the mettle to do it. Her second-to-none proofreading has saved me from innumerable mistakes and her vociferous encouragement has been the foundation upon which everything else is built. She is my lighthouse guiding me to safe harbor. My brothers and sisters-in-law have cocooned me in love, taken care of me in every way possible, and always made me laugh until I fell out of my chair. I'm grateful to my nieces Alma, Joanna, Lila, and Sophia and my nephew Elliott for all the hugs and questions that have served as a constant reminder that love and curiosity are the motor force of possibility.

Of the many happy surprises my recent marriage has brought, perhaps none has been so joyous as finding a second family as loving and magical as the one I've grown up with. Yasuko-san, Yoichi-san, Mizuki, Hiroaki, and Shizu-san have taught me that the deepest feeling is not constrained by language: love needs no translation. As I type these words I feel the strong clasp of Shizu-san's hand in my hand. I am inspired by Mizuki's breadth of learning about modern art, and the inventiveness of her scholarship motivates me to keep turning over new ideas. Yasuko-san's lyrical soul charges the surrounding world with a numinous electricity that daily expands my sense of the observable, of the dreamable, and of the beautiful. In her, I have found the dearest of friends and the most fascinating of conversationalists.

To say that this book of origins begins with its most devoted reader and dedicatee, Madoka, is literally true as her name greets the reader on its first page. We stand arm in arm at the entrance to this book, for we have shaped it together, reading draft after draft, side by side. We discussed, organized, polished, honed, reimagined, restructured, and recast every word, idea, and argument in this book together as a team. Her infinite love has taught me that the boundary between the congenital and acquired cannot be discerned, for all that I was and all that I am I have become with her. She is and has always been the origin of my happiness, my life, my love, my everything.

A version of chapter 1 appeared in *Criticism* in 2013. A version of chapter 5 appeared in *Modernism/modernity* in 2018. Portions of the introduction are contained in both of these pieces in addition to some parts of "Queer Modernism" in *A Handbook of Modernism Studies* (Wiley-Blackwell, 2013). A few paragraphs of my introduction, "The First Sexology?," to *Heinrich Kaan's "Psychopathia Sexualis" (1844): A Classic Text in the History of Sexuality*, appear in this book's afterword. I am grateful to the publishers for allowing me permission to reprint from these earlier publications. In addition to the aforementioned institutions, I would like to express my gratitude to the Harry Ransom Center for their Dorot Foundation Postdoctoral Research Fellowship in Jewish Studies, to the Sophia Smith Collection of Women's History, to the College of Physicians of Philadelphia for two Wood Institute travel grants, and to the Ruth Landes Memorial Research Fund at the Reed Foundation, all of which provided crucial material support in the research and writing of this project.

# Introduction

In the late nineteenth century sexologists fiercely debated a question crucial to homosexual rights and identity: namely, was homosexuality immutable, involuntary, inborn, and located in the body or was it mutable, voluntary, learned, and environmental?[1] In his *Contributions to the Etiology of Psychopathia Sexualis* (1902), the famed sexologist Iwan Bloch attempted to articulate the position that both male and female homosexuality are acquired rather than congenital in the strongest possible terms.[2] A partial list of the etiological influences that Bloch argued could lead to the development of male homosexuality included impotence, onanism, habitual alcohol consumption, opium indulgence, seduction, same-sex environments, warm climate, anal sex with women, wearing clothing of the opposite sex, looking in the mirror, celibacy, polygamy, religious belief, gonorrhea, flagellation, epilepsy, obscene literature and works of art, and the professions (deemed feminine) of actors, artists, landscape gardeners, decorators, cooks, hairdressers, ladies' tailors, and female impersonators. While Bloch's text is more encyclopedic in its detailing of etiological factors than those of many of his colleagues, none of these factors would have been considered anomalous to contemporary practitioners of sexual science (Benjamin Tarnowsky's *Pederasty in Europe* (1898), Auguste Forel's *The Sexual Question* (1905), and Edward Prime-Stevenson's *The Intersexes* (1908), for example, offer similar catalogs).[3] That is, many of these etiologies had already been put forward previously as conditions generating homosexuality and were understood

1

at the time as valid scientific arguments by sexologists. The sheer variety of Bloch's enumeration suggests the radical instability, unevenness, and messiness of the emergence of sexuality. Bloch's inventory of etiologies and those like it both generated and strove to understand inchoate conceptions of sexuality. Moreover, they were part of sexology's broader project to produce sexual knowledge and classify nonnormative sexual practices in order to shift sex away from the sphere of religious moral judgment.[4] This new sexual science helped judges and other members of the legal establishment to negotiate these seemingly new sexual acts and was instrumental in the formation of the new sexual subjectivities that we associate with modernism.[5]

*The Book of Minor Perverts: Sexology, Etiology, and the Emergences of Sexuality* contends that sexology's ever-multiplying enumeration of sexual causes both demands and provides the grounds for a new theory of sexuality: a historical etiology. A historical etiological approach recovers a multiplicity of patterns, models, and categories of sexuality, reconstructing their sites of production, tracing synchronic relations between sexual formations, and theorizing the contours of these sexualities by attending to accounts of their origins.[6] Instead of offering a causal narrative of (innate) homosexuality, my approach is etiological in the figural sense, providing an account of the concept of homosexuality by examining the forgotten intellectual systems and etiological assumptions from which it emerged. That is, rather than attempting to discover the etiology of homosexuality as Bloch and his contemporaries did, this book explores how specific etiological bases provide modalities for theorizing sexuality historically. In other words, I argue that these etiologies, which are often dismissed as homophobic or preposterous, record now (largely) vestigial models of sexuality.[7] Because this project understands the history of sexuality to be part of the history of science and aims to put the two disciplines more fully in dialogue, my account of the emergence of sexuality is necessarily provisional, nontotalizing, approximate, and open to adjustment and change (in the ways that historians of science have taught us to think about their objects).[8]

In addition to exploring these authoritative systems, this book's historical etiological approach is particularly interested in what Stephanie Foote calls, in another context, "vernacular sexology."[9] I repurpose Foote's term to describe the way that laypeople contest, define, and revise sexual subjectivity in relation to more official modes of sexology. As a field that "did not erect exclusionary credentials around its practice," sexology often eschewed expertise, putting "the narratives of the patients themselves center stage."[10] But rather than focusing on so-called "patient" narratives, this book theorizes sexology outside the clinic, reading literary texts as works of vernacular sexology. Mapping the interchange between vernacular and more official forms of sexology brings an important conceptual payoff: namely, understanding how these sexological categories were lived and experienced as well as produced. Take, for example, the modernist writer Djuna Barnes's famous statement "I'm not a lesbian, I just loved Thelma," referring to her longtime partner and fellow artist Thelma Wood.[11] Scholars generally read this declaration epistemologically: as a homophobic disavowal, as the result of Barnes's desire to resist the categorization of lesbianism, or even as patently false given her other female lovers.[12] However, I am interested in it as an etiological statement—how might Barnes be theorizing sexuality if we take her at her word? Such a sexuality's desiring field would not encompass a host of sexed bodies and objects, but a singular one. Sexual behaviors and acts performed with this singular object are unique, in no way indicating a pattern for future desires or pleasures. For Barnes, the object of desire *is* the cause of desire. In her telling, her love for Thelma is so great as to overcome both the social taboo of lesbianism and her alleged heterosexuality.[13] If Lauren Berlant has taught us that sexuality "is a set of patterns that align you to the world in a particular way," what surprisingly emerges in Barnes's account is a sexuality without patterns.[14] Given the expansiveness of Berlant's conceptualization of sexuality, Barnes's comment suggests that even our broadest theorizations of sexuality are too constrained.

As this reading has begun to suggest, this book theorizes a historical etiological method as an alternative to the epistemological approaches that play such a vital role in the field-imaginary of sexuality studies.[15] While obviously etiology is a kind of epistemology, my historical etiological approach reverses the polarity of sexuality studies, turning attention away from the effects of sexuality toward representations of its causes.[16] I argue that these etiologies carry not only the sediment of earlier sexual formations but also the genetic building blocks of modern sexuality. To put this differently, historical etiology is a crucial tool—if not *the* crucial tool—for periodizing and narrativizing what is variously referred to as the invention of sexuality, the birth of homosexuality, the formation of sexual subjectivity, the emergence of the homo/hetero binary, and more mockingly, in Eve Kosofsky Sedgwick's phrase, the "Great Paradigm Shift."[17] By the "Great Paradigm Shift," Sedgwick nominates the historical process by which "the gender of object choice" emerges as "*the* dimension" that provides sexuality with its basis for classification and definition.[18] At its broadest, this project seeks not to rationalize what Sedgwick calls "the unrationalized coexistence of different models" of sexuality, but to understand how their coexistence occurred.[19] To put this more plainly, I aim to show how an explosion of "unrationalized"—which is to say multiple and conflicting—explanations of sexuality came to exist simultaneously.

In order to examine this "unrationalized" field of sexuality, this book charts the relationship between acquired and congenital models of sexuality, arguing that congenital models are a catalyst for the coordination of the homo/hetero binary. Congenitality coordinates temporal (immutable), volitional (willful), and embodied (inborn) elements, occupying the body for biopolitical administration. This alignment enacts a double eclipse of, on the one hand, the acquired set of etiologies that Bloch and other sexologists enumerate, and on the other hand, the catalog of what Michel Foucault describes as "minor perverts" who fit "no order."[20] The biopolitical simplification and division of bodies into homo and hetero obscures and forecloses the possibility of "minor perverts." For Foucault these "thousand aberrant sexualities"—"zoophiles," "zooerasts," "auto-monosexualists," and many others now forgotten—constitute a speciation akin to that of the homosexual and embody the proliferation of discourse about sexuality.[21] Because Foucault focuses on the homosexual, he does not take up his own insight about the importance of the speciation of these minor perverts, instead exoticizing them as being "entomologized" with "strange baptismal names" and seeing them as the mere embodiments of the will to power.[22]

This book explores the meaning and value of this speciation, narrating the movement from a "thousand aberrant sexualities" to one: homosexuality. Foucault and much other sexuality studies scholarship typically perceives sexology as an inflection point for reverse discourse, in which homosexuality begins to speak on "its own behalf" instead of just understanding it to medically disqualify or pathologize.[23] I build on this insight to contend that this multiplicity of etiologies and "the numberless family of perverts" created by them also provide us with a new set of sexual coordinates and help us to see the formation of and competition between different models of sexuality.[24] That is, etiology enables us to narrate how the gender of object choice emerged as sexuality's dominant grammar.

While Sedgwick posits that "the gender of object choice" emerges as "*the* dimension denoted by the now ubiquitous category of 'sexual orientation,'" she is curiously reticent about how the division of humanity into the species of homo and hetero transpires.[25] She writes: *"Epistemology of the Closet* does not have an explanation to offer for this sudden, radical condensation of sexual categories; instead of speculating on its causes, the book explores its unpredictably varied and acute implications and consequences."[26] While Sedgwick's catalogs ordinarily exceed even the expansiveness of the Whitmanian, here, uncharacteristically, she doesn't strive to proliferate the categories being radically condensed. Instead, she suggests only that the development of object choice would not "have been foreseen from the viewpoint of the fin de siècle itself, where a rich stew of male algolagnia, child-love, and autoeroticism, to mention no more of its components, seemed to have as indicative a relation as did homosexuality to . . . sexual 'perversion.'"[27] Sedgwick's abdication of mentioning the components of the sexual domain—the ingredients of her "rich stew"—indexes precisely what is lost in queer theory's eschewal of etiology: namely, that we do not yet have a narrative of how object choice became the defining attribute of modern sexuality.[28] Constructing such a narrative promises to add to our sense of what other possibilities might have organized sexuality (or kept it from concretization at all), some of which have been so lushly charted by scholars like Hortense J. Spillers, Saidiya V. Hartman, Mark Rifkin, Elizabeth Freeman, Christopher Looby, and Peter Coviello.[29] Responding to the proliferation of sexual classifications and taxonomies at the turn of the twentieth century, I consider how narratives of sexual causality (offered by the sexual subjects themselves or narrativized for them) stabilize the emerging homo/hetero binary or provide errant models and organizations of sexuality. I am thus interested in both the models of sexuality that etiologies provide and the ways that etiologies narrate the history of the emergence of the homo/hetero binary. Because both etiologies and narratives of the emergence of sexuality are verboten objects of analysis for Sedgwick, this book engages in a sustained exploration of her work and thought in order to understand its impact on the formation of the field.

## Epistemology, Etiology, and Doing the History of Sexuality

In order to understand how an etiological approach differs from and, as I will argue, is constitutively excluded from an epistemological approach, I want to briefly summarize the nature of epistemological inquiry into sexuality.[30] While Sedgwick coins the term "epistemology of the closet" in the title of her 1990 book, she never exactly spells out what she means by it. I will argue that the epistemology of the closet actually names three imbricated processes:

1. It describes the way that sexuality is conflated with or comes to mean secrecy, privacy, and knowledge *tout court*, and thus locates sexuality at the center of modern subjectivity.
2. It describes the effects of homophobia (hence the term "closet") on "many of the major nodes of thought and knowledge in twentieth-century Western culture."[31]
3. It describes the negotiations of sexual knowledge, ignorance, opacity, and translucency in everyday life, what Lee Edelman calls "the social relations of knowledge."[32]

The first of these operations transforms the phrase "epistemology of the closet" into a tautology, arguing that the study of knowledge is the study of sexuality and vice versa.[33] Here, Sedgwick suggests that the performative power of knowledge and its twin sexuality—which is to say what they make happen and how—exposes all men to the universalizing, homophobic effects that she calls *"the homosexual question."*[34] By the homosexual question, Sedgwick means that because homosexuality is not precisely defined, men of all stripes are vulnerable to the "homophobic impulses" and exploitations of the closet, constructing their subjectivities in and through the closet's interrogative.[35] In the second operation, Sedgwick charts the entwinement of sexuality and knowledge-making in modernity. In particular, she examines homophobia's distorting impact on knowledge production, contending that knowledge is "structured by particular opacities."[36] These opacities take many forms—suppression, fear, reticence, politeness, etc.—but they also emerge from what Henry Abelove calls the "discomfiting dual feeling" that deductions and observations related to sexual knowledge—which is to say in Sedgwick's terms all deductions and observations—are both "too bizarre to be cogent" and "too obvious to be worth seeing and saying."[37] That is, this dual feeling prevents questions from being asked and answered, inhibiting and structuring knowledge fields. These impediments and organizations of knowledge bring us to the third intertwined operation of the epistemology of the closet, the quotidian negotiation of social relations between people and the way that such acknowledgments or eschewals of knowledge can license both vulnerabilities and kindnesses. For example, Sedgwick describes a man and a woman who freely canvas "the emotional complications

of each other's erotic lives," but "only after one particular conversa-
tional moment," a decade into their relationship, the friends felt "that
permission had been given to the woman to refer to the man . . . as *a
gay man*."[38] As this example suggests, the avowal or disavowal of sexual
knowledge can be alternatively cutting, affirming, or both.[39]

While Sedgwick understands sexual knowledge to be characterized
by ineluctable "opacity, obscurity, obstruction, and impasse," Marlon
Ross sees an unnamed and unanalyzed opacity at the heart of Sedgwick's epistemological project: namely "racial ideology."[40] His brilliant
essay "Beyond the Closet as Raceless Paradigm" (2005) argues that black
subjects are constitutively excluded from epistemological inquiry:

[T]he penchant for "epistemology" itself derives from a universalizing project that
covers up the racial ideology at work in constructing the psychological depth of
certain individual subjects (the minority of elite European males) constantly frus-
trated by their ideal objects of desire. Primitives, savages, the poor, and those un-
educated in the long history of epistemology are not normally represented as epistemological subjects. . . .[41]

Here, Ross contends that because racialized subjects ("primitives, savages") are not understood to be fully human under the project of enlightenment, they lack the interiority, "psychological depth," and
secrets that are the mainstay of sexuality studies' epistemological analysis and thus are excluded from such analysis.[42] Ross's critique sets the
parameters for my project. In particular, his incisive claim that sexology as an epistemological discourse is predicated on "racial sameness"
between "white sexologists" and white subjects in order to see sexual
difference (otherwise such sexual behavior would be attributed to racial difference) cautions me to delimit my claims about sexuality primarily to the white subjects that are the (nearly exclusive) objects of
Western sexological case histories.[43] Sexology does extend its purview
beyond these case histories in the form of sexual anthropology, but
these ethnologies take the form of less individuated lives, what he calls
*"mass"* lives (which explains why they do not appear in case studies).[44]
Ross's claims implicitly suggest why an epistemological approach has
excluded etiology; in its methodological focus on fully formed subjects,
sexuality studies as a field has not adequately examined the discourses
that forged sexual personhood, that performed the work of what Ian
Hacking calls "making up people."[45] This has meant both the exclusion
of racialized subjects as not fully human, as not people, but also the
exclusion of acquired sexual practices and minor perversions that have

not crystallized into varieties of personhood or come to be understood as congenital and biologized. Instead, my etiological approach attends to the ways that the multiplication of etiologies is uneven, coagulating around a handful of categories (male and female homosexuality, inversion, sadism, masochism, fetishism, and autoeroticism) that take shape in relation to a much wider field of minor perversions (for example, bestiality, kleptomania, nymphomania, necrophilia, dendrophilia, genius, sex with statues, etc.).[46] One of the contentions of this book is that understanding these central perversions in relation to their minor cousins will enrich our understanding of both by bringing into focus the ways that congenital homosexuality simultaneously effaces acquired etiologies and minor perverts.

My etiological approach calls for a sustained engagement with sexology as this sexual science puzzles, grapples, and strives to understand and categorize people. Too often the flowering of sexology in the latter third of the nineteenth century or the Oscar Wilde trials are said to stabilize the array of sexual possibilities. To take a representative and important example, Peter Coviello writes of "all that might have been lost at the close of the nineteenth century, all the errant possibilities for imagining sex that have sunk into a kind of muteness with the advent of modern sexuality."[47] While an etiological approach shares Coviello's desire to make these sexualities speak or, as Christopher Looby has beautifully put it, to animate these now "defunct sexualities," Coviello's suggestion that this muteness falls on the multiplicity of sexual models "at the close of the nineteenth century" seems all too early to me.[48] That is, next to the kind of "earliness" that Coviello brilliantly theorizes, an etiological approach posits a lateness of sexuality—one that is manifestly interested in the cast of minor perverts that stick around after the initial tentative articulations of the homo/hetero divide and in the kinds of proliferating sexual models that emerge as sexology conceptualizes and categorizes varieties of personhood. This lateness nominates the long process of coordination and solidification as sexuality congeals unevenly into the homo/hetero binary. In sum, sexology doesn't make the homosexual in any simple way; it posits, essays, theorizes, condenses, builds on, forges, debates, explores, and is baffled by a vast number of existing and new sexual formations and subjectivities and models. These models offer innumerable possibilities for tracing the history of sexuality as it fashions the homo/hetero binary and for tracing all the ways that it doesn't.

I have been arguing that queer theory has been remarkably incurious about etiology, and with good reason. Queer studies has not broached the subject of sexual etiologies chiefly because many of the legal rights and protections afforded gay Americans turn on the thorny legal question of equal protection: is homosexuality an "immutable characteristic"?[49] Because conferral of this designation would make gay people eligible for special protection, queer theory has been hesitant to discuss the fraught etiological history of sexuality.[50] Challenging this prohibition, this book sets out from the provocative position that we've forgotten half the history of sexuality. I mean half here to signify both historically (the history of sexuality in the chronological period from roughly 1844 to 1948) and etiologically, as in half of the fiercely contested debate in literature and sexology about whether sexuality is congenital or acquired.[51] This erasure of acquired models of sexuality has kept us from understanding this period's most lively debate in the history of sexuality and thus has obscured our ability to see the period at all. That is, in the service of a goal about which Michael Warner has taught us to be skeptical—namely, securing a rights-based normalization of gayness—we have strategically forgotten the longstanding and hard fought debate about the etiological status of sexuality.[52]

Sedgwick exemplifies such wariness in relation to etiological approaches; she states: "gay-affirmative work does well when it aims to minimize its reliance on any particular account of the origin of sexual preference and identity in individuals."[53] In particular, she fears that accounts of gay ontogeny are not easily divorced from "gay-genocidal nexuses of thought."[54] Similarly, David Halperin asserts that "the search for a 'scientific' aetiology of sexual orientation is itself a homophobic project" akin to describing "in genetic terms the capacities of the various human races."[55] Valerie Rohy's *Lost Causes: Narrative, Etiology, and Queer Theory* (2015) offers the most sustained engagement with the question of etiology, asserting that "the structuring role of etiology in today's discussions of civil rights is fundamentally homophobic, *whatever causality is claimed*."[56] Rohy's book makes a double gesture: on the one hand, she attacks the "liberal orthodoxy" of biologically determined and innate homosexuality ("born gay") as foreclosing a world where homosexuality is desirable, necessary, thinkable, and freely chosen; and on the other, she asserts that such choice is impossible (even as we must "demand our notational right to choose queerness") because we cannot distinguish between cause and effect, choose our desires, or act as free subjects.[57] Rohy dismisses etiology, arguing that it "will never yield equality" and that etiological positions ranging from the putatively pro-gay to antigay "share a heteronormative ideology."[58] She sees etiology—as her title puts it—as a "lost cause" and those who pursue its politics as misguided.[59] While I admire her inventive reading of causality as retrospective and retroactive, this dislodging and reversing of etiology's temporality ends up emptying etiology of its causal power, transforming every cause into a lost cause.[60] Her interest in lost causes leads her to shift away from "the question of *what causes homosexuality*" to "that of *what homosexuality causes*."[61] In contrast, my book will be concerned precisely with the causative force of etiology (rather than what I take to be Rohy's interest in effects), detailing the "plural" and "multi-capillaried" historical models of sexuality that etiology offers for theorizing sex and the broader domain of sexuality that these models make manifest.[62] Moreover, this book strongly disagrees with her contentions about etiology and the "harm[fulness]" of sexology, finding in etiology a much more affirmative sense of potentialities and discovering in sexology what Coviello might call errant, unlikely, extravagant, and unyarded models of sexuality.[63]

Let me be clear: I have no interest in deciding whether homosexuality is either congenital or acquired, nor am I interested in reaffirming sexological conclusions about etiology. Instead, my project aims to chart a historical, scientific, and political debate without regard to the "truth" of either the congenital or acquired position.[64] Thus, my historical etiological approach seeks to divorce etiology from the will to truth and its accompanying diagnostic certitude, illusions of objectivity, and pathologization. Rather, I want to retain etiology's cataloging energies and narrative capacities, particularly its ability to register the contingent and specific conditions of sexuality's production. I aim, thus, to forge a weak theory of etiology that finds the scientistic logic of taxonomy to play an important role in the construction of individuals' sexual lives and self-conceptions, without etiological nosographies being wholly determinative on the one hand, or having no impact on the other. In this way, I hope to sidestep the force of Sedgwick's, Halperin's, and Rohy's objections and to offer historical etiology as a tool for recasting the recent methodological debate in queer studies that asks "how to do the history of homosexuality."[65]

This methodological inquiry begins with a debate over the Great Paradigm Shift—whether it is possible and/or desirable to historicize the emergence of the homo/hetero divide. Sedgwick expresses two intertwined concerns about attempting to locate this historical emergence. First, she worries that it will inadvertently "*refamiliarize*," "*re-naturalize*," and "damagingly reify" "'homosexuality as we know it today,'" thereby obscuring "the present conditions of sexual identity."[66] Second, she fears that this calcification of the present installs alterity and supersession as the historiographical paradigm of the history of sexuality (rather than gradualism and change with coinciding and co-extensive sexual formations). In response to these important concerns, this project returns to a moment when scientists, writers, scholars, and sexologists were undecided about whether sexuality was congenital or acquired. I do so in order to shift sexual historiography away from what Valerie Traub calls "whole-scale diachronic change" toward "a manifestation of ongoing synchronic tensions in conceptualizations about bodies and desires."[67] Attending to lateral and horizontal competition between sexual models, I share Traub's and Sedgwick's skepticism about the singularity of the invention of sexuality. Instead, I read Sedgwick against the grain to posit a series of shifts (rather than one Great One) over more than three hundred years in order to capture the definitional incoherence of homosexuality even as I focus on the dawn of the twentieth century. By recovering and deploying the wide variety of period conceptions of sexuality, this book foregrounds dynamism and contestation in order to reconsider the emergence and transformation of synchronic and overlapping models of sexuality at the beginning of the twentieth century. A historical etiological approach thus proffers a genealogy of sexuality. However, where Foucauldian genealogy "opposes itself to the search for 'origins,'" a historical etiological approach includes narratives of origins as one element or force within what Foucault calls "the singular randomness of events."[68]

Not everyone, of course, has heeded Sedgwick's injunction against diachronic change. In the wake of Foucault, George Chauncey and David Halperin come closest to offering narratives of the Great Paradigm Shift. Chauncey claims that "gender status superseded homosexual interest as the basis of sexual classification in working-class culture" until World War II.[69] While he does not offer an explanation as to how homosexual interest (by which he means sexual interest in same-sex object choice) became the basis of classification after World War II, he does explain how object choice came to dominate middle-class culture. In the gendered construction of sexuality, men distinguish "themselves from boys," but by the late nineteenth century they move "to define themselves more centrally on the basis of their difference from women."[70] This shift from manhood to masculinity occurs because the manliness of middle-class men was besieged by three groups: women, working-class men, and queers and fairies.[71] Entering the workplace in greater numbers, struggling for and eventually winning suffrage, campaigning against the "manly entertainments" of boxing, prostitution, and alcohol, women "seemed to be breaching the division between the sexes' proper spheres and to be claiming or challenging the pre-rogatives of men" on virtually every front.[72] Likewise, the rough and tumble masculinity of working-class men and their growing political power in the labor movement and at the ballot box called into question the more sedentary masculinity of middle-class men. Middle-class men tried to restore this lost masculinity in many ways—for example, through bodybuilding and hunting and founding institutions that combated "overcivilization" like the Boy Scouts of America. But in terms of understanding how sexuality shifted from a gender-based system to an object-based system, no figure is as important as the fairie and the femininity and gender instability that he represented. The fairie assured men of their masculinity, confirming their normality (here the fairie is a minoritized figure segregated from the "normal" man). But the fairie also functioned as "the repository of their deepest fears" (here the fairie is a potentially universalizing position that any man can occupy), suggesting that in terms of gender men are not necessarily different or not that different from women.[73] Sex (*pace* Judith Butler) seemed to provide a more stable ground than gender on which to articulate masculinity; the desire for men could be confined to the fairie and to women, while the desire for women ("exclusive heterosexuality") could provide "a new, more positive way to demonstrate" manhood.[74] That is, heterosexuality disenfranchises the fairie from masculinity and thus from maleness.

Chauncey's account of the shift from an emphasis on manhood to an emphasis on masculinity dovetails with Halperin's claim that "something very significant happened when sexual object-choice became in the course of the twentieth century, at least in some social worlds, an overriding marker of sexual difference. That is an event whose impact and whose scope we are only now learning how to measure."[75] In other words, Halperin attempts to explain what Sedgwick calls the "radical and irreducible incoherence" resulting from "the unrationalized co-existence of different models" of sexuality.[76] He hypothesizes that the incoherence results from our retention of "at least four pre-homosexual models of male sexual and gender deviance, all of which derive from an age-old system that privileges gender over sexuality, alongside of (and despite their flagrant conflict with) a newer homosexual model derived from a more recent, comparatively anomalous system that privileges sexuality over gender."[77] These four models—effeminacy, "active" sodomy, friendship, and inversion—have been "obscured *but not superseded*" by homosexuality.[78] Halperin's emphasis on the "cumulative process of historical overlay and accretion" helps to make visible the diachronic tensions of sexuality, accounting for some of what Sedgwick calls the "overlapping, contradictory, and conflictual defini-tional forces" of homosexuality.[79] But in his emphasis on the "consis-tency" and "particularity" of these models, Halperin underestimates the "synchronic tensions" within homosexuality and within his "pre-homosexual models" that etiology makes visible, particularly the ten-sions between acquired and congenital models of sexuality.[80]

In order to get a sense of these synchronic tensions one need only look at the sexological terminology of male homosexuality: homosexu-alism, similisexualism, unisexuality, Urningthum, Uranian, inversion, philarrhenic nature, antipathic sexual instinct, Adhesiveness, contrary sexual feeling, reverse sexual instinct, psychosexual hermaphroditism, pederasty, man-manly love, Socratic love, homogenic love, and even lesbian love (all could be used to describe male-male sexual relations).[81] The list of terms for female homosexuality is similarly expansive and repurposes older terms like lesbian love, tribadism, tribadic love, trib-ady, Sapphism, and sapphic love and older figures like frictrices, fric-tionists, hetairistriae, dietairistriae, and the subagitatrix.[82] But sexology also conjures new terms for lesbianism—feminine homosexuality, fe-male homosexuality, female uranism, unisexuality, woman-womanly love, inversion, Adhesiveness—and new figures: the lady lover, the urninde, the female Urning, and the Urningin.[83] While these lists could no doubt be expanded, they provide a sense of the definitional instability of sexological conceptions of same-sex desire. Such instabil-ity would only be supplemented by including a similar catalog of ver-nacular terms.

Spelling out the messiness of homosexuality's definitional incoher-ence across a range of sciences and disciplines, Dana Seitler's "Queer Physiognomies; Or, How Many Ways Can We Do the History of Sexual-ity?" (2004) contends that these scientific discourses do not provide "a stable site of power/knowledge production for homosexual identity."[84] Instead, she suggests that "the unstable proliferation of the definitions and embodiments of perversity ultimately render the perverse body a hybrid and indeterminate one, formulating the variables of perver-sion into an unmanageable figure—a multiply produced, polyvalently diseased, indistinct image—thus calling into question the stability of sexual visibility itself."[85] As this quotation and Seitler's eponymous fo-cus on "physiognomies" suggest, she is interested in the visuality of perverse bodies.

Where Seitler sees these perverse bodies as figures of opacity within the history of sexuality, I am interested in understanding them as aris-

ing from a set of etiological assumptions. Over the course of the nineteenth century, as Harry Oosterhuis contends, "mental and nervous
disorders" shifted from being understood somatically as "the *result* of
'unnatural' acts" to being perceived psychiatrically as "the *cause* of
sexual aberrations," thereby effecting "a fundamental change in the
meaning of sexuality."[86] One implication of Oosterhuis's argument is
that a shift in the etiological underpinning of mental and nervous disorders produces sexual subjectivity (a topic I will explore in chapter 3).
This invention of subjectivity locates sexuality both inside and outside the confines of the body. Moreover, I contend that the competition
between etiologies, somatic and psychiatric, acquired and congenital,
produces the synchronic tensions in sexual definition. Recovering
these now vestigial models and perverse bodies enables us to trace the
development of the Great Paradigm Shift and, in so doing, etiology
massively expands what Coviello calls "the very *domain* of sexuality."[87]

### A *Temporary* Aberration?

In order to undertake this project, this book focuses on the opposition between congenital and acquired bases for sexuality in the period
between Carl Westphal's "Contrary Sexual Feeling" (1870) and Alfred
Kinsey's *Sexual Behavior in the Human Male* (1948).[88] In this historical moment homosexuality was understood as much as a habit, vice,
and addiction as a kind of personhood. Beginning with the case of
male homosexuality, I argue that the chronology of acquired modes
of sexuality that I propose differs markedly from those offered by historians. Robert Beachy describes Richard von Krafft-Ebing's view that
homosexuality was "an innate and largely fixed sexual orientation" as
"representative."[89] He then writes: "There were exceptions, of course.
The Munich psychiatrist Albert von Schrenck-Notzing viewed same-
sex eroticism as a perversion that might be cured through hypnosis
and suggestion. The distinguished Berlin psychiatrist Albert Moll—
while rejecting Krafft-Ebing's theory of degeneration—was hesitant to
view same-sex love as unambiguously congenital . . . Of course, Freud
launched his own theory with the publication of *Three Essays on the
Theory of Sexuality* in 1905 . . ."[90] This account, as I hope to show, dramatically underestimates the importance of acquired sexuality to the
history of sexology. Likewise, Jennifer Terry's *An American Obsession*
(1999) outlines three "etiological frameworks" for medicalized homosexuality: naturalists who understand homosexuality as "a benign

but inborn anomaly," degenerationists who understand homosexuals to "suffer from an inborn constitutional defect," and "psychogenists" who "regarded homosexuality as a psychogenically caused outcome of early childhood experiences."[91] Astoundingly, Terry's history leaves virtually no room for the models of acquired sexuality. While Terry's psychogenetic model is open to modes of acquisition in the form of "early childhood experiences," the confinement of these modes to childhood enormously restricts the domain of sexuality and is inadequate to the sexological literature. My account also flatly contradicts John D'Emilio's chronology, which stands as one of the few accounts of acquired sexuality: "From the late nineteenth century through the 1920s, congenital explanations dominated scientific inquiry. 'Contrary sexual instinct,' said the scientists, was hereditary and inborn. But scientists were at a loss to prove these assertions and, as Freudian theory became more influential, environmental theories of origins took hold."[92] Contra Beachy, Terry, and D'Emilio, I will contend that congenitality and acquisition stand on equal footing into the 1930s. I argue that the sexological production of congenitality crucially enables the implantation of sexuality in the body and thus plays a key role in the "radical condensation of sexual categories" into homo- and heterosexuality.[93] The demise of acquired modes of sexuality that I chart in this book therefore enables the conflation of the history of sexuality and the history of congenitality (though importantly not the history of sex). To put this differently, the intertwined conceptions of sexual inversion (primarily associated with congenitality and gender deviance) and homosexuality (primarily associated with acquisition and object choice) become increasingly fused as a congenital notion of object choice emerges under the name homosexuality.[94] While we know that "sexuality represents a seizure of the body by a historically unique apparatus for producing historically specific forms of subjectivity," I contend that the temporality of congenitality—its implicit "always"—produces the body as an especially productive site for sexual identity.[95] That is, congenitality helps to consolidate the operation of biopower.

In what is undoubtedly the most famous account of the formation of the homo/hetero divide and its relation to acquisition and congenitality, Michel Foucault notes sexology's constitutive role:

The nineteenth-century homosexual became a personage, a past, a case history, and a childhood, in addition to being a type of life, a life form, and a morphology, with an indiscreet anatomy and possibly a mysterious physiology. . . . Homosexuality appeared as one of the forms of sexuality when it was transposed from the practice of sodomy onto a kind of interior androgyny, a hermaphrodism of the soul. The sodomite had been a temporary aberration; the homosexual was now a species.[96]

While Foucault dates this speciation to 1870, historians and theorists of sexuality have dated it earlier, pointing to Ulrichs's coinage of the term "Urning" in 1864 and Kertbeny's coinage of the term "homosexual" in 1868.[97] In a 1975 lecture that Foucault gave while writing the first volume of *The History of Sexuality*, he himself suggests a chronologically earlier emergence: "With Heinrich Kaan's [1844] book we have then what could be called the date of birth, or in any case the date of the emergence, of sexuality and sexual aberrations in the psychiatric field."[98] We might begin to reconcile these persistent backdatings by turning to Halperin's *How to Do the History of Homosexuality* (2002). Halperin argues that while earlier figures might share aspects of gender presentation, deviant subjectivity, or other features of sexual morphology or subjectivity with the modern homosexual, it is the unique arrangement, compression, and interrelation of these characteristics that forge modern sexual identity.[99]

While I find Halperin's strategies invaluable for thinking about the emerging speciation of male homosexuality, they are also vital for thinking about the afterlife of the "temporary aberration" of the sodomite and persistence of noncongenital sexualities after the speciation of the homosexual. I argue that the homosexual, like the sodomite, was a temporary aberration well into the 1880s and beyond. While the species of the congenital homosexual exists by 1870, he is only recognizable as such for a handful of specialists and is not understood in those terms even by many within the sexological community until much later.

The historical dominance of acquired etiologies of homosexuality over congenital ones is evident in Havelock Ellis's account of sexology's development in his *Psychology of Sex* (1933):

The first and most fundamental difficulty [in the history of sexual inversion] lay in deciding whether sexual inversion is congenital or acquired. The prevailing opinion, before Krafft-Ebing's influence began to be felt, was that homosexuality is acquired, that it is, indeed simply a "vice," generally the mere result of masturbation or sexual excesses having produced impotence in normal coitus, or else (with Binet and Schrenck-Notzing) that it is the result of suggestion in early life. Krafft-Ebing accepted both the congenital and the acquired varieties of homosexuality, and the subsequent tendency has been towards minimizing the importance of acquired homosexuality.[100]

Ellis dates the rise of a congenital understanding of sexual inversion in exactly the same manner as Foucault: namely, to Karl Westphal's famous 1870 paper on "contrary sexual sensations."[101] While marking an early beginning for congenital understandings of sexuality, Westphal's influence does not demarcate a major historical break. Instead, there is a much longer period throughout which congenital sexuality and its effects are disseminated, challenged, and gradually adopted over time. Krafft-Ebing's *Psychopathia Sexualis* (1886), according to Ellis, marks a crucial step in this process. Albert Moll's *Perversions of the Sexual Instinct: A Study of Sexual Inversion* (1891) gives further momentum to Krafft-Ebing's attack on acquired sexuality. Moll's treatise "minimize[es] the importance of acquired homosexuality," as the "prevailing opinion" at that time "was that homosexuality is acquired."[102] As late as 1933, Ellis could assert that "many psycho-analysts still cherish the belief that homosexuality is always acquired, but . . . they also recognize that it is frequently fixed, and therefore constitutional, the difference of opinion becomes unimportant."[103] Thus, the early history of male homosexuality is a history of acquisition until at least 1891 and, as Ellis's account suggests, the question is not definitely settled in his mind into the 1930s when even differences of opinion become unimportant.[104]

While Ellis is undoubtedly right that Krafft-Ebing and Moll sought "to enlarge the sphere of the congenital," the final 1902 edition of Krafft-Ebing's *Psychopathia Sexualis* demonstrates just how much smaller that sphere was for women.[105] Even as Krafft-Ebing claims that "homosexual feeling" is "in most cases . . . congenital," he also writes that "[t]he majority of female homosexuals do not act in obedience to an innate impulse, but they are developed under conditions analogous to those which produce homosexuality by cultivation."[106] The reach of the congenital in Krafft-Ebing's work seems to extend almost exclusively to male homosexuality. Moll makes the case for congenital inversion more forcefully, claiming "that pure cases of acquired sexual inversion are rare. Almost all research workers are in accord on this point."[107] And yet, even into the 1930s Moll still wavers on the point of congenitality in women, holding open the possibility of congenital female inversion while writing that " [i]n many cases sexual inversion in women is found to be caused by accidental causes."[108] This debate occurs simultaneously in the literary sphere. Radclyffe Hall's *The Well of Loneliness* (1928) is at pains to establish a congenital basis for lesbianism, while Virginia Woolf's *Orlando* (1928) and Djuna Barnes's *Ladies Almanack* (1928) emphasize the possibility of noncongenital forms of sexuality.[109]

Even if "almost all research workers" agree on the rarity of acquired inversion among men (and Ellis's account gives us reason to be skeptical of such a claim), the question is far from settled in the popular imagination. This is evident in the renowned literary critic F. O. Matthiessen's 1924 description of "reading Ellis' volume on inversion": "for the first time it was completely brought home to me that I was what I was by *nature* [sexually inverted]."[110] Before that Matthiessen's close friends, with a single exception, "agreed that it was entirely a question of early environment, having been led into the wrong sexual channels by older boys at school."[111] Matthiessen's ability to change his mind—from seduction to congenitality—suggests the degree to which the debate remains open, a point underlined by his friends' almost unanimous sense that inversion was acquired. Similarly, a surprising scene in Ralph Werther's *Autobiography of an Androgyne* (1919) features Anthony Comstock—America's most infamous censor—declaiming about what Werther calls the "much discussed" question "as to whether sexual inversion is congenital or acquired":

In words which I [Werther] wrote down immediately after leaving his [Comstock's] presence, he declared: "These inverts are not fit to live with the rest of mankind. They ought to have branded in their foreheads the word 'Unclean. . . .' Are they assaulted and blackmailed? They deserve to be. Krafft-Ebing and Havelock Ellis know nothing about them if they say they are irresponsible. They are willfully bad, and glory and gloat in their perversion. Their habit is acquired and not inborn. Why propose to have the law against them repealed? If this happened, there would be no way of getting at them. It would be wrong to make life more tolerable for them. Their lives ought to be made so intolerable as to drive them to abandon their vices."[112]

Here, the transcription of Comstock (whatever its reliability) forecloses any congenital etiology of inversion.[113] He dismisses the congenital position attributed to Krafft-Ebing and Ellis and insists that inverts willfully engage in their vice. In spite of Moll's claim, Comstock, Matthiessen, and Werther all suggest that the question of congenital/acquired etiology is a live issue in the early years of the twentieth century.

Moreover, Alfred W. Herzog, editor of the sexological periodical *Medico-Legal Journal* and the editor of Werther's narrative, attests that Moll's virtual unanimity about the congenital basis of inversion among "research workers" is premature, claiming that "some cases of homosexuality are congenital . . . others are acquired in early childhood, while others again are the result of vice or sexual necessity, as among

soldiers, sailors, or in schools. . . ."[114] Similarly, Bloch "assails the theory
that homosexuality is congenital," while acknowledging that at the
moment the theory "that most sexual anomalies are acquired . . . is
rather in eclipse."[115] While the etiological underpinnings of sexuality
proposed by sexologists and laypeople were fiercely debated, what is
clear is that the advent of modernism and the invention of homosexuality occurred simultaneously. This simultaneity is not as coincidental
as it might first appear, since sexology's literary roots run deep.[116]

## Sexological Modernism

Although sexology is generally understood to stand at the intersection
of such varied disciplines as medicine, psychiatry, anthropology, foren-
sics, endocrinology, legal studies, and many others, it is less well known
that many of its earliest practitioners were themselves poets and novelists. While scholars like Ivan Crozier and Howard Chiang strive to
"isolate" and differentiate disciplinary "fields of discourse," *The Book
of Minor Perverts* moves in the opposite direction, understanding sexology in the broadest possible terms.[117] In particular, I attend to the
porous and flexible boundaries between literature, medicine, and science, noting the innumerable literary works produced by sexologists.
Inspired by the sexual frankness of Walt Whitman's verse, Edward Carpenter wrote his own Whitman-esque celebrations of same-sex love in
*Towards Democracy* (1902):

The love of men for each other—so tender, heroic, constant;
That has come all down the ages in every clime, in every nation. . . .
The love of women for each other—so rapt, intense, so confiding-close, so
burning-passionate. . . .[118]

Additionally, his sexological writings drew heavily from Whitman's
example; in *The Intermediate Sex* (1908) he praises Whitman as "the in-
augurator . . . of a new world of democratic ideals and literature."[119]
Similarly, John Addington Symonds wrote both poetry and the important privately printed sexological text *A Problem in Greek Ethics* (1883).
Likewise, Edward Prime-Stevenson privately printed the novel *Imre:
A Memorandum* (1908) whose conclusion features two men living together and also authored the sexological treatise *The Intersexes: A History of Similisexualism as a Problem in Social Life* (1908). Harry Oosterhuis
describes the contributors to the earliest homophile journal *Der Eigene*

(1896–1931) as "for the most part literary men."[120] One of a handful of female sexologists, Marie Stopes wrote poetry and plays in addition to the best-selling *Married Love* (1918).[121] Marc-André Raffalovich, too, wrote novels, plays, and poetry in addition to his sexological essays. The eminent American sexologist G. Frank Lydston wrote collections of short stories and a play. Similarly, Ellis wrote poems, edited Renaissance plays, and authored many of the most famous works of sexology.[122] These literary works suggest that literary scholars have a unique vantage from which to narrate the history of sexology.

Sexologists' literary works were not conceptually distinct from their medical and scientific writings but occupied an imbricated field of knowledge production. In fact, sexologists often drew their source material and case studies from literature.[123] W. C. Rivers's immediate apprehension of the "strong similarity" between Walt Whitman's *Calamus* poems and "confessions of homosexual subjects recorded in text-books on the human sex-instinct" suggests the proximity between the literary and sexological.[124] Likewise, the highly influential sexologist Krafft-Ebing coined the term "masochism" from the writings of the Austrian writer Leopold von Sacher-Masoch and the word "sadism" from the Marquis de Sade.[125] While the centrality of these examples is telling, they do not capture the range and extent to which sexology draws on literary material. This exchange is bidirectional, as modernist writing often takes sexology as its source material; Aleister Crowley's *White Stains* (1898) versifies Krafft-Ebing's *Psychopathia Sexualis*, Henry James's "The Author of *Beltraffio*" depicts John Addington Symonds's uneasy marriage, and the protagonists of Richard Bruce Nugent's *Gentleman Jigger* (written between 1928 and 1933), Aimée Duc's *Are They Women?: Novel about the Third Sex* (1901), Mae West's *The Drag: A Homosexual Comedy in Three Acts* (1927), Radclyffe Hall's *The Well of Loneliness* (1928), and Margareta Suber's *Two Women* (1934) read sexology books.[126]

This revolving door between literature and sexology suggests that we should understand modernist literary works as "vernacular sexology" that dispute, amend, shape, contribute to, and work through more institutionalized modes of sexology.[127] André Gide's *Corydon* (1911) finds the works of "Moll and Krafft-Ebing and Rafflovitch" unsatisfactory, "reek[ing] of the clinic."[128] The text's eponymous defender of the naturalness of homosexuality instead proposes to write the history of "normal homosexuals."[129] Likewise, Werther's *Autobiography of an Androgyne* uses his life experiences to supplement, corroborate, and argue with the findings of sexologists.[130] Thus, I follow Christopher Looby in attending to the importance of the "literariness of sexuality" even as the genealogy I have charted here carries a slightly different (and complementary) valence from the senses of literariness that Looby posits.[131] Given the inextricability of literature and sexology, it is unsurprising that literary discourse also provided vocabularies of sexual experience. E. M. Forster's Maurice, for example, describes himself as "an unspeakable of the Oscar Wilde sort" and Brian Howard and Harold Acton are described by a friend as looking "like a couple of Oscar Wildes."[132] Similarly, W. F. Snead refers to people "found guilty of Oscar Wilde's crime."[133] Radclyffe Hall's name, like Wilde's, became a byword for homosexuality: "Mrs. Arthur is a . . . is a . . . well, you know, Radclyffe."[134] Likewise, a lesbian journalist, Evelyn Irons, describes unpleasantly getting called "Miss Radclyffe Hall, Miss" by truck drivers when she "wore a collar and tie" immediately after the novel's publication.[135] While literariness does not itself create a notion of sexual interiority, it deepens this sense of interiority and furnishes these nascent sexological subjects with a vocabulary for narrativizing and narrating their sexual experiences, thereby fostering the development of sexual subjectivity. Thus, the literary is at the heart of the sexual and, importantly, at the heart of the sexological.[136]

This inattention to the literary suggests one of the ways that (with a handful of exceptions) sexuality studies has dramatically underthought the range and diversity of sexological discourse, notably its braiding of *psychopathia sexualis, anthropologia sexualis,* and *magia sexualis* (which I will discuss in the first three chapters, respectively).[137] Instead, sexuality studies has privileged individuals who are perceived to have resisted sexological categorization. This book shows individuals participating, innovating, creating, reimagining, accepting, exploring, engaging with, and otherwise working through sexological thought (in its vernacular, literary, and professional contexts) to find themselves.[138]

In mapping sexuality in its plurality, I suggest that the field of sexuality studies is too narrowly conceived, too limited to the modernist tropes of transgression and subversion. This is a point that I made in my first book, *Celibacies: American Modernism and Sexual Life,* and my ambition here is broader. Namely, that it is not just celibacy, chastity, and nonsexual forms that are written out of the modernist sexual domain, but a variety and multiplicity of strange, preposterous, and just plain odd understandings of sexuality that we need to account for in order to gain a better understanding of the history of sexuality. If in *Celibacies* I was interested in charting something like gay subjectivities without gay acts, this book began by exploring gay acts without gay subjectivity (before I realized how important subjectivity is to both etiology and the Great Paradigm Shift) in order to disrupt hierarchies of homosexuality. In the case of *Celibacies*, I counteracted the idea that active homosexualities are better than so-called "repressed," "closeted," or "latent" ones. In this book, I dispute the claim that congenital or consistent sexualities are in some way better than acquired or mutable ones. This last point seems especially salient at this moment of homonationalism when some gays are obtaining legal recognition and protections, leaving queer and trans folks with less of a coalition and without the same protections (legal and otherwise).[139]

Chapter 1, "The Walk-In Closet: Situational Homosexuality and the Always of Desire," explores female sexuality as a limit of congenitality. I argue that the early history of homosexuality must be recognized as what we would today refer to as situational homosexuality. A history of situational homosexuality will relocate the underpinnings of sexual identity from psychology and desire to the less savory foundations of boredom and starvation and recast the proximity between homo- and heterosexuality. I argue that period constructions of situational homosexuality as a behavior rather than as a psychology illuminate the operation of *psychopathia sexualis*—the psychologization of sexual aberrations—as dependent on an unchanging psychology. In particular, I examine Thomas Dickinson's *Winter Bound: A Play in Three Acts and Nine Scenes* (1929) and Lillian Hellman's *The Children's Hour* (1934) in order to theorize how object choice is stabilized temporally and geographically in the all-female environments depicted in the plays. I understand these plays to think through the clash between congenital and acquired forms of sexuality at the moment that congenitality is becoming increasingly codified and acquisition is becoming a minor perversion. In short, this chapter theorizes a nonsubjective homosexuality: a homosexuality not of persons, but of place—one that circulates like rumor attaching to bodies rather than one that emerges from within them. By turning toward identities that take temporality or migration as their conditions of possibility (rather than understanding these as threats to identity), I foreground the temporal and geographical situatedness of all sexualities.

Chapter 2, "*Anthropologia Sexualis*, Universalism, and the Macro Environments of Sex," argues that in spite of the dominance of the dynamic, humoral theory of the body for thousands of years, we still have little understanding of what role it plays in the invention of the homo/hetero binary. To this end, this chapter reads across a range of sexological writing encompassing Richard Burton's climate-based Sotadic Zone, Havelock Ellis's observation of a "special proclivity" for homosexuality in the "hotter regions of the globe," and Victor Segalen's claim that there is "[n]ot much Arctic Eroticism" to explore climate as the aspect of the permeable, humoral body with the longest afterlife.[140] I argue that an examination of what Iwan Bloch calls "Anthropologia Sexualis" will highlight the meanings of the shift from the humoral body to a germ theory of the body for the construction of sexuality.[141] Reading Thomas Mann's *Death in Venice* (1912) as a text that roots homosexuality in the competing epidemiological regimes of *anthropologia sexualis*'s humoralism and *scientia sexualis*'s germ theory, I read Mann's novella as providing a key switch point for understanding the divestment of sexuality in humoralism (a divesture that has roots dating back at least to the seventeenth century). Moreover, I contend that it provides rich models for theorizing sexuality as climatic on the one hand and microbial on the other.

Chapter 3, "*Magia Sexualis*, Sexual Subjectivity, and the Willfulness of Sexual Aim," argues that conceptions of magic, sorcery, witchcraft, and the occult have influenced constructions of sex and sexuality to a much greater extent than has been realized in the existing scholarship. I argue that *magia sexualis* and its notion of will in particular play an essential role in the construction of sexual subjectivity. The chapter begins by thinking about the possibilities of attraction without desire or sexuality by considering the quasi-magical/quasi-chemical idea of elective affinities in Baron Ludwig von Reizenstein's German-language American novel *The Mysteries of New Orleans* (1854/5). In the second section, I trace the afterlife of this sexual subjectivity and its relation to will in George du Maurier's bestselling *Trilby* (1894) in order to chart a genealogy of aim-based sexuality. I conclude by examining the now almost wholly forgotten African-American figure Paschal Beverly Randolph (1825–75), who pioneered sexual magic. Reading Randolph's novels and sexological writings, I argue that he is one of the earliest theorists and instantiators of sexual subjectivity. In particular, I argue that he constructs his vision of sexual subjectivity in relation to the specter of American slavery. In focusing on the eclipse of *anthropologia sexualis* in the previous chapter and *magia sexualis* in this chapter, I map the ways in which *scientia sexualis* gradually becomes synonymous with *psychopathia sexualis* as sexuality is increasingly located inside the body as a psychology rather than external to it.

Chapter 4, "Sex in the Age of Fordism: The Standardization of Sexual Objects," explores industrialization as an etiology of sexuality, charting how the compartmentalization of sexuality develops around sexual object choice. Taking a hint from scholars like John D'Emilio and Henry Abelove who understand economic forces to have an enormous impact on sexual life, this chapter examines industrialization's transformation not just of the ways that we produce objects, but also how industrialization is imagined to invent sexual objects. More specifically, I consider how Fordism was understood by Antonio Gramsci and Sherwood Anderson to standardize sexual object choice in order to create the hegemonic system of sexual orientation dominant in America and much of Europe. This chapter attends to the ways in which Anderson's text *Winesburg, Ohio* (1919) both locates consumer and sexual objects at the center of modern fields of desire and imagines the inhabitants of the small Ohio town to enact nonindustrialized and nonstandardized sexual pleasures.

Chapter 5, "Volitional Etiologies: Toward a Weak Theory of Etiology," explores the temporal structure of etiology, taking alcohol as its case study. Almost all acquired etiologies of sexual aberration operate under the assumption that heterosexuality or the normal operation of the sexual instinct precedes the etiological event that leads to sexual deviation or aberration. Acquired etiology, thus, is the central mechanism of sexology's sequencing practices. Reading the works of Iwan Bloch, Magnus Hirschfeld, Stella Browne, Edmund Bergler, and Auguste Forel, this chapter argues that sexologists have a difficult time establishing the sexual sequencing of homosexuality and alcohol. That is, they struggle to determine whether alcoholism causes homosexuality, homosexuality causes alcoholism, or whether they are simultaneous comorbidities. I am interested in how the inability to order cause and effect here (and in a range of other etiologies) suggests that sexuality is written under the sign of what Foucault would call "decompartmentalization."[142] That is, sexuality by the middle of the twentieth century has not yet been compartmentalized around object choice and incorporates a number of categories and patterns that will come to be written out of the sphere of the sexual: criminality, alcoholism, gambling, lying, and other vices.

My afterword, "After Sedgwick: The Gordian Knot of the Great Paradigm Shift," attempts to work through two fundamental impasses in the historiography of sexuality: (1) Does the invention of sexuality (what Sedgwick calls the Great Paradigm Shift) occur with the advent of the molly in the eighteenth century as one group of scholars (Randolph Trumbach, Mary McIntosh, Alan Bray, Michel Rey, Theo van der Meer, Michael Warner, Rictor Norton, Thomas King) argues or with the sexological figure of the homosexual as another group of scholars (Michel Foucault, David Halperin, Joseph Boone, Arnold Davidson,

Peter Coviello) proposes? (2) Scholars of sexuality working with more contemporary materials have assembled a vast scholarship on the role that race (Marlon Ross, Siobhan Somerville), class (Michael Trask, Margot Canaday), and gender (George Chauncey, Barry Reay) play in the construction of sexual object choice. However, there is no synthesis or mapping of the relations between these works. I argue that my etiological approach will help us to navigate these impasses. This book argues that an etiological approach will enable us to narrate the Great Paradigm Shift more fully. This afterword is my effort to do just that, and as such it is in many ways the culmination of the book.

Strikingly, many of the etiologies that this study considers remain current in contemporary America, echoing their distant though now subterranean earlier logics. Situational homosexuality still adheres in the same-sex environments of prisons ("gay for the stay"), women's colleges ("lesbian until graduation" [LUG]), and fraternities (bromosexual); the language of hotness ("having the hots for," "that's hot," etc.) as a discourse of sexuality echoes the language of climate; the rhetorical registers of magic and chemistry associated with elective affinity continue to characterize and structure fantasies of dating/romantic relationships in the contemporary US ("meeting her was magical," "We felt instant chemistry"); the relation between alcohol and homosexuality returns in the terms "three-beer queer," "gaysted," and "liquid lesbian." We might hear the current resonances of Djuna Barnes's assertion that she was only a lesbian for her partner in the common formulation "I would go gay for X celebrity." The contemporary formation of "gay for pay" summons a longer history of trade.[143] Similarly, the transformation inherent in the terms "hasbian," "yestergay," "bi for now," "heteroflexible," and "ex-gay" continues to suggest the labile and mobile currents of sexuality.[144] The seeming unrationalizability of these sexual formations with the homo/hetero binary suggests not just the irrationality and complexity of sexual desire, but that organizations around object choice have the potential to be just as unstable as these less familiar sexual configurations. Moreover, it also suggests a political value in recognizing the multiplicity of past configurations of sexuality ("minor perversions") at a moment (our own) when the homo/hetero binary is beginning to lose traction.

# ONE

# The Walk-In Closet: Situational Homosexuality and the Always of Desire

One function of identity is the management and expulsion of inappropriate acts, attributes, plans, feelings, morphologies, experiences, questions, strayings, thoughts, models, and desires in the service of continuity and coherence.[1] This chapter will detail the ways in which the forging of sexual identity's temporal "always" would come to require a constancy of desire and a constancy of the gender of object choice.[2] In order to understand the emergence of the stability of object choice in both registers, this chapter explores the diametric opposite of such stability: namely, the concept of "situational homosexuality." Borrowing Regina Kunzel's definition, I understand situational homosexuality to "describe same-sex practices produced by circumstance, architecture, and environment" and thus presumed not to have "a somatic or psychic origin."[3] In this way, situational homosexuality describes a nonnormative sexual practice that is not written under the sign of *psychopathia sexualis*—the psychologization of sexual aberrations—and helps us to understand that unchanging psychology is a crucial component of sexual identity.

In particular I examine two contemporaneous lesbian plays that are both about situational homosexuality— Thomas Dickinson's *Winter Bound: A Play in Three Acts and Nine Scenes* (1929) and Lillian Hellman's *The Children's*

*Hour* (1934).[4] These plays appeared amidst a spate of other plays featuring lesbian themes and were part of a "pansy and lesbian craze": Sholem Asch's *God of Vengeance* (1918); Harry Wagstaff Gribble's *March Hares* (1921); Arthur Hornblow Jr.'s *The Captive* (1926), which was adapted from Edouard Bourdet's *La Prisonnière* (1926); and William Hurlbut's *Sin of Sins* (1926).[5] These plays were accompanied by a slew of lesbian texts: Rosamund Lehmann's *Dusty Answer* (1927), Grete von Urbanitzky's *Der Wilde Garten* (1927), Djuna Barnes's *Ladies Almanack* (1928), Radclyffe Hall's *The Well of Loneliness* (1928), Elizabeth Bowen's *The Hotel* (1928), Compton Mackenzie's *Extraordinary Women* (1928), Wanda Fraiken Neff's *We Sing Diana* (1928), Warner Fabian's *Unforbidden Fruit* (1928), Virginia Woolf's *Orlando* (1928), Nella Larsen's *Passing* (1929), Natalie Clifford Barney's *Adventures of the Mind* (1929), Anna Weirauch's *Scorpion* trilogy (1919–1931), Lucie Delarue-Mardrus's *The Angel and the Perverts* (1930), Olive Moore's *Spleen* (1930), Wyndham Lewis's *The Apes of God* (1930), Dorothy Richardson's *Dawn's Left Hand* (1931), Christa Winsloe's *Girls in Uniform* (1931), and Colette's *The Pure and the Impure* (1932).[6] This flurry of lesbian representations suggests a grappling with the increasing and dawning realization of the existence of lesbianism (no doubt heightened by the *Well of Loneliness* obscenity trial).[7] This chapter will be particularly interested in the shifting status of lesbianism in relation to object choice: as a flickering impossibility, a passing phase, or an emergent identity rivaling heterosexual object choice in its stability.

In the first part of this chapter, I describe how sexologists' failure to naturalize the periodicity of desire through the language of the seasons inadvertently constructs modern heterosexuality as possessing a constant, unwavering desire. I argue that *Winter Bound* exemplifies the early-twentieth-century process by which periodicity becomes associated with lesbianism while heterosexuality is constructed as perennially unchanging. In the second part of the chapter, I turn back to the sexological debate between congenital and acquired understandings of sexuality that I explored in the introduction to examine the emergence of a congenital seat for lesbian sexuality. Reading Lillian Hellman's *The Children's Hour* (1934) as positioned at the confluence between congenital and acquired understandings of sexuality, the third part of the chapter charts the uneasy historical incorporation of acquired homosexuality into the increasingly congenital and identarian sexual matrix in the 1930s. I argue that the sexual regimes of the 1930s transmute acquired homosexuality into situational homosexuality.[8] Hellman's play pluralizes our sense of situational homosexuality, theorizing at least three competing and overlapping discourses of this sexual formation: the deprivation, transformation, and panic models. Finally, I close with a consideration of the little-known role of lesbianism in Hellman's famous feud with Mary McCarthy and what I argue are the dispute's unexamined sexual politics in order to consider how the meanings of once unstable object choice are transformed by the increasingly stable sexual order.

## Seasonal Sex

While this chapter will focus on the stabilization of the gender of object choice, I want to begin by exploring the sexological debate between the cyclicality of desire and the construction of the "always" of desire. In his book *Race and Rhythm in Modernist Poetry and Science* (2008), Michael Golston contends that a group of late-nineteenth- and early-twentieth-century scientists felt that "the circumstances of modernity compromise or even destroy organic human senses of rhythm."[9] While Golston doesn't attend to questions of sex and sexuality, sexologists and other period thinkers of sexuality were preoccupied by sexual rhythms: particularly the frequency of desire and the inconsistency of sexual object choice. These preoccupations with inconstancy were often combined.

In her massively popular 1918 sex manual *Married Love*, for example, Marie Stopes describes modernity's ill effects on organic human rhythm (aligning her with the set of thinkers that Golston describes):

There is no doubt that Love loses, in the haste and bustle of our modern turmoil, not only much of its charm and grace, but some of its vital essence. The evil results of the haste which so infests and poisons us are often felt much more by the woman than by the man. The over-stimulation of city life tends to "speed up" the man's reactions, but to retard hers. To make matters worse, even for those who have leisure to spend on love-making, the opportunities for peaceful, romantic dalliance are less to-day in a city with its tubes and cinema shows than in woods and gardens where the pulling of rosemary or lavender may be the sweet excuse for the slow and profound mutual rousing of passion.[10]

Here, modernity and the processes of urbanization hasten men and slow women, disrupting their ordinary synchronicity.[11] The pastoral scenes of a mythical yesteryear are gone and men and women are out of sync with the natural world.[12] Like Stopes, Dr. A. W. Johnstone similarly contends in an 1895 article for the *American Journal of Obstetrics* that humans have lost their ties to the natural world, declaring "woman is the only animal in which 'rut' is omnipresent."[13] The Australian sexologist William James Chidley advocates in his humbly named *The Answer* (1912) having sex only during the spring to "escape from our degeneracy" and return "to permanent happiness."[14] He understands "Spring love" to be "universally admitted to be a natural prelude to the act of coition" and that it "should *always* precede it. In other words, the fact it is dispensed with now—or *can* be dispensed with in our present mode of coition—proves that the act [sexual intercourse] is unnatural."[15] Similarly, Martyn Liadov, the rector of Sverdlov Communist University, the most prominent Communist Party school, argues in a 1924 book that nonseasonal sexual desire and, implicitly, menstruation have been inflicted by capitalism on the female body:

In no animal is sexuality a dominant emotion throughout the whole year. It appears only at a specific time, during the female's spring heat. [ . . . ] For a prolonged historical period (and this is clear from a wide range of historical sources) man, like all other animals, mated only once a year. [ . . . ] When a market economy developed, when private property began to be accumulated, then woman, too, was transformed into private property and had to be prepared to satisfy her master's demand at any time."[16]

The oddness of Liadov's argument that before capitalism humans mated only once a year aside, Liadov, Stopes, Johnstone, and Chidley share a sense that sex in its current state of modernity lacks periodicity and that this aseasonal quality indexes it as unnatural and pathological. These diverse commentators' nostalgic looks backward to a premodern and phantasmatic past when sex was in perfect rhythm with nature results in constructing modern heterosexuality as having a constant desire, an implicit temporal "always," without periodicity or seasonality.

Thomas Dickinson's play *Winter Bound* (1929), his only to reach Broadway, explicitly works through this opposition between the periodicity and constancy of desire. In spite of his short-lived career as a playwright, he was an English professor who was well known at the time as the author of several important critical works and anthologies about the contemporary theater, most famously *The Insurgent Theater* (1917).[17] While *Winter Bound* is all but forgotten today (it has never been published and has received little more than a passing mention or footnote since 1931), it was the last play produced by the famous avant-garde acting company the Provincetown Players.[18] The Province-town Players are widely regarded as one of the most important theatre groups in the history of American theater (one of the central batteries energizing New York modernism) and are particularly noted for their representation of queer lives and sexual and gender nonnormativity.[19] *Winter Bound* was no exception, described by one reviewer as "a case study out of Krafft-Ebing."[20]

The plot of *Winter Bound* centers around a feminist experiment: two women, Tony and Emily, decide to live together in a Connecticut farmhouse during the winter in order to prove that women can work and live without men. Sometimes mistaken for a man, Tony is a gruff masculine woman who insists she is not a woman at all ("I'd hate to think I was a woman") and approximates models of congenital inversion (a "he-woman").[21] Emily is described as "thoroughly feminine" and "healthy," with "no complexes."[22] The play writes the relationship between these women under two competing seasonal regimes: one underwriting asexuality (extreme cold freezes desire) and the other lesbianism (the loneliness of the cold itself generates desire).[23] In the first instance, Tony and Emily hope that the natural environment's "open air" will enable them to get their minds "off sex entirely."[24] In the second instance, the deprivation and loneliness of the snowbound farmhouse in which the rule is "no men allowed" threatens to inflame lesbian sexual desire.[25] Emily's susceptibility to situational homosexuality seems acute as the play describes her as "influenced by the latest strong spirit that comes into her orbit."[26] Much of the drama hinges on whether Tony and the bitter cold will lead Emily to lesbianism. When Tony asserts, for example, that "there is one difference anyway [between Emily and Tony and a married couple]. We don't eat each other up with sex passion."[27] Emily responds skeptically: "How do you know we don't eat each other up?"[28] The separatism of the women's feminist space is endangered when an injured and bleeding male neighbor Chet knocks on their door. Emily, not yet knowing of his injuries, begs Tony not to let him enter. After Tony opens the door, a triangular love plot ensues as Tony and Chet struggle over Emily. The play ends with the coming of spring and Emily leaving Tony to get married to Chet.[29]

The sex/gender imaginary of *Winter Bound* is highly seasonal. Just before embarking on the feminist experiment with Tony, Emily comments that she "loves autumn vegetables more than spring things . . . They're so sturdy and independent. . . . Garden flowers are the same. . . . They're made for cold weather."[30] Here, the cold weather vegetables are imagined to be as resilient and independent as Emily and Tony under-

stand themselves to be. The women repeatedly suggest that the frozen
deep environment is conducive to the creation of a utopic space outside
of sexual culture and sexual need. Along these lines, Tony says, "Some-
body's got to come out to the country and live clean."[31] The frosty cold
curtails not just the heat of desire but also forecloses reproduction
(heavy-handedly symbolized by the death of the farm's calving cow).
But in addition to this asexual vision of the winter, its lashing chill
and imprisoning snow ("as high as the house") isolates the women and
enables queer desire; Emily says, "Don't you see I'm lonely, lonely, so
lonely, I think that I could die."[32] Before Emily moves in with Tony, a
friend warns her that she'll wish she "had a man when the long winter
nights come on."[33] While the play's conclusion with Emily's marriage
to Chet seems to concur with this assessment, it also leaves open the
possibility that Tony's uncertain status as a man (as "neither man nor
woman . . . a he-woman") and her assertion that her love for Emily is "a
new kind[] of love" enable her to provide the absent warmth created by
"the long winter nights." [34]

The play's most explicit moment of lesbian erotics turns on the
question of Tony's uncertain maleness. The scene is both a literaliza-
tion of heterosexual frigidity with Emily suffering from her recurring
"little headache" and a variety of other hysterical symptoms in order
not to have sex and also a scene of lesbian caring. Tony lures Emily to
bed by softening her manliness:

Tony: I'll tell you what I'll do. I'll get some supper and you can have it in bed. Go to
bed in my room. It's warmer there.
Emily: You're sure you don't mind? It would be nice.
Tony: Mind! I should say not. It's fun to get supper. And I'll bring mine, and we'll
eat together. I'm sorry I'm hard bitten, kid. I don't mean to be. It's just my way.
You go to bed.
Emily: I have been awfully lonely—at night. Will you lock up?
Tony: Trust me. I'll take care of you. I'll bring your supper.
Emily: Don't be long.[35]

This passage crackles with eroticism with Emily saying she's "been
awfully lonely—at night" and Tony expressing excitement ("Mind! I
should say not") that the two will share the same bed. While Simone
de Beauvoir and other feminist commentators have taught us (rightly)
to read the history of frigidity as a tool of misogyny used to inculcate
women into compulsory heterosexuality and unwanted sexual relations, this same history might also construct frigidity as a productive

site for researching the history of lesbianism.[36] With regard to lesbianism, it is precisely Emily's feelings of coldness and loneliness that open her to the warmth of Tony's bed. This exchange ends the scene and the stage direction of the next scene says "A great change has taken place in Emily since the last scene," implying that the wintery chill leads to sexual consummation and happiness.[37]

*Winter Bound*'s obsessive foregrounding of the temporality of the seasons and the seasonality of desire implies that proper heterosexuality must eschew any seasonality. To echo Johnstone again, "woman is the only animal in which 'rut' is omnipresent" and heterosexuality is timeless, eschewing periodicity and cyclicality. Emily's marriage to Chet in the spring suggests that within the diegesis of the play, the perennial warmth of heterosexuality aligns winter more with asexuality than with queer desire. The marriage posits a steady temporality, extending into an unrepresented future that contrasts sharply with the seasonality of queer desire.

*Winter Bound* provides one example of the ways in which lesbian desire becomes increasingly associated with cyclical temporality in the late nineteenth- and early twentieth centuries. During this period seasonality is a crucial structure of lesbian feeling and one of the ways in which lesbianism differentiates itself from the perpetual timelessness of heterosexuality. Casting heterosexuality's temporality as monotonous, lesbian writers position their relationship as a rare seasonal delicacy. This hallmark of lesbianism erotics is evident in the subtitle of Djuna Barnes's *Ladies Almanack*: "showing their Signs and their tides; their Moons and their Changes; the seasons as it is with them; their Eclipses and their Equinoxes; as well as a full Record of diurnal and nocturnal Distempers."[38] Similarly, Sarah Orne Jewett's *A Country of Pointed Firs* (1896) begins with a "return" suggesting that the desire between the novel's two protagonists is a seasonal one much like Jewett's intervallic relationship with Annie Fields.[39] Moreover, in *Bequest from a Life: A Biography of Louise Stevens Bryant*, the American sexologist Lura Beam describes her lesbian partner as organizing her daily life around seasons: "On summer evenings, she ate dinner on the lawn or looking into thick woods to the North, in winter at a small table beside the open fire."[40] This seasonality and its absences carry a submerged erotic charge and govern the intimacy between Bryant and Beam:

The home routine in this setting was planned for rather separate lives. Most of our work was of the kind that only ripens by thinking and being alone. Therefore, we

had separate sets of rooms and if we were eating at home, had only dinner together. We commuted on different trains and we kept separate circles of friends
and had many separate trips and holidays. These habits continued until the last four
years when the needs of her failing strength made us inseparable.[41]

Here, the inseparability between Bryant and Beam is wrought from
a lifetime of their willed seasonal separation. Beam's use of the word
"ripens" suggests the preciousness of their seasonal time apart and the
way it enriches their time together. We must then understand the seasons as a crucial site of same-sex erotics and the eschewal of seasonality
as part of the production of modern heterosexuality and its constant
desire.

## The Invention of Situational Homosexuality

Building on my contention that periodicity is a crucial aspect of the
history of same-sex sexuality, I want to turn toward situational homosexuality and other identities that take ephemerality, mutability, tran-
sitoriness, and environmental factors as their condition of possibility
(rather than understanding impermanence as something that threatens identity). I will argue that the history of situational homosexuality brings the very situatedness of all sexualities (not just situational
homosexuality) into view.[42] I contend that situational homosexuality
operates at a particularly vexed jointure between acquired and congenital modes of sexuality and that congenitality underwrites identity's
temporal "always."

The conceptual difficulty of fitting these transitory models into
acquired and congenital histories of sexuality is evident in George
Chauncey's field-defining *Gay New York: Gender, Urban Culture, and the
Making of the Gay Male World, 1890–1940* (1994). I revisit this foundational text in order to argue that virtually all of the sexual types that
Chauncey understands as congenital or identarian can be understood
instead as acquired and ephemeral. Even though Chauncey argues
that his subtitle, "the Gay Male World," consists of "multiple social
worlds," his book is still centrally interested in arguing that gay men
imagine "themselves as linked . . . in their common 'queerness' and
their membership in a single gay world."[43] As Chauncey's discussion of
"trade" makes clear, membership in the gay world is a matter of men-
tality more than of particular sexual acts.[44] Given this focus on forms

of belonging, Chauncey's history excludes the "situational homosexual" in whom this chapter is centrally interested and who might be said to engage in gay acts without possessing the gay subjectivity that would qualify him for membership in the imagined community of Chauncey's gay world.[45] Chauncey refers to "situational homosexuality" as a "culturally blind concept" that does not take into account how ethnic and racial differences affect the likelihood and incidence of homosexual activity in same-sex environments.[46] While we must heed Chauncey's call to attend to the ways that situational homosexuality adheres to certain persons and bodies more readily than others, I contend that discounting the history of situational homosexuality might damage our sense of the history of homosexuality as a whole.

When we think about situational homosexuality at all (and sexuality studies very rarely does), we imagine it, as my reading of *Winter Bound* has begun to suggest, under the sign of what I call the deprivation model as a sexuality of last resort: growing out of geographic confinement or economic necessity.[47] The sexologist Stella Browne exemplifies this understanding of situational homosexuality emerging from confinement: "Artificial or substitute homosexuality [situational homosexuality] . . . is very widely diffused among women, as a result of the repression of normal gratification and the segregation of the sexes."[48] Similarly, one of the tramps comments in George Orwell's *Down and Out in Paris and London* (1933) that "'Homosexuality is general among tramps of longstanding'" because they can't afford to take a woman out or buy a prostitute's services.[49] Situational homosexuality annuls its autonomy, seeing its actions as predicated on a kind of biological necessity akin to hunger rather than on desire (in the sense of desirableness). Orwell's tramps engage in homosexuality, in Krafft-Ebing's phrase, "for want of something better."[50] Their sexuality is what Guy Hocquenghem calls "a poor man's sexuality, the sexuality of the oppressed"; it is an outlet to release the suffocation of desire or to fill the time—nothing more.[51] Hocquenghem's description accords with a late-nineteenth-century letter that Havelock Ellis quotes:

Passionate friendships among girls, from the most innocent to the most elaborate excursions in the direction of Lesbos, are extremely common in theatres, both among actresses, and even more, among chorus and ballet girls. Here the pell-mell of the dressing rooms, the wait of perhaps two hours between the performances, during which all the girls are cooped up, in a state of inaction and excitement, in a few crowded dressing-rooms, affords every opportunity for the growth of this particular kind of sentiment.[52]

Here, situational homosexuality makes time exciting and the theatre functions as a site of situational homosexuality. Its combination of boredom and excitement suggests that, as Heather Love puts it, "when it comes to sex, proximity and opportunity count for a lot."[53] The letter's emphasis on boredom also suggests that situational homosexuality provides a way to theorize sexuality without desire (a subject I will return to in chapter 3).

Implicit within the term "situational homosexuality" is the idea that "when the situation changed, so would the behavior."[54] As soon as a tramp has the money or, in the case of a prisoner, is released, he will return to "normal" heterosexual relations.[55] Regina Kunzel, one of the few commentators who historicizes situational homosexuality, claims that this account suggests "that the border between homosexuality and heterosexuality [is] slippery and permeable," eroding "confidence in a sexual binary and in the stability of sexual identity . . . just as those ideas were rising in prominence." [56] While in Kunzel's description situational homosexuality threatened to dissolve the nascent concept of sexual identity, I understand situational homosexuality to help solidify sexual identity. That is, situational homosexuality insulates heterosexual identity from same-sex behavior by re-soldering acts to identities when they become disaligned and thereby preserves the so-called "pre-situated" identity.[57] Thus, situational homosexuality stabilizes the homo/hetero divide and is central to the development of regimes of modern sexuality.

This emphasis on stability, on fixity, and on congenitality also pathologizes movement. In this register, "wanderlust" (which I discuss more in chapter 2) was understood to be a dangerous sexual pathology, eroticizing movement and transforming it into unnatural desire.[58] Moreover, Margot Canaday highlights the pathology of movement, arguing that vagrancy and sodomy were closely associated in America's early-twentieth-century sexual ideology because dominant sexual ideologies made the assumption that "men who were not self-governing in their sexual practices could not be self-governing in their labor."[59] Canaday argues that vagrants, transients, unattached persons, floaters, and the unmarried made up one side of a binary opposite those who are "settled down," where "settling down" connotes home, family, work, and reproduction.[60] She argues that "[t]his inchoate opposition between mobility and settlement evolved into an explicit differentiation between homosexuals and heterosexuals," suggesting one reason why tramps, sailors, and soldiers are associated with both homosexuality and, as I am arguing, situational homosexuality.[61]

In addition to the tramp, sailor, and soldier, perhaps the figure most closely associated with situational homosexuality was that of "trade." The term "trade" shifts in the middle third of the twentieth century from meaning "'straight' men who had sex with queers or fairies for pleasure rather than money" to mean increasingly "'straight' male prostitutes."[62] The tramps described by Orwell condense both meanings, engaging in sex with each other for pleasure (because they have no opportunities to have sex with women) and for money or food out of destitution. Sailors, soldiers, and trade all play a crucial role in both the practice of homosexuality and its modes of fantasy (functioning as ideal objects of desire for fairies and queers).[63] Likewise, the linked figures that Chauncey identifies as "wolves" and "punks" pair up in the virtually all-male sites associated with situational homosexuality: ships, prisons, and on the road.[64] Chauncey defines "wolves" as "combin[ing] homosexual interest with a marked masculinity" while "punks" "denoted a physically slighter youth who let himself be used sexually by an older and more powerful man, the wolf, in exchange for money, protection, other forms of support."[65] Perhaps part of what differentiates working-class sexuality from middle-class sexuality, then, is that same-sex sociability was more central to working-class life than middle-class life further into the twentieth century.

My claims that acquired modes of homosexuality (of which situational homosexuality is a type) describe much of the early history of homosexuality and are crucial to the etiology of homosexuality expound on and dovetail with Canaday's claim that movement itself becomes aligned with the homo side of the homo/hetero binary at midcentury. Situational homosexuality marks the incorporation of movement in Canaday's terms, or acquired homosexuality in mine, into congenital frameworks of sexuality. The stabilizing effects of situational homosexuality suggest the tremendous stigma with which it is burdened. That is, situational homosexuality helps to rationalize what Sedgwick has called "the unrationalized coexistence of different models [of sexuality]."[66] Situational homosexuality bears not just the shame of homosexuality, but also the shame of shoring up the systems of stigmatization themselves, making it complicit in the censure of queer sexualities by promising that homo- and heterosexuality are starkly differentiated.

Thus, situational homosexuality resides at the heart of homosexuality.[67] This is nowhere clearer than in Werther's etymology of the word "fairie":

The term "fairie" is widely used in the United States by those who are in touch with the underworld. It probably originated on sailing vessels of olden times when voyages often lasted for months. While the crew was either actually or prospectively suffering acutely from the absence of the female of the species, one of their number would unexpectedly betray an inclination to supply her place. Looked upon as a fairy gift or godsend, such individual would be referred to as "the fairy."[68]

Werther astonishingly implicates the fairie—apparently the most congenital of homosexuals—in the history of situational homosexuality.[69] While the "purported heterosexuality" of trade locates him both inside and outside of Chauncey's gay world, the fairie is central to any history of modern homosexuality.[70] The "fairie," for Werther, emerges out of an environment of sexual deprivation where "the crew was . . . suffering acutely from the absences of the female of the species." Situational homosexuality is strikingly valued as a "gift or godsend" even as it emerges out of suffering. Werther's use of the word "unexpectedly" to describe the fairie's "betray[ed] . . . inclination" modifies a desire that is both surprising to the sailor-turned-fairie (the acute sexual deprivation of the ship induces homosexuality) and surprising for the crew (they had not expected one of their number to be capable of such desires). Growing out of one of the quintessential environments of situational homosexuality, the etiology of the fairie is situational, cementing my claim that the "homosexual," like the sodomite, was a "temporary aberration" well into the twentieth century. Werther's example suggests that situational homosexuality needs to be thought in a universalizing register; even the fairie (that most minoritized of homosexuals) can be understood to be situational.[71] Having remapped all of the figures— trade, punks, wolves, and fairies—that Chauncey has identified as central to the existence and erotic system of the working-class gay world, we must understand that there is a profound overlap, if not identity, between situational homosexuality and homosexuality so called in the early decades of the twentieth century.

## Contracting Homosexuality

Because congenitality, as I argued in the introduction, emerges as an etiological underpinning for female homosexuality so much later than for male homosexuality, this overlap is particularly pronounced in the case of lesbianism. This is one reason why few texts have as much to teach us about situational homosexuality as Hellman's *The Children's Hour*. This wildly successful play was produced during a historical moment in which acquired sexuality was shifting from being a competitor of congenital sexuality to its bulwark (in its new instantiation as situational homosexuality). But even more than this historical shift, the entwinement of lying and homosexuality in Hellman's text makes it a particularly rich site for thinking about the history of acquired homosexuality, since the sexological terms "false," "spurious," and "pseudohomosexuality" were used interchangeably with situational homosexuality.[72] Situational homosexuality was often referred to as "artificial" or "imaginary," elaborating a logic by which the "truth" of the sexual self (as in the phrase "true invert") adheres in congenital identity, while the falsehood of vice is quarantined as an act.[73]

This logic is especially important given Hellman's assertion that "This is not really a play about lesbianism but about a lie."[74] Hellman implicitly sets the truth of lesbianism against the lie of the play, suggesting an attempt to substitute an event or situation for sexuality. She seeks to separate them even as her phrasing "not really . . . about" suggests their imbrication.[75] Hellman's play features two women in their late twenties who run a school: Karen, who is attractive and engaged, and Martha, who is nervous and unmarried. Their pupil, Mary, spreads a rumor that Karen and Martha are lesbians, or, at least, in what importantly amounts to the same accusation, are doing certain dirty or unnameable things together. Amidst an atmosphere that understands children to be without sexual knowledge unless, as is the presumed case here, they are initiated into it first hand, Mary's lie is immediately believed. The plausibility of this lie is enhanced by fears that, as Diana Fuss has chronicled, schools are breeding grounds for lesbian contagion.[76] Mary's grandmother, Mrs. Tilford, disseminates the lie out of such a fear of infection, explaining her reasoning to Karen and Martha: "*You've* been playing with a lot of children's lives, and that's why I stopped you."[77] Mary's lie destroys her teachers' lives: the students are pulled out of the school, causing the financial and emotional hardship of its closure, the public humiliation when the women lose a libel suit, and the dissolution of Karen's engagement. The most damaging effect of the lie, however, is Martha's realization that she is in fact a "lesbian" who is in love with Karen, the trauma of which leads her to suicide.[78]

While the exodus of pupils engineered by Mrs. Tilford and the other parents is orchestrated in the hope that a change of situation will change their daughters' (potentially contaminated) behavior (conforming to our deprivation model), the impact of Mary's lie on Martha seems to suggest a second model of situational homosexuality—the transformation model. Here, the situation unlocks a desire, perhaps a repressed or melancholic desire; or, the situation renovates the receptors of desire, creating new modes of and opportunities for desiring.[79] This second model or version of situational homosexuality suggests that once one has engaged in same-sex acts or, in Martha's case, desires, one is, in the pathologizing language of the period, "addicted" to homosexuality, becoming a homosexual.[80] In this model, the walk-in closet is emphatically not a walk-out closet.[81] The discourses of habit and addiction echo Ellis's association of acquired homosexuality and vice. We might think of "habit" and "addiction" as middle terms between acts and identities, the repetition of a habit, embodying the reiterative doing that Judith Butler has taught us to understand as the basis of identity.[82] Bad habits are associated at the turn of the century with particular locales—the billiard hall as a den of vice or the school as a hotbed of lesbianism—suggesting a more labile vision of homosexuality, a homosexuality not of persons but of place.[83] That said, this version of situational homosexuality is perhaps closest to the coming-out narrative of the closet; where the closet puts forward continuity—the homosexual is gay all along—this version of situational homosexuality posits that the situation effects a fundamental change of identity, reorganizing desire and pleasure and forestalling the first model's easy movement across the homo/hetero divide. In the Tiresias-esque choice between homo and hetero, the transformation model suggests the superiority of homosexuality for those who have experienced both.[84]

Rather than the transformation model, I am more inclined to read Martha under a third model in which situational homosexuality has a shorter period of onset as well as a shorter duration—namely "homosexual panic." Characterizing "homosexual panic" in the same vein as situational homosexuality may seem peculiar given that Sedgwick has (rightly) taught us to understand this term as a justification for violent antigay crime, stemming from the onset of a momentary "pathological psychological condition" brought on by the threat of sexual advance.[85] While Sedgwick characterizes this defense (which emerged in the late 1970s) as taking its name from "a rather obscure and little diagnosed" condition, the American Edward Kempf actually coined the term in 1920 and describes it as a common diagnosis:

The mechanism of homosexual panic (panic due to the pressure of uncontrollable perverse sexual cravings) is of the utmost importance in psychopathology because of the *frequency* of its occurrence wherever men or women must be grouped alone for prolonged periods, as in army camps, aboard ships, on exploring expeditions, in prisons, monasteries, schools, and asylums.[86]

The panic is identical to the other descriptions of situational homosexuality with the difference that it may last "from a few hours to several months."[87] This question of timing as well as its connection to either outward violence or suicide makes it a particularly apt descriptor of *The Children's Hour*'s conclusion since the ending differs primarily in terms of pacing from the other models of situational homosexuality that I have elaborated.

Whereas the first two models of situational homosexuality (deprivation and transformation) occur over a long period of time, developing and gestating in processes of institutionalization, Martha's sexual revelation is instantaneous:

It's funny; it's all mixed up. There's something in you, and you don't know it and you don't do anything about it. Suddenly a child gets bored and lies—and there you are, seeing it for the first time. . . . It all seems to come back to *me*.[88]

Martha's description of Mary's lie as occurring "suddenly" is crucial here, for a moment later a pistol shot is heard. Martha diagnoses herself instantly, "the night," Martha says, "we heard" Mary's lie.[89] From diagnosis to contagion to suicide—it all happens in a moment—the space of half a page. Martha attempts to contain the suddenness—in a clash between the transformation and panic models—when she says "It all seems to come back to *me*." Here, the transformation model understands the temporality of truth to arrive from the past (it is located within her body as "something" in her, something congenital), while the panic model understands identity as occurring in the present (in the action of boredom and lying).[90]

Even before Martha's immediate self-diagnosis and suicide, contagion is, as Mikko Tuhkanen has pointed out, instant.[91] When Karen, Martha, and Joe confront Mrs. Tilford about spreading her granddaughter's lie, Mrs. Tilford does not want to let them in her house. She is worried that she might catch lesbianism; this fear is shared by Mrs. Burton, who "wait[s] outside" while her daughter Helen's belongings are packed because she doesn't "want to enter a place like [the school]."[92] Similarly, all of the girls are pulled out of the school instantaneously—one student is requested home "right away"—a fact echoed in the events on which Hellman bases her play.[93] Additionally, the pupils at the real-life Scottish model for the Wright-Dobie school (with the exception of one) were unable to find places at other schools for fear that the knowledge of lesbianism that they had gained, if not the contagion itself, could cause an outbreak at another school.[94]

While the play makes several attempts to quarantine lesbianism in Martha's body, ultimately it cannot be compartmentalized. For example, Mrs. Tilford's expression of love for her granddaughter Mary—that she loves her "[a]s much as all the words in all the books in all the world"—is colored by the copy of *Mademoiselle de Maupin* (1835) that circulates among the school girls and from which Mary gains her partial knowledge of lesbianism.[95] Even Karen, whose surname "Wright" and fiancé (though suspiciously not a husband) provide protections against lesbianism, is implicated in the sexologically influenced description of Martha as "about the same age as Karen. She is a nervous, high-strung woman."[96] Martha's meddling aunt expands Martha's case, grounding her "unnatural" fondness for Karen in the longer history of her childhood: "You don't like their [Karen and Joe's] being together. You were always like that even as a child. If you had a little girl friend, you always got mad when she liked anybody else. Well, you'd better get a beau of your own now—a woman of your age."[97] Even this lesson in heterosexuality where Martha is instructed to "get a beau" of her own contains a slippage where the phrase "a woman of your age" might be read as a prescription to acquire a lesbian lover rather than the incitement to maturity that it is manifestly meant to be. Therefore, while Martha is largely contained within the logic of the case, within an embodied congenitality, lesbianism in *The Children's Hour* constantly exceeds the sphere of the congenital. Thus, even if by the play's conclusion Martha is a modern lesbian firmly ensconced in *psychopathia sexualis* with "a past, a case history, and a childhood," she is in the minority.[98] All of the other women and children in the play are in the sphere of situational or panicked homosexuality: Karen Wright, Mrs. Lily Mortar, Mrs. Tilford, Mary Tilford, and all of the other girls. As late as 1934, lesbianism is still, as Krafft-Ebing and Ellis have suggested, predominately situational rather than psychological, even if the lesbian has become a species.[99]

## Making the Case

From within the context of this panicked model of situational homosexuality, I want to read not just *The Children's Hour* but one of the most important moments in Hellman's career: namely, the American author

Mary McCarthy's famous charge against Hellman that—"[e]very word she writes is a lie, including 'and' and 'the.'"[100] This statement provoked Hellman to sue McCarthy in February 1980 for 2.25 million dollars and sparked one of the most colorful and exciting literary controversies of the decade. A range of luminaries including Stephen Spender, Norman Mailer, and Christopher Hitchens weighed in publicly on the controversy, and many more discussed it privately. While Hellman died leaving the lawsuit without resolution, virtually every commentator on the case felt that it was in some or multiple ways unjust or excessive: McCarthy's charge was absurd, Hellman's quest for such a large pecuniary sum was overblown, the case generated an unconscionable infringement on the First Amendment, and so on.[101]

By reading McCarthy's charge in light of representations of situational homosexuality in Hellman's *The Children's Hour*, we can understand this excess as growing out of Hellman's sexual panic or crisis of sexual identity. Much to Hellman's chagrin, McCarthy's charge of lying does not inhere in a specific act of writing but rather has the globalizing structure of identity—Hellman's writing stands accused of being a lie *tout court*.[102] Rather than evaluating whether this claim is defamatory or not (a legal standard that would also explore its truth or falsity), I want to suggest that Hellman's *The Children's Hour* does not exactly equate lesbianism and lying so much as it opens up a relay between the two related vices.[103]

Since McCarthy attended and admired the original production of Hellman's play, the figuration of lesbianism through lying seems well within the realm of possibility and may begin to explain what virtually all commentators on the suit perceive to be its excessive quality.[104] That Hellman and her circle understood it in precisely this way is borne out most clearly in a set of letters about the defamation suit that Hellman exchanges with her friend and fellow writer William Styron. Styron writes to Hellman expressing his wish that she had met McCarthy's charge with silence:

What she said about you was loathsome and, of course, in itself a lie but so outlandishly hyperbolic as to be absurd. Had she said—just for example—that you were a card carrying Party member until the year 1960 (or that you were a lesbian, or that you had committed a fraud) you would probably have a sound case.[105]

Uncertainly interrupted by a set of dashes as "just" examples, Styron's list of accusations that would provide Hellman with "a sound case" seems neither "hyperbolic" nor "absurd." Instead, his list of hypothetical charges reads more like an elaboration of the connotations of McCarthy's charge. Hellman was sympathetic to the Communist Party well through the 1960s, famously standing up to the House Un-American Activities Committee in 1952.[106] Indeed, numerous commentators in the press had already suggested that a disagreement between Hellman and McCarthy about communism dating from the Spanish Civil War was the "real" motivation for the lawsuit.[107] Similarly, since Hellman was famous for her nonfiction memoirs, McCarthy's charge was also certainly one of fraud. Given the plausibility of the charges of communism and fraud and their dissemination in the public sphere, Styron's list implies that McCarthy's charge carries the insinuation of lesbianism.

In this light, we might return to Hellman's statement that her play is not "about lesbianism but about a lie," seeing it as an anxious attempt to deflect attention from her homoerotic feelings or to bracket homosexuality in a minoritizing gesture, delimiting it as what D. A. Miller calls, in a different context, *a homosexuality of no importance.*"[108] Hellman's statement feels particularly anemic inasmuch as even a partial rendering of *The Children's Hour*'s plotting would say that it is not about lesbianism, but about a lie fabricated out of a French novel and eavesdropping that is corroborated by blackmail enabled by a theft.[109] From the title of Robert M. Kaus's *Harper's Magazine* article about the Hellman-McCarthy suit "The Plaintiff's Hour," we see that the translation of lying from its diegetic 1934 context in which Martha and Karen lose a libel suit to the defamation suit in 1980 is an easy one.[110] Moreover, the titling of Kaus's article might suggest that the larger public sphere—not just Hellman and Styron—considered lesbianism the central issue of the McCarthy suit. In this reading, we might understand McCarthy to summon an earlier sexual regime, refunctioning Hellman's 1930s sexual vocabulary ("lying" as a sign of "lesbianism") to castigate the Hellman of the 1980s. Such a profound shift in sexual valence also occurs in relation to *The Children's Hour*'s libel suit. It signals the moment in the play (with the exception of Martha's suicide) when homosexuality is most clearly figured within the realm of fixity, permanently staining the reputations of Martha and Karen. That is, if lesbianism in *The Children's Hour* takes place in a largely acts-based system of sexuality, the judge's codification of the women's "sinful sexual knowledge of one another" provides the moment in which the emergent identarian system is most visible.[111] The play ends with Karen despondent over her future, even as Mrs. Tilford is more hopeful, suggesting slightly less permanence and the possibility for transformation.

Mrs. Tilford's hopefulness is only possible, though, after envisioning that the court has issued a public apology, and even then, Karen has her doubts about the future of her reputation.[112]

While I have anatomized and separated three different models of situational homosexuality (deprivation, transformation, and panic) to explore them more fully, they intermix and overlap. All three models offer a non-identity-based understanding of sexuality—a homosexuality of rumor that comes and goes (as in the first and third models) or, if it sticks, is about choosing one pleasure over another, about getting addicted (as in the second model). As suggested by my reading of the Hellman-McCarthy suit, these non-identity-based models have gradually been folded into the emerging hegemony of the congenital model. The eclipse of situational homosexuality in the latter half of the twentieth century was crucial to the increasing solidification of the homo/hetero binary, for this regime is undergirded by the popular belief that all sexuality is congenital—innate, adhering in bodies.[113] For instance, a 2015 Gallup poll found that the majority of Americans think that "people are born gay or lesbian."[114] Likewise, Suzanna Walters asserts that "a belief in the biological immutability is now . . . the mother's milk of gay rights discourse" and John D'Emilio similarly claims that "During the 1990s, the notion that homosexuality is biological, that lesbians and gay men are 'born this way,' has spread through American culture with amazing rapidity."[115] While Walters and D'Emilio and many others express skepticism about the politics of such a position, there is no denying that it is the most commonly held belief. One effect of this assertion of congenitality is the erasure of sexuality's situatedness, naturalizing sexuality as inborn without circumstance or environmental factors. Recovering models of situational homosexuality helps us to trace the historical inauguration of a congenital seat in order to understand the history of sexuality more fully and to develop our understanding of the relationship between acquired and congenital bases of sexuality.

TWO
——

# *Anthropologia Sexualis,* Universalism, and the Macro Environments of Sex

This chapter narrates the broad shift from conceptions of an unstable, open body to one that is solid, biologized, and impermeable by exploring how the dynamic, humoral body is refashioned into an ironclad container of sexuality.[1] This solidification of the body is important for three reasons: (1) it underwrites sexuality's seizure of the body by forging a stable vessel in which to domicile sexual personhood;[2] (2) it facilitates the dominance of congenital conceptions of sexuality; (3) it enables the production of sexuality in relation to age similitude rather than age difference (the mutability of the aging body will be especially important for our inquiry in this chapter).

Male and female bodies at the turn of the twentieth century were remarkably porous, impressionable, and mutable. These bodies were able to move up or down the evolutionary chain, becoming more "civilized" or experiencing what Cesare Lombroso calls "atavistic retrogression."[3] In this evolutionary-devolutionary register, bodies might be fortified through the eugenic process that Havelock Ellis and Caleb Williams Saleeby call "race-regeneration" or might degenerate into animals through what Bénédict Augustin Morel, Emil Kraepelin, and other scientific racists call the degeneration of the race.[4] In addition to this mutability along the human-animal axis, bodies in the late nineteenth and early twentieth centuries were capable of transformation in relation to sex. For example, George Beard's *Sexual Neurasthenia* (1884) suggests that when "sex is perverted . . . men become women, and women men, in their tastes, conduct, character, feelings, and behavior."[5] Parodying the fears of thinkers like Beard, the feminist and novelist Sarah Grand humorously catalogs the effects of women who enter the public sphere: "we shall be afflicted with short hair, coarse skins, unsymmetrical figures, loud voices, tastelessness in dress, and an unnatural appearance and character generally."[6] The threat of the masculinization of women and effeminization of men was only heightened by the emerging possibility that the sexes were not distinct. Such indistinction is evident in Edward Carpenter's conception of intermediate sexes, Magnus Hirschfeld's intermediate sexual types, Ulrichs's idea of "a woman's soul in a male body," and Sigmund Freud's universal bisexuality that posited that, as Joanne Meyerowitz puts it, "all males had female features and all females had male features."[7] Moreover, experiments in endocrinology by Ernest Starling (who coined the word "hormone") posited that the removal or addition of testes could change the sex or gender behavior of the body.[8]

In order to understand these elastic bodies, it is important to contextualize them in the history of humoral theory. Early modern and eighteenth-century scholarship has charted the way that humoral theory and its legacies have constructed sex (Laqueur), sexuality (LaFleur, Nussbaum), emotion (Paster), and race (Chiles, Curran, Floyd-Wilson, Wheeler) as "transformable."[9] These accounts contend that the mutability of humoralism increasingly dissipates in the nineteenth century as the rise of genetics, eugenics, and racial sciences like anthropometry and craniometry forge sex, sexuality, and race as largely biological and biologized concepts. In this chapter, I push these histories of mutability forward into the twentieth century, contending that the putative immutability of these concepts, particularly race and sexuality, has been overstated. To this end, this chapter explores climate as the aspect of the permeable, humoral body with the longest afterlife. I mean "climate" here in the broad humoral sense to encompass the seasons, weather, temperature, air, but also the so-called "non-naturals": food, exercise, sleep, immediate environment, excretion, and venery.[10] Humoral and climate theory worked in tandem to create the balance of humors because humors were profoundly susceptible to outside influences. Roxann Wheeler argues that this idea of bodily regulation that she calls "climate/humoral theory" "provided the most important rubric for thinking about human differences in the eighteenth century."[11]

I build on this contention to argue that the persistence of "climate/ humoral theory" as an explanation of human difference into the twentieth century requires that we explore the important role that the humoral body plays in the invention of the homo/hetero binary.[12]

In the first section, this chapter expands outward from the institutional settings of situational homosexuality (the schoolroom, the barracks, the prison) discussed in the previous chapter to explore how sexuality is acquired at a much larger scale. I argue that climate is an etiology of sexuality well into the twentieth century and that an exploration of what Iwan Bloch calls "Anthropologia Sexualis" will highlight the meanings of the shift from the humoral body to a germ theory of the body for the construction of sexuality.[13] In the second section, I read Thomas Mann's *Death in Venice* (1912) as a text that roots homosexuality in the competing epidemiological regimes of *anthropologia sexualis*'s humoralism and *scientia sexualis*'s germ theory.[14] Mann's novella thus provides a key switch point for understanding the final disaggregation of sexuality and humoralism and provides rich models for theorizing sexuality as climatic on the one hand and microbial on the other.[15] I argue that the humoral theory of the body with which climate is associated was expunged in the service of stabilizing sexuality for biopolitical control. In the final section, I reframe this climatological narrative in the terms of its contemporary critics to suggest that this stabilization of the biological body also entails a movement away from age-differentiated sexuality.

At bottom, this chapter is interested in the construction of *anthropologia sexualis* as a universalizing model of sexuality that stands in contradistinction to the minoritizing model of *scientia sexualis*.[16] Bloch posits that all people regardless of race, class, or nation have the same relation to pathological sexuality.[17] This *anthropologia sexualis*'s attunement to the "physical foundation" of the "idiosyncrasies" of "sex . . . in every time and clime" suggests climate as the chief motor force and explanation for sexual variety in and across large geographic areas and historical periods.[18] Against *scientia sexualis*'s "limited circles of . . . sexual perversions," Bloch's *anthropologia sexualis* "establish[es] universal, human phenomenon."[19] Where the minor perverts of the *scientia sexualis* individuate and minoritize, the "general human phenomenon" characteristic of *anthropologia sexualis* universalizes, suggesting both the enormity of its designs on sexuality and the important function of climate in the construction of modern sexuality.[20]

### Some Like It Hot

The medical establishment was in virtual unanimity in the late nineteenth and early twentieth centuries that climate had an enormous impact on sexual life and possessed the differentiating function that Bloch theorized. In *Sexual Inversion* (1897), for example, the famed sexologists Havelock Ellis and John Addington Symonds observe a "special proclivity" for homosexuality in "the hotter regions of the globe."[21] Similarly, Iwan Bloch contends that "there can be no doubt that in the hotter regions of the earth the normal sex impulse and the abnormal expression of it appear earlier and more intensely as well as more extensively than in the colder zones."[22] Eugen Steinach describes the "sex life" of inhabitants of "warm latitudes" as manifesting "more intensive and rapid development than in the more temperate zones."[23] Moreover, the sexologist Auguste Forel asserts: "A good deal has been said concerning the hot blood of warm climates, and on the whole it appears true that people who inhabit these climates have a more violent and more precocious sexual temperament than those who live in cold regions."[24] These sexologists repeatedly assert that hot climate is associated with sexual precocity: for Bloch, the sexual impulse manifests "earlier," "more intensely," and "more extensively," for Steinach, "more intensive[ly]" and rapidly developing, for Forel "more violent[ly]" and "more precocious[ly]."[25] I will return to hot climate's impact on the sexual life course and its hastening of puberty shortly, but for now I just want to note that the causal relation between hot climate and sexual licentiousness dates back at least to Montesquieu's *The Spirit of the Laws* (1748), where he writes of "the vices of [hot] climate."[26] Robert Tobin recovers the signifier "warm brothers" as a way to discuss male-male sexual relations in eighteenth-century Germany and W. H. Auden uses the word *schwül* (meaning humid) as a signifier for "gay" in 1929 Berlin.[27] Victor Segalen further extends this association, noting under the heading *"Sexual Exoticism"* in his "Essay on Exoticism" (1918) that there is "Not much Arctic Exoticism."[28]

This model of climatic sexuality infuses not only the medico-legal-anthropological work of sexology, but also literature. In *Venus in Furs* (1870), for example, one character posits that "Hot climates produce more passionate temperaments, and warmth itself acts as a bodily excitant."[29] James Joyce's *Ulysses* (1922) features one such "passionate temperament[]," described by Leopold Bloom as "com[ing] from the great heat, climate generally."[30] Similarly, E. M. Forster recorded his impressions of India, writing: "The climate soon impaired my will; I did not suffer from the heat in other ways, but it provoked me sexually."[31] One of the characters in Nancy Mitford's *Love in a Cold Climate* (1949) also suffers from India's sexual heat and holds out the possibility that sexual desire will abate when she moves to London's cooler climate.[32] These examples suggest that even as other areas of medicine had long abandoned humoral explanations of disease, sexuality provided a strange reserve of residual climatological thinking.

With this climatological construction of sexuality in mind, I want to turn to the infamous explorer and translator Richard Burton, particularly his "Terminal Essay" (1886), in which he outlines his climatological theories. Named for its place at the end of his translation of *The Arabian Nights* (an important *ars erotica* text), Burton's essay theorizes the existence of a Sotadic Zone (after the Greek poet Sotades's homoerotic verse) in which certain areas of the globe incline visitors and inhabitants toward homosexuality. I take Burton as my guide, understanding him as theorizing an anthropological and climatic model of sexuality rather than one rooted in *scientia sexualis* or *psychopathia sexualis*.[33] Burton's *anthropologia sexualis* associates certain parts of the globe with particular sexualities, while employing climate as a discourse to explain variety and variegation. While this now seems difficult to conceptualize, historically individual sexual practices have often been associated with particular geographies (for example, lesbianism is associated with Lesbos, sodomy with Sodom, and "buggering" as a corruption of the word "Bulgar" is associated with the heretics of Bulgaria).[34] Similarly, certain climates could induce varieties of sexual behavior; Bloch, for example, describes "tropical frenzy" as constituting "a peculiar cause for sadistic behavior."[35] He continues: "It is a recognized fact that some Europeans who have been known in their homeland as peaceful, harmless and humane individuals and have taken up residence in some tropical region, have suddenly revealed themselves as brutal, bloodthirsty and degenerate tyrants."[36] We might read Bloch's account of this minor perversion as an example of the impact climate has on sexuality, and it begins to suggest the persistence of the thinking that Felicity Nussbaum describes as the sexualization of "whole areas of the world."[37]

But Burton's theorization of the Sotadic Zone also constitutes an amplification of the thinking that links geographies and sexualities. The sheer mind-boggling expansiveness of the Sotadic Zone—its universalizing scope and its powers of queer world-making—are profoundly unlike anything that has preceded it. Burton charts the limits of sexuality as coterminous with huge sections of the earth:

1. There exists what I shall call a "Sotadic Zone," bounded westwards by the northern shores of the Mediterranean (N. Lat. 43°) and by the southern (N. Lat. 30°). Thus the depth would be 780 to 800 miles including meridional France, the Iberian Peninsula, Italy and Greece, with the coast-regions of Africa from Marocco to Egypt.
2. Running eastward the Sotadic Zone narrows, embracing Asia Minor, Mesopotamia and Chaldaea, Afghanistan, Sind, the Punjab and Kashmir.
3. In Indo-China the belt begins to broaden, enfolding China, Japan and Turkistan.
4. It then embraces the South Sea Islands and the New World where, at the time of its discovery, Sotadic love was, with some exceptions, an established racial institution.
5. Within the Sotadic Zone the Vice is popular and endemic, held at the worst to be a mere peccadillo, whilst the races to the North and South of the limits here defined practise it only sporadically amid the opprobrium of their fellows who, as a rule, are physically incapable of performing the operation and look upon it with the liveliest disgust.[38]

Climatology furnishes Burton with a way to draw distinctions between human beings whose common monogenetic, Adamic origin should make them the same.[39] That is, it provides a middle position between monogenetic and polygenetic understandings of race, not yet positing what M. F. Ashley Montagu will understand as the genetic homogeneity of race, but also eschewing much of the racism of the polygenetic position (that different races come from different species).[40] The classificatory work of the Sotadic Zone (using climate as a technique of differentiation) simplifies and categorizes *The Arabian Nights*'s incredible range of stories from many national origins into a single kind of pleasure: pederastic.[41] This simplification imagines a set of sexual proclivities rooted in climatic forces, suggesting the extent to which his theory of sexuality is, in his words, "geographical and climatic, not racial." Furthermore, the slow panoramic glide of Burton's present-tense description of the Sotadic Zone ("There exists," "the belt begins to broaden," "It then embraces," etc.), as if he were narrating a map, suggests the movement of sexuality within the zone itself and the particular susceptibilities of a traveler's sexuality. That is, a traveler's sexuality takes new shapes as it enters new geographies and climates.

The Sotadic Zone provided a springboard for future sexological and literary engagements with climate (even as I am arguing that it also codified earlier beliefs). Expounding on Burton's work in a section with the heading "Sotadic Zone of Extravagant Vice," Bloch offers perhaps the fullest explanation for what he calls "the influence of a warmer climate in hastening sexual development and intensifying the sexual sensations."[42] While it is never exactly explained why the heat is associated with an increased sex drive—this idea enjoys unanimous approbation in the sexological community—Bloch does explain that "the earlier appearance and greater intensity of the *libido* [in warm climates] more frequently necessitate such means of increasing titillation."[43] Since warm climates increase sexual appetite and drive, they also generate sexual aberration because desiring subjects are willing to engage in any act no matter how "gross and unnatural" to satisfy their lust.[44] Thus, Bloch claims that the "earlier appearance" of libido "is extremely conducive to the origin and fixation of sexual aberrations" because the beginning of puberty marks "[t]he time in which the imagination displays its richest activity" and its most creative envisaging of new sexual aberrations.[45] Additionally, the need for increased titillation creates a preference for anal sex because "the [warm] climate causes the genitals of the southern women to become lax very early."[46] Bloch understands this genital deformation as "plainly a step in transition toward homosexuality" since men "seeking greater friction-titillation" will engage in "*coitus analis* with a woman or with a boy."[47] Here, Bloch ascribes a motive for desire that is less psychological and more rooted in the functionality of sex ("friction-titillation") in a foreign locale.[48] In other words, an *anthropologia sexualis* rather than a *psychopathia sexualis*.

It would not be difficult to find colonial ideology lurking behind Burton's and Bloch's climatic sexuality. We might note, for example, that Burton describes "Sotadic love" in the South Sea Islands and the New World as largely "an established racial institution," thereby installing a racial underpinning to the system (or at least a part of it) that Burton insists is climatic. This determinism between race and sexual practice is also evident in the Sotadic Zone's exclusion of sub-Saharan Africa, promulgating the period myth that Africans were too innocent, natural, and unsophisticated to practice homosexuality.[49] Similarly, Bloch asserts that the Orient "has been a hot-house of sexual excess" since "time immemorial."[50] While he sees this excess as being "chiefly climatic," religious prejudice and fantasies of *ars erotica* are smuggled in when he comments on Islamic teachings as "permeated with sensuality."[51] The questioning of these climatic claims is in fact the tack taken by Burton's contemporary, the sexologist John Addington Symonds. In his book *A Problem in Modern Ethics* (1891), Symonds attempts to recast and supplement Burton's evidence in order to shift the etiology of homosexuality. Symonds argues that homosexuality "takes place universally" and conjectures that it is "tolerated in certain parts of the globe, which he [Burton] defines as the Sotadic Zone."[52] He suggests instead that "[t]he problem is therefore not geographic and climatic, but social."[53] While I will return to Symonds's effort to read the social as replacing the climatic, for the moment I want to recover the affordances, particularities, and theoretical potentialities of the climatic as well as its historical impact on the construction of the homo/hetero binary. Thus, this chapter is less interested in either the internal consistency or truth of Burton's, or Bloch's, or Symonds's climatic theories than in the set of theoretical and historical possibilities that they open up for modeling sexuality and for thinking about how these models are incorporated in the homo/hetero binary. That is, I am interested in how humoral organizations of sexuality are recast with the invention of sexuality and the effect that they have on age-differentiated constructions of sexuality in particular.

## Susceptible Subjects

A number of period texts link climate, queer sexuality, orientalism, and disease, but I focus on Mann's *Death in Venice* because it showcases epidemiological models that compete with the humoral. By the time of the novella's composition, humoral understandings of disease— whether emanating from an imbalance of the humors or from the miasma theory of "bad air" or "pestilential air"—were on the wane.[54] Miasmatic theory has its origin with Hippocrates and posits that "bad air" or "pestilential air" steaming "from swamps and stagnant waters, filthy and crowded living conditions and putrefaction of organic matter" caused disease.[55] This older set of ideas was being replaced by a new microbial understanding of disease.[56] This emerging germ theory—made possible by the research of Louis Pasteur and others in the 1860s—understood microbes to be the agents of disease. Pasteur's ideas took an exceptionally long time to gain acceptance.[57] I call attention to the epidemiological competition between the microbial and the miasmatic because *Death in Venice* moves uneasily between them. It memorably and robustly analogizes homosexuality and cholera, illustrating how different epidemiological models offer different etiologies of sexuality.

*Death in Venice* shares characteristics with Priscilla Wald's "outbreak narrative," which features "the identification of an emerging infection" and "includes discussion of the global networks throughout which it travels."[58] That said, the novella does not conclude with "the epidemiological work that ends with its containment."[59] Instead the narrative turns toward the hushed tones of a cover-up, a kind of secret outbreak narrative. After Gustav von Aschenbach arrives in Venice, he realizes that the Venetian authorities and local populace are attempting to conceal the cholera outbreak, pretending that nothing more is happening than some unseasonably hot weather:

> They're trying to keep it quiet! But at the same time, he was happy about the adventure awaiting the world around him. For the established order and well-being of normal life run counter not only to crime but also to passion, which welcomes, and vaguely hopes to benefit from, any loosening of the bourgeois fabric, any confusion and affliction of the world. So Aschenbach felt a dark satisfaction about what was happening in the filthy alleys of Venice, about the official cover-up and the city's nasty secret—a secret that blended with his own most private secret and that he, too, was intent on guarding. For the lover had only one anxiety: that Tadzio might leave Venice; and Aschenbach realized, not without dismay, that he would not know how to go on living if that occurred.[60]

Mann articulates Aschenbach's queer desire for Tadzio in the language of climate and disease, creating a homology between the "city's nasty secret" (the "oppressive" [342] weather is actually a disguise for a cholera "cover-up") and Aschenbach's "private secret" (that he stays in Venice not to improve his health, but to desire a young boy).[61] Both the city's secret and Aschenbach's secret "run counter" to "normal life" and "well-being," queerly rending the "bourgeois fabric" and opening the possibility for dark adventures and "passion" that borders the criminal.[62] This shared necropolitical project culminates in Aschenbach's death and the homologous deaths of many of Venice's inhabitants. Such analogies between disease and vice were common and can be heard even more explicitly in the title of Julius Rosenbaum's *The Plague of Lust* (1901). Similarly, Burton's text repeatedly uses the language of disease to describe homosexuality, referring to "periodical outbreaks" in "London, Berlin and Paris" and characterizing the spread of homosexuality in epidemiological language: "[o]utside the Sotadic Zone, I have said, Le Vice is sporadic, not endemic."[63]

The articulation of homosexuality through humoral theory's epidemiological language in Burton and Mann reaches its apotheosis in the description of what Wald would understand as the "global networks" moment of Mann's outbreak narrative. This description of the travels of the cholera outbreak corresponds substantially with the Sotadic Zone's climatic cartography of desire:[64]

For several years now, Indian cholera had been showing a greater and greater tendency to spread and wander. Originating in the hot morasses of the Ganges Delta. . . . the epidemic had raged and raged with unusual vehemence throughout Hindustan, spreading eastward to China and westward to Afghanistan and Persia; and then, following the main caravan routes, it had carried its horrors to Astrachan and even Moscow. But while Europe was terrified that the specter might travel there by land, it had been transported overseas by Syrian merchant ships, cropping up almost simultaneously in several Mediterranean ports. Next, it had reared its head in Toulon and Málaga, showed its mask at several points in Palermo and Naples, and apparently settled in for good throughout Calabria and Apulia. However, the northern part of the peninsula had been spared. (354)

Here "the hot morasses of the Ganges Delta" suggest a miasmatic understanding of cholera, with the swampy morasses expelling pestilential air.[65] Mann's depiction of cholera does not function as a mere vehicle for depicting deviant sexuality but imagines cholera itself to be associated with such sexuality.[66] Writing about the cholera epidemics that engulfed Europe in the 1820s, Frank Mort chronicles the attribution of the disease to "the physical and moral habits of the poor."[67] In Scotland, for example, Mort recounts the story of a mill girl who "had been living 'very perniciously' with an Irishman named Murray" and their subsequent deaths.[68] Mort records how these deaths were described by a local doctor as a result of "the couple's irregular conduct, 'living in the closest intimacy.'"[69] Similarly, Bloch concurs with and lauds the "immortal service of [Johann Ludwig] Caspar and [Richard] von Krafft-Ebing to have insisted energetically upon the fact that numerous individuals whose *vita sexualis* is abnormal are persons suffering of disease."[70] Bloch here suggests a causal link between disease and abnormal sexuality, that they are comorbidities.[71]

Likewise, Mann's conjunction of Orientalized miasma and sexualized cholera begins to suggest a humoral etiology of sexuality. In this humoral model, everyone in a given climatic area is susceptible to becoming a homosexual. Rather than imagine sexuality starting and ending with the limits of the body or defining it through the body's contours and geometries, climate imagines a very different origin and distribution of sexuality.[72] A climate motivates a specific performance, inducing and affecting subjects within its circumference to different degrees (depending on their susceptibility to the climate's power). We might understand this profoundly environmental sexuality as offering a forgotten nonsubjective organization of sexuality, one that answers Foucault's famous call for "a counterattack against the deployment of sexuality" not with "bodies and pleasures" but with environments and temperatures.[73]

Positioned within this humoral model, Aschenbach is susceptible to Venice's climatic force, noting that "years ago . . . such weather had afflicted him, wrecking his health so badly that he had been forced to abscond from Venice like a fugitive" (315).[74] Before he sets out for Venice, Aschenbach is in Munich feeling "overwrought" and experiencing "the growing depletion of his strength" (287). His constitution is described as "anything but robust" (294) (accounting in part for this susceptibility) and city life saps his energy, inducing the exhaustion of modern life that Max Nordau characterizes as degeneration.[75] In order to rejuvenate himself, he takes some "fresh air and exercise" to "restore his energy" (287). The fresh air and exercise (both of which might be considered non-naturals) imply a humoral imbalance, borne out by Aschenbach's dread of the upcoming "summer in the country" and "the mountain peaks and mountain walls that would again surround his sluggish dissatisfaction" (292). In his enervated state he has a miasmatic vision: of "a tropical quagmire under a steamy sky, muggy, luxuriant, and monstrous, a primordial jungle of islands, morasses, and alluvial inlets," populated with "rank and rampant ferns," "stagnant waters," and "a crouching tiger" (290). While the fetid ferns and stagnant water suggest the corrupting influence of ill health on the humoral system, Aschenbach settles on a change of climate, one which is "not too far, not all the way to the tigers" (292). But he ends up journeying farther than he had initially planned.

We might read Aschenbach's unexpected journeying as resulting from another minor perversion: what the text terms "wanderlust" [*Reiselust*].[76] In the context of the humoral body, wanderlust is a sexological perversion because the humoral body is susceptible to change (even as its ego-ideal is unchanging equilibrium). The wanderlusting subject in his physical, geographical movement externalizes the plasticity of the humoral body when it is in disequilibrium. That is, wanderlust is a vice because it suggests an openness (and perhaps even a willingness) to change. For example, in *The Feebly Inhibited; Nomadism, or the Wandering Impulse, with Special Reference to Heredity* (1915), the prominent eugenicist and biologist Charles Davenport argues that "all cases of nomadism can be ascribed to one fundamental cause—that those who show the trait belong to the nomadic race."[77] Davenport transforms movement into a racial characteristic that is defined by "the absence of the germinal marker that makes for sedentariness, stability, [and] domesticity."[78] Given that Aschenbach's depiction is based on the Jewish composer Gustav Mahler (with whom he shares a first name and appearance), we might understand Aschenbach's wanderlust as a racialized representation of Mahler as a Wandering Jew.[79] Lacking the impulses of stability and domesticity that are the hallmarks of normative family life, the Jewish Aschenbach's wanderlust is a sexual pathology that, Davenport explains, is associated with "uncontrolled eroticism, leading to various unsocial acts in the sex-realm."[80] While Davenport understands wanderlust as a kind of gateway onto other sexual perversions, another doctor, P. R. Vessie, describes wanderlust as itself a perversion, characterized by a lack "of selfrestraint" [sic] and as gratifying "the natural instinct called lust."[81] Similarly, the famous Chicago School sociologist Robert E. Park characterized the movements of the hobo as suffering the pathology of wanderlust: "The hobo is, to be sure, always on the move, but he has no destination, and naturally he never arrives. Wanderlust, which is the most elementary expression of the romantic temperament and the romantic interest in life, has assumed for him, as for so many others, the character of a vice."[82] Here, Park and Vessie contend that wanderlust's peripatetic and sexual aimlessness (movement without direction) and its objectlessness (having "no destination") suggest it as a perversion in and of itself. Aschenbach's wanderlust seems closer to Davenport's nosography; the artist's "forbidden penchant that was entirely antithetical to his mission" suggests a kind of openness to perversion or a kind of will to perversion (318).

This destinationless wandering and inability to arrive afflicts Aschenbach as he moves rapidly from one location to another, first entertaining the possibility of "leav[ing] Europe," (290) then imagining "some cosmopolitan resort in the charming south" (292) before deciding "to spend the evening poring over maps and timetables" (292). But all this reflection leaves him as unsettled and uncertain as ever. He instructs "his servants to prepare his mountain cottage," boards "the night train to Trieste," sails "to Pola," before heading to "an Adriatic island . . . not far off the Istrian coast" (301). After he arrives there, he is still "haunted by an anxious longing to move on" without "knowing where" and studies the "boat routes . . . for an idea" (301). All these peregrinations and divagations eventually lead him to Venice. Even when arriving in Venice, Aschenbach has trouble reaching his destination (arguing with the gondolier over how to arrive at his hotel), not "unpack[ing] fully" (315), deciding to leave again, and then staying in Venice when he realizes "it was Tadzio who had made it so difficult for him to leave" (328). Here, his aimless, objectless wanderlust takes Tadzio as its object.

This attachment to Tadzio is framed as a universal admiration of classical beauty and located within the tradition of age-differentiated (homosexual) love (Mann's text incorporates both classical references and Greek metrical patterns).[83] In contradistinction to this universalizing, humoral model of sexuality, the text also posits a minoritizing model of sexuality—associated with germ theory—that divides people between sick and healthy. As Robert Tobin argues the text features a number of "characters with a series of shared characteristics": they have "snub noses," "large Adam's apples," "yellowish, slightly sickly skin," reddish hair, too-prominent teeth, and tend to "signal their membership in this group with a number of fashion markers—rakishly titled and colorfully beribboned straw hats, red ties[,] and sailor's outfits."[84] While these characteristics are a polythetic set, they begin to suggest that these men are infected with the disease of homosexuality manifesting the same symptoms. This model of contagion from one individual to another (rather than the predisposition of climate) suggests a different penumbra of sexuality, one organized around stranger sociability and, in the case of *Death in Venice*, foreign lines of transmission.[85]

On his journey to Venice, Aschenbach repeatedly expresses his disgust for one of these infected, homosexual men "wearing an overly fashionable, pale-yellow summer suit, a red tie, and a flippantly up-tilted panama hat encircled by a colorful scarf. . . . But no sooner did Aschenbach focus on him than, somewhat shocked, he realized that this was a bogus youth. The man was old, there was no doubting it. . . . Horrified, Aschenbach watched him and the way he associated with his friends" (303). Noticing his makeup, toupee, dyed facial hair, dentures, and rings, Aschenbach feels that "he had no right to wear . . . colorful dandyish clothes, no right to pretend he was 'young'" (303). In spite of this horror, by the end of the story Aschenbach becomes one of these men, donning a red necktie, wearing makeup, and dying his hair until it "was as black as in his youth" (360). We might read Aschenbach's transformation as embodying a shift from a universal, humoral model of sexuality to a minoritized, implantation model rooted in germ theory, suggesting that humoral theory and germ theory offer differing and competing medical models of sexuality.[86] That is, in the earlier part of the text homosexuality is understood as environmentally constituted, affecting a humorally susceptible subject but without changing the fundamental constitution of the subject (leaving the environment will free him of its climactic influence). In contrast, at the end of the text, under the rubric of germ theory, homosexuality has become a disease that permanently modifies the subject's constitution once he is infected. The increasing dominance of germ theory is underwritten

by a profound stabilization that is crucial for the implantation of homosexuality in the body. By this I mean that this stable body provides
the foundation for the temporal always of the homo/hetero binary that
I discussed in chapter 1. That is, these desires are constructed as unchanging and immutable, as rooted in and through the body, forging a
sturdy foundation for sexual identity.

## Climate's Governmentality

This shift from the open humoral body to the closed germ theory body
is part of a larger stabilization of the body that I described at the beginning of this chapter (even as I argue that it is held open longer than
commentators usually suggest). In this section, I chart how *Death in
Venice* maps a second stabilization of the body: namely, the shift from
an aging body moving through sexual stages to one that roots sexual
identity in age similitude and consent. In charting the stability of the
sexual body across age, I hope to demonstrate how age consistency
attempts to neutralize or circumscribe the aging and still-changing
closed congenital body. This de-emphasis on age is crucial to forging
biological sex as the primary diacritical marker of object-choice sexuality. That is, it forges an age-consistent model of congenital homosexuality as against an age-differentiated, acquired model.

Aschenbach's first sighting of Tadzio immediately establishes their
relationship within the age-differentiated conventions of classical pederasty: "Aschenbach was amazed to see that the boy was absolutely
beautiful. His face, pale and of a graceful reserve, surrounded by honey-
colored curls, with its straight nose, lovely lips, earnest expression,
sweet and godly, all recalled Greek statues of the noblest era . . . he had
never encountered such perfection in nature or in the arts" (312). Here,
Tadzio embodies the highest and most ennobling aesthetic ideals; he
is an object to be gazed on, one analogized to Greek statues. Mann's
repeated invocation of Tadzio as a statue—radiating with "the yellow
shimmer of Parian marble" (316), "his armpits were still as smooth as
a statue's" (332)—underlines Tadzio as, to borrow David Halperin's
description of the boy's role in classical pederasty, "sexually inert."[87]
As Halperin explains: "Neither boys nor women were thought to possess the sort of desires that would impel them to become autonomous
sexual actors in their relations with men."[88] At the text's outset, Tadzio
exemplifies this classical model: "a nonexpressive divinity" (319). However, as the narrative progresses the relationship between Aschenbach

and Tadzio changes dramatically, becoming instead a model of identity and age similitude. The visuality of the "bogus youth" and of Aschenbach after the barber dyes his hair and applies makeup to him suggests that age is less and less essential as a diacritical marker of object choice. Similarly, since Tadzio looks "ill" and dons a "sailor suit" festooned with "loops, braids, and embroideries" (313), he shares the visual characteristics of the adult men infected with homosexuality. In short, the bodies of Aschenbach and Tadzio increasingly resemble each other. Moreover, Tadzio's encouragement of Aschenbach when Aschenbach is following him ("walking behind his family . . . he would peek back over his shoulder with his peculiar, twilight-gray eyes to make sure his lover was trailing him") (362) suggests that, as Jeffrey Masten writes in another context, this "is not the blank slate that boy-subjectivity is said to be in classical pederasty" but rather something closer to a consenting desire.[89] Tadzio's desire is, by the story's end, nearly indistinguishable from Aschenbach's desire. In other words, the text concludes by imagining the desires of Aschenbach and Tadzio as enmeshed in the minoritized discourse of the *scientia sexualis* rather than the universality of the *anthropologia sexualis* (mutable only in relation to climate).

We might understand this shift from age difference to age similitude as mapping the collision of what Symonds would understand as two social systems of sexuality: namely, what is tendentiously called "Western sexuality" and what is called the "Mediterranean" or "Greek" model of age-differentiated sexuality.[90] The text's setting in Venice—with its historical role as Europe's trading portal to the Byzantine Empire and much of the Muslim world—makes it ideal for considering the relationship between so-called Western and Eastern systems of sexuality.[91] In the gender-based Mediterranean model, sex was "not knit up in a web of mutuality, not something one invariably has *with* someone," but something one *does* to someone.[92] In the late nineteenth and early twentieth centuries, the active/insertive/masculine male was not regarded as homosexual while the passive/receptive/feminine male was regarded as possessing a distinct identity, one characterized as unmanly and queer. In contrast, the Western model was not age differentiated and saw both partners, active and passive, as homosexual.[93] With this difference in mind, Symonds's reading of the social highlights the question of age in *Death in Venice* and Burton's "Terminal Essay," particularly in light of Aschenbach's pursuit of the adolescent Tadzio and Burton's description of "Le Vice" as "pederastic."

Throughout this chapter I have been reading homosexuality and pederasty ("the sexual pursuit of adolescent males by adult males") as synonymous, and there is good reason to do so since the terms were used interchangeably in the period.[94] However, in this section, I differentiate homosexuality and pederasty because I agree with Kadji Amin that modern pederasty "has been undertheorized within queer scholarship."[95] In particular, modern pederasty has been overly conflated with both homosexuality and its ancient instantiations.[96] Attending to the differences between homosexuality and modern pederasty without losing sight of their imbrication enables us to conceptualize what I have been describing as the shift from humoral to germ theory as also an eclipse of Eastern/Mediterranean models of sexuality by Western models. To put this differently, I want to argue that Symonds's idea of the social reframes this competition as one between modes of governmentality: as an encounter between perceptions of Western democracy and Oriental despotism. Venice's status as a gateway between both East and West highlights this clash. In particular, I will argue that the moment of the invention of Western sexuality is one of increasing sexual egalitarianism that is contrasted with the imagined authoritarianism of the Orient (a tyranny that, as I argued earlier, is also associated with "tropical frenzy"). Additionally, I contend that the figure of the youth—on the border between consent and submission—became increasingly charged in this perceived opposition between East and West. This understanding of the youth will also help us to clarify the Foucauldian distinction between *scientia sexualis* and *ars erotica*, bringing these two formulations of sexuality into focus as itself an *anthropologia sexualis*.

Ars erotica and *scientia sexualis* represent for Foucault two "procedures for producing the truth of sex."[97] The *ars erotica* draws truth from pleasure, is learned from a master, and is largely associated with the East, while *scientia sexualis* draws its knowledge from "the bond, the basic intimacy in discourse between the one who speaks and what he is speaking about."[98] *Scientia sexualis* is learned from below in the "slow surfacing of confidential statements" and is associated with the West.[99] Having set up this opposition, Foucault suggests that the *scientia sexualis* is in fact a "subtle form" of *ars erotica*, one that takes its "pleasure in the truth of pleasure."[100] Building on Foucault's theorization of these two traditions, Sanjay K. Gautam's important book *Foucault and the Kamasutra* (2016) argues that these traditions articulate "a conflict over the primacy or sovereignty" of truth and pleasure.[101] That is, *ars erotica* posits pleasure as superordinate to truth whereas *scientia sexualis* posits truth as superordinate to pleasure. Or as Gautam puts it, "Thus, in *ars erotica*, the notion of truth finds itself subordinated to that of pleasure, a situation exactly the reverse of *scientia sexualis*, in which truth is the sovereign category."[102]

We could understand the relationship between *ars erotica* and *scientia sexualis* as also mapping two types of governmentality. That is to say, *ars erotica*'s emphasis on mastery associates it with perceptions of Oriental/Asiatic despotism, whereas *scientia sexualis*'s emphasis on egalitarian access to the truth of one's subjectivity associates it with Western democracy. Alain Grosrichard traces the long history conflating despotism and Asia, locating the seraglio/harem as its central precinct:

> Oriental despotism is essentially bound up with a certain kind of relation between the sexes, with a certain sexual economy. . . . The sexual *jouissance* without limits which is allowed him [the despot] as an exclusive right is also the means of his absolute power and the fundamental explanation of the form this power takes. . . . [T]he heart of despotic power in the Orient, extending over vast empires, is hidden in that very place where the despot exercises his *domestic* power: in that walled space, forbidden to the gaze, saturated by sex and structured by it—the seraglio.[103]

Here, the historical imbrication between Asia and despotism is understood to be structured by a particular sexual economy (the harem) and, as Grosrichard makes clear, a particular climate: namely the hot weather that thinkers from Aristotle to Montesquieu associate with docility and slavery.[104] That is, the warm climate makes its inhabitants particularly vulnerable to the enslaving despot.

Deploying this vision of absolute despotic pleasure as a foil, Anglo-American sexuality was gradually fashioning itself in a variety of spheres as more consent-based and thus increasingly democratic and egalitarian (thereby bolstering Western colonial ambitions). The slow erosion of coverture—the fiction that "a wife's legal existence was merged into that of her husband at the moment of marriage" and that her property and legal capacities were his alone—in England and America in the nineteenth century paved the way for marriages to be less hierarchical.[105] The 1857 legalization of civil divorce in England reformed marriage to make it a more "plastic institution," one that was based on, as Sharon Marcus explains, "a dissoluble contract based on equality, rather than an irrevocable vow that created hierarchy."[106] As marriage became increasingly consent-based, the mid-1880s witnessed concomitant changes in the age of consent in the United States and England. Nayan Shah evocatively describes the last decades of the nineteenth century and the first decades of the twentieth in America and Canada as "undergoing a cataclysmic shift in social consciousness and legal protections for girls and their relations with adult men."[107] This reorganization was consent- and status-based as it increased the size of the class of individuals who could not consent ("minors" and "children") in order to reinforce the consent of those who could ("adults"). The age of male-female consent was gradually and unevenly raised upward in the United States (and similar changes transpired in England contemporaneously).[108] This necessity for consent underlines not just pedophilia but also necrophilia, bestiality, dendrophilia, and sex with statues as bad objects (since such bad objects cannot consent).

The contrast between the vision of the despotic Orient and the freely consenting West is written into the racist 1875 Page Law that sought primarily to arrest the flow of Chinese prostitution into the US, requiring immigration officials to distinguish between wives and prostitutes. The distinction was extremely difficult for US officials to police because the Chinese sex/gender system operated very differently from US norms, resulting in the barring of the majority of Chinese women:

[D]uring hard times in China, women and girls were commonly sold into domestic service, concubinage, or prostitution, and one form of sale could lead to another. Yet not all domestic servants, called *mui tsai*, were resold; some continued providing domestic service until freed through marriage. But the practice of selling women, and the difficulties of differentiating between various kinds of sales, led immigration officials to assume that all girls traveling in groups were surely prostitutes, rather than, for example, *mui tsai*. A further source of confusion to officials was the fact that some Chinese men had concubines, in addition to first wives. Concubines, who were usually of lower social status and acquired through purchase, were legal members of the family, and their children were their father's legal heirs. But concubinage, which reflected a sex and gender system that was different from the dominant US culture, contributed to officials' beliefs that virtually all immigrant Chinese women were enslaved prostitutes.[109]

Here, the Western fantasy of the Orient produces the East as a space of nonconsent and sets the consenting West in relief. This fantasy, as Gayatri Spivak has famously argued, was used as a justification for colonialism inasmuch as it suggests, in Spivak's famous phrase, "[w]hite men saving brown women from brown men."[110]

While this difference of consent has been primarily figured in relation to women's bodies, Mann's and Burton's texts suggest that the figure of the male youth (who, in the Western imaginary, cannot consent) is essential to understanding the relation between Western and Mediterranean/Oriental models of sexuality and, as I will argue, *scien-*

*tia sexualis* and *ars erotica*. Here I follow Joseph Boone's contention that "the beautiful boy. . . . consistently threads its way throughout Oriental and Orientalist homoerotics" in order to consider how *ars erotica* and *scientia sexualis* conceptualize the figure of the child differently, making the disarticulation of homosexuality and pederasty crucial.[111]

In Foucault's *History of Sexuality*, he argues that children provide "a basis for constructing a science that is beyond their grasp," suggesting that children are the lynchpin of *scientia sexualis*.[112] Their centrality is a result of their position both inside and outside of *scientia sexualis*'s knowledge economy: "practically all children indulge or are prone to indulge in sexual activity; and that, being unwarranted, at the same time 'natural' and 'contrary to nature' . . . children were defined as 'preliminary' sexual beings, on this side of sex, yet within it, astride a dangerous dividing line."[113] Thus, the changing status of the relationship between childhood and sexuality in the West (indexed by age of consent laws) marks the figure of the child as crucial to the construction of sexual subjectivity (inasmuch as subjects can be defined increasingly as consenting or not). Through the figure of the Western child and its contrast with the fantasy of Eastern despotic (read: unlimited) pleasure, we begin to see how same-sex relations shifted from a model of age-differentiated pederasty to a model of age-similar homosexuality. That is, the Western model envisions sexual relations that are less power differentiated (here age difference indexes power) in contrast to the fantasy of Eastern sexuality as characterized by anti-egalitarian impulses, even as, of course, Western sexuality is constituted in and through power, particularly in relation to race, class, and gender.[114]

We can witness this transformation in sexual subjectivity by looking at how US laws criminalized same-sex contact with minors at the close of the nineteenth and advent of the twentieth centuries. William N. Eskridge Jr. has detailed how these laws became increasingly consent-based, effecting a dramatic shift in legal constructions of sexuality:

In 1881 Indiana amended its sodomy law to include enticement of minors "to commit masturbation," and in 1897 Michigan created a separate and more serious crime for sodomy with boys. After 1900 most states adopted criminal laws protecting the sexual purity of male as well as female children. In 1897 Illinois criminalized "any immoral, improper or indecent liberties with any child of either sex, under the age of fifteen years". . . . Most popular were statutes making it a crime to "contribute to the delinquency of a minor," a concept inaugurated by Massachusetts in 1906. Nineteen states, mostly with urban centers, had such statutes by the end of World War I.[115]

These laws were fueled in part by sensationalistic journalism, what Philip Jenkins terms "a wave of journalistic accounts of notorious sex crimes and serial killings."[116] But they were also constructed in response to a small group of sexologists like that of Charles Gilbert Chaddock, who rendered Krafft-Ebing's *Psychopathia Sexualis* (1886) into English in 1892 and who argued that "[r]ape of children is the most frequent form of sexual crime."[117] Similarly, W. Travis Gibb asserted in 1894 that assaults on children occurred "much more frequently than is generally supposed" by men and women against children of both sexes.[118]

These fears about vulnerable children also gave birth to a homophile strategy to shift same-sex sexuality away from a model of age-differentiated pederasty to a model of same-sex contact organized around similitude: homosexuality. In her work on age-differentiated homosexuality, Jana Funke argues that Symonds expressed his concerns about homosexuality's relationship to "equality, consent[,] and the influence and corruption of youth" in his poetry of the 1860s and that it continued to be a concern throughout his career.[119] Symonds felt that homosexuality's putative corruption of youth provided an easy avenue for opponents of same-sex love to attack homosexuality and thus he deployed a congenital basis of sexuality as "part of a wider strategy to defend same-sex desire against accusations of corruption."[120] Similarly, Jay Grossman, Betsy Erkkila, Kevin P. Murphy, and Robert Caserio have argued that Walt Whitman's idea of same-sex comradeship was underpinned by or at least aspired to a vision of democracy and what Masten has called in a different context the "hierarchy-averse discourse of equality and identicality" if not also of age consistency.[121] Caserio, for example, traces a tradition from Walt Whitman that forges an "alliance of same-sex love with egalitarian possibility" that "dominates the imaginations of queer modernists."[122] Against this tradition, the specter of nonconsent that Symonds worried over continued to organize relations between men throughout much of the twentieth century. Whether in terms of Sedgwickian homosexual panic that is underpinned by a fear of rape, or in terms of the corruption of children who cannot by definition consent, the homosexual's association with figurations of nonconsent operates as a foil for the model of heterosexual sexuality built on the notion of consenting adults.[123]

This chapter has sought to explore what Valerie Traub has called "the historical interarticulation and coimplication of Eastern and Western bodies, desires, aesthetic traditions, and analytical paradigms."[124] In particular, I have striven to describe two technologies of universalism—climate/humor theory and *anthropologia sexualis*—that operate at this East-West intersection. These technologies broaden and produce the concept of sexuality outside of, quoting Bloch again, "limited circles of . . . sexual perversions," instead theorizing sexuality as a universal property that everyone possesses.[125] This understanding of sexuality as widespread and comprehensive provides a crucial foundation for the increasing hegemony of the homo/hetero binary.

THREE

# *Magia Sexualis*, Sexual Subjectivity, and the Willfulness of Sexual Aim

Sexuality studies has lost the ability to hear the magical properties inherent in past vocabularies of sex and sexuality. The historical trace of this magic is evident, for instance, in the figure of the "fairie." In a passage from *Autobiography of an Androgyne* (which I also examined in chapter 1), Ralph Werther writes:

The term "fairie" is widely used in the United States by those who are in touch with the underworld. It probably originated on sailing vessels of olden times when voyages often lasted for months. While the crew was either actually or prospectively suffering acutely from the absence of the female of the species, one of their number would unexpectedly betray an inclination to supply her place. Looked upon as a fairy gift or godsend, such individual would be referred to as "the fairy."[1]

Here, Werther's genealogy of the fairie has the structure of a fairy tale, beginning in "olden times" and positing a magical etiology in its reference to "a fairy gift or godsend." As the *OED* tells us, a fairy gift is "a wonderful or valuable gift that arrives unexpectedly or in a seemingly magical way." This association is strengthened further by Werther's frequent reference to his lovers as demigods and subdieties.[2] A number of other period texts similarly link the fairie to magic. For example, the collaborative novel

66

*Teleny* (1893), conventionally attributed in part to Oscar Wilde, describes an all-male orgy (a "symposium" in which "women are never admitted") as transporting its participants "into the magic realms of fairy-land."[3] Robert Scully's novel *A Scarlet Pansy* (1932) opines upon "a real live fairy, not the story-book kind" and imagines fairies who "wave their magic wands and give you everything you want."[4] Likewise, the diarist Donald Vining records a 1939 account of his love interest being described to him in the following way: "Now he's a real one (fairy). You're just a make-believe one, no matter what you say, but damned if he's not a real one."[5] Similarly, a 1938 newspaper account describes a drag performer as "a fairy, but not the kind the Grimm Brothers collected tales about . . . they dubbed her Snow White."[6] An account of an "ultra-ultra speak[easy]" notes that it "isn't Ireland even if the faires may be seen there."[7] These examples begin to suggest the degree to which the fairie is associated with magic and magical properties.

The fairie—this chapter will argue—is far from the only late nineteenth- and early twentieth-century figure to entwine sexuality and magic. Edward Carpenter's *The Psychology of the Poet Shelley* (1925), for example, demonstrates the inextricability of genius, homosexuality, and magic. Commenting on Shelley's "inversion," Carpenter argues that he "suffered from a repression of homosexual impulses" and asserts that he "belonged to the class of double-natured, or intermediate, types—a class which embraces many artists of very diverse qualities: for example, Leonardo, Michelangelo, Wilde and Tchaikowsky."[8] As this list of queer artists suggests, Shelley's homosexuality was for Carpenter inseparable from his genius. Likewise, Andrew Elfenbein has argued that Lord Byron's "reception created, popularized, and disseminated an image of the 'homosexualized' genius."[9] By homosexualized genius, Elfenbein means the "association between genius and mysteriously unfathomable depths of erotic transgression."[10] For Carpenter, "Shelley's genius" is certainly homosexualized, which is not merely to say that Shelley was for Carpenter both a genius and a homosexual but rather that Shelley's genius is a product of his homosexuality.[11] Along these lines, Carpenter contends that "the blending of the masculine and feminine temperaments does undoubtedly in some cases produce persons whose perceptions are so subtle and complex and rapid as to come under the head of genius."[12] This blending of masculine and feminine produces "a higher order of consciousness" that Carpenter calls both "*Cosmic consciousness*" and "*divination*."[13] Here, Shelley's homosexualized genius is linked to magic: Carpenter understands him as a "visionary" possessing the power to see the future with "Second Sight."[14]

In *Days with Walt Whitman* (1906), Carpenter also attributes this combination of genius, homosexuality, and cosmic consciousness to Walt Whitman: "With Whitman . . . [i]t is probable indeed that never in historical times has the cosmic intuition found a fuller and more complete utterance."[15] For Carpenter, Whitman is the apotheosis of humanity and human evolution.[16]

By attending to these magical cadences in the sexual lexicon, I argue that sexuality studies has underestimated the importance that *magia sexualis*—a term I borrow from the title of the nineteenth-century sexual magician Paschal Beverly Randolph's most famous book to denote magic, occultism, sorcery, supernaturalism, and witchcraft in the most capacious senses—has played in the construction of modern sexuality and sexual subjectivity.[17] This absence of consideration of *magia sexualis* in sexuality studies is all the more surprising inasmuch as many commentators have noted the interarticulation of sexual anomalies and the supernatural. Alan Bray, for instance, has taught us that early modern subjects showed "no hesitation in speaking in the same breath of a sodomite, a werewolf, and a basilisk."[18] Similarly, in histories of modernist sexuality, Pamela Thurschwell understands hypnotism and other alternate states as a "trope and ground" for sexuality.[19] Likewise, Andreas Sommer and Heather Wolffram have charted how sexologists like Albert von Schrenk-Notzing and Cesare Lombroso were proponents of research into "supranormal" activity.[20] And Jodie Medd has demonstrated that Radclyffe Hall was accused of being a "grossly immoral woman" for seducing the married Una Troubridge "through psychical research" (involving mediumship, séances, and trances).[21]

In spite of this excellent work on the relationship between sex and magic, scholars are yet to grapple with the seismic influence *magia sexualis* had on period constructions of sexuality.[22] Joy Dixon comes closest to such an understanding, arguing for the mutual constitution of spirituality and sexuality. She establishes that *"simultaneously* religious and sexual" impulses characterize a broad tradition of "mid-to-late nineteenth-century Anglo-America[n]" thought: encompassing religious revivals, communitarian experiments, strains of Protestantism, free love, and spiritualism (which involves communication with the dead).[23] Other scholars similarly explore individual aspects of the relation between magic and sexuality. Building on this work, I take a much more capacious view, seeing these phenomena as part of a unified field, and instead chart the imbrication between sexuality and mesmerism, animal magnetism, telepathy, elective affinities, spiritualism, witchcraft, and shamanism.[24] Foregrounding this range of magical reference,

I argue that *magia sexualis* plays a formidable role in forging the grammars of sexual attraction and the formation of sexual subjectivity. In particular, I will argue that it is precisely such a concept of attraction and later desire that effects a shift from what Michel Foucault terms the deployment of alliance (marriage, kinship, inheritance) to the deployment of sexuality (sensations, pleasures, and impressions).[25]

The first section of this chapter explores erotic possibilities prior to the formation of sexual subjectivity, attending in particular to the notion of elective affinities. Reading Baron Ludwig von Reizenstein's *The Mysteries of New Orleans* (1854/5), I argue that elective affinity provides a model of attraction that does not clearly differentiate between subject and object. The second section continues to trace this genealogy of desire without objects and thus, as I will argue, without subjects in George du Maurier's bestselling novel *Trilby* (1894). I attend in particular to the villainous Svengali's magical powers and understand him to exemplify an aim-based sexuality. In the final section of this chapter, I examine the literary and sexological work of Paschal Beverly Randolph to argue that he is one of the earliest theorists of a concept of sexual subjectivity. I argue that his concept of sexual subjectivity evolves from his belief in a nearly omnipotent sexual will.


## Sexuality without Desire

In order to explore the relationship between sexuality, magic, and subjectivity, I want to turn to Foucault's account of the emergence of sexual subjectivity in *History of Sexuality, Vol. 1*, in which he argues that "from the eighteenth century onward" "mount[ing] in the nineteenth century," the deployment of sexuality "was superimposed on . . . without completely supplanting" the deployment of alliance.[26] Foucault contends that "[t]he family is the interchange of sexuality and alliance" and describes incest—its constant solicitations and refusals—as the dispensation of eros under the transition between alliance and sexuality.[27] Because for Foucault "the family is the most active site of sexuality," he understands sexuality to be "'incestuous' from the start" and for sexuality to be entwined with alliance.[28] In this section, I argue for the existence of a second erotic organization under this transition, one that will enable us to understand the relationship between *magia sexualis* and sexual subjectivity: namely, elective affinity.

The concept of elective affinity comes from chemistry and means "the tendency of a substance to combine with certain particular substances in preference to others" (*OED*). Johann Wolfgang von Goethe's *Elective Affinities* (1809) famously translates this chemical process into a description of human relations. While Goethe foregrounds the compulsion and fatalism of elective affinity, I contend that elective affinity mediates between desire and compulsion, providing a switch point between the deployment of sexuality and the deployment of alliance. That is, election's emphasis on desire (choice, volition) points toward the deployment of sexuality, while affinity points toward alliance (the *OED* describes "affinity" as meaning "kinship between people or families that results from marriage").

Baron Ludwig von Reizenstein's German-language American novel *The Mysteries of New Orleans* (1854/5), a text permeated with sex magic, narrates the making of sexual (and magical) subjectivity through elective affinity. Born in Bavaria in 1826, Reizenstein emigrated to America in 1848 seeking adventure and riches (and fleeing his father's disdain for his profligacy and/or his possible same-sex desire).[29] *Mysteries* was serialized in January of 1854 and was completed in March of 1855.[30] The episodic and meandering narrative centers on a German family moving to New Orleans just before a yellow fever epidemic overcomes the city. The novel features arson, murder, adultery, miscegenation, incest, cross-dressing, lesbianism, child prostitution, parturition during a lynching, necrophilia, and many other titillating and taboo subjects. Central to the convoluted plotting of this novel is the figure of the magician Hiram, who is approximately 250 years old and possessed of extraordinary powers: mind reading, harnessing the energy of the moon to burn someone's face off, projecting scenes from the past onto a cinema-like screen, commanding a rat to murder a baby child, and unleashing a plague of yellow fever on the city of New Orleans. Hiram's magic is associated with sex in many registers; the text describes his "limitless perversity" and understands his magic powers to derive from a queerly reproducing plant called the *Mantis religiosa* that "blooms every year . . . but only bears seeds on particular years."[31] As I have argued elsewhere, in the mid-nineteenth century botany was a highly sexualized discourse (we might think of Walt Whitman's *Leaves of Grass*).[32] The text's persistent sexualization of botany underlines the queerness of the *Mantis religiosa* and Hiram's sexual magic. In a chapter entitled "Lesbian Love," for example, the language of botany is used to describe lesbianism (the text's usage of the term "lesbian" predates the *OED*'s entry in part because the text was initially written in German): "Nature herself is responsible for having wandered from the path when she creates flowers whose pistils will not accept masculine pollen, whose pistils in fact leave their flower cups in order to join one with another."[33] Here, we see botany both constituting and instantiating a language of sex and sexuality.

But more than these instances of the sexual connotations of Hiram's "black magic," his magic exudes eroticism because his chief aim in carrying out all of his nefarious deeds is to make two lovers fall in love.[34] This love will produce a child named Toussaint L'Ouverture who will end slavery in the United States (as his namesake did for Haiti during the Haitian revolution). In his prophecy Hiram outlines his plan to end slavery and describes what in fact occurs between Emil and Lucy:

Today is the twenty-first of April, 1853. In this year, in this month, and on this day, a Caucasian and an Ethiopian shall bathe in the source of the Red River. They shall walk across the mesa and fall lovingly into each other's arms. They shall then conceive a son, who shall be the liberator of the black race: thus it is written in the book of Hiram II, the Freemason.[35]

This passage's foretelling of the lovers magically falling "lovingly into each other's arms" emphasizes the agentless attraction of "fall[ing]" (particularly in the fated context of prophecy) on the one hand and the agential choosing of "lovingly" on the other. This liminal space of sexuality without desire, of elective affinity, characterizes Hiram's kinship/progeny-oriented goal of the deployment of alliance as well as the loving/desiring goal of the deployment of sexuality. In short, elective affinity, like incest, stands at the intersection of alliance and sexuality.

But perhaps sexuality without desire isn't quite right; perhaps sexuality is the wrong word. Perhaps the novel might be said to describe attraction without desire, or attraction with a modicum of desire. We might rather understand the novel's modalities of attraction—elective affinities—as modeling an earlier model of desire. Michael Bibler has characterized "elective affinity as an orientation . . . toward a particular person, but it is not exclusively a homo or a hetero orientation. . . . [I]t may not even be exclusive to just one person."[36] Here, Bibler understands that elective affinity is not organized around the gender of object choice but moves easily across genders. I would add that this movement across genders is facilitated by the grammar of attraction of elective affinity. That is, because the magnetism of elective affinities is a mutual force, it does not divide the two agents into subject and object, or between active and passive. As the two poles of active-subject and passive-object are traditionally gendered masculine and feminine, this subjectless and objectless mode of attraction moves easily across genders. Under Hiram's spell, Emil and Lucy are drawn to each other: "While Emil pressed his way through the exhausted dancers, Lucy advanced toward Emil."[37] The simultaneity of their advancement and their movement "hand in hand" suggests that neither functions as active subject or passive object, facilitating the genderlessness of their attraction.[38]

We see elective affinity's mode of attraction travel across genders in the opening chapters of *Mysteries*. In these chapters, Emil witnesses Lucy (cross-)dressed in his clothes and he is struck by a mimetic desire and decides to dress in her clothes:

Emil was pretty. Perhaps too pretty for a man. Even Apollo's clear, pure face would have turned yellow with envy at the sight of this ideal body with its elastic shape and roundness of limbs. Phidias would have thrown away his mallet in shame, and the Venus de Medici would not have hidden her charms with her hands, or rather she would have fallen about Emil's neck at first glance.

If Lucy had seen him now, standing half-naked in front of the mirror . . . as he sought to press his arm through a sleeve that was a bit too narrow for a man's arm—she would have gone half mad. And Emil? Emil had not lowered his thyrsus-staff, and if Leda's swan had been female this time, Juno rather than Zeus would have abandoned Olympus and descended to earth.

True beauty always deserves our wonder, whether it gleams from a woman or a man. It's all the same![39]

This densely allusive passage imagines a male god, a female god (in the form of a swan), a male sculptor, a female sculpture, and a woman all overpowered by attraction for a(n) (effeminate) man in the midst of dressing himself in female clothes. Emil's beauty—undifferentiated by gender—possesses a kind of irresistible, magical attractive power. Moreover, the botanical description of Emil's erect penis—"his thyrsus-staff"—that will enable his (imagined) rape by Juno suggests his own attraction to Lucy who is herself "half mad" with what the text describes in the previous scene as "a supernatural sexual intoxication that raged in her."[40] The novel's depiction of Lucy and Emil possessing not merely the same wardrobe but also the "same" beauty hints that elective affinity's elasticity in relation to the gender of object choice is characterized by nonindividuation. That is, we might understand elective affinity's nondistinction between subject and object as stemming in part from its de-individualizing function.

This is clearest in the text's lesbian scene between Claudine and Orleana (both minor characters extrinsic to the novel's central plotting). Orleana is said to resemble Queen Elizabeth's female object of desire:

There are many fables about Elizabeth and Raleigh, and the *Chronique Scandaleuse* has sought, in vain until now, to plumb the motives that led the Virgin Queen to show disfavor to Sir Walter.

Until now no one has discovered—or no one has dared to confess—that the cause was her jealousy of Raleigh due to his relationship with a lesbian lady.

In the Cabinet of Beauties of the new royal palace in Munich is a portrait of this competitor, and her surprising resemblance to Orleana can only be the result of an elective affinity, for Lesbos "produces no children."[41]

Though Orleana is not related to the unnamed "lesbian lady," she resembles her nevertheless.[42] The novel's theorization of a nonagential, fated resemblance between lesbians stands opposed to a nexus that links individuality, subjectivity, and desire. To put this more plainly, the text understands desire to individuate and forge sexual subjectivity. Where lesbians in the novel are imagined to be a collective, an affiliation (writing as a group from the *"Headquarters of the Lesbian Women"* and gathering "in clubs"), their lack of desire keeps them from individuation.[43]

In contrast, such an emerging individuating subjectivity is evident as Lucy ponders the "supernatural sexual intoxication that raged *in her.*"[44] This interiorization of the elective affinity she feels for Emil is important because later in the text Hiram will assert that his magic had nothing to do with their desire for each other, saying to Emil: "'You make every earthly effort to deceive your lord that you are guiltless and that I was the one who enticed you into your infidelity and your flippant promiscuity. You appear to have forgotten that you admired and made love to Lucy long before I drew you into the charmed circle of the *Mantis religiosa.*'"[45] Here, Hiram claims that it was not his magic ("the *Mantis religiosa*") that made Emil unfaithful to his wife but Emil's desire for Lucy (a claim Emil denies). While the text does not resolve whether this elective affinity emerges from exterior (Hiram's magic) or interior (Emil's desire) forces, this very irresolution clears a space for an emergent sexual subjectivity that will gradually take more definite shape over the course of the nineteenth and twentieth centuries. That is, elective affinity's movement away from its roots in chemistry toward magic suggests a shift from outside, natural forces (analogized to the social forces of the deployment of alliance) to increasingly interiorized forces (analogized to desires, libido, and sexual subjectivity) associated with *magia sexualis*.[46] Before detailing this evolution of an interiorized sexual subjectivity, I will, in the next section, continue to narrate this story of objectless desire in *Trilby* and its historical afterlife, tracing its role in the development of the homo/hetero binary.

## The Willfulness of Sexual Aim

George du Maurier's magic-suffused novel *Trilby* (1894) set a new standard for publishing success—it was a sensation and, as one critic put it, "The [financial] rewards to the publishers . . . were heretofore unheard of. Seldom had a single book produced so much revenue for a publisher."[47] But it was also a cultural phenomenon, sparking Trilby paintings, tableaux, photographs, parodies (*Frilby*, *Thrilby*, *Drilby Re-Versed*, and *Biltry*), spinoffs, and plays (twenty-four productions of *Trilby* ran simultaneously in 1896 in the United States).[48] A town in Florida was christened Trilby, streets and squares and lakes were named after *Trilby*'s characters, and advertisers sold Trilby sausages, hams, calendars, hearth brushes, and, of course, the famous Trilby hat that to this day carries its name.[49] Likewise, its magician villain Svengali is famous for being one of the most anti-Semitic characters in the history of literature and for introducing the word "Svengali" into English.

I want to dilate on one aspect of this craze: attempts to represent and sell what the novel calls Trilby's "astonishingly beautiful feet."[50] Trilby's feet encapsulate the novel's complex relation between sexual subjectivity and objecthood. Ranging from fantasies of embodying (part of) Trilby by selling ice cream and scarf pins in the shape of her feet to the marketing of shoes called "the Trilby," and contests to find women with the most Trilby-like feet, these popular happenings depict Trilby as at once part and whole, object and subject.[51] Because Trilby's feet both are and aren't her, they posit her as a kind of incomplete subject (only encapsulated in parts rather than as a whole); when she poses in "the altogether," her phrase for "in the nude," she describes her own fragmentation as "*l'ensemble*, you know—heads, hands, and feet,—everything—especially feet."[52] As Emma V. Miller and Simon J. James point out: "The term [altogether], then, is not suggestive of a whole/altogether but rather more all together, a sum of mutilated, fetishised body parts."[53]

This anatomization of Trilby into parts (the word "Trilbies" even became slang for feet) is key to the novel's theorization of objectless desire.[54] That is, one of the central claims of this chapter will be that a sharp differentiation between subject and object is necessary for the creation of sexual subjectivity: having an object is a precondition of becoming a subject. The popular commodification of Trilby's feet begins to suggest that one afterlife of elective affinity's subjectless and objectless desire is what, following Freud, we might think of as sexuality characterized by aberrant "sexual aim" (since the fetishization of the foot provides one of Freud's central examples of "the abandonment of sexual aim [the desire for heterosexual intercourse]").[55] But I prefer to call such sexual organizations "aim-based sexuality" (rather than object-based) so as not to stigmatize them. While I will argue that the Jewish magician Svengali is the central agent of the novel's theorization of aim-based sexuality, for now I want to take the hint that *Trilby* and the *Trilby* craze's obsession with feet point toward desire that does not clearly differentiate between subject and object.

*Trilby* depicts the friendship of a circle of bohemian artists—most prominently Taffy, the Laird, and Little Billie. All three friends are in love with the artist's model and laundress Trilby O'Ferrall. While many other artists and musicians move in and out of the friends' circle, visiting their studio, the plot is animated by the much disliked musician Svengali. He attempts to keep Trilby away from the other three friends while simultaneously striving to become known as the world's greatest musician. He trains protégés—notably Mimi la Salope and Gecko—but neither is a worthy vehicle for his magical powers. Instead, he hypnotizes Trilby, who has the world's most beautiful voice and is completely tone deaf and thus unable to sing in key. His magic transforms her into La Svengali—the world's most beautiful singer. As part of his hypnotic control, she will remember absolutely nothing of her time as La Svengali.

In one register, we might understand the novel as being about a kind of failed subject making. Svengali attempts to hypnotize and transform Trilby into a female version of himself, La Svengali. Svengali sets himself a particularly difficult task since the essence of what the novel calls "Trilbyness" is her "singularly impressionable nature"; her amorphousness and mutability elude the processes of subjectification.[56]

When the reader first encounters Trilby, she is wearing "a strange medley of garments" and her voice "might almost have belonged to any sex (even an angel's)."[57] The text seems manifestly unable to classify her sex and even her humanity (she might be an angel): she is "a very tall and fully developed young female clad in the grey overcoat of a French infantry soldier," wearing "a huge pair of male slippers" and possessing "a very healthy young face, which could scarcely be called quite beautiful," a "mouth too large," a "chin too massive," "[b]ut a small portion of her neck . . . was of a delicate privet-like whiteness."[58] In addition, "she had a very fine brow," and "her broad cheeks were beautifully modelled"; she would, the novel tells us, "have made a singularly handsome boy."[59] I draw attention to this lengthy description of Trilby as a woman, angel, and boy in the clothes of a man (with "massive" mannish features) to suggest her instability as a gendered and even human subject. Thus, we might read the text as Svengali's effort to turn Trilby into a fully gendered subject, stabilizing her "irrepressible Trilbyness" and forging her into a subject through his all-encompassing hypnotic power.[60] This stabilization has the ironic effect of stripping Trilby of what is most essential to her: her ever-changing Trilbyness. While Svengali might either be said to fail to turn Trilby into La Svengali (here we might read her as returning to her mutable self after Svengali's death) or to succeed (hypnotizing her through his photograph after his death), in either case I am interested in how Svengali's desire is routed through and in relation to this highly unstable subject.

Svengali's desire to forge Trilby as his ego-ideal exemplifies one possible afterlife of elective affinity, a desire without a clear differentiation between object and subject: an aim-based sexuality. Modernist studies and sexuality studies have unduly ignored the concept of sexual aim in part because in the archives of psychoanalysis and sexology, there is very little pathology around aim (in the way that there is around object choice).[61] According to Freud, "The normal sexual aim is regarded as being the union of the genitals in the act known as copulation, which leads to a release of the sexual tension and temporary extinction of the sexual instinct—a satisfaction analogous to the sating of hunger."[62] As Arnold Davidson points out in his reading of this passage, the normal operation of the aim requires genital-genital contact (rather than oral-genital, oral-anal, anal-genital, oral-oral, etc.) and copulation.[63] Thus, we begin to see another reason that sexual aim has not received much scholarly attention: namely, that sexual aim is largely a handmaiden for and bulwark of sexual object choice for Freud. That is, in spite of the fact that Freud asserts that the relation between the two "requires thorough investigation," we can see that his description of normal sexual aim already encodes and shores up opposite sex object choice.[64] The proximity for Freud between object and aim is further illustrated in the *Three Essays* (1905) when he contends that many of his examples of deviations of the sexual aim might "from the point of view of classification" have been better mentioned "in respect of the sexual object."[65] In this section, I want to explore sexual aim beyond the Freudian clinic, mapping aim-based sexuality in an expanded field without confining it to sexual acts. With this more capacious sense of sexual aim in mind, I literalize the concept to ask broader questions: What do we want to do with sex? What are the goals of sex?

Svengali's desire to control Trilby offers one such model of sexual aim that does not take shape in sexual acts.[66] In order to understand the aim-based sexuality of Svengali, we must examine his promiscuous and nondiscriminating relation to his sexual objects. The novel intimates that Svengali is attracted to everyone; the narrator seems to shudder almost visibly at the thought of his giving music lessons to women, writing in parenthesis "(not at ladies' schools, let us hope)."[67] We also see Svengali ogling Little Billie in the bath "tickled and interested by the sight" and asking Billie when he would bathe again as he "would much like to come and see him do it."[68] He also watches Taffy in the bath, leading Taffy to threaten violence and to curse him as a "filthy black Hebrew."[69] Svengali is attracted to virtually every character in the novel and thus emits a kind of polymorphous perversity. In the history of the development of sexual object choice, we can understand polymorphous perversity as an intermediate step between Foucault's "thousand aberrant sexualities" and the birth of the homosexual.[70] That is, it represents an internalization of what had been mostly external and acquired and becomes positioned as a necessary stage on the way to the development of normal object choice.

Svengali's sexuality is not organized by objects but rather is structured by sexual aim. Even though our sexual imaginary—genitally organized as it is—might not immediately register it as "sexual" aim, his desire to achieve musical perfection is also a desire for mastery. His relations with his protégés Gecko, Mimi, and especially Trilby, whom he holds "spellbound" so she "could not move," are scenes of mastery (the same could be said of the voyeuristic bath scenes where he teases Little Billie and Taffy).[71] This desire for mastery begins to explain why the damage to Svengali's nose (resulting from the scuffle with Taffy after Svengali belittles him) is so traumatic—it functions as a kind of unmanning or unmastering in the context of the anti-Semitic conflation of the Jewish nose and the Jewish penis.[72] Svengali's desire for mastery is an objectless aim, since it does not matter to him whom he is mastering—the objects are more or less interchangeable. More or less because Trilby is, of course, his privileged object. Trilby is his preferred object of mastery only because she will enable him to most fully realize his aim of musical greatness. Hence, the novel and Svengali in particular depict a sexuality of pure aim.

One way to understand the eros of Svengali's aim—and particularly his use of Trilby as a medium—is in relation to the text's repeated description of Svengali's power as "mesmerism."[73] As Alex Owen argues, "The very vocabulary of trance mediumship oozed sexuality. Mediums surrendered and then were entered, seized, possessed by another."[74] The eroticism of Svengali's mesmeric enslavement of Trilby is clearest in Gecko's account as the novel concludes:

He [Svengali] had but to say *"Dors!"* and she suddenly became an unconscious Trilby of marble, who could produce wonderful sounds—just the sounds he wanted, and nothing else—and think his thoughts and wish his wishes—and love him at his bidding with a strange, unreal, factitious love . . . just his own love for himself turned inside out—*à l'envers*—and reflected back on as from a mirror . . . It was not worth having! I was not even jealous![75]

Though erotically charged, the scene here stages the relation between Trilby and Svengali as standing outside the logics of subject and object. The image of the mirror instead creates a confusion between subject and object, between Svengali and La Svengali. She projects his love, but it is a narcissistic love, "just his own love for himself turned inside out." Instead, what Trilby offers is an amplification of his aim, thinking Svengali's thoughts and wishing his wishes with him. She is, as Gecko tells us, "just a singing-machine—an organ to play upon—an instrument of music—a Stradivarius—a flexible flageolet of flesh and blood—a voice, and nothing more—just the unconscious voice that Svengali sang with."[76] Trilby is so identified with Svengali, so inseparable from him, so much a projection of him, that she is called La Svengali and Gecko tells us "it was not worth having! I was not even jealous."[77] Svengali's narcissistic, identificatory erotics understands Trilby as mere instrument and nothing more, literally a Stradivarius or a flageolet. But this is Gecko's account and it is one that seems firmly ensconced in notions of object choice, of wanting a love object to possess subjectivity and return the gaze of love. There is every reason to believe that Svengali was not just content with his aim-based sexuality but overjoyed by it. Gecko describes how she sang for "kings and queens in royal palaces," how people went "mad to hear her," and how "Svengali fell down in a fit of sheer excitement" at all the adulation.[78] I understand this ecstatic fit, this orgasmic collapse as a representation of a fully satisfied aim-based desire, a desire without a subject or an object.[79]

## The Magician's Will and the Emergence of Sexual Subjectivity

Mediumship and its concomitant nondifferentiation between subject and object (that we have explored in *Trilby*) is strongly rejected by the sexual magician Paschal Beverly Randolph. Almost wholly unknown in both literary studies and sexuality studies, Randolph was a prolific novelist and, as Hugh Urban puts it, "[a]rguably the most important figure in the rise of modern sex magic."[80] Born in 1825 in New York City, he was a free person of color, abolitionist, autodidact, and self-described genius. He claimed to be the descendant of William Randolph—who counts among his descendants President Thomas Jefferson, Supreme Court Justice John Marshall, General Robert E. Lee, Congressman John Randolph of Roanoke, and a host of other distinguished heirs.[81] Paschal Beverly Randolph's proposed "school of sexual science" (which long predates Iwan Bloch's concept of *"Sexualwissenschaf"*) and his *magia sexualis* were forged in large part by his extensive travels in the East (where he visited Egypt, Syria, Turkey, Persia, Arabia, Jerusalem, and many other locales).[82] Learning the "secrets" of the East, Randolph sold mail order pamphlets detailing his system of *magia sexualis*.[83] Randolph's oeuvre—consisting of a profusion of pamphlets, treatises, and novels—promised the attainment of dozens and dozens of magic powers; he asserts that "copulative union and its mutual ending . . . possesses the key to all possible Knowledge, the mighty wand of White Magic—may defy disease, disaster, keep Death itself at bay, regain lost youth and wasted power, challenge permanent defeat, gain all good ends, reach the ultimate Spaces, commune with highest seraphs, bathe in the crystal seas of God's Infinite Love, and be in truth Sons and Daughters of the Ineffable Lord of glory!"[84] Here, Randolph argues that a plethora of magical powers can be attained through sexual training and will, in contradistinction to Spiritualists, who believed mediums were necessary to practice magic. In this section, I will argue that Randolph's denunciation of mediumship and his limitless faith in will are key to his *magia sexualis* and, more importantly, provide insight into how he became, as I will argue, one of the earliest theorists and instantiators of sexual subjectivity.

A central tenet of Randolph's magic is a limitless faith in personal will. Randolph writes: "The will is Lord of man's accidents and incidents, and if his reason guide it well, nothing can withstand its force."[85] Later in the same text, Randolph commands: *"Try! the soul groweth tall and comely, and waxeth powerful and strong only as it putteth forth its Will!"*[86] Here, Randolph suggests omnipotent will enables access to magical powers and new freedoms—"the triple white magic of Love, will, and persistent trying."[87] Elsewhere Randolph asserts that *"constant trying means eventual success"* and then glosses it with a footnote that reads: "This is *the secret of the ages.* No one can fail who truly consistently continues to *TRY.* The reaction to action—the efforts made though sometimes long delayed, must and *will* ultimately bring the desired result."[88] This small sampling of Randolph's faith in the unlimited agential powers of will are constructed as explicit foils for mediumship and slavery. He writes in 1860 on the eve of the Civil War that whoever engages in mediumship "is on the high road to a slavery far more fearful than even Southern bondage is to the poor black victims of its dreadful sway,—and God knows *that* is almost past endurance."[89] Randolph's profound diminishment here of the horror, suffering, and trauma of slavery speaks to his hatred of mediumship as an abdication of the limitless agency of the will. The specter of the will-less condition of slavery haunts mediumship's unfreedom as does Randolph's ancestry. While I will say more about Randolph's description of himself as a "SANG MÉLÉE"—with "not less than twelve strains of blood rush[ing] through [his] veins"—later in the chapter, for now I want to flag that he elevates the status and power of unfettered will compensatorily to disavow his overly proximate "African ancestry" and to assert that he is not a slave.[90]

Randolph's unbounded faith in personal agency leads him to conceptualize and propound a version of an all-powerful sexual subjectivity as a set of erotic techniques that can be learned, mastered, and acquired by force of will. As his biographer puts it, "the fundamental secret of Randolph's sexual magic" is that "at the instant of intense mutual orgasm [of a man and a woman] the souls of the partners are opened to the powers and energies of the cosmos, and anything then truly willed is accomplished."[91] This limitless will is both a set of sexual techniques that can be taught and learned (for the attainment of simultaneous orgasm) and also a space of sexual and spiritual interiority.[92] Randolph's emphasis on techniques of pleasure enables us to revisit Foucault's claim that "*scientia sexualis* is but an extraordinarily subtle form of *ars erotica.*"[93] To put this differently, Randolph's theorization of a nearly omnipotent sexual personhood repurposes and extends the teachings of *ars erotica* he encountered during his Eastern journeys into a "SCHOOL OF SEXUAL SCIENCE," suggesting that his *scientia sexualis*—which is among the earliest in the world—derives, as Foucault suggests, from *ars erotica.* Importantly, then, Randolph's *magia sexualis* marks a departure from the desirelessness of elective affinity to forge a desiring sexual subjectivity. This sexual subjectivity is actively cultivated, prepared for, and produced through a series of bodily and spiritual practices involving abstinence, diet, deep breathing, sleep regimens, and so on to prepare for the moment of mutual orgasm. Randolph describes the birth of such subjectivity most extensively in *The Ansairetic Mystery: A New Revelation Concerning SEX!* (1873):

[N]o real magic (magnetic) power can, or will, descend the soul of either, except in the mighty moment—the orgasmal instant of BOTH—not one alone! for then, and *then only*, do the mystic doors of the SOUL OPEN TO THE SPACES. . . . The eternal spark within us . . . finds its human body only when Sex-passion opens the mystic door for it to enter the man—through him, the woman, through her the world, through THEM, the Spaces, and through it again Allah, GOD—*not* as a drop of infinite ocean of Mind, but as a Being in the Heavenly hierarchies![94]

Here, the soul (what Randolph calls "the eternal spark within us") enters the man's body through simultaneous orgasm ("the orgasmal instant of BOTH") that is then transferred to the woman's body. The (heterosexual) sex act itself inaugurates the creation of subjectivity ("SOUL") while it maintains the gender hierarchy since the man transfers interiority to the woman. In short, simultaneous orgasm produces sexual subjectivity. As the title *The Ansairetic Mystery* (which "refers to the Ansaireh, a Shi'i group in the Levant that is today sometimes called the Alawites or Nusaris") and the references to Allah make clear, this sexual subjectivity emerges from a set of putatively Eastern erotic techniques, providing further evidence for Foucault's hypothesis that *scientia sexualis* is a form of *ars erotica*.[95]

Since the harmonious mixing of simultaneous orgasm crucially powers Randolph's *magia sexualis*, his racial identity as a *"sang melée,"* as Christine Ferguson argues, proves a boon to his magic because it increases his proximity to amalgamation:

I owe my successes,—mental—to my conglomerate blood; my troubles and poverty to the same source. . . . My mother was once a beautiful *sang mêlée* of various strains of blood. She had some Madagascan, French, Spanish, Indian, and Oriental in her, all of which I have, and several others besides, as English, Celtic, Cymrian, Teutonic, Moorish.[96]

Ferguson eloquently argues that Randolph proudly asserted his mixed ancestry and espoused a polygenesist account of humanity despite its clear associations with racism because the blending of bodies and especially of soul requires difference.[97] For Randolph, this blending is emblematized by the self-shattering of simultaneous orgasm. I am wholly persuaded by Ferguson's account and would add that by embodying all races (except notably the "inferior" sub-Saharan African), Randolph lays a cosmopolitan claim to universality.[98] He imagines that his very mixedness voids race and color, authorizing the universality of his sexual system and sexual subjectivity.

But not all mixing was advantageous for Randolph. In his earlier work, he imagines a potential misalignment between body and spirit that in fact predates even the earliest sexological constructions of inversion. Westphal coins his term "contrary sexual feeling" in 1869 and the Italian specialist Arrigo Tamassia used the phrase "inversion of the sexual instinct" by 1878.[99] But earlier than Westphal and Tamassia, Karl Heinrich Ulrichs coins his term Urning in 1864 and explains in 1869 that it means: "Men who, as a result of their inborn nature, feel themselves attracted by the impulse of their sexual desire exclusively to male individuals. . . . The Urning is a riddle of nature. He is a man only by the build of his body, not according to his sexual drive. His sexual drive is, rather, that of a female being."[100] In 1862, prior to conceptualizing the Urning, Ulrichs began exploring Franz Anton Mesmer's theories of animal magnetism in order to understand attraction; Mesmer's work would also shape conceptualizations of elective affinity and Randolph's work. The language of attraction, magnetism, and sparking desire would continue to inspire Ulrichs's thought, suggesting the influence of *magia sexualis* on some of the earliest ideas of sexology.[101]

But Randolph's conceptualization of misattuned bodies and souls that we would now understood as inversion predates Ulrichs's conception:

I have often wondered if it were not possible for a woman to bear a child, the body of which might be attributable to one man, and its spiritual part to another? A case is now before me of the daughter of a courtesan, whose mother had two intrigues. One man was a German, the other an Italian; and the girl, *physically*, is the image of one, and in a hundred things, *mentally*, the exact counterpart of the other! May it not be possible for a woman to bear the body of a child to one, and yet draw the spiritual elements—indeed everything except the mere flesh and bone—from some other man, or men, and that, too, altogether without coverture by the latter, but by virtue of a certain mysterious sympathia, analogous in some degree to that other wonderful principle by which certain peculiar physical marks are impressed upon the child by the mental states of the mother. Here is a nut for the Philosophers to crack, if they can. Certainly the thing is not *impossible*, however *improbable* it may be.[102]

In this passage from *The Grand Secret; Or, Physical Love in Health and Disease* (1861) Randolph extrapolates from the example of "the daughter of a courtesan" to envision the possibility, even the probability, of a woman having a body and a spirit from (at least) two different fathers.[103] While this misalignment is not organized around object choice or sexuality or even the forms of misattunement that we usually understand to be part of the early history of inversion, David Halperin importantly points out that "inversion . . . was defined as a psychological orientation without a sexuality."[104] Halperin supports his claim by attending to Westphal's assertion that "'contrary sexual feeling' *does not always coincidentally concern the sexual drive as such* but simply the feeling of being alienated, with one's entire inner being, from one's own sex."[105] The daughter of the courtesan is imagined to have precisely a psychological orientation with a different national and gendered character ("mentally" a man) than her physical appearance (a woman who resembles a different man), creating two different kinds of alienation between her inner and outer being. That is, her mental connection to the first man neither aligns with her embodiment as a woman (familiar to us from other models of inversion) nor with the physical resemblance to the second man (distinct to Randolph's conception of inversion). Another example of inversion appears in Randolph's novel, *Dealings with the Dead* (1861/2), where he explains that in "the Soul-world," "it is found that many who, as if by accident, had worn the physical characteristics of one, were really, at soul, of the opposite sex."[106] Randolph continues to develop this theory of inversion in *Eulis!* (1874) when he writes that "Now accidents and inversions, aversions and perversions, occur in all departments of nature, but none so glaring and positive as are encountered among human beings; and the mis-sexing of them is one of the most common forms of mal-construction . . . in which case the body of the child will be of one gender, its soul and spirit of the opposite one."[107] With this "mis-sexing" in view, we must then understand Randolph as the first theorist of inversion.

I have been arguing that the nexus between *magia sexualis*, will, and sexual subjectivity remains an underexplored strain of thinking about sexuality (one that will be taken up by such diverse thinkers as Richard Maurice Bucke, Mary Butts, Edward Carpenter, Aleister Crowley, Julius Evola, William James, and William Sharp). This intellectual through line of *magia sexualis* is in need of a much fuller study since it plays a key role in the construction of sexual subjectivity and has a crucial influence on the development of core conceptualizations of sexuality like inversion and attraction. Moreover, I hope that this chapter has elucidated the ways in which the increasing disarticulation of subject and object (united in theories like elective affinity) strengthens both sexual subjectivity and object choice. In other words, the emergence of sexual subjectivity consolidates the object-choice-based organization of sexuality. And the way that the magical operation of desire— alighting upon particular objects in ways that pass understanding, that feel supernatural or alchemical or just plain enchanting—serves to codify their difference.

# FOUR

# Sex in the Age of Fordism: The Standardization of Sexual Objects

The word itself [homosexuality], as Havelock Ellis noted, is a barbarous neolo-
gism sprung from a monstrous mingling of Greek and Latin stock; as such,
it belongs to a rapidly growing lexical breed most prominently represented
by the hybrid names given to other recent inventions—names whose mere
enumeration suffices to conjure up the precise historical era responsible for
producing them: e.g., "automobile," "television," "sociology."

DAVID HALPERIN, *ONE HUNDRED YEARS OF HOMOSEXUALITY*

Sexuality studies has taught us that economic forces have
a tremendous impact on the shape of sexual life. In John
D'Emilio's famous essay "Capitalism and Gay Identity"
(1983), for example, he claims that the shift from a system
of interdependent family production to a free labor system
of capital enables the emergence of gay identity.[1] With the
gradual development of free labor, economic subsistence
no longer required men, and to a lesser extent women,
to live at home, enabling concentrations of men in large
cities and networks of same-sex meeting outside family
surveillance. Likewise, Henry Abelove's "Some Speculations on the History of Sexual Intercourse during the Long
Eighteenth Century in England" (1989) argues that the
population explosion in England between 1680 and 1830
is attributable to the increased popularity of "cross-sex
genital intercourse (penis in vagina, vagina around penis,

with seminal emission uninterrupted)" or what he memorably nominates "sexual intercourse so-called."[2] Abelove speculates that this new popularity of intercourse so-called is linked to the capitalist forces that are commonly referred to as the Industrial Revolution. Rather than seeing a causal connection between production and reproduction, Abelove speculates that they are "aspects of the same phenomenon": "production became discursively and phenomenologically central in ways that it had never been before."[3]

Given the constitutive force of capital on sexuality posited by D'Emilio and Abelove, Fordism seems particularly ripe for such analysis since it explicitly aims to normalize worker's bodies into more efficient capitalist subjects.[4] In order to undertake such an investigation in this chapter I want to take a hint from Jonathan Ned Katz, who argues that

Between 1877 and 1920 Americans were embarked on *The Search for Order*, documented in historian Robert H. Wiebe's book of that title. Though Wiebe doesn't mention it, this hunt for regularity gave rise in the arena of sex to the new, standard model heterosexuality. This paralleled early-twentieth century moves to standardize railroad tracks widths, time zones, business and manufacturing procedures (discussed by Wiebe), as well as to test and regularize intelligence and femininity and masculinity.[5]

Rather than consider the regularization of heterosexuality that Katz is interested in, this chapter will consider industrialization's transformation not just of the ways that we produce objects, but also how industrialization is imagined to invent sexual objects. In the first section, I will explore the perceived force of industrialization on sexual life, particularly its impact on our object-based sexual system. More specifically, I will consider how Fordism was understood by Antonio Gramsci and Sherwood Anderson to standardize sexual object choice.[6] Arguably more than any other modernist figure, Anderson evinces a profound understanding of the motor force of industrialization and its influence on daily life, particularly sexual life.[7] In the second section, I will explore two alternative sexual formations that Anderson posits as nonstandardized and thus, for him, less regimented. In a 1921 letter, discussing his most famous work, *Winesburg, Ohio: A Group of Tales of Ohio Small-Town Life*, Anderson describes what he would often call the "Winesburg form" as enabling him to capture the "large, loose sense of life."[8] This form famously depicts a short story cycle that depicts a small town of people loosely organized around a young newspaperman named George Willard, to whom the townspeople confess their life stories. But the "new looseness" that the Winesburg form enables also operates as a rebuttal to what Anderson sees as the standardization of industrialism, particularly sexual standardization.[9] The chapter concludes by speculating on how industrialization is understood to play an important role in the emergence of the object-based system of sexuality that provides the dominant framework for conceptualizing American sexuality in the twentieth and twenty-first centuries.

## Fordist Sexuality

Fordism is characterized by both its automation of the assembly line and its commitment to pay workers a wage that enables them to afford the goods they produce. As David Harvey puts it, "what was special about Ford . . . was his vision . . . that mass production meant mass consumption."[10] Fordism is thus both a style of production and a modality of consumption. In his *Prison Notebooks* (written in the late 1920s and early 1930s), in a section called "Americanism and Fordism," Gramsci argues:

It is worth drawing attention to the way in which industrialists (Ford in particular) have been concerned with the sexual affairs of their employees and with their family arrangements in general. One should not be misled, any more than in the case of prohibition, by the "puritanical" appearance assumed by this concern. The truth is that the new type of man demanded by the rationalization of production and work cannot be developed until the sexual instinct has been suitably regulated and until it too has been rationalized.[11]

In discussing Ford's regulation of his workers' sexual lives, Gramsci refers to the infamous Sociological Department of the Ford Motor Company, which at its peak in 1919 had 150 agents investigating the so-called "private" lives of its workers through unannounced home visits. Homes were checked for cleanliness (particularly those of immigrant workers) and whether Ford employees were teaching their children English and thus adequately Americanizing them. In addition, the department investigated alcohol use, gambling habits, finances, and, of course, whether or not employees bought Model Ts. Harvey explains that the "'new man' of mass production" had to have "the right kind of moral probity, family life, and capacity for prudent . . . and 'rational' consumption to live up to corporate needs and expectations."[12] For our purposes though, the most important aspect of the Sociological

Department's surveillance was its scrutiny of Ford employees' sexual lives.[13] Gramsci elaborates:

It seems clear that the new industrialism wants monogamy: it wants the man as worker not to squander his nervous energies in the disorderly and stimulating pursuit of occasional sexual satisfaction. The employee who goes to work after a night of "excess" is no good for his work. The exaltation of passion cannot be reconciled with the timed movements of productive motions connected with the most perfected automatism.[14]

While Gramsci sees industrial capitalism as an etiology of monogamy (and here he is proximate to Freud's 1930 *Civilization and Its Discontents*), I am more interested in the regularization of sexual object choice as one of a series of products made uniform by Fordism. In short, this chapter will explore how industrialization was understood to standardize object choice.

Anderson is particularly helpful in understanding this process because his work provides a rich representation of the overlapping and interconnected sexual cultures of rural life, small town existence, and urban experience. Born in the small Ohio town of Camden in 1875, he is most famous for his 1919 collection of short stories, *Winesburg, Ohio*. He is also well known for his influence on Ernest Hemingway, William Faulkner, and José García Villa. He had an outsized role in the early careers of Hemingway and Faulkner in particular, recognizing their talents and helping them to find venues for some of their most pivotal early publications. His modernist sensibility was deeply rooted in his experience of both the industrial and consumer economies (working in both factories and the advertising industry). Throughout his writing career, Anderson expresses his fear of industrialization and its ensuing forces of standardization. In 1928, he writes: "There is in America just now a tremendous movement toward standardization of all life and all thought. . . . We all dress alike, read the same kinds of newspapers and magazines, talk alike, live in towns that all look alike and we all pretty much think alike."[15] In another essay, he describes wanting to resist the "one iron groove" of industrialization in order to "re-open the channels of individual expression."[16] In one register, his preoccupation with industrialization can be said to be a hallmark of modernism, for, as Michael Denning argues, "modernism itself might be understood as the culture of Fordism."[17] Read in this light, Ezra Pound's imperative to "Make it new" rails against Fordism's efforts to "make it the same."[18] Along these lines, Shane Vogel reads Langston Hughes as theorizing the sexual and temporal register of "afterhours" in defiance of industrial capitalism's regulation of bar "closing time."[19]

Like Hughes, Anderson works within the strictures of industrialization, loosening its grip to open spaces of deregulation and improvisation. That the normalizing and regularizing of dress, information, speech, living space, and even thought is also a fear of sexual standardization is evident in Anderson's contention in *The Modern Writer* (1925) that

Although the modern man and woman of the streets has been pretty effectually standardized as regards his hat, the cigarette he smokes, the automobile he drives, he cannot in reality be standardized. Few of us as yet order our wives from a mail order house. Although in America and during the long period which we have all been so busy conquering the mechanical world we have in general looked upon the poet or the artist as rather a sissy, a nut, a man who had better be brushed aside, we all have something of the poet and lover in us.[20]

Here, Anderson posits writing (in the figure of the gender dissident "sissy" poet and artist) and sex (in the figure of the lover) as two sites that resist the effectual standardization of modern man and woman.[21] The conditionality of "as yet," which threatens to shade into a future anterior in Anderson's contention that "Few of us as yet order our wives from a mail order house," suggests his anxiety that sexuality too will become standardized.[22]

In *Winesburg, Ohio*—Anderson's most famous reflection on the occurrence of "a tremendous change in the lives and in the habits of thought of our people of Mid-America"—he investigates the effects of sexual standardization.[23] In the story "Paper Pills," for instance, Anderson describes a "very beautiful" young woman whose parents die, leaving her with money (9). The combination of wealth and beauty brings numerous suitors, one of whom impregnates the girl. In an attempt to have an abortion, she visits old man Doctor Reefy. Unhappy with her other suitors, she marries the doctor and then dies shortly thereafter. The depiction of the unusual marriage between the girl and the doctor is drawn in counter-distinction to the routinization of desire in the city. Anderson represents the courtship as an example of the idiosyncratic desires of small town life, characterizing it as

delicious, like the twisted little apples that grow in the orchards of Winesburg. . . . The apples have been taken from the trees by the pickers. They have been put in barrels and shipped to the cities where they will be eaten in apartments that are filled with books, magazines, furniture, and people. On the trees are only a few gnarled apples that the pickers have rejected. They look like the knuckles of Doctor Reefy's hands. . . . Only the few know the sweetness of the twisted apples. . . . She [the beautiful girl] was like one who has discovered the sweetness of the twisted apples, she could not get her mind fixed again upon the round perfect fruit that is eaten in the city apartments. (10, 12)

The story analogizes the standardization of a commodity (apples) to the standardization of desire. Desiring the old doctor, the beautiful girl can't get her mind right to desire a proper suitor (analogized to the round city apple). This conflation of consumer desire and sexual desire suggests that some of the pleasures of small town life remain unstandardized (albeit still governed by an ethos that John D'Emilio and Estelle Freedman describe as keeping "sexuality . . . properly confined to the marital relationship.")[24] The passage imagines the city apples being eaten in apartments "filled with books, magazines, furniture, and people." The odd final inclusion of "people" in this list of products suggests that the people of the city are themselves standardized by the processes of industrialization and consumer capitalism, indistinguishable and self-identical like the merchandise of capitalism, like pieces of furniture. In contrast, the nonstandardized pleasures of small town life are embodied in the sweetness of the twisted apples.[25] These pleasures are focalized through the figure of the hand, the way that the twisted apples are said to resemble the hands of Doctor Reefy.

### Nonindustrial Desires

Within *Winesburg*, the hand emblematizes a nonindustrialized economy. While one could easily imagine a genealogy in which the hand is associated with lifeless mechanization, urbanization, and deadening repetition (W. H. Auden's "Casino" (1936) offers one such vision where "Only their hands are living"), Anderson's representation of the hand as a modality for escaping sexual standardization is not unique.[26] For example, his contemporary William Carlos Williams writes *In the American Grain* (1925): "Machines were not so much to save time as to save dignity that fears the animate touch. . . . a mechanism to increase the gap between touch and thing, *not* to have a contact."[27] For Williams, contact nominates sexual vitality and connection (so much so that he launched a little magazine called *Contact* in 1920).[28] Likewise, C. P. Cavafy's "He Asked About the Quality" (1930) suggests a similar erotic economy in which hands and touch provide a sexual reprieve from the dreariness of work and poorly made goods.[29]

Part of what makes hands and their corollary, nonindustrialized sexuality, eccentric to the larger sweep of sexual modernity is their fashioning of not just artisanal and distinct objects, but vague objects. By vague objects I mean sexual objects that do not have clearly delimited outlines and yet nevertheless have a certain amount of concreteness. In "Paper Pills," for example, the story takes its title from the little scraps of paper on which the doctor wrote "thoughts, ends of thoughts, beginnings of thoughts" (10). He stuffs the papers into his pocket until they "became little hard round balls" resembling his hands, which themselves look "like clusters of unpainted wooden balls" (10). He then onanistically (or excrementally) dumps the paper pills onto the floor, or throws them at his friend in an act of queer sociability. These thoughts are not given a definite shape but are mere "scraps," recording endings and beginnings without taking a particular form, having a set function, or being part of a larger narrative (10). They typify the vague objects that are associated with Winesburg and with the hand in particular.

*Winesburg* constructs a sexual universe that is not genitally organized but structured instead around the sexuality of hands and touch.[30] While Anderson's text is often understood as embodying "The Book of the Grotesque" (xix) described in the preface's title, with each of the interlaced tales depicting grotesques, I read *Winesburg* at least as much under the sign of its first story, "Hands." "Hands" narrates the story of a gifted schoolteacher named Adolph Myers. His touch is associated with an eroticized celibacy and inspires his pupils.[31] "Here and there," Anderson writes, "went [Myers's] hands, caressing the shoulders of the boys, playing about the tousled heads. . . . By the caress that was in his fingers he expressed himself. . . . Under the caress of his hands doubt and disbelief went out of the minds of the boys and they began also to dream" (7). But this dream-inducing touch becomes a nightmare as it is interpreted as a queer desire for the boys. Pursued by shouts of "'I'll teach you to put your hands on my boy, you beast'" and "'[k]eep your hands to yourself'" (7), Myers does "not understand what happened" but feels "that the hands must be to blame" (8). He changes his name to Wing Biddlebaum, flees to Winesburg, and goes "timidly about, . . . striving to conceal his hands" (8).[32]

If "Hands" tells "The story of Wing Biddlebaum's hands," which is described as being "worth a book in itself" (5), then I want to suggest that *Winesburg, Ohio* is the book described in this moment—the story of the hands of the inhabitants of a small town in Ohio. Anderson contends that his text features "a related group of people, their lives touching, never quite touching," and as if to enact this fleeting, tangential touching, every story in *Winesburg* (with the exception of the preface) contains the word "hand" or "hands."[33] I understand the repetition of the word "hand" and its loose connectivity to describe the Winesburg form and its resistance to the standardization of American life. Biddlebaum's hands in their originality, creativity, and movement lend a loose shape to the form of *Winesburg* itself. Rather than see the text as merely "touching the reader" as Aaron Ritzenberg's *The Sentimental Touch* (2013) contends, or as "without sentimentality" as Edwin Fussell puts it, I see it as forging an affective and sexual vagueness, one that is "touching, never quite touching."[34] Within Winesburg's sexual economy, hands function as both part and whole, suggesting that hands are neither reducible to fetishized sexual objects (in the logic of part as whole) or to what Eve Kosofsky Sedgwick calls *"erotic localization."*[35] By *"erotic localization,"* I understand Sedgwick to mean that the sphere of the sexual is entirely encompassed by a localized site such as the hand (in the logic of the whole embodied in the part). Instead, hands act as conduits for an objectless sexuality, or at least one in which desire is fully present but the object or set of objects remains largely inchoate, vague—a directionless yearning.[36]

Hands embody the particularities of small town desire—a desire that is fundamentally nonpurposive. In "Surrender," for example, Louise Bentley leaves her family farm "wanting love more than anything else in the world" (50) and moves in with her father's friend to get an education in Winesburg. The narrator traces the vague shape of her desire:

Day and night she thought of the matter, but although the thing she wanted so earnestly was something very warm and close it had as yet no conscious connection with sex. It had not become that definite, and her mind had only alighted upon the person of John Hardy because he was *at hand* and unlike his sisters had not been unfriendly to her. (53, my emphasis)

Louise's desire for John Hardy is characterized as being "at hand," emerging out of the adjacency and proximity of "rural community" (96) rather than from a "definite" desire for sex or for the man (or from the foreclosed lesbian erotics in reference to Hardy's sisters). The inhabitants of Winesburg largely lack the means and the opportunities for sexual exploration, or even, in Louise's case, the awareness of such opportunities. Instead, Louise and the other members of the Winesburg community are groping and grasping for sexual knowledge beyond their reach.

In a psychoanalytic frame, Louise's desire occupies a space between polymorphous perversity and the sexually standardized object choice of industrialization, but she does not know what she seeks: "so vague was her notion of life that it seemed to her just the touch of John Hardy's hand upon her own hand would satisfy" (55–56). Here, what Freud would understand as a lack of a clear sexual aim amplifies the vagueness, fuzziness, and indistinction around object choice. As I argued in chapter 3, sexual aim, from its inception in Freud, shores up object choice because intercourse so-called, the only desirable aim in the psychoanalytic imaginary, presupposes different-sex genital contact.[37] Thus, Louise's aimlessness suggests that vague objects are also interchangeable and replaceable. Her desire's relation to objects (if not frequency and intensity) is perhaps closest in the sexological literature to nymphomania—another of the "thousand aberrant sexualities"— which was "not directed at a particular individual object . . . but toward others in general."[38] Though Louise escapes the logic of mimetic desire, not desiring what others desire, her sadness is that in eschewing the standardized modes of desire, she cannot articulate her desires or make them understood. In the opening sentence of "Surrender," a title that will come to describe Louise's affective state, Anderson tells us that "The story of Louise Bentley . . . is a story of misunderstanding" (50). It also seems like a story of sexuality prior to industrialization's forging of desire as a force for reification. In this register, we might understand industrialization to hasten the demise of sexual formations characterized by undefined object choices. That is, these sexual formations are perhaps made less possible with the increase of industrialization.

Industrialization's increasing foreclosure of the desiring of vague objects is even clearer in "Hands," where Biddlebaum's hands are described as "fluttering pennants of promise" (6) and the source of his "elusive individuality (5)."[39] When Biddlebaum is in need of a normalcy that he does not fully understand, he implicitly reaches out to the normalizing energies of industrialization. That is, when he rechristens himself, he chooses the name Biddlebaum "from a box of goods seen at a freight station as he hurried through an Eastern Ohio town" (8). Here, Biddlebaum constructs his new identity through the homogenizing forces of industrialization. With this understanding of the hand as a site of individuality in the face of effectual standardization, we can recast *Winesburg*'s famous trope of the grotesque as that which cannot be standardized. In this reading, *Winesburg* describes and recounts sexual variation—voyeurism in "The Strength of God," exhibitionism in "Adventure," pedophilia in "Hands," the condition of being "stage-struck" (18) in "Mother," excessive alcohol consumption in "Tandy," etc.—without classifying or codifying this into a nosography as a kind of weak theory version of Krafft-Ebing's *Psychopathia Sexualis*. That is, Anderson's "The Book of the Grotesque" refuses the universalization and standardization of Krafft-Ebing's encyclopedic catalog by valuing these figures as singularities.

If the hand operates as one site of looseness against what Gramsci has helped us to see as the rationalization and regulation of the sexual instinct, Anderson's romanticization of America's landscape offers a second alternative to industrialism's sexual regime. One of its clearest articulations comes in Anderson's 1933 introduction to Walt Whitman's *Leaves of Grass*, where he juxtaposes the deleterious forces of industrialization to what he calls "land hunger, river hunger, sea and sky hunger":

If I, an American man, cannot learn to love one strip of countryside, turn of a flowing river, white farm house on a slope in an apple orchard, if I cannot love some one spot . . . (if I am a strong man perhaps a dozen such spots) how can I love America . . . ?

. . . or a woman or a brother man?

. . . The great sweet land that Walt Whitman sang so lustily is still here. People now forget what America is . . . why forget how huge, varied, strong, and flowing it is? We gather too much and stay too long in holes in cities. We forget land-love, river and sky-love.[40]

Here, the hunger for America's lands, rivers, and skies—its landscape—offers a way out of the standardization of industrialization. Anderson privileges variety and multiplicity—the strong man can love a dozen spots instead of one—over the sameness of the industrialized city.[41] Once the lover of land has recaptured the variegation of the "great sweet land" sung "so lustily" by Whitman, then he is ready to love a woman or a brother man outside of the prescribed molds forged by Henry Ford and offered by, as the apple orchard here suggests, city apples.

Anderson's novel *Many Marriages* (1923) begins with such a vision of land hunger, which facilitates the protagonist John Webster's sexual awakening. Webster is a washing machine manufacturer who suddenly realizes the meaninglessness of his monogamous and monotonous industrial life when he has a vision triggered by looking at some wooden boards in his factory.[42] He is able to see "the land from which the boards came" and the men singing and enjoying the work they do (in contrast to industrialized modes of labor).[43] This vision leads John to an epiphany:

One could not be just a manufacturer of washing machines in a Wisconsin town . . . One became a part of something as broad as the land in which one lived. . . . He himself was a man standing . . . but . . . within his body . . . there was something, well perhaps not vast in itself but vaguely indefinitely connected with some vast thing.[44]

Having reconnected with land hunger, river hunger, and sky hunger, John is able to experience a spiritual and erotic connection with others—the many marriages of the novel's title—in ways that were not possible while he lived his industrious and industrialized life. To put this differently, Anderson's title inserts a slipperiness into the idea of what a "marriage" is (this certainly is not the monogamy that Gramsci has in mind as the handmaiden of industrialism). We might think of this passage as offering an etiology of sexuality "vaguely indefinitely connected with some vast thing." Land love is diffuse, refusing the sexual concentration of the city, and is not attached to a single object, but instead comingles easily with river love and sky love. It becomes the medium for other connections and offers a tutorial for human sexuality.

Edward Carpenter's *Civilization: Its Cause and Its Cure* (1889) similarly figures land love through the trope of the hand as a way out of the disease of civilization. He conjures instead a "new human life":

always the work of man perfecting and beautifying the lands, aiding the efforts of the sun and soil, giving voice to the desire of the mute earth—in such new communal life near to nature. . . . In such new human life then—Mutual help and combination will then have become spontaneous and instinctive: each man contributing to the service of his neighbor as inevitably and naturally as the right hand goes to help the left in the human body—and for precisely the same reason. Every man—think of it!—will do the work which he *likes*, which he desires to do, which is obviously before him to do, and which he knows will be useful, without thought of wages or reward; and the reward will come to him as inevitably and naturally as in the human body the blood flows to the member which is exerting itself.[45]

Here, the desires of "the mute earth" and the "new human" operate together and correspond exactly, suggesting that Carpenter's vision of a new society emerges at the intersection of landscape, desire, and unalienated labor. Moreover, such a nexus is as natural "as the right hand goes to help the left in the human body," suggesting that the vehicle of the hand embodies land love and a life outside the alienation of wage labor.

While hands suffuse the eros of *Winesburg* and also formally organize the text by touch, land love too animates the text's erotic economy and structures its form. To put this differently, the representation of the town of Winesburg itself constitutes a lusty singing of "land-love, river and sky-love." This is nowhere clearer than in Winesburg's depiction of a fairground:

There is something memorable in the experience to be had by going into a fair ground that stands at the edge of a Middle Western town on a night after the annual fair has been held. The sensation is one never to be forgotten. On all sides are ghosts not of the dead, but of living people. Here, during the day just passed, have come the people pouring in from the town and country around. Farmers with their wives and children and all the people from the hundreds of little frame houses have gathered within these board walls. Young girls have laughed and men with beards talked of the affairs of their lives. The place has been filled to overflowing with life. (171–72)

Here, the text's movement from the specificity of Winesburg to the abstraction of the experience of standing "at the edge of a Middle Western town" after an annual fair itself performs the way loving "one strip of countryside" (Winesburg) is a way of loving America, a woman, and a brother man. While my etiological reading has helped us to explore sexuality in its less familiar shapes, as resistant to standardization and rationalization, I want now to explore those dominant forces and their impact on sexuality.

## Objects and Objects

I have been arguing that industrialization might be understood as having a hastening effect and operating as a catalyst for both the processes of sexual standardization and the dominance of an object-based organization of sexuality. In George Chauncey's influential account, this system exists simultaneously with and will come largely to supersede the gender-status system. Moreover, Chauncey argues, this object-based system comes into focus for middle-class individuals much earlier: "exclusive heterosexuality became a precondition for a man's identification as 'normal' in middle-class culture at least two generations before it did so in much of Euro-American and African-American working-class culture."[46] Chauncey's account cautions that we not ascribe a single cause to the emergence of an object-based system (since it seems to have emerged at least twice). Because Fordism creates what Simon Clarke calls "a growing 'new middle class' of managerial, technical[,] and supervisory workers," we might conjecture that this new upward mobility accelerates the object-choice-based system's rate of diffusion to the working classes.[47] That is, we might imagine that as the "new middle class" encounters the older middle class, they adopt their sexual cultures in order to assimilate (among other reasons) while they maintain their kinship and friendship ties to working-class cultures, which subsequently come to look more like middle-class sexual cultures. With this supposition in mind, I want to conclude by arguing that *Winesburg*'s story "Queer" offers a complementary conjecture and will help us to understand better the transition between these two systems.

"Queer" is set in a store called "Crowley & Son," which sells "everything and nothing" (134); it is "a queer jumble" (138). The story revolves around a strange incident: Ebenezer Crowley, the senior proprietor in the eponymous store, is speaking with a traveling salesman who is offering him an exclusive on selling a "substitute for collar buttons" (134–35). Ebenezer receives this salesman's offer with the fear that always accompanies such visits for him: "He was afraid, first that he would stubbornly refuse to buy and thus lose the opportunity to sell again; second that he would not be stubborn enough and would in a moment of weakness buy what could not be sold" (134). Like so many characters in *Winesburg*, Ebenezer has an ambivalent relation to objects; he is both afraid to desire objects and afraid not to desire them. In the midst of this decision, his younger son, Elmer, brandishes a gun and demands that the salesman leave, shouting "We ain't going to buy any more stuff until we begin to sell. We ain't going to keep on being queer and have folks staring and listening" (135). Objects, here, are at the center of modern fields of desire: the father's inability to navigate the object worlds of industrialization makes him queer. He is unable to read, let alone incite, consumer desire. But his most egregious offense against the rules of normalcy is the coat that he wears "constantly" (134). "[B]rown with age" and "covered with grease spots," it makes him feel "dressed up and ready for the day in town" (134). This shabby coat exemplifies Ebenezer's inability to discern the meanings and values of objects. This is particularly dire in the age of Fordism since the transformation of workers into consumers heightens commodification and the resemblance between persons and objects.

His son Elmer also struggles to find his object. His rage at the salesman (who Anderson refers to as Elmer's "immediate object") is meant for George Willard, the journalist for the *Winesburg Eagle*, who he imagines is staring and otherwise paying undue attention to Elmer and the exchange in the store (135). This staring, or, more likely, fantasy of staring, carries a homoerotic current, leading him, in a scene of Sedgwickian homosexual panic, to pummel George at the end of the narrative.[48] But even George is not the right object; the narrator tells us that Elmer "had no special feeling concerning" George (136). This slippage between objects, its inability to find the proper one, suggests a homology between the father's failure to choose suitable material objects for sale and the son's "passion" toward the wrong social and sexual objects (136). That is, the father and son suggest a homology between right modes of material desire and the routes of sexual desire.

That these circuits of desire are in some way crossed, powering each other, is evident in the father's outburst as Elmer leaves the store after brandishing the gun. Ebenezer says, "'Well, well, I'll be washed and ironed and starched'" (136). The conflation here between Ebenezer and dirty linen operates in the sexual register of soiled clothing, but also suggests the way that that register is channeled through the conduit of the object world.[49] Rather than adjudicating between the polysemous meanings of the story's title—"Queer"—I am interested in how they laminate onto one another, how ineptness facing the forces of industrialization and consumerism can lead to queerness in object-based sexual economies and how sexual queerness can keep one from understanding consumer desires.[50] Or to put this in the language of my epigraph, I see the common origin of words like "automobile," "sociology," and "homosexuality" as bespeaking not merely a shared etymology, but a shared etiology.[51]

Anderson helps us to see both the emerging dominance of an object-based sexuality and the ways in which his depiction of rural sexuality resists the genital structure of desire that Sedgwick describes as characterizing modern life:

It is a rather amazing fact that, of the very many dimensions along which the genital activity of one person can be differentiated from that of another (dimensions that include preference for certain acts, certain zones or sensations, certain physical types, a certain frequency, certain symbolic investments, certain relations of age or power, a certain species, a certain number of participants, etc. etc. etc.), precisely one, the gender of object choice, emerged from the turn of the century, and has remained, as *the* dimension denoted by the now ubiquitous category of "sexual orientation."[52]

The Winesburg citizens' gestural repertoire of sex provides a glimpse of a set of modalities of desire not yet short-circuited by the invention of sexual object choice.[53] In recovering and reconnecting these circuits of desire, we can begin to imagine sex before it is canalized into more familiar tracks of sexuality. Anderson's depiction of the vagueness of object choice is important because it captures a historical stage in which sexuality is "of one person" but hasn't yet solidified or selected one "of the very many dimensions" outlined by Sedgwick. This is encapsulated succinctly by a stranger in *Winesburg* who claims wistfully: "I am a lover and have not found my thing to love" (97). That is, sexuality has become interiorized as something individuals possess (being "a lover" as the stranger says), but its desires have not become focalized on a particular individual or kind of individuals (the stranger has "not found" his "thing to love"). Moreover, what is sought to love is here a "thing" rather than a "person," suggesting the profound imbrication between material and sexual objects. As capacious as Sedgwick's mapping is—with its reverberating etceteras—we need an even broader consideration of nongenital forms of sexuality in order to understand the formation of sexual orientation that she describes.

FIVE

# Volitional Etiologies: Toward a Weak Theory of Etiology

To discuss weak theory in relation to etiology seems an oxymoron. What, after all, could be stronger than etiology's causative force? And yet the key text of weak theory in sexuality studies, Eve Kosofsky Sedgwick's "Paranoid Reading and Reparative Reading, or, You're So Paranoid, You Probably Think This Essay Is About You" (1997), begins precisely with a moment of etiological inquiry. During the height of the AIDS epidemic, Sedgwick asks her friend Cindy Patton about the "sinister rumors about the virus's origin"—the conspiracy theories that AIDS had been deliberately spread, that it was a military plot, or that it emerged from similarly dastardly motives.[1] Patton responds with what Sedgwick calls her "congenial, stony pessimism":

I just have trouble getting interested in that. I mean, even suppose we were sure of every element of a conspiracy: that the lives of Africans and African Americans are worthless in the eyes of the United States; that gay men and drug users are held cheap where they aren't actively hated; that the military deliberately researches ways to kill noncombatants whom it sees as enemies; that people in power look calmly on the likelihood of catastrophic environmental and population changes. Supposing we were ever so sure of all those things—what would we know then that we don't already know?[2]

For Sedgwick this is an epiphanic moment about the performativity of knowledge, the way that it does things, makes things happen, rather than being "only" true. Knowledge, Sedgwick writes, "does not intrinsically or necessarily enjoin . . . [one] . . . to any specific train of epistemological or narrative consequences."[3] This enjoining is for Sedgwick strong theory, generating a single course of action: an etiology that creates one sequence of events, one set of narrative consequences, a single causal chain. In contrast, weak theory offers a narrative profusion, a set of possible sequences, "causes and effects": "They might," Sedgwick writes, "but then, they might not."[4] Weak theory in this context means an account of causality that is *sufficient* but not *necessary*, and thus plural or provisional, or virtual rather than definitive.

Guided by the title of another of Sedgwick's essays, "Privilege of Unknowing" (1988), I'm also interested in the way that this anecdote might suggest that not knowing, too, triggers a multiplicity of narrative sequences rather than, say, an imperative to uncover or unmask conspiracies.[5] Neither knowledge nor ignorance creates universals; both, instead, engender parallel knowledges that stand co-present. To put this differently, weak theory is generative rather than right (though it might also be right), offering different paths and different futures that all stand in a nonhierarchical relation to one another. It presents a minority report, offering simultaneous rather than consecutive and supersessionary knowledge. Understanding sexual etiologies in this way—with various etiological narratives offering not competing truth claims, but rather coexisting possibilities—places them within a larger history of causation and modernity. In *A Cultural History of Causality: Science, Murder Novels, and Systems of Thought* (2004), Stephen Kern details the deterioration of positivist knowledge across an enormous range of disciplines at the turn of the twentieth century (with particular attention to modernist fiction). Kern contends that causal understanding took on "increasing specificity, multiplicity, complexity, probability, and uncertainty."[6] Following Kern in seeing sexology as part of this transformation in the history of theories of causation, I argue that etiology in its weakness will enable us to loosen the totalizing force of sexuality's seizure and inhabitation of the body.[7]

In order to chart the operation of this weakness, this chapter focuses on a particular class of etiologies that confused sexologists' narratives of causality during the heyday of etiological theorizing about sexuality. These etiologies are acquired, but they are volitional rather than environmental—gambling, smoking, celibacy, criminality, donning "excessive" or opposite-gender clothes, opium and hashish indulgence, or overindulgence in food—and can be understood to operate at the boundary of self-control.[8] In other words, these etiologies occupy the paradoxical space between choice and compulsion, between voluntarity and involuntarity, and between active and unconscious action. I understand this class of volitional etiologies to embody the difficulties that sexologists grappled with as they attempted to establish etiological priority. By "etiological priority," I mean the clear ordering of cause and effect, of illness and symptom. I understand these etiologies to exemplify a moment when—to borrow from Sara Ahmed—"the history of will crosses the history of sexuality."[9] The willfulness of these etiologies, their errancy and unruliness, keeps them from obeying (what will become) the logics of sexual orientation and narrative subjectivity whereby congenital desire leads to sexual object choice.

In the first part of this chapter, I read across a variety of sexological and literary texts to demonstrate that alcoholism could occupy a range of sequential positions in relation to homosexuality: inducing it, being simultaneous with it, following from it, and even generating it in others. Volitional etiologies, thus, exist within a multidirectional, serially organized temporal field. I borrow the term etiolation (referring to plants weakened by a dearth of sunlight) from botany—a classificatory discourse that I have argued elsewhere provided the basis for sexology's sexual catalogs—to suggest that these volitional etiologies require an especially etiolated theory of etiology (one that is even weaker than the weak theory of etiology that I described in the introduction).[10] This weakened theory of etiology helps us to describe the multiple temporal sequences created by volition. In the final section, I offer a reading of Charles R. Jackson's alcoholic novel *The Lost Weekend* (1944) because I understand it to embody precisely such an etiolated etiology. My reading traces the counter-etiological narrative of Jackson's work in order to outline a weak theory of sexuality predicated on etiology's powers of etiolation. I conclude with a meditation on this weak sexuality, exploring the relationship of sexual sequence to the emergence of sexual object choice as the governing system of sexual organization.

## Etiological Priority

I understand the abdication of sequence, then, as a crucial component of weak theory because it is constituted by parallel knowledges. In her pathbreaking book *Inconsequence: Lesbian Representation and the Logic of Sexual Sequence* (2002), Annamarie Jagose argues that "sexology's founding definitional project" is "its production of sexuality as a sequential effect."[11] Here, Jagose contends that sexology secures the "primacy and originality" of heterosexuality over homosexuality.[12] Dana Seitler further elucidates the operation of sexual sequence, arguing that "[f]or Ellis, sexual deviance could only be cognized relationally, or more to the point *serially*."[13] By this she means that nonnormative sexual difference for Ellis is "fundamentally serial," because knowledge about it is conceptualized through other pathologized "structures and types" in relation to race, gender, animality, criminality, intelligence, economic status, and so forth.[14] This insight suggests a second sense in which the homo/hetero binary in particular is fundamentally sequential. "Without a concept of gender," Sedgwick writes, "there could be, quite simply, no concept of homo- or heterosexuality" (even if gender is not as central to broader understandings of sexuality).[15] Thus, the homo/hetero binary is already infused with secondariness and, paradoxically, depends on its erasure of sequence (in the movement away from acts, behavior, and choice toward congenitality, orientation, and involuntariness).

Following Jagose, I aim to enrich our understanding of sexual sequence and its relation to both the construction of sexuality and the sexological project, arguing that etiology is at the heart of sexology's sequencing energies. Acquired etiology is central to this mechanism of sexual sequencing because most acquired etiologies of sexual aberration operate under the assumption that heterosexuality—which is to say the "normal" operation of the sexual instinct—precedes the etiological event that led to sexual deviation or aberration. In other words, acquired sexual etiologies provide the ground for the production of the "sequential effect" that Jagose describes.

Because of the limited archives of Jagose and Seitler (they both focus on Ellis and Freud), I develop a weak theory of sexuality across a broad range of literary and sexological texts to draw out the different relation that volitional etiologies have to the processes of sequencing. These texts enable us to articulate an etiolated etiology that asks questions about origins without establishing a cause or causes and which is open to the possibility of etiology without identifiable cause.[16] To put this differently, since each sequence of acquired sexuality suggests a different etiology and because the sequences are reversible and multidirectional, these volitional etiologies require a theory of etiology that does not dictate a causal chain. Moreover, Sedgwick's mapping of the "historical interimplications" "both structurally and temporally" of

"the addict identity and the homosexual identity" suggests that volition might provide a further avenue for weakening the causal logics of
sexuality and their sexual orderings.[17] One implication of Sedgwick's
argument is that the artificiality of the addict's desires or the homosexual's desires (called "addictions")—as opposed to the naturalness of
reproductive desires (called "needs")—places sexuality's processes and
technologies of sovereignty within a weakened field of mastery.[18]

Alcohol is among the most prevalently debated etiologies in such
a sexual field and thus offers a wide range of sequential orderings.[19] I
chart the cultural prevalence of these etiological sequences in order to
suggest the scrambling of cause and effect and the nondominance of
any one of them. Magnus Hirschfeld's *The Homosexuality of Men and
Women* (1914) posits one such ordering, contending that

Alcoholic beverages which, when consumed in moderate amounts, stimulate the
sex drive. . . . Beginning in ancient times, excesses in drinking and love-making
have been considered to go hand in hand. In addition to that, of course, alcohol appears to reduce the power of inhibition by dulling the senses. So, that explains why
heterosexual men occasionally state that they had intercourse with a man because
they were under the influence of alcohol, and why homosexuals say they can have
intercourse with a woman when they are drunk.[20]

Here, Hirschfeld seems to offer at least two different rationales for
alcohol-induced homosexuality. Firstly, he proposes that alcohol stim-
ulates the sex drive. While this might lead to immoderate heterosexual
sex, this increased desire will not stop there in its pursuit of alleviation,
of an outlet. That is, if heterosexual intercourse is unavailable, alcohol and the gnawing desire it induces might lead a supposedly heterosexual individual to make a homosexual object choice. This is what I
called in chapter 1 "the deprivation model"; in the absence of a desired
alternative, the drive must be satisfied and object choice becomes a secondary consideration. In this account of sexual decision-making, alcohol is such a stimulant to desire that it can override presumptive sexual
object choice.[21] Secondly, Hirschfeld contends that alcohol dulls the
faculties of reason and reduces inhibition. In this model, the imbibing
subject possesses an innate queerness, which exists prior to the consumption of alcohol. This queerness is blocked in some way, perhaps
by the social stigma attached to making homosexual object choices.
Drinking alcohol dispels these reservations and social costs, unlocking
queerness in this disinhibition model. For Hirschfeld, these possibilities need not be contradictory; there exists a complementarity between

this increase in drive and the willingness to buck social taboos while acting on one's desires.

Iwan's Bloch's *Contributions to the Etiology of Psychopathia Sexualis* (1902) shares much of Hirschfeld's understanding of the relationship between alcohol and homosexuality:

Undoubtedly certain stimulants and drugs possess an etiological importance in *psychopathia sexualis*. Alcohol and opium demand first attention.

The occurrence of numerous aberrations and transgressions in acute alcoholic intoxication is well known and requires no further exposition. Actually pedication, sodomy, and other kinds of unnatural vice as direct consequences of alcoholic intoxication have occurred in cases of individuals at other times sexually normal.

More important is the fact that chronic alcoholism has a decisively unfavorable influence on the *vita sexualis*. Alcoholism can even, without consecutive neurasthenia, cause *spermatorrhea* in a man, sterility in a woman. Gradually in both the potency is decreased while on the other hand the *libido sexualis* is increased. Thus very really the ground is prepared for the appearance of sexual anomalies. The sexual imagination of the alcoholic becomes more extravagant (*ut vino calefacta Venus, tum saevior ardet luxuries*, as the proverb goes) and more receptive of suggestions. As to the latter, von Schrenck-Notzing has pointed out in his book on the importance of narcotics in hypnotism that alcohol, morphine, hasheesh, create a favorable pre-disposition for the reception of suggestions and auto-suggestions. Thus it is obvious that the chronic alcoholic lets suggestions influence him also in the matter of sex, and by this means the development of sexual perversions in him is fostered. It is very significant that in Zanzibar the Suaheli [Swahili] word *walevi* (drunkard) is used directly for "pederast," the active as well as the passive pederasts among the negro population of Zanzibar being habitual sots.[22]

Here, Bloch offers two additional etiologies. The first—that of suggestion—shares, with Hirschfeld's account, alcohol's ability to reduce powers of decision-making. However, where Hirschfeld's drinker finds desire within himself that alcohol enables, the drinker under the influence of suggestion eschews his own desire and adopts that of someone else. The second model proposed by Bloch operates differently, offering an almost vitalist principle of exhaustion. The physical effects of alcohol have left the body of the drinker unable to perform, and thus repeated attempts at sexual satiation result in failure (impotence, sterility, etc.) In order to achieve satisfaction the drinker tries something new, stimulating his or her imagination to ever more unusual perversions in an attempt to find satiation and recover potency.[23] Thus, the sexual subject's predilections are reorganized by his encounter with alcohol, exemplifying what I called "the transformation model" in chapter 1.

All of the models that I have discussed in this chapter so far more or less proceed from the idea that alcohol induces homosexuality, that alcohol is the cause of homosexuality or, in a weaker register, facilitates it.[24] However, these two passages also begin to suggest an additional temporal possibility: namely, simultaneity. Hirschfeld's contention that "excesses in drinking and love-making have been considered to go hand in hand" suggests that alcohol is not prior to homosexuality, but synchronous with it. Moreover, Bloch's contention that the Swahili "word *walevi* (drunkard) is used directly for 'pederast'" suggests a similar temporal coinciding (albeit one with a specifically racial/regional inflection) carried in the simultaneously summoned multivalence of the word's usage.

The possibility that alcohol functions as a kind of comorbidity with homosexuality is further expounded in a 1925 letter the painter Russell Cheney wrote to his partner, the literary scholar F. O. Matthiessen:

I have dodged the issue of my character this 10 or 15 years and my character has steadily deteriorated in will power. It is lack of will power which keeps me from reaching what I want in painting. That shows mostly in the two indulgences, in drink and sex. For some reason the drink business seemed to suddenly adjust itself, after you left. I just felt: here, you can't go on this way, quit it—and I have. Dev [Matthiessen], even while you were here with me I was cheating you on it—my sense of decency was about gone. I slipped a new bottle of cognac for the old empty one and you never knew I emptied it. When you went to the [bathroom] several mornings, I slipped a good solid drink and brushed my teeth so you wouldn't know—really lying to you, that's what it was, and I have had bitter, bitter shame the last couple of days since I came to. Sorry, Dev. It's all over—it will never come back, because this change in me is not a temporary effort of the will but a change in me.[25]

Cheney's use of the language of "character" makes evident that he conceptualizes both alcoholism and homosexuality as vices (though he also uses the less stigmatizing term "indulgences"). Earlier in this same letter Cheney has proposed that the two no longer share physical relations ("I definitely say that . . . the relation between us has got to be that of two regular [friendly] fellers, as far as actual physical connection goes").[26] This imperative for celibacy suggests that Cheney understands himself to have "quit" the vice of alcoholism as he has quit having sex with Matthiessen. The two vices are linked as matters of "will power," operating as catalysts for one another as indexed by Cheney's "change" occurring at the moment of his separation from Matthiessen.[27] Though possibly out of politeness or possibly because he doesn't know or doesn't conceptualize it in these terms, Cheney doesn't ascribe a cause ("for some reason") to the sudden adjustment that occurs.[28] But Cheney's "change" also exceeds the logic of the will. Possessing an involuntariness that is contrasted with "a temporary effort of the will," Cheney's "change" is described as "a change in me," suggesting that such involuntarity consolidates identity and functions as a necessary component of sexual subjectivity—the unconscious—alongside the agency that I charted in chapter 3.

Leon Pierce Clark, who served as president of the American Psychopathological Association, describes yet another etiological sequencing, namely that homosexuality causes alcoholism. Recounting a case of a man who takes to drink after the death of his beloved uncle, Clark writes:

His first severe alcoholic spree followed immediately after the uncle's death, and he had feelings of anxiety and fear which drove him to drink. Doubtless the fear resulted from the repressed feeling for the uncle, and the desire to drink was additionally conditioned by memory of previous drinks with him. The fear and restlessness which introduce socalled [sic] dipsomanic attacks are usually rooted in conflicts and repressions of the sexual desire.[29]

Instead of reading this as a case of coping through drink in the face of tremendous loss, Clark forecloses the innocence of this possibility with the certainty of the word "doubtless." Rather, Clark contends that repressed desire for his uncle is the cause of his alcoholism and then generalizes that such dipsomania "usually" is rooted in such repressed (homosexual) desires. Moreover, the memory of previous drinks with the uncle is also given a "subconscious homosexual tendency" when Clark poses the rhetorical question: "Can it be merely chance that men so much enjoy being among themselves and drinking together, sometimes roughly, sometimes in more refined manner?"[30] In his references to roughness and refinement Clark here suggests that homosexuality, however "subconscious," causes alcoholism across classes.[31] In an article on homosexuality and alcoholism Simon Weijl echoes Clark, noting that "latent homosexual drives are directly connected with the causes of compulsive drinking."[32] Where Clark and Weijl see repressed desire as the motive for drink, Ernest Hemingway records Gertrude Stein saying that disgust with homosexuality is the cause: "The main thing is that the act male homosexuals commit is ugly and repugnant and afterwards they are disgusted with themselves. They drink, take drugs, to palliate this, but they are disgusted with the act and they are always changing partners and cannot be really happy."[33] Whether the root cause is the repression of homosexuality or disgust with it, both of these sequences suggest that homosexuality could be understood by medical professionals and lay people alike in the first half of the twentieth century as causing alcoholism.[34]

These three etiological sequences—alcohol causes homosexuality, alcohol and homosexuality are simultaneous with one another, homosexuality causes alcoholism—all concern individual rather than alloerotic desire.[35] However, Malcolm Lowry's *Under the Volcano* (1947) provides examples of alcoholism making one attractive to another person or people. Here, alcoholism magnetizes desire toward the drinker rather than directing it or producing it.[36] In his "Introduction" to *Under the Volcano*, Stephen Spender describes the protagonist Geoffrey Firmin's "suppressed homosexual tendency," capturing the novel's atmospheric homosexuality—its homoerotic traffic in women, its references to Oscar Wilde, Jean Cocteau, A. E. Housman, its phobic sodomy jokes, and its detailing of inadequate heterosexuality.[37] The scene that I am most interested in, however, features a very inebriated Firmin being watched ("he had been observed too") and then having a conversation with a retired walnut grower named Quincey while Quincey tends his garden.[38]

The imagery is heavy-handed, featuring a "fruit tree," a garter snake, and Firmin drunkenly pontificating on and recasting the story of the Garden of Eden.[39] As Firmin theorizes alternative understandings of Adam's knowledge, Quincey is staring at another metaphorical snake in the garden: namely, Firmin's penis visible through his "open fly."[40] While Firmin at first understands Quincey's prolonged staring as assent to his Edenic theories, it clearly carries a sexual valence (even if Firmin doesn't realize this):

[Firmin] greeted Mr. Quincey's cat . . . "hello-pussy-my-little-Priapusspuss, my-little-Oedipusspusspuss," and the cat, recognizing a friend and uttering a cry of pleasure, wound through the fence and rubbed against the Consul's [Firmin's] legs, purring. . . . "Animals not fit for food and kept only for pleasure, curiosity, or whim—eh?—as William Blackstone said—you've heard of him of course!—" The Consul was somehow on his haunches half talking to the cat, half to the walnut grower, who had paused to light a cigarette. "Or was that another William Blackstone?"[41]

With references to Priapus, Oedipus, and a pussy that rubs and purrs, this passage hums with desire, saturated and suffused as it is with excessive and illicit sexuality. But the sexual possibility most animated by the passage is sodomy—in the senses of male-male penetrative sex and of cross-species intimacy. The word "somehow" ("The Consul was somehow on his haunches") draws an incredulous attention to Firmin's unusual drunken posture, while the simultaneous humanity and animality of the word "haunches" threatens, in the baroque wordplay of the passage, sodomitical "intercourse" with both the cat and with Quincey as Firmin talks partly to each of them. The sodomitical wordplay is picked up a few sentences earlier when Firmin mentions "the abominations" in the Garden of Eden.[42] This is activated again in the reference to the widely influential legal scholar William Blackstone and his characterization of sodomy as an abominable crime, "the very mention of which is a disgrace to human nature," as well as in the possibility of keeping animals "only for pleasure."[43] In the context of the open fly, this passage suggests that alcohol can generate homosexual desire for someone else in addition to its other individual etiologies. Alcohol, in short, can be both auto- and alloerotic.[44]

This model of homosexuality magnetized by alcoholism is also evident in Lowry's biography. Douglas Day, Lowry's biographer, notes that some of the dialogue given to Quincey was originally spoken by Lowry's mentor, guardian, and fellow writer Conrad Aiken.[45] This biographical fact amplifies the homoerotics of the novel's scene; Lowry was introduced to his first wife Jan Gabrial by Aiken, an introduction that was framed as a homoerotic trafficking in women. Aiken's autobiographical novel *Ushant* (1952) recounts how, in Day's paraphrase, "Aiken admits . . . that it has been his 'visceral and feculent scheme' to hand her [Jan Gabrial] to Lowry, so that—vicariously, at least—he could possess her too."[46] Gabrial also reports being "fairly flung at other men" and would taunt Lowry for his lack of sexual prowess.[47] In addition to this homoerotic "sharing" of Gabrial, Lowry was propositioned by homosexual men. His friend Paul Leonard Charles Fitte asked him to have sex and threatened suicide if he declined. When Lowry refused, Fitte's suicide immediately followed, leaving Lowry with a lifelong "recurrent sense of guilt."[48] Lowry's drunkenness is also said to have functioned as an aphrodisiac for the two men whom Day describes homophobically as "a pair of aggressive English homosexuals . . . who were hoping to get him [Lowry] drunk enough to submit to them."[49]

Together the four models I have enumerated (alcoholism can induce homosexuality, be simultaneous with it, follow from it, or can make one sexually attractive) enable us to think about what is at stake in positing that sexual sequence is ultimately not determinable. The fact that these four models can coexist suggests the fictionality of the sexual self's narrative. Against the sequencing project of sexology, the indeterminate causality posed by volitional etiologies enables us to see the tenuousness of the developmental narrative of sexual subjectivity, and thereby assert that, perhaps, no sexuality is secondary or derivative. We can, as Annamarie Jagose puts it, "denaturalize the apparently self-evident priority of heterosexuality."[50] That is, the particular value of these etiolated etiologies is that they (potentially) begin to unthread the prioritization and thus provide one axis along which the stigma of nonnormative sexualities, particularly homosexuality, can operate.

## The Counter-Etiological Imaginary and the Decompartmentalization of Sex

In order to theorize the importance of etiology to sexual sequence, I turn in this final section to Charles R. Jackson's *The Lost Weekend* (1944), a book that contains all four of the etiologies I discussed above as well as others. *The Lost Weekend* is arguably the most famous literary depiction of alcoholism and was made into a wildly successful 1945 film that won Academy Awards for Best Picture, Best Director, Best Actor, and Best Screenplay. The novel narrates the story of Don Birnam as he lies, steals, pawns, and intimidates his way through a besotted long weekend—the eponymous lost weekend—making sure that he never runs out of alcohol or money for more alcohol. At the time, the editor of the *Journal of the American Medical Association*, Dr. Morris Fishbein, asserted that the book captured "the very soul of the dipsomaniac."[51] As the language of the soul suggests, if dipsomania had been a temporary aberration, the alcoholic was—under one etiological regime put forward by Fishbein—rapidly becoming a species.

Over and over again *The Lost Weekend* tantalizingly promises to reveal the secret cause or etiology of its protagonist Don's drinking. In fact, it obsessively multiplies such etiologies, while often laminating the secret of his drinking onto that of homosexuality:

1. His genius and precociousness
2. The influence of dangerous reading (particularly James Joyce's *Dubliners*)

3. Fate (Don's surname is associated with *Macbeth*)
4. Homosexuality
5. The shock of expulsion from his fraternity for expressing same-sex desire
6. Narcissism (associated with looking in the mirror and homosexuality)
7. Anxiety about masculinity
8. Arrested development
9. Boredom/desire for stimulation
10. An absent father
11. Incestuous desire for his brother
12. Overinvestment in his mother

Virtually all of these enumerated etiologies (though the list is by no means exhaustive) might be understood as indexing homosexuality, and Don's drinking has often been ascribed to such repressed desire. For example, Jaime Harker's reading of the novel contends "that Don's heavy drinking is related to his suppressed sexuality (Don began drinking after he was kicked out of his fraternity for a too-intensive friendship with a fellow fraternity brother, though he never makes this connection)."[52] Similarly, Robert J. Corber understands Don's alcoholism to be "caused by a false accusation that he had a homosexual relationship with a fraternity brother."[53] While the text does, in one register, tantalizingly solicit these readings, I am interested in the way that these etiologies have their own consistency, density, and meaning, which cannot be fully subsumed under the sign of homosexuality or even sexual subjectivity.[54] To paraphrase Scott Herring in a different context, I understand *The Lost Weekend* to run contrary to generic expectations, queering the genre of the etiological case study, turning it against itself, using it to manipulate homosexual identifications, and frustrating the compulsion to reveal sexual knowledge.[55] This foiling of sexual knowledge, this thwarting of confession (the central technology of *psychopathia sexualis*), frustrates the project of sexual self-making. That is, in contrast to interpretations that seek the cause of Don's drinking, my reading explores the novel's counter-etiological bent—the way it avoids singling out the cause of Don's drinking by multiplying prospective causes. These etiologies resist the promise of unlocking or explaining. Thus, while the novel begins with James Joyce's line from "Counterparts" (1914)—"'The barometer of his emotional nature was set for a spell of riot'"—representing it as inducing a drinking spree, the narrator later says that Don "couldn't lay the blame on a phrase in a book."[56] Here, any etiological force initially attributed to literature or to reading dissipates and becomes ineffectual.

The moment when the novel most clearly foregrounds its status as a counter-etiological narrative arrives just before the novel's conclusion:

> Why were drunks, almost always, persons of talent, personality, loveable qualities, gifts, brains, assets of all kinds (else why would anyone care?); why were so many brilliant men alcoholic?—And from there, the next one was: Why did you drink?
>
> Like the others, the question was rhetorical, abstract, anything but pragmatic: as vain to ask as his own clever question had been vain. It was far too late to pose a problem with any reasonable hope that it would be worth listening to or prove anything at all. It had long since ceased to matter Why. You were a drunk; that's all there was to it. You drank; period. And once you took a drink, once you got under way, what difference did it make Why? There were so many dozen reasons that didn't count at all; none that did. Maybe you drank because you were unhappy, or too happy; or too hot, or too cold; or you didn't like the *Partisan Review*, or you loved the *Partisan Review*. It was as groundless as that. To hell with the causes— absent father, fraternity shock, too much mother, too much money, or the dozen other reasons you fell back on to justify yourself. They counted for nothing in the face of the one fact: you drank and it was killing you. Why? Because alcohol was something you couldn't handle, it had you licked. Why? Because you had reached the point where one drink was too many and a hundred not enough.[57]

Here, the novel parodies the very idea of etiological explanation as "groundless" in its enumeration of conflicting mundanities—"too hot," "too cold," "unhappy," "too happy." The fact that some of these etiologies have been threaded throughout the narrative—"absent father" and "fraternity"—while others such as "lik[ing] the *Partisan Review*" are being introduced for the first time seems to undermine the explanatory force of all the etiologies on offer. Or if they are not groundless then they are too far removed from their origins to matter anymore in the face of assertions that "It was far too late" and "It had long since ceased to matter Why." Here, the novel's search for causes is overwhelmed by their effects, dissolving the value of causes altogether.

The counter-etiological structure of the novel tells us something important about etiological thinking, particularly for thinking about the question of etiological priority. The novel answers the question of why one drinks by saying: "You were a drunk; that's all there was to it. You drank; period." This tautological and counter-etiological explanation refuses both cause and effect, defeating epistemology and the question of "Why?" at the moment that it refuses etiology. This etiological refusal or spoiling of the case study is made more pronounced in light of the unstable ordering of the sexological and literary examples that I examined in the first section.[58] That is, the multidirectional temporality of etiology here begins to expound a weak(er) theory of etiology—namely, one articulated through what Michel Foucault calls "decompartmentalization."[59]

While Foucault does not define decompartmentalization, I take him to mean the process by which one sexual formation is interconnected with or fused with others (for example, that masturbation and homosexuality were part of the same pathology).[60] With this in mind, I would argue that queer studies and the historiography of sexuality have tended to over-compartmentalize individual sexual formations. Sexology is more diverse than the scholarly focuses on inversion, homosexuality, and sadomasochism would suggest and these formations are more interconnected with, more serially constructed through adjacent sexual formations than, is ordinarily discussed. That is, in isolating a particular identity or practice from the sexological network and from the nosography in which it is enmeshed, we have narrowed the domain of sexuality as it existed at the turn of the twentieth century and into the mid-twentieth century.[61] Rather than reading this enmeshment, sexuality studies has persistently ignored the sheer range and variety of sexology's will to knowledge and its interarticulated constructions of sexuality. To put it simply, we diminish the complexity of any given sexual formation if we understand it without reference to what Foucault calls the "thousand aberrant sexualities."[62]

In *The Lost Weekend*, for instance, we must read Don's theft, lying, alcohol abuse, literariness, precocity, and homosexuality as existing together in a decompartmentalized sexual formation, as all part of a unified domain of sexuality, the same network of desire and behavior.[63] In other words, we must conceptualize them as standing in a relation of complexity rather than as singularities, producing sexuality as an assemblage.[64] This is precisely how Bloch understands the sexuality of one masochist who describes himself "as a clothes- and shoe- fetichist, as a fancier of cunnilinctus and passive pedication!"[65] Bloch theorizes sexuality here to be decompartmentalized, encompassing what he calls "complex aberrations" and "complex perversion[s]."[66] Referring to these individuals possessed of complex aberrations, Bloch describes them as "embodying the entire *psychopathia sexualis*" and as "a walking '*psychopathia sexualis*'" and suggests that they are "the best proof that sexual perversions are acquired, since it is inconceivable that all sexual abnormalities could be simultaneously inborn in one individual."[67] This claim is less important for our purposes in relation to the debate between acquisition and congenitality, which Bloch was in the process of losing, than for suggesting that sexuality is not monocausal. Multiple sexual etiologies suggest "the unrationalized coexistence of different models of sexuality," at its most unrationalized.[68] In this moment, Bloch underlines the necessity of a weak(er) theory of etiology that can incorporate many causes and which does not attempt to establish etiological priority or sequence.

Even as historical forces are solidifying and delimiting the sexual subject—in relation to constancy (chapter 1), boundedness (chapter 2), agency (chapter 3), and standardization in relation to objects (chapter 4)—volition scrambles sequential unfolding, pluralizing sequences to create not just what Guy Hocquenghem calls in a different context "non-limitative horizontal relations," but also non-limitative temporal ones.[69] To put this differently, volition participates in a structure of sexual sequentiality that demands *some* order or arrangement while lacking any *particular* sequence or definite ordering. This weak sequentiality without the imperative to any particular sequence begins to rupture even the difference between acquisition and congenitality that I have been charting. The early twentieth-century sexologist Auguste Forel writes, "[T]he difference between hereditary and acquired sexual anomalies is only relative and gradual, so that it is necessary to avoid opposing one against the other."[70] If the difference between heredity and acquisition is fundamentally a temporal one in which heredity precedes acquisition, then the scrambling of sequence suggests their uneasy disaggregation. It presents the utopian possibility that all sexualities might be imagined in a single plane without hierarchy, sequence, or priority.

# After Sedgwick: The Gordian Knot of the Great Paradigm Shift

Sexuality . . . depends on the mutual redefinition and occlusion of synchronic and diachronic formulations. EVE KOSOFSKY SEDGWICK, *BETWEEN MEN*

The title of my afterword embeds an interrogative: "What does it mean to be after Sedgwick?" I want to think of this condition of being "after" as not merely a chronological succession, but perhaps afterness as being "in Sedgwick's wake," or "in the style of Sedgwick," or even for some, "in pursuit of Sedgwick" (erotic or otherwise).[1] Sedgwick repeatedly says in *Epistemology of the Closet* that "we can't know in advance."[2] With this refrain in mind, what does it mean to speak after, or to after-speak someone who understands their work as engaged in a continual process of future unfolding?[3] That is, to speak after someone, to borrow Jonathan Goldberg's pun, who is perennially articulating "the Eve of the future."[4] One possible risk of speaking after Sedgwick is, of course, disappointment. Another might be boredom. With such dangers in view, I take Sedgwick's words in my epigraph as an Archimedean point for both reframing the project of this book and for reorienting Sedgwick's body of work. I strive to do so in the style of Sedgwick and in homage to the consequence and power of her work.

One aim of this book has been to give a synchronic

account of what is ordinarily framed as a diachronic event: the invention of the homo/hetero binary, or the Great Paradigm Shift, as Sedgwick jokingly put it. In this afterword, I want to return to the diachronic nature of this event to see how it looks in light of this book's remapping of what Valerie Traub has called the "synchronic tensions" between acquired and congenital models of sexuality.[5] As I argued in the introduction, the debate between acquisition and congenitality and its recasting of "the very domain of sexuality" makes a reconsideration of these changes all the more imperative.[6] Taking up Sedgwick's challenge (articulated in my epigraph), this afterword examines how the synchronic expansion of sexuality necessarily reconfigures our account of sexuality's diachronic change. One of the central claims of this afterword will be that the Great Paradigm Shift is not a single shift, but a process of gradual and sloping change.

In the introduction I traced Sedgwick's hesitancy about proposing a narrative of the Great Paradigm Shift in *Epistemology of the Closet*. Inasmuch as *Between Men* might be said to offer precisely such a narrative (describing the historical period just prior to that examined by *Epistemology*), we might understand this reluctance as a repudiation of her earlier work. Critics have tended to overlook this submerged historical narrative in favor of focusing on *Between Men*'s exploration of mimetic desire and erotic triangles in spite of the book's contention in its opening paragraph:

I will be arguing that concomitant changes in the structure of male "homosocial desire" were tightly, often causally bound up with other more visible changes; that the emerging pattern of male friendship, mentorship, entitlement, rivalry, and hetero and homosexuality was in an intimate and shifting relation to class; and that no element of that pattern can be understood outside of its relation to women and the gender system as a whole.[7]

I might gloss Sedgwick's sentence here to mean that she will track the shifting meanings of male bonds in all their forms in relation to women, gender, and class in the period stretching from the mid-eighteenth to the mid-nineteenth century.

*Between Men* divides "Victorian men among three rough categories according to class": (1) aristocratic men (associated with effeminacy) who have long had access to secrecy and what Sedgwick calls "a distinct homosexual role and culture"; (2) educated middle-class men who "had a good deal of objective sexual freedom" but seem "not to have had easy access to the alternative subculture, the stylized discourse, or the sense of immunity of the aristocratic/bohemian sexual minority"; (3) working-class men who serve as objects of fantasy and "sexual value to more privileged men."[8] *Between Men* focuses on the second group, educated middle-class men, exploring their emergence as older patriarchal structures are collapsing. She charts this group's shifting relation to women and effeminacy, arguing that there is a large-scale cultural shift from William Wycherley's *The Country Wife* (1675), which compulsorily routes "homosocial desire through women," to a mid-nineteenth-century culture, exemplified by Walt Whitman's *Leaves of Grass* (1855), which explores "a range of forms and intensities of male homosocial bonds . . . without admitting culturally defined 'femininity' into them as a structuring term."[9] In particular, Sedgwick considers how the shift from the patriarchal/feudal family to the nuclear family produces middle-class men who stand in anxious relation to femininity, effeminacy, and homosexuality: "no man must be able to ascertain that he is not (that his bonds are not) homosexual."[10] That is, in the period between the late seventeenth century and the mid-nineteenth century all men became vulnerable to the charge of homosexuality.[11]

Sedgwick's account here of what she will later call the Great Paradigm Shift is important for two reasons. First, in the context of Sedgwick's thought, it helps us to see that her axioms in *Epistemology of the Closet* are, as I intimated in the introduction, not necessarily places where sexuality studies must begin or end its thinking, especially given that Sedgwick often took a different tack earlier or later in her career. This is true not merely of the Great Paradigm Shift, but also of etiology. Despite her axiomatic admonition about etiology, both *Between Men* and *Tendencies* (1993) are significantly more open to the political possibilities of etiological analysis (*Tendencies*, for example, includes an essay titled "How to Bring Your Kids Up Gay: The War on Effeminate Boys").[12] With this in mind, this book seeks to formulate not a new set of axioms for sexuality studies but a new set of hypotheses.[13]

The second reason to recapitulate Sedgwick's narrative of the Great Paradigm Shift is that it directly conflicts with the account—to the extent that there is one—in *Epistemology of the Closet*. In this later book, Sedgwick posits 1891 as "a moment from the very midst of the process from which modern homosexual identity and a modern problematic of sexual orientation could be said to date."[14] Elsewhere the text contends that "The year 1891 is a good moment to which to look for a cross-section of the inaugural discourses of modern homo/heterosexuality" and that the terms of "the crisis of sexual definition . . . were crystalizing so rapidly by 1891."[15] While Sedgwick makes several other references to 1891 as the *annus mirabilis* of the homo/hetero binary in *Epistemology*, I am less interested in her violation of her own axiom than in the yawning gap between the chronology of the periodizing claims about the invention of sexuality in this book and in *Between Men*.

While Sedgwick's two accounts begin to bring the story of the Great Paradigm Shift into view, they also emblematize wider tensions in the field of sexual historiography as Sedgwick appears at different times on both sides of what I see as a cleavage in accounts of sexual history. This afterword, then, argues that the historiography of (male) sexuality continues to be riven by two fundamental impasses. First, there is a group of eighteenth-century scholars (Trumbach, McIntosh, Bray, Rey, van der Meer, Warner, Norton, King) for whom the modern regime of male sexuality coalesced at the end of the seventeenth century, while a similar agreement exists among scholars working with more contemporary materials (Foucault, Halperin, Boone, Davidson, Coviello) that sexuality emerged at the end of the nineteenth century.[16] Randolph Trumbach, for example, asserts that "By 1880 modern Western homosexuality and heterosexuality had existed for nearly two hundred years. The new names therefore only represent a new stage in the public discussion of these roles, however much the discussion may have changed the political environment in which the roles were enacted."[17] This view stands in pointed contradistinction to the title and argument of Halperin's book *One Hundred Years of Homosexuality* (1990). My sense is that these two bodies of scholarship are not put in dialogue in part because of Sedgwick's argument (discussed in the introduction) for not seeking the Great Paradigm Shift.[18] Second, among those who understand homosexuality to emerge around the turn of the twentieth century, there is no scholarly consensus about what role race (Ross, Somerville), gender (Chauncey, Reay), and class (Heap, Trask, Canaday) play in the construction of sexual object choice. While it is widely agreed that these three categories have an enormous impact on the construction of object choice, there is as of yet no synthesis or mapping of their interrelation. This afterword will attempt to explore these impasses—if not cutting the Gordian Knots, at least describing them more diagnostically and thinking through them relationally.

## Impasse 1: Two Hundred and Fifteen Years of Homosexuality?

The eighteenth-century figure of the molly—a word that signified both female prostitutes and effeminate and sodomitical men—is at the center of the periodization of the invention of homosexuality. Describing the network of meeting places (known as molly houses) for these men, Trumbach writes, "there is no doubt that in the great cities of Europe in the 18th century, in London as well as Paris, men who engaged in homosexual behavior constructed around themselves a protective subculture."[19] Similarly, Alan Bray describes the London molly houses and other sites of meeting for casual same-sex contact as a "specifically homosexual world."[20] Bray understands this world to be organized around sociability and sex: "Sex was the root of the matter, but it was likely to be expressed in drinking together, in flirting and gossip and in a circle of friends as in actual liaisons."[21] In eighteenth-century Holland, Theo van der Meer maps a similar subculture of "public meeting sites" and "private parlors, pubs, and brothels" where "effeminacy and camp-like behavior" are "rampant."[22] Michel Rey describes "congregations of homosexuals" gathering in Parisian taverns in populous districts at least as early as 1706 and increasing in the 1730s.[23] The visibility of these subcultures in England, Holland, and France constitute what Stephen Shapiro calls "the moment of the molly."[24]

What was it then that was happening in eighteenth-century northwestern Europe?[25] The subcultures in England, France, and the Netherlands were terrorized by unprecedented crackdowns at the beginning of the eighteenth century. Bray describes the English molly houses as experiencing "persecution on a scale and of an immediacy unknown before," resulting in raids and mass arrests in 1699, 1707, and 1726.[26] While the London raids have the richest historiography, similar sets of arrests occur in France and the Netherlands.[27] For example, Bryant T. Ragan chronicles the use of undercover agents to harass and entrap Parisian sodomites between 1720 and 1789, noting 234 arrests in the year 1749 alone.[28] In Holland, too, van der Meer argues that "throughout a major part of the eighteenth century Holland staged the most severe prosecutions of men engaging in same-sex [sexual] behavior in early modern Europe."[29] Between 1730 and 1732, 350 men were prosecuted and between 80 and 100 were put to death.[30]

Describing the London campaign, Bray makes a startling claim (and one which is importantly applicable to the French and Dutch cases as well): "As a social phenomenon they [the mass arrests] were something new; they are in marked contrast to the circumstances that prevailed in England up to the last quarter of the seventeenth century. . . . Something fundamental has changed that needs to be looked at more closely."[31] Though Bray does not specify this "something new" that swept northwest Europe, his second book *The Friend* (2003) seems to suggest that it is the suspicion of the bonds between men, which arose as the structure of friendship declined.[32] This claim would also dovetail with Sedgwick's account in *Between Men*. How can we square this timeline of suspicion with the more familiar and later emergence of homosexuality that Foucault so famously charts?

A number of scholars of both camps position these earlier sexual categories—the molly and the sodomite—as highly proximate to, and for some importantly different from, the conceptualization of the homosexual. For example, David Halperin describes the figure of the molly as "verging on the homosexual," even as he notes that the molly does not "distinguish systematically between sexual deviance and gender deviance."[33] In the same vein, Michael Warner sees London molly houses as sites "where something like a modern homosexual culture was developing."[34] Likewise, van der Meer sees the "rise of a same-sex proto-something," positing "a homosexual self-awareness" that is not a "modern identity."[35] He does, however, see sodomites forming "a category in their own right," resisting the negative associations of sodomy and transforming them "in order to look upon themselves as morally responsible human beings."[36]

The self-awareness that van der Meer sees as a harbinger of "something" is even more prominent in the self-defenses of those who were accused of same-sex practices. Hal Gladfelder, for example, discovered a 1749 pamphlet by Thomas Cannon that features sodomites speaking "feelingly of their desires and in spirited defense of their practice."[37] While Gladfelder asserts that Cannon's text is the earliest known printed defense of sodomy, Bray analyzes an earlier document that records a defense of buggery: namely, John White's *The First Century of Scandalous, Malignant Priests* (1643).[38] White's attack on the venality of the Anglican Church cites one hundred examples of abuse (the "century" of his title) and records John Wilson, Vicar of Arlington, as having "*openly affirmed, that Buggery is no sinne.*"[39] While Wilson's words are heavily mediated by White's account, we might read the series of offenses leveled against Wilson as providing some clue to the grounds of this early affirmation of sodomy:

[H]e in most beastly, divers times attempted to commit buggery with *Nathaniel Browne, Samuel Andrewes*, and *Robert Williams* his Parishioners, and by perswasions and violence, laboured to draw them to that abhominable sinne, *that* (as he shamed not to professe) *they might make up his number eighteene*, and hath professed, that he made choice to commit that act with man-kind rather then with women, to avoide the shame and danger that oft ensueth in begetting Bastards; and hath also attempted to commit Buggery with a Mare, and at a Baptizing of a Bastard child, blasphemously said, openly in the Church, *That our Saviour as he was in the flesh, was a Bastard;* and usually preachth, *That Baptisme utterly taketh away originalle sinne . . . and that men should pray with Beades,* and hath openly said, *that the Parliament were Rebells, and endeavoured to starve the King, and whatsoever the King commands, wee are all bound to obey, whether it be good or evill,* and hath openly affirmed, *that Buggery is no sinne,* and is a *usuall frequenter of Ale-houses and a great drinker.*[40]

White's account accuses Wilson of buggery with three named parish-ioners (and fifteen others), buggery with a mare, of baptizing a bastard, of blasphemy, of heresy, of treason, and of insobriety. Where Bray reads Wilson as "an entirely Orthodox Laudian clergyman" "his sexual be-haviour apart," I see White's catalog of charges as suggesting that Wilson was perhaps engaged in a more concerted attempt to engage in treason and heresy.[41] While sodomy tends to be a curiously object-less practice (not differentiating between persons and animals) and a curiously aim-less practice (encompassing all nonreproductive sexual acts), this pas-sage begins to distinguish objects (separating the meanings of buggery "with man-kind rather then with women") and treats transgression of monarchial and divine power as a kind of aim (in the capacious sense I outlined in chapter 3). While I'll say more about aim later in this after-word, for now I want to note that the advent of aim might provide a cru-cial bridge between acts and identities in the emergence of sexual sub-jectivity forged of "sexual tastes, preferences, inclinations, or desires."[42]

We will have to wait almost eighty years before hearing another de-fense of sodomy in England. In 1718, John Bowes was caught in the act of sodomy with a man named Hugh Ryly; when Bowes was teased ("Rallying them for so vile a practice"), he riposted: "'Sirrah[!] what's that to you, can't I make use of my own Body? I have done nothing but what I will do again.'"[43] Similarly, William Brown, upon being en-trapped and apprehended for sodomy and questioned as to his motive, replied in 1726, "I did it because I thought I knew him, and I think there is no crime in making what use I please of my own body."[44] Here, both Bowes and Brown seem to articulate a kind of self-possession or sense of ownership over their own bodies and its desires. Given the title *Der Eigene* (which might be translated as "the self-owner") of what is often identified as the first multi-issue homophile periodical, we would do well, as Michael Bibler has ingeniously argued, to attend to the role of property in the construction of sexuality.[45] While the hermeneutic focus of these quotations is generally placed on Butlerian (repeated) use (Bowes's suggestion that he will perform such acts "again"), Brown's sense that he thought he "knew" the man who entrapped him might multiply the set of hermeneutic possibilities around the encounter. Does such a claim suggest merely that Brown recognized him or that they had engaged in sexual relations before (the man who entrapped him says in his deposition that he "was well acquainted with the Methods they [sodomites] took in picking one another up")?[46] In the second instance, is this "knowing" part of a discourse of repeated use, or does "knowing" him connote some purported understanding of his character, which has obviously failed Brown in this instance? That is, does it suggest something closer to the "category" of persons that van der Meer describes (an embodied personhood in some way assumed by Brown to be legible)?

Henry Abelove's groundbreaking essay "Some Speculations on the History of Sexual Intercourse during the Long Eighteenth Century in England" (1989) begins to help us to understand the relation between repeated use and personhood. Abelove speculates that the demographic explosion in England between 1680 and 1830 (the population grew from 4.93 million to 13.28 million) is attributable to

a remarkable increase in the *incidence* of cross-sex genital intercourse (penis in vagina, vagina around penis, with seminal emission uninterrupted) during the late eighteenth century in England. I mean that this particular kind of sexual expression, which we moderns often tendentiously name "sexual intercourse," became more popular at that time in England, so much more popular that by means of that enhanced popularity alone, without any assistance from a decline in mortality, England's population could have doubled in a relatively short span. With the assistance of a decline in mortality, the population actually more than doubled.[47]

For Abelove the new popularity of cross-sex genital intercourse is linked to the capitalist forces that are commonly referred to as the Industrial Revolution. Rather than seeing a causal connection between production and reproduction, Abelove sees them "as aspects of the same phenomenon," fascinatingly forging a relay between biopolitical governance, "sexual intercourse so-called," capitalism, and modernity.[48] But what interests me most is his suggestion that "the tradition of very diverse cross-sex sexual behaviors . . . are reorganized and reconstructed in the late eighteenth century as foreplay."[49] This movement from many aims to one aim—(re)production—begins to construct an aim-oriented, interiorized sexual subjectivity (organized around "use"). I want to speculate that this aim-oriented sexual practice may provide a vital link between acts and identities since, as I argued in chapter 3, sexual aim outlines the shape of a fantasy, of what kind of person one wants to be.[50] Thus, when Brown asserts, "I think there is no crime in making what use I please of my own body" he begins to deploy a self-possessed sexual aim to forge his sexual subjectivity through repeated use, and may even do so against a congealing sense that the proper use of the body is reproduction.

A few decades later, the 1757–59 sodomy trial of the Calvinist minister Andreas Klink—a centerpiece of van der Meer's argument—offers a different kind of concretization, not one of sexual subjectivity but of sexual morphology. Klink's trial offers us a rich archive for exploring the reconfiguration of sexual understanding in Europe and the forms of its embodiment. Klink drew on the belief that "strong impressions on pregnant women affected the fetus and could result in giving birth to disformed children, even monsters" to argue that sodomy "was proper to his nature, while his mother, when pregnant with him and while his father not being at home, had had such a strong mind and desire for her husband, which he had inherited from her."[51] Here, Klink's description of himself as "disformed" roots his sodomitical nature in his body. While Klink also drew on the example of "David and other 'great men' in the Bible" to establish his moral probity, I am struck by the way that his former claim establishes a kind of congenitality and sketches him as possessing a sexual morphology.[52] In 1776 at another sodomy trial, Gerrit van Amerongen stated: "men who held on to it [sodomy] were like being born with it and they can be as amorous to one another as man and wife can be."[53] In a slightly different register from Klink, Amerongen posits a kind of functional congenital—"like being born with it"—that I think begins to explain why Trumbach understands these eighteenth-century figures as homosexuals in all but name. In short, congenitality is mistaken for identity.

To put it another way, the "something new" that happens during "the moment of the molly" is the emergence or, more properly, the pre-emergence in the Raymond Williams sense, of an idea of congenitality, of the innateness of sexuality.[54] This interiorization sometimes looks like a sexual morphology that is legible on the body, as is the case with Klink and Amerongen, but sometimes looks like a possessive category or expressive capacity emerging from a sexual subjectivity, as exemplified by Brown and Bowes. This emergence of interiority (becoming increasingly expressive) exists contemporaneously with same-sex community, persecution, and spirited defenses of sodomy, making this sexual configuration look like homosexual identity for a handful of eighteenth-century subjects (even when these elements stand in parallel rather than in conjunction). To put this more colloquially, the ingredients of homosexuality are all there; they just haven't been baked together. That is, they have not been ordered, arranged, and fused by what Arnold Davidson calls sexuality's "very particular style of reasoning."[55] As I have argued throughout this book, congenitality, constancy, boundedness, agency, and a clear differentiation from objects also constitute essential ingredients in the making of modern sexual identity. The modern homosexual, as David Halperin argues, insists "on the *conjunction* of sexual morphology and sexual subjectivity."[56] While I cannot agree with Kim M. Phillips and Barry Reay, who write that they "remain unconvinced by the historical prominence of the molly," I instead claim that the emergence of sexuality will have to wait until the nineteenth century.[57] Homosexuality's formation will be assembled from many building blocks—including the molly—over time. I understand congenitality as one of "the conditions of emergence *for*" homosexuality even if it does not itself constitute that emergence.[58] To put this differently, sexual self-possession and congenitality unexpectedly precede sexuality.

**Impasse 2: How Intersectional Is Object Choice?**

As I have been arguing throughout this book, object choice is essential both to the construction of sexual subjectivity and to modern sexual identity. Given object choice's prominent role, we need to account for the intersectional construction of embodiment, particularly as object choice is about the desiring of some bodies over others. My remapping of the Great Paradigm Shift then brings us to our second set of impasses in the history of sexuality. Namely, what relation do race, class, and gender have to object choice for men in the late nineteenth- and twentieth-century US context? While I will say more about this male focus shortly, I concentrate on the United States both because it has the richest sexual historiography and because it is the central context for this book. While I could explore other axes of identity (disability, religion, age, etc.), my sense is that disability's longstanding history as a variety of perversion—and here I am thinking of the history of teratology—predates the emergence of "the interrelated concepts of norm, normal, and normativity" that "underwrite the new taxonomies of heterosexuality and homosexuality" by many centuries.[59] Likewise, while Chauncey, Peter Coviello, and others have pointed to the variance of sexual cultures among religions, these questions have not been taken up systematically or broadly enough to consider them here.[60]

We are perhaps closest to being able to write a history of age's relation to the homo/hetero binary. In *Psychopathia Sexualis* (1886), Krafft-Ebing states, "The term violation [of individuals under the age of fourteen], in the legal sense of the word, comprehends the most horrible perversions and acts, which are possible only to a man who is a slave to lust and morally weak."[61] While Krafft-Ebing here suggests that sex with individuals under fourteen is "horrible," he implies that having sex with a youth over such an age is barely a perversion. Up until the early years of the twentieth century, at which point sex with youths was transformed into a great evil, this position was widely held by sexologists. Expressing the position that pederasty (as opposed to pedophilia) is not (much of) a vice, Havelock Ellis writes: "A sexual attraction for boys is no doubt, as Moll points out, that form of inversion which comes nearest to normal sexuality, for the subject of it usually approaches nearer to the average man in physical and mental disposition. The reason of this is obvious: boys resemble women, and therefore it requires a less profound organic twist to become sexually attracted to them."[62] The capacity to "take boys for women" that Stephen Orgel charts in Renaissance England is here associated with late nineteenth-century England and, in Ellis's citation of Moll, with Germany.[63] In this account, love for boys approximates or approaches "normal sexuality." Bloch's *The Sexual Life of Our Time* (1906) seems to share this view of pederasty, describing how a homosexual informant explains to him that pederasty is "'the most natural and least harmful means of gratification.'"[64] The anarchist and founder of the first homophile journal—*Der Eigene*—Adolf Brand, who often opposed the sexologists, was even more supportive of pederasty, advocating a "closer connection of the man with the youth and of the youth with the man."[65] Similarly, in 1913, Magnus Hirschfeld writes, "We understand the words Plato puts into Phaedrus's mouth in the *Symposium*, 'I know of no greater blessing than a young man just stepping into the world having a virtuous lover or a lover having a beloved young fellow. For the principle by which all people who want to live a noble life should be guided, this principle, I say is neither kinship nor honor nor wealth nor any kind of motive other than love.'"[66] In the same text, Hirschfeld divides the majority of the homosexual population into two categories—ephebophiles (who desire youths between the ages of fourteen and twenty-one) and androphiles (who desire men "at the beginning of manhood up to the beginning of old age") and notes that the difference in age preference between the ephebophile man and the gerontophile "(who likes people fifty and older)" makes them "almost as foreign as a person of the opposite sex."[67] In metaphorizing age as biological sex, Hirschfeld here undermines his own taxonomy of age, instead supplementing the increasing diacritical power and coalescence around gender of object choice.

Thinking about this diminishment of age in relation to the shift from manhood to masculinity that I discussed in chapter 2 might account for the disappearance of the age differentiation of the wolf/punk relation and the emergence of the age similitude of the homo/hetero binary. That is, men's definitional shift from being defined in relation to boys to being defined in relation to women cements both the gender differentiation for the homo/hetero binary as well as its age consistency. This reading is further supported by the raising of the age of consent in the mid-1880s from ten or twelve to sixteen or eighteen in the United States and similar numbers in England in order to reduce the potential age span between partners.[68] One possible reason for the emergence of this idea of consent might be that this is also the period that sees the rise of highly publicized ransom kidnappings (Charley Ross was famously kidnapped in 1874).[69] But the relation between age of object choice and gender of object choice remains an area for further inquiry.

The role race played in the construction of sexual object choice has been a topic of lively scholarly debate. Ann Laura Stoler, for example, has suggested that "an implicit racial grammar underwrote . . . sexual regimes."[70] Such a grammar became explicit with the advent of *Plessy v. Ferguson* and its Jim Crow system of "separate but equal" in 1896. Marlon Ross contends that "Jim Crow is as much a regime of sexual classification as it is a form of racial imposition."[71] Siobhan Somerville similarly argues that "the simultaneous efforts to shore up and bifurcate categories of race and sexuality in the late nineteenth and early twentieth century were deeply intertwined."[72] For Ross and Somerville, "the color line was fundamentally eroticized in the early twentieth century."[73] This eroticization occurs because the enforced separation of black and white bodies charges those on both sides of the color line with forbidden desirability. Thus, while *Plessy* institutionalized existing practices of racial hierarchization, Ross and Somerville rightly understand it as effecting a sea change in the relation between race and sex: linking blackness and perversion. This imbrication of racial and sexual "deviance" was a new formation, markedly different from the discourse that had hitherto dissociated blackness from perversion. As Marc Epprecht argues in *Heterosexual Africa?* (2008), throughout the late eighteenth century and up through the late nineteenth century, "Africans south of the Sahara" were understood by Europeans to be too innocent to "practice same-sex sexuality," making them "virtually unique in the

world."[74] The "vast generalizations" detailed by Epprecht that understand sub-Saharan Africa to be devoid of homosexuality underwrote
Richard Burton's 1886 conceptualization of the Sotadic Zone (which I
discussed in chapter 2), particularly his depiction of a homosexuality-
less sub-Sahara. Eschewing this narrative of innocence, *Plessy* codifies a
new narrative of the human, one that converts a range of racial identities (in the case of Homer Plessy, creoleness) into a vilified blackness and
pathologizes race, in part by associating it with sexual licentiousness.

The biologization of whiteness enabled this lamination of blackness
and perversion. As Cheryl Harris famously argues, *Plessy* transfigured
whiteness into "status property."[75] Building on this insight, Madoka
Kishi contends that "insofar as whiteness is defined by . . . exclusively
white ancestry . . . whiteness is imagined not simply as property, but
more specifically as family property. In this sense, race is not just 'repro-
ducible'; rather, it can *only* be reproduced from the supposed original—
unable to be produced, acquired, or alienated unlike other forms of
property—inherited exclusively by means of heterosexual reproductive intercourse."[76] Here, Kishi articulates the alignment of whiteness
and heterosexuality, suggesting heterosexuality as the sole modality of
whiteness's production. Moreover, blackness as a disqualification from
"full citizenship" was "legally systematized" by settling on what Ross
describes as the rhetoric of "sexual deviance and consequentially [the]
social irresponsibility of black men's desires and ambitions," particularly their "unreliable passions and unaccountable impulses."[77] Here,
*Plessy* constructs relays between heterosexuality and whiteness on the
one hand and sexual deviance and blackness on the other hand. This
dovetails with Magnus Hirschfeld's assertion in 1914 that Americans
"frequently blame one or the other ethnic group for homosexuality,"
suggesting that the logics of race and sex were inextricable and interarticulated.[78] Ross pushes further than Hirschfeld, however, to argue that
the subjectivities of people of nonwhite races are constructed as signs of
undifferentiated perversion, forging nonwhiteness itself as a marker of
sexual deviance. Specifically, he argues that the "assumed racial sameness" between sexologists and their subjects enables the identification
and classification of sexual difference.[79] In contrast, white sexologists
attribute sexual difference—like homosexuality—in racialized subjects
to "perceived racial difference," thereby "overdetermin[ing]" and short-
circuiting the interdependence of race and sexuality and explaining
why sexology so rarely explores the case histories of black subjects.[80]

The near identification between racialization and sexual deviance
was not limited to the production of blackness, but extended to a host

of nonwhite bodies, particularly those of immigrants.[81] For example, the Page Law of 1875 excluded virtually all Chinese women as suspected prostitutes, strengthening the ties between nonwhiteness and perversion and solidifying the bonds between whiteness and normative heterosexuality.[82] Similarly, Margot Canaday's discussion of early twentieth-century US immigration policy finds strong links between nonwhiteness, poverty, and perversion—especially homosexuality. As Canaday details, virtually the state's only tool for excluding homosexuals was the "likely to become a public charge" clause.[83] This clause had a low burden of proof and thus could be wielded against a majority of immigrants (most of whom were poor). The law effectively linked poverty, homosexuality, and nonwhite bodies in the early years of the twentieth century, suggesting that "men who were not self-governing in their sexual practices could not be self-governing in their labor."[84] Thus, aliens suspected of sodomy were deported "without much investigation into their actual economic circumstances."[85] The circuits of thought that Canaday maps exemplify what Seth Koven describes as the "insistent eroticization of poverty."[86] Michael Trask similarly outlines the ways in which early twentieth-century fears of class contact and mobility were conceptualized through the vocabularies of sexual deviance: "elites . . . chose to couch class difference in the language of sexual illicitness, viewing innovative and unsettling social arrangements as an extension of the irregular or perverse desires that sexology deliberated."[87]

This nexus between homosexuality, poverty, and nonwhite bodies became especially important for the construction of the homo/hetero binary with the advent of and widespread popularity of the practice of slumming (the touring and exploration of working-class, immigrant, and nonwhite metropolitan neighborhoods by heterosocial groups of mostly white middle- and upper-class men and women).[88] Chad Heap understands slumming to effect an "increasing heterosocialization of urban leisure" away from the "rowdy male homosociality" of "sporting male-culture" (consisting of drinking, gambling, pugilism, cockfighting, and importantly "cross-class camaraderie . . . maintained in large part by men's shared access to the sexual favors and paid services of working-class women").[89] "[C]ombining the reform movement's engagement of respectable white middle-class women with the sporting-male culture's unabashed pursuit of pleasure," the heterosocial practice of slumming began to undermine the nineteenth-century gender ideology of separate spheres and—even more importantly for our purposes—the gendered ordering of sexuality that Chauncey has detailed (and that I recounted in the introduction).[90]

The turn of the century vogue for slumming in bohemian areas and the culture of bohemianism (with its attention to sexual equality and pleasure, rejection of traditional gender roles and traditional gender presentation) "undermined the very foundations of gender difference" and signaled "the imminent shift from a gendered sexual regime to the now-hegemonic hetero/homo sexual binary."[91] In particular, what Heap describes as "the pansy and lesbian craze" in the 1920s and 1930s helped to cement this process, particularly as pansies and lesbians performed together at the same clubs.[92] This shared performance, Heap argues, "undeniably contributed to the codification of the now-dominant hetero/homo sexual binary by allowing white lesbians and pansies to construct a shared communal identity in opposition to slumming heterosexuals (and vice versa)."[93] Heap's claim dovetails with the arguments of Trask, Koven, and Canaday as this differentiating gesture constructs lower-class bodies as perverted/homosexual and middle-class bodies as heterosexual.

The relationship between gender and sexuality is even more complicated than sexuality's relation to class and race, not least because, as Sedgwick points out, "gender is *definitionally* built into determinations of sexuality."[94] "Without a concept of gender," Sedgwick writes, "there could be, quite simply, no concept of homo- or heterosexuality."[95] And yet the differences between histories of sex focused on sexuality and those focused on gender create an impasse in the dating of the Great Paradigm Shift. Foucault posits the advent of an object-based system (homo/hetero) said to emerge by 1870. This dating is at odds with the dominance of a gender-based system of sexuality (chronicled by Chauncey well into the 1930s) that does not differentiate by the sex of sexual object, but by the gender of act: either active/insertive/masculine or passive/receptive/feminine. Chauncey articulates a class-differentiated understanding of this discrepant timeline: "exclusive heterosexuality became a precondition for a man's identification as 'normal' in middle-class culture at least two generations before it did so in much of Euro-American and African-American working-class culture."[96] While the chronology of "at least two generations" is somewhat imprecise, Chauncey seems to want his history to align with Foucault's narrative (for middle-class individuals), thus marking the emergence of object-choice-based sexuality in the last third of the nineteenth century.

As I suggested in chapter 4, however, there was less distinction between middle-class and working-class homosexualities than is ordinarily posited by scholars like Chauncey. Of course, there was a time lag between the middle- and working classes as to the advent of object-choice sexuality, which has to do, in part, with what Rictor Norton calls "the slowness of [sexuality's] medicalization."[97] In other words, Norton suggests that it takes elite sexological constructions of sexuality a long time to filter down to working-class experience and adoption of these sexological conceptions. And this was certainly the case. But as I argue in chapter 1, this emergence of object choice also had to await the widespread adoption of congenitality; Foucault's speciation is also a congenitalization. The crucial insight of recognizing the interrelation between congenitality and object choice is this: the long process of congenitalization suggests that the acquired modes of sexuality that I have argued characterize many of Chauncey's working-class sexual figures also characterized middle-class sexual figures (a cross-pollination no doubt effected in part because of the prevalence of slumming). That is, both middle-class and working-class sexualities were characterized by acquisition. My claim that (working-class) homosexuality is situational homosexuality suggests that even that most congenital of figures—the fairie—was more in the sphere of acquisition than has hitherto been recognized. This is to say, the dominance of sexual object choice for both middle- and working-class individuals has been overemphasized and emerged later for both groups, even though its advent came slightly earlier for the middle class.

In spite of this increasing convergence between middle- and working-class understandings of sexuality, it is clear that working-class and gender-based sexuality has a long (if residual) afterlife. In *Sexual Behavior in the Human Male* (1948), for example, Alfred Kinsey writes: "Mouth-genital contacts between males and females are certainly heterosexual, even though some persons may think of them as homosexual. And although one may hear of a male, 'who has sex relations with his wife in a homosexual way,' there is no logic in such a use of the term, and analysis of the behavior and of the motivations of the behavior in such cases do not show them necessarily related to any homosexual experience."[98] Kinsey disavows understanding the logic that would enable a man to describe having sex with "his wife in a homosexual way"; however, the logic is clearly that of sodomy. Any nonreproductive act is categorized as sodomitical and thus here is associated with homosexuality. By dismissing the logic of "such a use of the term," Kinsey aims to stabilize the meaning of homosexuality around object choice rather than around reproduction. Barry Reay's pioneering account of sexual trade in *New York Hustlers* (2010) further complicates the hegemony of object-choice-based sexuality over gender-based models. Charting the persistence of gender-based understandings of sexuality into the late 1960s (and perhaps even later), Reay extends the genealogy of acquisition that I have been tracing. Along these lines, Gore Vidal writes in 1985: "there is no such thing as a homosexual or a heterosexual person. There are only homo- or heterosexual acts."[99] Following Reay, I understand this declaration not as a tenacious denial or resistance to categorization (though it might also be those things), but as an articulation of a foreclosing sexual organization, of which Vidal was one of the last adherents.[100]

With these stories of protracted sexual organizations, emergent formation, diachronic changes, and synchronic tensions in view, I want to offer a first draft of the story of the Great Paradigm Shift (at least as it occurred for men in the United States).[101] My narrative, however, is largely limited to male sexuality. I focus on men because as Chauncey argues the idea of object choice as structuring female sexuality had less prominence at the turn of the twentieth century: "doctors were less willing—perhaps culturally less able—to distinguish a woman's behavior in sexual relations from other aspects of her gender role."[102] We might understand this conflation of women's gender and object choice (despite sexology's radical reconceptualization of object choice for men) as helping to account for what Valerie Traub explains as the prominence of the alterist position (foregrounding historical break) in studies of male homosexuality as compared with the prominence of the continuist position (foregrounding historical continuity) in studies of female homosexuality.[103] Moreover, Judith Bennett's characterization of the history of women as one *"of change without transformation,"* held in "patriarchal equilibrium," further suggests that we might understand the Great Paradigm Shift as less applicable to women.[104] Theresa Braunschneider has suggested that to the extent that there is a historical break for women, we might understand it as emanating from the eighteenth-century development of companionate marriage and its accompanying transformations of choice and desire.[105] But an inquiry into this latter question is outside of the scope of this project. With these limitations in mind, I begin to narrate this shift for the history of male homosexuality.

## Toward an Account of the Great Paradigm Shift

A conception, a notion, or an idea of sexual object choice as an organizing rubric of sexuality was put forward sometime between Heinrich Kaan's *Psychopathia Sexualis* (1844) and Carl Westphal's "Contrary Sexual Feeling" (1870).[106] This time span encompasses the early sexual theorizations of the homophile activists Karl Heinrich Ulrichs and Karl-Maria Kertbeny. Additionally, because Kaan supplies what Foucault calls "the first great global dynasty of sexual aberrations" and because all of these aberrations might be understood as modes of deviant object choice (masturbation, pederasty, lesbian love, necrophilia, bestiality, and the violation of statues), my account disputes Chauncey's claim that inversion (by which he means gender deviance broadly construed and including homosexual object choice) is in any way prior to object choice.[107] Moreover, my claim dovetails with Sedgwick's account in *Between Men* inasmuch as the shift from a model of mimetic desire routed through a woman to one that excludes women might be understood as a movement from what we might later call an aim- and object-based model to an object-based model. I understand mimetic desire as aim-based and object-based because, in Sedgwick's formulation, "the choice of the beloved is determined in the first place, not by the qualities of the beloved, but by the beloved's already being the choice of the person who has been chosen as a rival."[108] Here, the rival is the object, but rather than desire the rival directly, one desires his desire (aim). The qualities of the beloved, which is to say the determinant in an object-based system, are relatively unimportant in the mid-eighteenth century and take on increasing significance by the middle of the nineteenth century (tracking the rise of object choice as an increasingly exclusive focus).

During the mid-nineteenth century the idea that "the natural function of the sexual instinct . . . [is] propagation" enjoys what Arnold Davidson calls "virtually *unargued unanimity*."[109] This is why, Davidson contends, "sadism, masochism, fetishism should be treated as a species of the same disease . . . [even as] they have no essential features in common."[110] Returning to Abelove's account of the increasingly sharp line between sodomitical and reproductive sex acts, I understand this narrative of eighteenth-century sexual reorganization to explain how such unanimity emerges. That is, this valuation of reproduction locates propagation at the center of the sexual instinct. In this register, we might understand the crackdowns on mollies as part of a broader biopolitical effort to encourage "sexual intercourse so-called" and to police modes of sexuality that fall outside this precinct.[111]

This unanimity around reproduction as the constitutive feature of the sexual instinct would remain until 1905 when Sigmund Freud innovatively broke the sexual instinct into two: dividing it into sexual object and sexual aim. According to Freud, "The normal sexual aim is regarded as being the union of the genitals in the act known as copulation, which leads to a release of the sexual tension and temporary extinction of the sexual instinct—a satisfaction analogous to the sating of hunger."[112] Freud's eschewal of reproduction in his definition of normal sexual aim in favor of mere copulation or what Abelove terms "sexual intercourse so-called" clears the way for the emergence of sexuality organized around sexual objects. To put this differently, sexual aim and reproduction were demoted or stripped out to construct object-based sexuality. They instead came to support the centrality of object choice.

Of the nonreproductive sexualities that Davidson describes, masturbation is undoubtedly the most prominent. Sedgwick hypothesizes that it was "uniquely formative" in the construction of sexual identities: "the masturbator may have been at the cynosural center of a remapping of individual identity."[113] Kaan's *Psychopathia Sexualis*—which is both an anti-onanist tract and the first sexological text—fills in the historical details of Sedgwick's supposition that the masturbator was one of many sexual identities "subsumed, erased, or overrriden" by the homo/hetero binary.[114] It serves as an intermediate step and thus provides a roadmap for how a preoccupation with the regulation of homosexuality in the later nineteenth and early twentieth centuries gradually replaced an obsession with masturbation in the eighteenth and early nineteenth centuries.

Kaan's *Psychopathia Sexualis* fuses masturbation, homosexuality, and other perversions together, uniting them under the rubric of imagination. This notion of imagination—which always, in Foucault's phrase, "overflows" the anatomical functions of the physical body—fosters sexual subjectivity and the psychic life of sexuality separate from biological and evolutionary explanations (indeed, highlighting their inadequacy)[115]:

[I]n every distortion of the sexual instinct, it is the imagination that supplies the path that fulfills it, contrary to the laws of nature. All these types of deviation are merely different forms of one and the same thing, and they cross into one another. Boys who are given to onanism, even if dissuaded from this habit at a later age, most easily fall into other aberrations of the sexual drive; and among primitive peoples, one type occurs at the same time with others.[116]

Kaan's text sets the stage for masturbation and homosexuality to bleed into one another ("all these types of deviation are merely different forms of one and the same thing"). This fusion enables the demise of antimasturbation rhetoric as a mode of discipline and the rise of the regulation of homosexuality as its replacement in maintaining the social order. While Kaan is far more concerned with masturbation than any of the other aberrations in his taxonomy, his text accents masturbation differently than his predecessors, imagining it as alloerotic (or threatening to be so) as well as autoerotic. Onanism, for Kaan, ceases to be merely a problem in and of itself (of dissipation, of self-control, of self-absorption—though it also poses these dangers) and instead obtains a new and crucial position as a kind of gateway to other vices, occurring, Kaan says, "at the same time with others [aberrations]" and "cross[ing] into one another."[117] This newly hierarchized understanding of masturbation (onanists "fall into other aberrations") suggests that guarding against onanism is tantamount to the prevention of other aberrations of the sexual instinct. Once Kaan's text opens the possibility that masturbation and other aberrations (especially homosexuality) are terms in a sequence, the movement from Kaan's position (that onanism facilitates or occurs at the same time with other aberrations) to a position in which those other aberrations are themselves the central problem requires only a shift in emphasis (perhaps explained by Chauncey's account of the movement from manhood to masculinity). In short, Kaan's text enables us to see how sexuality is interiorized and becomes primarily alloerotic.[118]

But how did alloeroticism align with gender to forge the gender of sexual object choice? [119] Michael Lynch's important essay "'Here is Adhesiveness': From Friendship to Homosexuality" (1985) begins to help us with this question, arguing that phrenology plays an important role in the development of object choice in America. He charts phrenology's theorization of the "Adhesive" faculty, which measured one's congenital capacity for affectional bonds, particularly friendship, and which explained attraction.[120] As soon as it was established as a faculty of mind, phrenologists began to worry about its abuse. Lynch traces how Walt Whitman seizes on such abuse to recast Adhesiveness in the 1856 edition of *Leaves of Grass*:

For the phrenologists, Amativeness was opposite-sex but could be abused into same-sex activity; Adhesiveness was possible between the sexes, but was most often described in same-sex examples. Whitman's restriction of Adhesiveness to male-male relationships opened the way for an understanding of same-sex expression of a sexual instinct that was polar to an opposite-sex expression of it. . . . Whitman's male-male Adhesive love was alone able to "rival" male-female Amative love.[121]

As Lynch makes clear, for the earlier phrenologists, the gender of object choice did not characterize the nature of the relation and it was possible to have Amative and Adhesive feelings toward men and women as well as both at the same time. But Whitman's reconceptualization foregrounds the gendering of these relations and makes them putative opposites, suggesting that Whitman's version of Adhesiveness begins to provide sexuality with its dimorphic structure. Because phrenology aimed to read the brain through the body, this development of dyadic object choice was also a congenitalization that located sexuality in the mind, and thus provided a crucial hinge between what Davidson calls "anatomical and psychiatric styles of reasoning."[122]

The idea of object choice, however, did not catch fire or become common knowledge for a surprisingly long period of time. Its conception of sexuality had few adherents (like Whitman and Kaan) and ebbed slowly outside the medical establishment. Foucault has suggested that "as early as 1877" fetishism modeled how "the instinct became fastened to an object," but object choice did not really begin to take shape for middle-class individuals until the 1890s with the first usage of the word "homosexuality" in English and the Wilde trials.[123] The Eulenburg Scandal in 1907, which carried accusations of homosexuality to the highest reaches of German government, brought increasing awareness of and adoption of this sexual system.[124] During this period, there was an increasing dominance of congenital conceptions of sexuality and a minimalization of acquired modes of sex (at least for middle-class individuals). While the initial constructions of congenitality and the naturalness of same-sex desire date back to the seventeenth century (as we examined in impasse 1), this idea would come slowly to dominance and would not be definitively settled until the 1930s. And as we have seen, acquired modes of sexuality continued to persist in residual form long after that. During this protracted period of medicalized congenitalization from about 1844 or 1870 until roughly the 1930s, homosexuality was profoundly intertwined with conceptions of race and ethnicity, class, and gender. While Bloch's *anthropologia sexualis* posited that "sexual aberrations and perversions are ubiquitous, diffused throughout the entire world, just as much among primitive races as civilized nations" and "[s]exual perversions are just as widely diffused among the lower classes as among the upper," this version of sexuality delinked from race and class remained a minority position.[125]

The entwinement of race and class with sexuality began to unravel with the ascendancy of congenitalization in the 1930s and 1940s. The *OED* indexes the dominance of the congenital model, furnishing by 1946 an example of the term "sexual orientation" to mean "a person's sexual identity in relation to the gender to whom he or she is usually attracted." Moreover, John Money's 1955 coinage of the term "gender role" provides one index of the separation of sexuality from gender.[126] As Canaday argues, by 1952, with the passage of the McCarren-Walter Act, a major immigration and naturalization bill, homosexuality was severed from race, class, and gender. Canaday contends that the most important transformation for the consolidation of the homo/hetero binary in the post–World War II era was not homosexuality's construction as "a discrete identity . . . distinct from class and race" but rather its construction as a discrete legal identity, what Canaday calls "a non-medical category."[127] She traces the ways in which McCarren-Walter came to simplify and solidify a diverse range of gender and sexual practices, neatly dividing the human race: "one was either heterosexual or one was homosexual."[128] Over the course of the 1960s as McCarren-Walter was litigated, the courts created a legal equation between homosexual acts and homosexual status. Reay's narrative dovetails with Canaday's history of the foreclosing possibility of engaging in same-sex acts while identifying as heterosexual, charting, as he does, the decline of the heterosexuality of the hustler in the 1970s and 1980s.

The hardening of the homo/hetero binary reaches its apex as this decline of the heterosexual hustler is coupled with the conceptualization of the AIDS epidemic of the 1980s as a gay plague (underwritten by its early description as "gay compromise syndrome" in the medical literature or as GRID—gay-related immune deficiency—in newspapers).[129] At the beginning of the AIDS crisis the national (heterosexual) imaginary envisioned gay people in terms of absolute difference as contagious, inhuman monsters. This difference was biologized as the gay gene or the gay brain in the research of Dean Hamer, Simon LeVay, and others in the early 1990s, literalizing Foucault's formulation of the homosexual as a separate species.

But this essentialized alterity between gay and straight did not last very long. With the emergence of queerness and the concomitant proliferation of sexual and gender identities and bodily morphologies (trans, down low, genderqueer, asexual, etc.), the homo/hetero binary's grip on sexuality has been loosening. The precipitous rise of the phrase "sexual orientation" from 1980 to 2000 when mapped in the Google Ngram Viewer (with usage increasing ninefold) and its falling usage after the height of 2000 (slipping by more than 15 percent by 2008, the last year of available data) marks both the concretization of the homo/hetero binary in the face of the AIDS crisis and its loosening with the growing dissemination of queerness as a nonidentity.[130] While evidence provided by the Google Ngram Viewer is flawed for a number of reasons (the unevenness of the corpus, technical difficulties with optical character recognition, etc.), these numbers, however rough, begin to substantiate both the dominance of the inborn, congenital model of the homo/hetero binary at its apex and its fall.[131]

There are political and affective reasons for wanting to chart the Great Paradigm Shift—the desire for connection to the past, the possibility of activating the past in the present's Benjaminian moment of danger, the need to know the history of an identity that has been important to so many for so long (even if it was never simply an identity or even set of identities). I hope my project facilitates many of these historiographical, theoretical, and affective investments and recovers new connections to the past and ways of feeling our way into the past. Deploying a historical etiological approach to examine the Great Paradigm Shift enables us to anatomize "the unrationalized coexistence of different models" of sexuality.[132] We can see which models were available—garnering a clearer sense of what Coviello calls "the very *domain* of sexuality," but also ascertaining an inventory of its constitutive parts.[133] Halperin has registered these "genetic traces," mapping and making available some of the diachronic models that have shaped sexuality over the *longue durée*.[134] Recent critics have added additional models (even if they wouldn't necessarily put it in precisely these terms): Michael Bibler has added property, Barry Reay has added masculinity, and I have added celibacy elsewhere.[135] Historical etiology also helps us to see that the synchronic explosion of sexual models at the turn of the twentieth century emerges out of the congenital-acquired debate in sexology. Behaviors, acts, beings, diseases, environments, circumstances, historical forces, identities, embodiments, perversions, and varieties of gender that from a twenty-first-century vantage might appear to be outside of sexuality's domain or appear on its margins are brought to its center. Historical etiology makes clear that we need a sexual historiography that is capacious enough to accommodate approaches to sexuality that are simultaneously continuist and open to historical alterity. This, then, is the promise of etiology—that we can bring into focus the etiolated, overlapping, unrationalized, diachronic, synchronic, collaged, messy contours of sexuality.

# Notes

1.  As Howard Chiang points out, sexologists occupied a range
    of positions in relation to homosexuality, "from pathologi-
    zation to normalization to glorification." In spite of these
    divisions and uneven conceptualizations, sexology consti-
    tuted in many ways the first homophile discourse. Howard
    H. Chiang, "Liberating Sex, Knowing Desire: *Scientia Sexu-
    alis* and Epistemic Turning Points in the History of Sexual-
    ity," *History of the Human Sciences* 23.5 (2010): 46.
2.  The first volume is translated under the more colorful title
    *Anthropological Studies in the Strange Sexual Practises of All
    Races in All Ages*, trans. Keene Wallis (New York: Anthro-
    pological Press, 1933). The second volume is translated as
    *Anthropological and Ethnological Studies in the Strangest Sex
    Acts in Modes of Love of All Races Illustrated*, trans. Ernst Vo-
    gel (New York: Falstaff Press, 1935). The volumes were origi-
    nally published in German in 1902 and 1903, respectively.
    On the translation and American distribution of these titles
    and similar books, see Jay A. Gertzman, *Bookleggers and
    Smuthounds: The Trade in Erotica, 1920–1940* (Philadelphia:
    University of Pennsylvania Press, 1999), 193.
3.  Benjamin Tarnowsky, *Anthropological, Legal, and Medi-
    cal Studies on Pederasty in Europe* (New York: Falstaff Press,
    1933); Auguste Forel, *The Sexual Question: A Scientific,
    Psychological, Hygienic, and Sociological Study* (Brooklyn, NY:
    Physicians and Surgeons Book Company, 1931); Edward
    Prime-Stevenson, *The Intersexes: A Study of Similisexualism
    as a Problem in Social Life* (privately printed, 1908).
4.  While it focuses on the nonnormative, sexology is also
    quite loquacious about the normal and the normative. On

the relationship between sexology and the normal, see Peter Cryle and Elizabeth Stephens, *Normality: A Critical Genealogy* (Chicago: University of Chicago Press, 2000), 261–93; Julian B. Carter, *The Heart of Whiteness: Normal Sexuality and Race in America, 1880–1940* (Durham: Duke University Press, 2007); and Karma Lochrie, *Heterosyncrasies: Female Sexuality When Normal Wasn't* (Minneapolis: University of Minnesota Press, 2005), 1–25.

5. Harry Oosterhuis, *Stepchildren of Nature: Krafft-Ebing, Psychiatry, and the Making of Sexual Identity* (Chicago: University of Chicago Press, 2000), 43. For historical overviews of sexology, see Chris Waters, "Sexology," in *Palgrave Advances in the Modern History of Sexuality*, eds. H. G. Cocks and Matt Houlbrook (New York: Palgrave, 2006), 41–63; Joseph Bristow, *Sexuality* (New York: Routledge, 1997), 12–61; and Howard H. Chiang, "Historicizing the Emergence of Sexual Freedom: The Medical Knowledge of Psychiatry and the Scientific Power of Sexology, 1880–1920," *Journal of the North Carolina Association of Historians* 16 (2008): 35–76.

6. Historical etiology owes much to Arnold Davidson's idea of historical epistemology. Arnold I. Davidson, *The Emergence of Sexuality: Historical Epistemology and the Formation of Concepts* (Cambridge: Harvard University Press, 2004).

7. As Matt Houlbrook points out, the category of homophobia is "ahistorical" since it is often used to describe violence against queer subjects before the conceptual stabilization of homosexuality. Matt Houlbrook, *Queer London: Perils and Pleasures in the Sexual Metropolis, 1918–1957* (Chicago: University of Chicago Press, 2005), 222.

8. See, for example, Bruno Latour, *We Have Never Been Modern*, trans. Catherine Potter (Cambridge: Harvard University Press, 1993); and Ian Hacking, *The Social Construction of What?* (Cambridge: Harvard University Press, 1999).

9. Stephanie Foote, "Afterword: Ann Aldrich and Lesbian Writing in the Fifties," in Ann Aldrich, *We Walk Alone*, ed. Marijane Meaker (New York: First Feminist Press, 2006), 158.

10. Kate Fisher and Jana Funke, "British Sexual Science Beyond the Medical: Cross-Disciplinary, Cross-Historical, and Cross-Cultural Translations," in *Sexology and Translation: Cultural and Scientific Encounters Across the Modern World*, ed. Heike Bauer (Philadelphia: Temple University Press, 2015), 105; Oosterhuis, 17.

11. The provenance and dating of Barnes's famous assertion about Thelma is very murky as it is attributed to her by one of her biographers, Andrew Field, who describes the statement as something she "told a close friend nearly a half century later [after her relationship with Thelma]" without a citation. Thus, the claim about Thelma exists in the semi-apocryphal realm of legend. Andrew Field, *Djuna: The Life and Times of Djuna Barnes* (New York: G. P. Putnam's Sons, 1983), 37.

12. In a 1936 letter to Lady Ottoline Morrell, Barnes writes that she "was not offended in the least to be thought lesbian." Quoted in Shari Ben-

stock, *Women of the Left Bank: Paris, 1900–1940* (Austin: University of Texas Press, 1987), 245. Barnes's archive houses a copy of an article dated June 7, 1971, from *Gay* newspaper on which Barnes wrote "Nice article—disgusting paper," quoted in Daniela Caselli, *Improper Modernism: Djuna Barnes's Bewildering Corpus* (Burlington, VT: Ashgate, 2009), 153n17. Monique Wittig sees Barnes's later disidentification with lesbianism as stemming from a dread "that lesbians should make her *their* writer, and that by doing this they should reduce her work to one dimension." Monique Wittig, *The Straight Mind and Other Essays* (Boston: Beacon Press, 1992), 63, her emphasis.

13. My reading here rhymes with Maggie Nelson's discussion of this passage in *The Argonauts* (Minneapolis: Graywolf Press, 2015), 9.

14. Lauren Berlant, interview with David K. Seitz, "On Citizenship and Optimism," *Society and Space*, March 22, 2013, http://societyandspace .org/2013/03/22/on-citizenship-and-optimism/. Lytton Strachey's quip about Edmund Gosse and Gosse's lover William Hamo Thornycroft that Gosse wasn't homosexual but "Hamo-sexual" suggests that desire oriented around an individual rather than sex of object choice was available as a model of sexuality to sexual subjects other than Barnes. Quoted in Michael Matthew Kaylor, *Secreted Desires: The Major Uranians: Hopkins, Pater, and Wilde* (Brno, CZ: Masaryk University Press, 2006), 143. Barnes suggests another diacritical system of sexuality in 1935 when a friend asked her if she were "really Lesbian" and she replied: "I might be anything. If a horse loved me, I might be that." Here, Barnes suggests a model of sexuality determined not by the desire of the desiring subject but by the receptivity of the beloved. Quoted in Daniela Caselli, "Literary and Sexual Experimentalism in the Interwar Years," in *The Cambridge Companion to American Gay and Lesbian Literature*, ed. Scott Herring (Cambridge: Cambridge University Press, 2015), 106.

15. I borrow the phrase "field-imaginary" from Donald E. Pease, "New Americanists: Revisionist Interventions into the Canon," *Boundary 2* 17.1 (1990): 11. For an important critique of these epistemological approaches, see Marlon B. Ross, "Beyond the Closet as Raceless Paradigm," in *Black Queer Studies: A Critical Anthology*, eds. E. Patrick Johnson and Mae G. Henderson (Durham: Duke University Press, 2005), 161–89. In the last fifteen years, queer of color critique has arisen as an important alternative to these epistemological approaches. See Roderick A. Ferguson, *Aberrations in Black: Toward a Queer of Color Critique* (Minneapolis: University of Minnesota Press, 2004).

16. On sexuality's relation to effects, see Susan S. Lanser, *The Sexuality of History: Modernity and the Sapphic, 1565–1830* (Chicago: University of Chicago Press, 2014), 3. To the extent that one might think of Sedgwick and Butler as setting the agenda of the field, both are focused on effects. Butler is notoriously anti-originary and Sedgwick writes: "*Epistemology of*

*the Closet* does not have an explanation to offer for this sudden, radical condensation of sexual categories; instead of speculating on its causes, the book explores its unpredictably varied and acute implications and consequences." Eve Kosofsky Sedgwick, *Epistemology of the Closet* (Berkeley and Los Angeles: University of California Press, 1990), 9. I will discuss this quotation in greater detail later in the introduction.

17. Sedgwick, 44.
18. Sedgwick, 8, her emphasis.
19. Sedgwick, 47.
20. Michel Foucault, *The History of Sexuality*, vol. 1, *An Introduction*, trans. Robert Hurley (New York: Vintage Books, 1990), 43.
21. Foucault, 44, 43. These thousand sexualities are also a period idea; for example in Friedrich Karl Forberg's *Manual of Classical Erotology* (1824), he asks on the opening page: "For how is it possible to specify the thousand modes, the thousand forms of Love, on which the inventive satiety of pleasure ventures?" Friedrich Karl Forberg, *Manual of Classical Erotology*, vol 1. (New York: Grove Press, 1966), 4–5.
22. Foucault, 43.
23. Foucault, 101.
24. Foucault, 40.
25. Sedgwick, 8, her emphasis.
26. Sedgwick, 9.
27. Sedgwick, 8–9.
28. I borrow the word "domain" from Peter Coviello, who repurposes it from Foucault; see Peter Coviello, *Tomorrow's Parties: Sex and the Untimely in Nineteenth-Century America* (New York: New York University Press, 2013), 4.
29. Hortense J. Spillers, "Mama's Baby, Papa's Maybe: An American Grammar Book," *Diacritics* 17.2 (1987): 64–81; Saidiya V. Hartman, *Scenes of Subjection: Terror, Slavery, and Self-Making in Nineteenth-Century America* (Oxford: Oxford University Press, 1997); Mark Rifkin, *When Did Indians Become Straight? Kinship, the History of Sexuality, and Native Sovereignty* (Oxford: Oxford University Press, 2011); Elizabeth Freeman, *The Wedding Complex: Forms of Belonging in Modern American Culture* (Durham: Duke University Press, 2002); Christopher Looby, "Strange Sensations: Sex and Aesthetics in 'The Counterpane,'" in *Melville and Aesthetics*, ed. Geoffrey Sanborn and Samuel Otter (New York: Palgrave, 2011), 65–84; and Coviello. In claiming that we do not yet have a narrative of the rise of object choice, I agree with Jonathan Ned Katz (in substance if not in tone) that "Sedgwick and later students of the queer have shown little interest in the empirical history of the homo/hetero divide—little interest in researching, documenting, and analyzing the detailed evidence of homo/hetero's origins and construction over time." "Envisioning the World We Make, Social-Historical Construction, A Model, A Manifesto," outhistory.com, accessed April 22, 2017.

30. My etiological project also differs markedly from ontological approaches to sexuality, which tend to be less historical, taking "being" as a transhistorical category.

31. Sedgwick, 1.

32. Lee Edelman, "Unnamed: Eve's *Epistemology*," *Criticism* 52.2 (2010): 185.

33. Along these lines, Sedgwick writes: "The process . . . by which 'knowledge' and 'sex' become conceptually inseparable from one another—so that knowledge means in the first place sexual knowledge; ignorance, sexual ignorance; and epistemological pressure of any sort seems a force increasingly saturated with sexual impulsion—was sketched in Volume I of Foucault's *History of Sexuality*. In a sense, this was a process . . . of exfoliating the biblical genesis by which what we now know as sexuality is fruit—apparently the only fruit—to be plucked from the tree of knowledge." Sedgwick, 73. Valerie Traub calls this the "'sex-as-knowledge relation'" in *Thinking Sex with the Early Moderns* (Philadelphia: University of Pennsylvania Press, 2015), 3. Lee Edelman importantly notes "the interdependence of epistemology and the closet." Edelman, 185. On the relation of homosexuality to secrecy and privacy, see Sedgwick, 71; and David M. Halperin, *Saint Foucault* (Oxford: Oxford University Press, 1995), 34–38.

34. Sedgwick, 246, her emphasis.

35. Sedgwick, 246.

36. Sedgwick, 8.

37. Henry Abelove, "Some Speculations on the History of Sexual Intercourse during the Long Eighteenth Century in England," in *Deep Gossip* (Minneapolis: University of Minnesota Press, 2005), 24.

38. Sedgwick, 4, her emphasis.

39. Sedgwick, 80. My analysis here is indebted to Edelman's reading of this passage. Edelman, 186. For an important discussion of the role of epistemology in Sedgwick's thought, see Drew Daniel, "'Why Be Something That You're Not?': Punk Performance and the Epistemology of Queer Minstrelsy," *Social Text* 31.3 (2013): 24–28.

40. Traub, 3; Ross, 170.

41. Ross, 171.

42. Ross, 163. This claim for the partial and/or excluded humanness of the black subject dovetails with much scholarship in black studies following in the wake of Spillers. See, for example, Achille Mbembe, "Necropolitics," trans. Libby Meintjes, *Public Culture* 15.1 (2003): 11–40; Alexander G. Weheliye, *Habeas Viscus: Racializing Assemblages, Biopolitics, and Black Feminist Theories of the Human* (Durham: Duke University Press, 2014); and Robert F. Reid-Pharr, *Archives of Flesh: African America, Spain, and Post-Humanist Critique* (New York: New York University Press, 2016).

43. Ross, 168. While I think Ross is absolutely correct about "racial sameness" as the ground for differences in sexuality, I would modify his references to sexologists' "whiteness" and "Anglo-Saxon[ness]" slightly to allow for

the racialization of Jewish sexologists and Jewish sexological subjects. On the relationship between Jews, race, and sexology, see, for example, Matti Bunzl, "Sexual Modernity as Subject and Object," *Modernism/modernity* 9.1 (2002): 165–75; and Erwin J. Haeberle, "The Jewish Contribution to the Development of Sexology," *Journal of Sex Research* 18.4 (1982): 305–23. While there is an abundance of anthropological evidence (which I will discuss in chapter 2) of and discussion about racialized bodies in the sexological archive, I have only come across a handful of American articles from the first quarter of the twentieth century where the author hints that he has examined black bodies (even if they are not exactly case studies of individual black subjects). See Charles H. Hughes, "Homo Sexual Complexion Perverts in St. Louis," *Alienist and Neurologist* 28.4 (1907): 487–88; Charles H. Hughes, "An Organization of Colored Erotopaths," in *Gay American History: Lesbians and Gay Men in the USA*, ed. Jonathan Ned Katz (New York: Crowell, 1976), 42–43; Margaret Otis, "A Perversion Not Commonly Noted," *Journal of Abnormal Psychology* 8.2 (June-July 1913): 113–16; Perry M. Lichtenstein, "The 'Fairy' and the Lady Lover," *Medical Review of Reviews* 21 (1921): 369–74. Similarly, in Robert Latou Dickinson's and Lura Beam's important *A Thousand Marriages*, only two of the more than one thousand American subjects are classified as "negroes." Robert Latou Dickinson and Lura Beam, *A Thousand Marriages: a Medical Study of Sex-Adjustment* (Baltimore: The Williams and Wilkins Company, 1931), 27. I thus agree with Melissa Stein that though sexological work on "interracial sexual relationships" has "received considerable attention from queer scholars" "these writings make up a very small portion of American scientific work on homosexuality." Melissa N. Stein, *Measuring Manhood: Race and the Science of Masculinity, 1830–1934* (Minneapolis: University of Minnesota Press, 2015), 200. For a work that more extensively features case studies of "negroes," see George W. Henry, *Sex Variants: A Study of Homosexual Patterns* (New York: Paul B. Hoeber, 1948). Henry's text (which was importantly assisted by Jan Gay and to a lesser extent by Thomas Painter) features five negro cases out of its sample of eighty. On Henry, Gay, and Painter, see Henry L. Minton, *Departing Deviance: A History of Homosexual Rights and Emancipatory Science in America* (Chicago: University of Chicago Press, 2002), 33–57.

44. Ross, 172, his emphasis.

45. Ian Hacking, "Making Up People," in *Historical Ontology* (Cambridge: Harvard University Press, 2002), 99–114. Reading Sedgwick's axioms and her "axiomatic reasoning," Melissa Hardie writes: "Axioms are assumptions that must be taken at face value: they must be conceded without interrogation. They point, here, to their history [coming from Foucault] but not to their etiology." Here, Hardie suggests that Sedgwick's axiomatic method may itself be anti-etiological. See Melissa Jane Hardie, "Post-Structuralism: Originators and Heirs," in *The Cambridge Companion to American Gay and*

*Lesbian Literature*, ed. Scott Herring (Cambridge: Cambridge University Press, 2015), 216.

46. On these major categories, see Davidson, 63. Scott Herring's account of material deviance provides an indispensable case study of how one kind of minor pervert creates what Foucault calls "a world of perversion" (40). See Scott Herring, *The Hoarders: Material Deviance in Modern American Culture* (Chicago: University of Chicago Press, 2014).

47. Coviello, 20.

48. Christopher Looby, "Marmoreanism," paper presented at the MLA Convention, Philadelphia, January 6, 2017.

49. My thinking here has been influenced by Janet Halley's searing critiques of immutability: Janet E. Halley, "Sexual Orientation and the Politics of Biology: A Critique of the Argument from Immutability," *Stanford Law Review* 46.3 (1994): 503–68; and "The Politics of the Closet: Towards Equal Protection for Gay, Lesbian, and Bisexual Identity," *UCLA Law Review* 36 (1989): 915–76. See also Kendall Thomas, "Beyond the Privacy Principle," *Columbia Law Review* 92.6 (1992): 1431–516; Toni M. Massaro, "Gay Rights, Thick and Thin," *Stanford Law Review* 49.1 (1996): 45–110; and Lisa Duggan, "Queering the State," *Social Text* 39 (1994): 1–14.

50. For an important exception, see Valerie Rohy's discussion of the contemporary politics of etiology in *Lost Causes: Narrative, Etiology, and Queer Theory* (Oxford: Oxford University Press, 2015), 22–55.

51. The debate between congenital and acquired homosexuality actually begins a bit earlier. In 1852, Johann Ludwig Caspar publishes "the first scientific case study" of sodomites and suggests that for some of them the inclination is innate (by 1858 he understands a majority of cases to be innate). In opposition, August Tardieu posits homosexuality as a "vice" "not an innate constitution or mental illness" in 1857. Johann Ludwig Casper, "Ueber Nothzucht und Päderastie und deren Ermittelung Seitens des Gerichtsarztes," *Vierteljahrsschrift für gerichtliche und öffentliche Medicin* 1 (1852): 21–78; Ambroise-Auguste Tardieu, *Étude medico-légale sur les attentats aux mœurs* (Paris: J.-B. Baillière, 1857). On this debate, see Robert Beachy, "The German Invention of Homosexuality," *Journal of Modern History* 82.4 (2010): 810–13.

52. Michael Warner, *The Trouble with Normal: Sex, Politics, and the Ethics of Queer Life* (Cambridge: Harvard University Press, 2000). Laura Doan's characterization of the reception of sexology as "always [understood to be] a unified, coherent, and spurious form of knowledge" begins to suggest that this debate has been forgotten because the scholarship on sexology has conceptualized it to be overly "unified" and "coherent." Laura Doan, *Disturbing Practices: History, Sexuality, and Women's Experience of Modern War* (Chicago: University of Chicago Press, 2013), 67. Michael Moon and Sedgwick also describe the way in which such a process frames "the *phylo-*

*genic question*, which asks about centuries-long processes—linguistic, institutional, intergenerational . . . as if it were identical to the *ontogenic* question: the question of 'how did *such-and-such a person* come to be,' shall we
say, gay rather than straight." My project aims to provide a phylogenic
account of the concept of homosexuality. Michael Moon and Eve Kosofsky
Sedgwick, "Divinity: A Dossier, A Performance Piece, A Little-Understood
Emotion," in *Tendencies* (Durham: Duke University Press, 1993), 226.
53. Sedgwick, 41. Thinking of *Epistemology of the Closet* as a text published in
1990 supplies two other reasons why queer theory seems wary of talking
about etiology. (1) In the context of the mass death resulting from the
AIDS epidemic in its first decade in the US, the word "etiology" seems
too loaded with associations with disease and death and perhaps was
understood to reify the connection between homosexuality and disease,
and (2) given queer theory's early indebtedness to deconstruction, the
study of origins would have been anathema to its intellectual project. On
the relation between queer theory and deconstruction, see Hardie, "Post-
Structuralism," 206–23.
54. Sedgwick, 40. Sedgwick exhibits more faith in etiological approaches in
Eve Kosofsky Sedgwick, "How to Bring Your Kids Up Gay: The War on
Effeminate Boys," in *Tendencies* (Durham: Duke University Press, 1993),
154–64. While Leo Bersani finds the "suspicion in gay studies of inquiries
into the etiology of homosexuality" "well founded" he also suggests that
"we might do well to consider the disadvantages of turning our backs on
these inquiries," in *Homos* (Cambridge: Harvard University Press, 1995),
56, 57, 58.
55. David M. Halperin, *One Hundred Years of Homosexuality and Other Essays on
Greek Love* (New York: Routledge, 1990), 49, 50. Diana Fuss is also skeptical of etiology, understanding "debates over etiology" to be "pointless."
Diana Fuss, "Freud's Fallen Women: Identification, Desire, and 'A Case of
Homosexuality in a Woman,'" in *Fear of a Queer Planet: Queer Politics and
Social Theory*, ed. Michael Warner (Minneapolis: University of Minnesota
Press, 1993), 45.
56. Rohy, 98.
57. Rohy, 40, 186, 189. Rohy's assertion that "born gay" ideology "is itself
a lost cause, useless to advance queer equity" strikes me as particularly
overblown. Rohy, 79.
58. Rohy, 54, 24.
59. While queer theory's engagement with etiology is largely condemnatory
or haphazard, there are important exceptions. I'm thinking of Kathryn Kent's work on lesbian recruitment, David Halperin's work on the
transmission of gay culture, Guy Hocquenghem's work on homosexual
production, Michael Warner's work on posterity, and Sedgwick's work on
gay childrearing. See Kathryn R. Kent, *Making Girls into Women: American
Women's Writing and the Rise of Lesbian Identity* (Durham: Duke Univer-

sity Press, 2003); David M. Halperin, *How to Be Gay* (Cambridge: Harvard
University Press, 2012); Guy Hocquenghem, *Homosexual Desire*, trans.
Daniella Dangoor (Durham: Duke University Press, 1993); Michael Warner, "Irving's Posterity," *ELH* 67.3 (2000): 773–99; and Sedgwick, "How to
Bring," 154–65. There also exists a body of criticism on what I would call
the "generational imaginary" of sex—the way that sexuality is thought to
be transmitted across generational lines. See, for example, Dana Seitler,
*Atavistic Tendencies: The Culture of Science in American Modernity* (Minneapolis: University of Minnesota Press, 2008); Kyla Schuller, *The Biopolitics
of Feeling: Race, Sex, and Impressibility in the Nineteenth Century United States*
(Durham: Duke University Press, 2017); Lynn Wardley, *Lamarck's Daughters: Fiction, Feminism, and the Power of Life* (unpublished manuscript).
While the transmission of sexuality across generations is often understood negatively—within the parameters of degeneration—Georg Hirth's
conception of "hereditary enfranchisement" and Iwan Bloch's idea of
"self-regeneration" might suggest new registers in which to understand
this generational sexuality. Georg Hirth, *Entropie der Keimsysteme und
erbliche Entlastung* (Munich: G. Hirth's Verlag, 1900); and Iwan Bloch, *The
Sexual Life of Our Time in Its Relations to Modern Civilization*, trans. M. Eden
Paul (London: Rebman Limited, 1909), 462.
60. Rohy, 83.
61. Rohy, 79, her emphasis. Rohy also fascinatingly suggests that both "born
gay" and homophobic theories "make causality a *means to an end*, a way to
promote an ideological cause" (78–79, her emphasis).
62. Sedgwick, *Epistemology*, 44. On the politics of homosexual causality,
see Lance Wahlert, "The Burden of Poofs: Criminal Pathology, Clinical
Scrutiny, and Homosexual Etiology in Queer Cinema," *Journal of Medical
Humanities* 34.2 (2013): 149–75; and Timothy Murphy, *Gay Science: The
Ethics of Sexual Orientation Research* (New York: Columbia University Press,
1997).
63. Rohy, 40; Coviello, 10.
64. Valerie Rohy makes an interesting claim in a slightly different register:
"Science will never find the biological cause of homosexuality, not because there is no biological cause, but because there is no homosexuality:
what the term names is too heterogeneous to totalize." Rohy, 14. For a
sexuality studies project that is interested in exploring the biological and
neurological basis of sexuality, see Elizabeth A. Wilson, *Psychosomatic:
Feminism and the Neurological Body* (Durham: Duke University Press, 2004),
49–62.
65. I have been particularly influenced here by David M. Halperin, *How to Do
the History of Homosexuality* (Chicago: University of Chicago Press, 2002),
104–37; Valerie Traub, "The Present Future of Lesbian Historiography," in
*A Companion to Lesbian, Gay, Bisexual, Transgender, and Queer Studies*, eds.
George Haggerty and Molly McGarry (Oxford: Blackwell, 2007), 124–45;

Dana Seitler, "Queer Physiognomies, or How Many Ways Can We Do the History of Sexuality?" *Criticism* 46.1 (2004): 71–102; Jeffrey Masten, "More or Less Queer," in *Shakesqueer: A Queer Companion to the Complete Works of Shakespeare*, ed. Madhavi Menon, (Durham: Duke University Press, 2011), 309–18; Scott Herring, "Catherian Friendship; Or, How Not to Do the History of Homosexuality," *Modern Fiction Studies* 52.1 (2006): 66–91; Carla Freccero, "Undoing the Histories of Homosexuality," in *Queer/Early/Modern* (Durham: Duke University Press, 2006), 31–50; Christopher Looby, "The Literariness of Sexuality: Or, How to Do the (Literary) History of (American) Sexuality," *American Literary History* 25.4 (2013): 841–54, and Lanser, 1–29.

66. Sedgwick, *Epistemology*, 45, 44.
67. Traub, "Present Future," 135.
68. Michel Foucault, "Nietzsche, Genealogy, History," in *The Foucault Reader*, ed. Paul Rabinow (New York: Pantheon Books, 1984), 77, 88.
69. George Chauncey, *Gay New York: Gender, Urban Culture, and the Making of the Gay Male World, 1890–1940* (New York: Basic Books, 1994), 87. This world organized by gender status operates on what Chauncey calls the "phallocentric presumption that a man's sexual satisfaction was more significant than the gender or character of the person who provided that satisfaction in definitions of sexual identity." Chauncey, 85.
70. Chauncey, 114.
71. On the shift between manhood and masculinity, see Michael Kimmel, *Manhood in America: A Cultural History* (Oxford: Oxford University Press, 2012).
72. Chauncey, 112.
73. Chauncey, 115.
74. Chauncey, 116, 117.
75. Halperin, *How to Do*, 17.
76. Sedgwick, *Epistemology*, 85, 47.
77. Halperin, *How to Do*, 109.
78. Halperin, *How to Do*, 109. In *Celibacies*, I argued that we ought to consider celibacy an additional prehomosexual pattern or model. Benjamin Kahan, *Celibacies: American Modernism and Sexual Life* (Durham: Duke University Press, 2013), 33–38.
79. Halperin, *How to Do*, 106; Sedgwick, *Epistemology*, 45.
80. Halperin, *How to Do*, 109; Traub, "Present Future," 135.
81. On homosexualism, see Jean-Claude Féray and Manfred Herzer, "Homosexual Studies and Politics in the 19th Century: Karl Maria Kertbeny," trans. Glen W. Peppel. *Journal of Homosexuality* 19.1 (1990): 35. On similisexualism, see Prime-Stevenson. On unisexuality, see Marc-André Raffalovich, *Uranism and Unisexuality: A Study of Different Manifestations of the Sexual Instinct* (New York: Palgrave, 2016). On Urningthum, see Hubert Kennedy, *Karl Heinrich Ulrichs: Pioneer of the Modern Gay Movement* (San Francisco:

Peremptory Publications, 2002), 160. On the male Uranian, see Edward
Carpenter, *The Intermediate Sex: A Study of Some Transitional Types of Men
and Women* (New York: Mitchell Kennerley, 1931), 13. On inversion, see
Havelock Ellis and John Addington Symonds, *Sexual Inversion: A Critical
Edition*, ed. Ivan Crozier (New York: Palgrave, 2008). On philarrhenic nature, see Prime-Stevenson, 377. On antipathic sexual instinct, see Richard
von Krafft-Ebing, *Psychopathia Sexualis: With Especial Reference to the Antipathic Sexual Instinct*, trans. Franklin S. Klaf (New York: Stein and Day, 1965).
On Adhesiveness, see Robert Macnish, "Adhesiveness," *Lancet* 2 (6 August
1836): 633. On contrary sexual feeling, see Halperin, *How to Do*, 127. On
reverse sexual instinct, see Charles H. Hughes, "Homo Sexual Complexion
Perverts in St. Louis," *Alienist and Neurologist* 28.4 (1907): 488. On psycho-
sexual hermaphroditism, see Ellis and Symonds, 190. On pederasty, see
Jana Funke, "'We Cannot Be Greek Now': Age Difference, Corruption of
Youth and the Making of Sexual Inversion," *English Studies* 94.2 (2013): 140.
On man-manly love, see Karl Heinrich Ulrichs, *The Riddle of "Man-Manly"
Love: The Pioneering Work on Male Homosexuality*, vol. 1, trans. Michael A.
Lombardi-Nash (Buffalo: Prometheus Books, 1994), 34. On Socratic love,
see Ralph Werther, *The Female-Impersonators* (New York: Arno Press, 1975),
28; and Forberg, 159. On homogenic love, see Edward Carpenter, *Homo-
genic Love and Its Place in a Free Society* (London: Redundancy Press, 1980).
On lesbian love, see Heinrich Kaan, *Heinrich Kaan's "Psychopathia Sexualis"
(1844): A Classic Text in the History of Sexuality*, trans. Melissa Haynes, ed.
Benjamin Kahan (Ithaca: Cornell University Press, 2016), 22–23, 79.

82. On lesbian love, see Kaan, 22–23, 79; and Krafft-Ebing, 406. On tribadism
and tribadic love, see Bloch, *Anthropologial Studies*, 237. On tribady, see
Krafft-Ebing, 407. On Sapphism, see Bloch, *Anthropological Studies*, 236. On
Sapphic love, see Bloch, *Anthropologial Studies*, 210; and Iwan [Ivan] Bloch,
*Marquis de Sade: The Man and His Age* (Magnolia Books, 2013), 89. On frictrices, see Forberg, *Manual* vol. 2., 149. On frictionists, see Forberg, *Manual*,
vol. 2, 109. On hetairistriae, dietairistriae, see Forberg, *Manual*, vol. 2., 109;
and Halperin, *How to Do*, 68–71. On the subagitatrix (also spelled subigi-
tatrix), see *Manual*, vol. 2., 129; and George M. Gould, *A Dictionary of New
Medical Terms* (London: Bailliere, Tindall, and Cox, 1905), 517.

83. On feminine homosexuality, see Bloch, *Anthropological Studies*, 236. On
female homosexuality, see Ellis and Symonds, 163. On female uranism,
see Ulrichs, *Riddle*, vol. 1., 162. On unisexuality, see Raffalovich; and
Elisabeth Ladenson, "Colette for Export Only," *Yale French Studies* 90
(1996): 25–46. On woman-womanly love, see Ulrichs, *Riddle*, vol. 1., 239.
On inversion, see Ellis and Symonds, 159. On Adhesiveness, see Macnish.
On the lady lover, see Lichtenstein, 369–74. On the urninde, see Bloch,
*Anthropological Studies*, 239. On the female urning, see Ulrichs, *Riddle*,
vol. 1, 173. On the Urningin, see Ulrichs, *Riddle*, vol. 1., 173.

84. Seitler, 79.

85. Seitler, 97.

86. Oosterhuis, 40.

87. Coviello, 4.

88. Carl Westphal, "Die conträre Sexualempfindung, Symptom eines neuro-pathischen (psychopathischen) Zustandes," *Archiv für Psychiatrie und Nerven krankheiten* 2 (1870): 73–108. While Westphal's article has a publication date of 1870, it actually appeared in 1869; see Halperin, *One Hundred*, 155n2. Alfred C. Kinsey, Wardell B. Pomeroy, and Clyde E. Martin, *Sexual Behavior in the Human Male* (Bloomington: Indiana University Press, 1975).

89. Beachy, "The German Invention," 819.

90. Beachy, "The German Invention," 819.

91. Jennifer Terry, *An American Obsession: Science, Medicine, and Homosexuality in Modern Society* (Chicago: University of Chicago Press, 1999), 42–43. The history of American sexology before Kinsey is in need of scholarly work and remains comparatively underdeveloped in relation to the sexological historiographies of England and Germany. This is particularly surprising given that both the terms "sexology" and "sexual science" were coined in America in 1867 and 1869, respectively. For the earliest usage of the word "sexology," see Elizabeth Osgood Goodrich Willard, *Sexology as the Philosophy of Life: Implying Social Organization and Government* (Chicago: J. R. Walsh, 1867). The term "sexual science" is first used by the phrenologist Orson Squire Fowler in *The Practical Phenologist*. There he advertises his forthcoming volume on sexual science: "[S]ee this whole subject of adaptations and sexual relations thoroughly discussed in the author's work on 'Sexual Science and Restoration. . . .'" O. S. Fowler, *The Practical Phenologist* (Boston: O. S. Fowler, 1869), 171.

92. John D'Emilio, "Born Gay?" in *The World Turned: Essays on Gay History, Politics, and Culture* (Durham: Duke University Press, 2002), 162.

93. Sedgwick, *Epistemology*, 9.

94. George Chauncey, "From Sexual Inversion to Homosexuality: Medicine and the Changing Conceptualization of Female Deviance," *Salmagundi* 58/59 (1982–83): 116.

95. Halperin, *How to Do*, 103.

96. Foucault, 43.

97. Jonathan Ned Katz, *The Invention of Heterosexuality* (New York: Dutton, 1995), 51–52.

98. Michel Foucault, *Abnormal: Lectures at the Collège De France, 1974–1975*, ed. Valerio Marchetti and Antonella Salomoni (New York: Picador, 2003), 282. See also my edition of Heinrich Kaan's text.

99. Halperin, *How to Do*, 104–137.

100. Havelock Ellis, *Psychology of Sex: A Manual for Students* (New York: Emerson Books, 1937), 223–24.

101. Ellis, *Psychology of Sex*, 222.

102. Albert Moll, *Perversions of the Sex Instinct: A Study of Sexual Inversion*, trans. Maurice Popkin (Newark: Julian Press, 1931).

103. Ellis, *Psychology of Sex*, 224.
104. This narrative bolsters Douglas Mao's claim in *Fateful Beauty* that "from the late nineteenth century through the early twentieth, the scarcely registered workings of environment on the developing human being were a preoccupation of many kinds of people, from artists to scientists, from writers of fiction to crafters of policy, from experts pondering national problems raised by juveniles to parents gnashing their teeth over domestic ones." Douglas Mao, *Fateful Beauty: Aesthetic Environments, Juvenile Development, and Literature, 1860–1960* (Princeton: Princeton University Press, 2008), 5.
105. Ellis and Symonds, 200.
106. Krafft-Ebing, 221–22 and 406. Cultivated, institutional, casual, pseudo, false, and temporary homosexuality were all roughly synonymous terms for acquired modes of sexuality.
107. Moll, 147.
108. Moll, 234.
109. While congenitality is not the only model of lesbianism in *The Well of Loneliness*, it is the dominant one. For an overview of congenitality in Hall's text, see Laura Doan, "'The Outcast of One Age is the Hero of Another': Radclyffe Hall, Edward Carpenter, and the Intermediate Sex," in *Palatable Poison: Critical Perspectives on The Well of Loneliness*, eds. Laura Doan and Jay Prosser (New York: Columbia University Press, 2001), 162–78. For alternative interpretations of Hall's text that position it in relation to transness and female masculinity rather than lesbianism, see Jay Prosser, *Second Skins: The Body Narratives of Transsexuality* (New York: Columbia University Press, 1998), 135–70 and Judith (Jack) Halberstam, *Female Masculinity* (Durham: Duke University Press, 1998), 75–110. On acquisition in Barnes's text, see Kent, 126–37.
110. F. O. Matthiessen and Russell Cheney, *Rat and the Devil: Journal Letters of F. O. Matthiessen and Russell Cheney* (Brooklyn: Shoe String Press, 1978), 47. On the intersection between queerness and nature, see Sam See, "The Comedy of Nature: Darwinian Feminism in Virginia Woolf's Between the Acts," *Modernism/modernity* 17.3 (2010), especially 644–45.
111. Matthiessen and Cheney, 47.
112. Ralph Werther, *Autobiography of an Androgyne*, ed. Scott Herring (New Brunswick: Rutgers University Press, 2008), 36, 33.
113. One hesitation about the verisimilitude of the story is that Werther records a very similar story in which another man calls for the branding of the word "UNCLEAN" on the foreheads of fairies in his *The Female-Impersonators*. Werther, *The Female-Impersonators*, 162. That said, Werther does say of his narrative that when "definite memory fails me, I have had recourse to my sea of general memories," opening the possibility that the Comstock story is being used to fill out this second account. Werther, *The Female-Impersonators*, 198.
114. Werther, *Autobiography*, 8–9.

115. Bloch, *Anthropological*, 6, 15.
116. On the circulation of sexology and erotic literature in the United States, see Gertzman.
117. Ivan Crozier, "Nineteenth-Century British Psychiatric Writing About Homosexuality before Havelock Ellis: The Missing Story," *Journal of the History of Medicine and Allied Sciences* 63.1 (2008): 67. Chiang's work is more nuanced than Crozier's, "differentiat[ing] and analyz[ing] the parameters of science and medicine in turn-of-the-twentieth-century sexology." Chiang, "Historicizing," 35.
118. Edward Carpenter, *Towards Democracy: Complete Edition in Four Parts* (London: George Allen and Unwin Limited, 1918), 396–97.
119. Edward Carpenter, *The Intermediate Sex*, 70. Some commentators would not consider Carpenter a sexologist because he lacks medical credentials and instead would understand him as a social activist and sex reformer. Building on Gayle Rubin's claim that Carpenter was "heavily cited" in "the medical texts," I understand Carpenter as a sexologist, taking the broadest possible view of sexology in order to apprehend the multidisciplinary and interdisciplinary nature of sexological discourse, the way it moves across the sciences, social sciences, humanities, and professional fields like law and medicine. Gayle Rubin, "Geologies of Queer Studies: It's Déjà Vu All Over Again," in *Deviations: A Gayle Rubin Reader* (Durham: Duke University Press, 2011), 352. For an argument for Carpenter as a sexologist, see Kate Fisher and Jana Funke, 103–7. For a heated debate over what counts as sexology and Carpenter's status in particular, see Ivan Crozier and Heike Bauer, "Sexology, Historiography, Citation, Embodiment: A Review and (Frank) Exchange," *History of the Human Sciences*, June 27, 2017, http://www.histhum.com/?p=367.
120. Harry Oosterhuis, *Homosexuality and Male Bonding in Pre-Nazi Germany*, trans. Hubert Kennedy (New York: Harrington Park Press, 1991), 4.
121. On female sexologists, see Kirsten Leng, *Sexual Politics and Feminist Science: Women Sexologists in Germany, 1900–1933* (Ithaca: Cornell University Press and Cornell University Library, 2018).
122. Will Fisher understands the simultaneous emergence of the discourses of the Renaissance and of sexology to be intertwined in the homophilic project of valorizing homosexuality as the pinnacle of civilization (which begins to explain why the sexologist Havelock Ellis edited a series of early modern plays). Will Fisher, "The Sexual Politics of Victorian Historiographical Writing about the 'Renaissance,'" *GLQ* 14.1 (2008): 52.
123. On sexologists' use of literary sources, see Anna Katharina Schaffner, "Fiction as Evidence: On the Uses of Literature in Nineteenth-Century Sexological Discourse," *Comparative Literature Studies* 48.2 (2011): 165–99; and Heike Bauer, "Literary Sexualities," in *The Cambridge Companion to the Body in Literature*, ed. David Hilman and Ulrika Maude (Cambridge: Cambridge University Press, 2015), 101–15.

124. W. C. Rivers, *Walt Whitman's Anomaly* (London: George Allen & Company, 1913), 1. On the centrality of Whitman to the literariness of sexuality, see Eve Kosofsky Sedgwick, *Between Men: English Literature and Male Homosocial Desire* (New York: Columbia University Press, 1985), 28, 206.

125. Krafft-Ebing, 87, 69. In the preface to the first edition of *Psychopathia Sexualis*, Krafft-Ebing claims that "the poet is the better psychologist" (xiii). For a history of the early usage of the term "sadism," see Alison M. Moore, *Sexual Myths of Modernity: Sadism, Masochism, and Historical Teleology* (Lantham, MD: Lexington Books, 2016), 26–34. On masochism as a "literary disease," see Amber Musser, "The Literary Symptom: Krafft-Ebing and the Invention of Masochism," in *Mediated Deviance and Social Otherness: Interrogating Influential Representations*, ed. Kylo-Patrick Hart (Newcastle, UK: Cambridge Scholars Publishing, 2007), 286–94, especially 287.

126. In *The Memoirs of a Sexologist* (1951), Ludwig Levy-Lenz writes that the dramatist and novelist Arthur Schnitzler reportedly said to him—after Lenz told him stories of his practice—"'There is plenty of material to last several playwrights and novelists their whole life long.'" Ludwig L. Lenz, *The Memoirs of a Sexologist: Discretion and Indiscretion* (New York: Cadillac Publishing Co, 1954), 344.

127. Foote, 158.

128. André Gide, *Corydon*, trans. Richard Howard (New York: Open Road, 2015), 8, 18. The text was published partially in a 1911 private edition, fully in a 1920 private edition, and publicly in 1924.

129. Gide, 115.

130. Werther, *Autobiography*, 40. In *The Female-Impersonators*, he refers to his three works (*Autobiography*, *Impersonators*, and *The Riddle of the Underworld*) as "books on sexology." Werther, *Female-Impersonators*, 3. On *The Riddle of the Underworld* (1921), see http://outhistory.org/exhibits/show/earl-lind/manuscript. On the relationship between autobiography and sexology, see Oosterhuis, *Stepchildren*, especially 127–230; and Katie Sutton, "Sexological Cases and the Prehistory of Transgender Identity Politics in Interwar Germany," in *Case Studies and the Dissemination of Knowledge*, ed. Joy Damousi, Birgit Lang, and Katie Sutton (New York: Routledge, 2015), 85–103.

131. Looby, 841.

132. E. M. Forster, *Maurice: A Novel* (New York: W. W. Norton & Company, 1993), 159; and Martin Green, *Children of the Sun* (London: Constable, 1977), 115.

133. Iwan [Ivan] Bloch, *Sexual Life in England: Past and Present* (Hertfordshire, UK: Oracle, 1996), 418.

134. The halting ellipses here and the stuttering "well" suggest the searching for a vocabulary that Hall's novel furnishes. Laura Doan, *Fashioning Sapphism: The Origins of a Modern English Lesbian Culture* (New York:

Columbia University Press, 2001), 194. In the early 1930s, in an interview conducted between a graduate student of the sociologist Ernest Burgess and an anonymous homosexual man, the man describes reading a number of gay novels including "Weel of Lonlienss" [sic] because he "wanted to find out more about the life [that] was in the book[s]" and because he "would like to live their live[s]." Ernest Watson Burgess Papers, University of Chicago Library, Box 128 Folder 7. Conversely, Mildred J. Berryman's unpublished thesis *The Psychological Phenomena of the Homosexual* (written between 1916 and 1939) describes some of the negative impact of the publication of Hall's novel: "At the time there was a great deal of gossip and effort being made to classify every woman who wore a suit and was seen in the company of a girl companion and every man who had curly hair and might have a little more than a feminine walk or a flare for bright colored ties. This commotion was the result of . . . "THE WELL OF LONLINESS" by RADECLIFF HALL [sic]. Literature has done much harm to these individuals and little has been gained because the problem has been presented in the wrong light." Taken together these two examples suggest that literature fosters the development of community and sexual subjectivity as well as surveillance and punishment. Mildred Berryman Papers, Library Special Collections, Charles E. Young Research Library, University of California, Los Angeles, UCLA MSS 2170, Box 1, Folder 4.

135. Quoted in Doan, *Fashioning*, 123. The doubled use of the word "miss" here bookending Radclyffe Hall's name anxiously calls into question Irons's unmarried status and her womanhood.

136. On the literary dimensions of sexology, see also Heike Bauer, *English Literary Sexology: Translations of Inversion, 1860–1930* (New York: Palgrave, 2009).

137. As my emphasis on the imbrication of these discourses suggests, I am resistant to approaches like that of Paul Peppis, who separates the sciences of ethnography, sexology, and psychology. Paul Peppis, *Sciences of Modernism: Ethnography, Sexology, and Psychology* (Cambridge: Cambridge University Press, 2014). I am grateful to Jana Funke for this point. On the historically later formation of *administrative sexualis*, see Roderick A. Ferguson, *The Reorder of Things: The University and Its Pedagogies of Minority Difference* (Minneapolis: University of Minnesota Press, 2012), 223–26.

138. Carter Bealer's diary offers an example of an individual accepting rather than contesting or resisting sexological classification: "For years and years I have been this way—have loved and worshipped silently other boys and youths, some older, some younger than myself—sexual inversion Havelock Ellis calls it. . . ." Quoted in Genny Beemyn, *A Queer Capital: A History of Gay Life in Washington, DC* (New York: Routledge, 2014), 14.

139. On homonationalism, see Jasbir K. Puar, *Terrorist Assemblages: Homonationalism in Queer Times* (Durham: Duke University Press, 2007).

140. Ellis and Symonds, 112; Victor Segalen, *Essay on Exoticism: An Aesthetics of Diversity* (Durham: Duke University Press, 2002), 13.

141. Iwan Bloch, *Marquis de Sade's Anthropologia Sexualis of 600 Perversions, 120 Days of Sodom; or, the School of Libertinage* (New York: Falstaff Press, 1934).

142. Michel Foucault, *Abnormal: Lectures at the Collège De France, 1974–1975*, trans. Graham Burchell (New York: Picador, 2003), 282.

143. On gay for pay, see Jeffrey Escoffier, "Gay-for-Pay: Straight Men and the Making of Gay Pornography," *Qualitative Sociology* 26.4 (2003): 531–55.

144. The fact that many of these contemporary acquired terms might be understood as insults suggests the continuing dominance of congenitality as a framework for sexuality. On ex-gay, Tanya Erzen, *Straight to Jesus: Sexual and Christian Conversions in the Ex-Gay Movement* (Berkeley: University of California Press, 2006).

CHAPTER ONE

1. This list owes something to David Halperin's catalog of not-quite-identities: "partial identity, emergent identity, transient identity, semi-identity, incomplete identity, proto-identity, or subidentity" (*How to Do*, 43). Elizabeth Freeman argues that "ordinary gender" identities "erase the passage of time," transforming "identification into identity." Elizabeth Freeman, "Packing History, Count(er)ing Generations," *New Literary History* 31.4 (2000): 733. See also D. A. Miller, *Place for Us (Essay on the Broadway Musical)* (Cambridge: Harvard University Press, 1998), 26.

2. In her reading of Kate Chopin's *The Awakening* (1899), Madoka Kishi suggests another vector of stability (the object's identicality with itself), arguing that the novel depicts "the instability of . . . object-desire . . . directed toward variety itself." Madoka Kishi, "The Erotics of Race Suicide: The Making of Whiteness and the Death Drive in the Progressive Era, 1880–1920," PhD diss., Louisiana State University, 2015.

3. Regina Kunzel, "Situating Sex," *GLQ* 8.3 (2002): 253.

4. *Winter Bound* was composed in 1917 and performed for the first time in 1929. The Library of Congress manuscript has a copyright date of 1928. On the composition of *Winter Bound*, see Helen Deutsch and Stella Hanau, *The Provincetown: A Story of the Theatre* (New York: Farar and Rinehart, 1931), 183.

5. Chad Heap, *Slumming* (Chicago: University of Chicago Press, 2009), 82. Sholom Asch's *Got Fun Nekomeh* was originally performed in Yiddish in America in 1907 before being translated into English as *God of Vengeance* in 1918 and performed on Broadway by the Provincetown Players in 1922/3. While it had been performed in Yiddish without incident, the Broadway cast was arrested on the charge of obscenity. See also Alan Sinfield, *Out on Stage: Lesbian and Gay Theatre in the Twentieth Century* (New Haven: Yale University Press, 1999), 177–78.

6. I borrow this list in its entirety from Susan S. Lanser's "1928: Sapphic Modernity and the Sexuality of History," in "What is Sexual Modernity," ed. Benjamin Kahan, special issue of *Modernism/modernity Print-Plus* 1.3, October 25, 2016, https://modernismmodernity.org/forums/posts/1928 -sapphic-modernity-and-sexuality-history.

7. On the recurring newness of lesbianism, see Susan S. Lanser, *The Sexuality of History: Modernity and the Sapphic, 1565–1830* (Chicago: University of Chicago Press, 2014), 33, 40.

8. Though the criminologist Charles A. Ford does not use the term situational homosexuality, he refers to sex between inmates as "situations" in 1929. The new importance of situational homosexuality is also evident in his comment that though lesbian relationships are well known in penal settings, only one article has ever been written on the subject (Margaret Otis's essay discussed later in this chapter). This observation will mark a turn toward the increasing exploration and theorization of situational homosexuality by criminologists. Charles A. Ford, "Homosexual Practices of Institutionalized Females," *Journal of Abnormal Psychology* 23.4 (1929): 447, 442.

9. Michael Golston, *Race and Rhythm in Modernist Poetry and Science* (New York: Columbia University Press, 2008), 10.

10. Marie Carmichael Stopes, *Married Love: A New Contribution to the Solution of Sex Difficulties* (London: A. C. Fifield, 1919), 12–13.

11. On Stopes's research into the rhythm of the sex-impulse, see Laura Doan, "Marie Stopes's Wonderful Rhythm Charts: Normalizing the Natural," *Journal of the History of Ideas* 78.4 (2017): 595–620.

12. In a beautiful reading of this passage, Annamarie Jagose argues that Stopes offers simultaneous orgasm as a practice that not only brings men and women into alignment with each other but also secures a host of "wider affiliative connections" with the nation, the "race," and with the rhythms of modern life. Annamarie Jagose, *Orgasmology* (Durham: Duke University Press, 2012), 67.

13. A.W. Johnstone, "The Relation of Menstruation to Other Reproductive Functions," *American Journal of Obstetrics* 32 (1895): 38. This view is shared by Heinrich Kaan: "While man is able to perform intercourse at a specific time (in the morning, on account of new energy acquired as a result of the preceding sleep, in midday as a result of nutrition, and at night with the help of the imagination), a woman is ready at any hour. Hence it is necessary for the man to solicit sexual pleasure, but for the woman to reject him so as to amplify his desire." Heinrich Kaan, *Heinrich Kaan's "Psychopathia Sexualis" (1844): A Classic Text in the History of Sexuality*, trans. Melissa Haynes, ed. Benjamin Kahan (Ithaca: Cornell University Press, 2016), 75. For a slightly different account of the relationship between women and rut, see B. S. Tamley, "Female Exhibitionism: A Psychosexual Study," *American Journal of Urology and Sexology* (1917): 216–17.

14. William James Chidley, *The Answer: A Philosophical Essay* (Sydney, Australia: A. J. Tomalin, 1912), 37. For more on Chidley, see Frank Bongiorno, *The Sex Lives of Australians: A History* (Collingwood, Australia: Black Inc., 2012), 60.
15. Chidley, 7, his emphasis. He emphasizes the "naturalness" of sex in the spring, by asserting that the "love embrace . . . will of course come about in the Spring, as with other animals." Chidley, 11.
16. Quoted in Eric Naiman, *Sex in Public: The Incarnation of Early Soviet Ideology* (Princeton: Princeton University Press, 1997), 1.
17. Kaier Curtin, *"We Can Always Call Them Bulgarians": The Emergence of Lesbian and Gay Men on the American Stage* (Boston: Alyson Publications, 1987), 141.
18. Deutsch and Hanau, 309. The exception to this scholarly lacuna is Curtin, 140–53. See also Alan Sinfield, *Out on Stage: Lesbian and Gay Theatre in Twentieth Century* (New Haven: Yale University Press, 1999), 57.
19. There is a growing body of scholarship about the Provincetown Players. See, for example, Robert Karoly Sarlos, *Jig Cook and the Provincetown Players: Theatre in Ferment* (Amherst: University of Massachussets Press, 1982); Barbara Oziebio, *Susan Glaspell: A Critical Biography* (Chapel Hill: University of North Carolina Press, 2000); Cheryl Black, *The Women of Provincetown, 1915–1922* (Tuscaloosa: University of Alabama Press, 2002); Travis Bogard and Jackson R. Bryer, eds., *The Provincetown Players and the Playwrights' Theatre, 1915–1922* (Jefferson, NC: McFarland, 2004); J. Ellen Gainor, *Susan Glaspell in Context: American Theatre, Culture, and Politics, 1915–1948* (Ann Arbor: University of Michigan Press, 2004); Brenda Murphy, *The Provincetown Players and the Culture of Modernity* (Cambridge: Cambridge University Press, 2005); Linda Ben-Zvi, *Susan Glaspell: Her Life and Times* (Oxford: Oxford University Press, 2007); and Emeline Jouve, *Susan Glaspell's Poetics and Politics of Rebellion* (Iowa City: University of Iowa Press, 2017). See also Kevin Mumford's treatment of Eugene O'Neill in Kevin Mumford, *Interzones: Black/White Sex Districts in Chicago and New York in the Early Twentieth Century* (New York: Columbia University Press, 1997), 121–32.
20. Alison Smith, "Other New Plays," *World* (November 18, 1929): 15.
21. Thomas Dickinson, *Winter Bound: A Play in Three Acts and Nine Scenes*, Library of Congress, unpublished manuscript, PS3507.I3537 W5 (Rare Bk Coll), act 1, scene 3, page 5; and Dickinson, act 3, scene 2, page 6.
22. Dickinson, act. 1, scene 1, page. 1.
23. This tension between asexuality and homosexuality is bitterly fought in the play's reviews as the critic John Anderson fights with Dickinson that the play depicts abnormality. See Curtin, 148–50. On the relationship between celibacy, asexuality, and homosexuality, see Benjamin Kahan, *Celibacies: American Modernism and Sexual Life* (Durham: Duke University Press, 2013).

24. Dickinson, act 1, scene 1, page 16.
25. Dickinson, act 1, scene 1, page 19.
26. Dickinson, act 1, scene 1, page 1.
27. Dickinson, act 1, scene 2, page 12.
28. Dickinson, act 1, scene 2, page 12.
29. When the play is mentioned at all, it is said to be derivative of D. H. Lawrence's *The Fox* (1920). *Winter Bound* and *The Fox* share a number of elements—both feature two women living on a farm and a visiting man who falls in love with one of them. The correspondences between the two texts lead Alan Sinfield to write after describing *Winter Bound*'s plotting that "This sounds very like D. H. Lawrence's novella *The Fox*," and Lillian Faderman similarly comments that Dickinson's play "seems to be influenced by D. H. Lawrence's novella" (Sinfield, 57, and Lillian Faderman, "Lesbian Chic: Experimentation and Repression in the 1920s," in *The Gender and Consumer Culture Reader*, ed. Jennifer Scanlon [New York: New York University Press, 2000], 163n5). Given the production of *Winter Bound* in 1929 and the writing of Lawrence's novella in 1920, this reading is certainly plausible. However, the first account of the Provincetown Theatre (written almost contemporaneously in 1931 by participants in the theatre company) states emphatically that "'Winter Bound' has been written some twelve years before its production" (Deutsch and Hanau, 183). The authors state this at some length to protect Dickinson against the charge of "timid[ity]" and to suggest that his work is not in fact derivative of *The Captive* and *The Well of Loneliness* (Deutsch and Hanau, 183). This assertion of its being written in 1917 raises four possibilities: that the authors of this early history of the Provincetown are mistaken/misremembering the story of *Winter Bound*'s composition, that Lawrence somehow knew about *Winter Bound* and that *The Fox* is derivative of Dickinson's work, that the two works both share plotting derived independently, or that *Winter Bound* was drafted initially in 1917 but was revised in relation to Dickinson's later reading of *The Fox*. Whatever the compositional relationship between the two texts, *The Fox* shares with *Winter Bound* a seasonal imaginary of desire.
30. Dickinson, act 1, scene 1, page 5.
31. Dickinson, act 1, scene 2, page 10.
32. Dickinson, act 1, scene 2, page 11.
33. Dickinson, act 1, scene 1, page 6.
34. Dickinson, act 3, scene 2, page 6.
35. Dickinson, act 1, scene 2, page 3; and Dickinson, act 1, scene 2, page 14.
36. For more on the relation between frigidity and lesbianism, see Benjamin Kahan, "Unqueerness," *Feminist Formations* 28.2 (2016): 162–65.
37. Dickinson, act 1, scene 3, page 1.
38. Djuna Barnes, *Ladies Almanack: showing their Signs and their tides; their Moons and their Changes; the seasons as it is with them; their Eclipses and their*

NOTES TO PAGES 32–34

*Equinoxes; as well as a full Record of diurnal and nocturnal Distempers* (New York: New York University Press, 1992).

39. Sarah Orne Jewett, *The Country of Pointed Firs and Other Stories* (New York: Signet Classics, 2009), 1. On the relationship between Jewett and Fields, see Heather Love, *Feeling Backward: Loss and the Politics of Queer History* (Cambridge: Harvard University Press, 2009), 92.

40. Lura Beam, *Bequest from a Life: A Biography of Louise Stevens Bryant* (Baltimore: Waverly Press, 1963), 133.

41. Beam, 135.

42. Jonathan Ned Katz contends "[t]he term [situational homosexuality] is fallacious, if it implies that there is some 'true' homosexuality which is *not* situated. All homosexuality is situational, influenced and given meaning and character by its location in time and social space." Jonathan Ned Katz, *Gay American History: Lesbians and Gay Men in the USA* (New York: Crowell, 1976), 11. Vernon Rosario also discounts the study of situational homosexuality entirely, contending that sexuality studies has virtually no interest "merely in any same-sex sexual activity (for example . . . 'situational' homosexuality . . .)." Instead, he writes, "It is the more elusive issue of same-sex desire or sexual orientation. . . . that is the matter of concern." Vernon A. Rosario, "Homosexual Bio-Histories: Genetic Nostalgias and the Quest for Paternity," in *Science and Homosexualities*, ed. Vernon A. Rosario (New York: Routledge, 1997), 7. Katz, Rosario, and, as I will argue later, George Chauncey fail to recognize situational homosexuality as a historically specific term that is part of the history of sexuality, whether or not it fits into their respective political programs. I see situational homosexuality as a tool for exploring what David Halperin calls "the irreducible definitional uncertainty about what homosexuality itself really is" (*How to Do*, 105).

43. George Chauncey, *Gay New York: Gender, Urban Culture, and the Making of the Gay Male World, 1890–1940* (New York: Basic Books, 1994), 3.

44. While Chauncey includes a discussion of "trade," he is careful to mark them as not part of the gay world: "The most striking difference between the dominant sexual culture of the early twentieth century and that of our own era is the degree to which the earlier culture permitted men to engage in sexual relations with other men, often on regular basis, without requiring them to regard themselves—or to be regarded by others—as gay." Chauncey, 65.

45. Chauncey claims that "gender status superseded homosexual interest as the basis of sexual classification in working-class culture" until World War II. Chauncey, 87. While the prominence of gender in this early twentieth-century narrative is deserved, one of its side effects has been that certain kinds of homosexual interests have received too little attention.

46. Chauncey, 91. The data set of Wooden and Parker on which Chauncey bases his claim that situational homosexuality is culturally blind dates from 1979 and 1980, significantly after the period and sexual shifts

under discussion here and in Chauncey's work. Wayne S. Wooden and
Jay Parker, *Men Behind Bars: Sexual Exploitation in Prison* (New York and
London: Plenum Press, 1982). Chauncey replicates Wooden's and Parker's
assumption that sex in prison has remained "relatively unchanged" for
the past 150 years. Wooden and Parker, 205. What is striking to me about
Wooden and Parker's data is that of the self-identified heterosexual men
surveyed, 55 percent engaged in some form of male-male sexual activity.
While the disparity between white men (38 percent) and black men (about
81 percent) suggests, as Chauncey does, the strong pull of the importation model [cultural specificity], I would contend that the total percentage
(55 percent) suggests the power of environmental factors, or what Wooden
and Parker call the deprivation model. That is, while some subjects are
more likely, more congenitally disposed to homosexuality, or more culturally inculcated against the taboos of homosexuality, a huge percentage
engage in homosexuality in the absence of women. Where Chauncey only
emphasizes the importation model when he calls situational homosexuality blind, Wooden and Parker emphasize the work of both—"[t]he results
of our study demonstrate that both these processes [deprivation and im-
portation] are at work in this prison setting" (44). Chauncey's underesti-
mation of the deprivation model extends outside his work on prisoners to
encompass seamen, hoboes, and transient laborers who, he argues, chose
"the road or . . . sea" out of a "desire to live in a social milieu" accepting of
homosexual relations rather than understanding these travelling sociali-
ties as helping to generate this milieu. Chauncey, 91.

47. Henning Bech evocatively describes this model and suggests instead that
"situational homosexuality" emerges from emotional deprivation and
insecurity. Henning Bech, *When Men Meet: Homosexuality and Modernity*
(Chicago: University of Chicago Press, 1997), 17–22. See also Jane Ward,
*Not Gay: Sex Between Straight White Men* (New York: New York University
Press, 2015), 99–107.

48. Stella Browne, *The Sexual Variety and Variability Among Women and Their
Bearing Upon Social Reconstruction* (London: C. W. Beaumont: 1915), 11.

49. George Orwell, *Down and Out in Paris and London* (New York: Harcourt
Brace Javanovich, 1961), 147.

50. Richard von Krafft-Ebing, *Psychopathia Sexualis: With Especial Reference to
the Antipathic Sexual Instinct*, trans. Franklin S. Klaf (New York: Stein and
Day, 1965), 188. Another tramp in Josiah Flynt's essay "Homosexuality
among Tramps" comments that he has sex with boys "'Cause there ain't
women enough. If I can't get them I've got to have the other." Josiah
Flynt, "Homosexuality among Tramps," in Havelock Ellis and John Addington Symonds, *Sexual Inversion: A Critical Edition*, ed. Ivan Crozier (New
York: Palgrave, 2008), 298.

51. Guy Hocquenghem, *Homosexual Desire*, trans. Daniella Dangoor (Durham: Duke University Press, 1993), 141, 113. For an economic theory of

sexuality, albeit a controversial one, see Richard A. Posner, *Sex and Reason* (Cambridge: Harvard University Press, 1992).

52. Quoted in Sinfield, 11. As Sinfield notes, the letter was likely written by Havelock Ellis's wife, the playwright Edith Ellis. She had a number of same-sex relationships.

53. Heather Love, "Made for TV," in "Virtual Roundtable on *Orange is the New Black*," *Public Books*, May 15, 2014. http://www.publicbooks.org/virtual -roundtable-on-orange-is-the-new-black/.

54. Regina Kunzel, *Criminal Intimacy: Prison and the Uneven History of Modern American Sexuality* (Chicago: University of Chicago Press, 2008), 102. While Kunzel dates the term "situational homosexuality" to the 1940s, I understand the concept to emerge much earlier (as I demonstrate later in the chapter) and thus use the term more broadly.

55. See Krafft-Ebing, 188; and Estelle B. Freedman, "The Prison Lesbian: Race, Class, and the Construction of the Aggressive Female Homosexual, 1915– 1965," in *Feminism, Sexuality, and Politics* (Chapel Hill: University of North Carolina Press, 2006), 143.

56. Kunzel, "Situating Sex," 265; and Kunzel, *Criminal Intimacy*, 92. Situational homosexuality is crucial to understanding heterosexuality, particularly since its role as a pure drive that overcomes social taboos in a single-sex environment functions as the direct counterpart to "compulsory heterosexuality" (which is rooted in social pressure overpowering desire in a heterosocial environment). Adrienne Rich, "Compulsory Heterosexuality and Lesbian Existence," *Signs* 5.4 (1980): 631–60. See also Kadji Amin, *Disturbing Attachments: Gender, Modern Pederasty, and Queer History* (Durham: Duke University Press, 2017), 45–75.

57. While Kunzel mentions that situational homosexuality has been "occasionally buttressing . . . of a modern sexual system in the making," she does not take up this suggestion. Kunzel, "Situating Sex," 256.

58. Margot Canaday, *The Straight State: Sexuality and Citizenship in Twentieth-Century America* (Princeton: Princeton University Press, 2009), 98; and Michael Trask, *Cruising Modernism: Class and Sexuality in American Literature and Social Thought* (Ithaca: Cornell University Press, 2003), 3, 16, 24, 115. The novel *Goldie* (1933) asks, "was it the usual thing for perverts to be restless, to seek to unbind themselves from old places and old friends. [sic]" Kennilworth Bruce, *Goldie* (New York: William Godwin, 1933), 83.

59. Canaday, 41.

60. Canaday, 98.

61. Canaday, 15. On the association between deviance and mobility, see also Chad Heap, "The City as Sexual Laboratory: The Queer Heritage of the Chicago School," *Qualitative Sociology* 26.4 (2003): 457–487; Todd DePastino, *Citizen Hobo* (Chicago: University of Chicago Press, 2003); and Trask.

62. Chauncey, 70. For a different time line, see Barry Reay, *New York Hustlers: Masculinity and Sex in Modern America* (Manchester: Manchester Univer-

sity Press, 2010), which I discuss further in the afterword of this book. In Glenway Wescott's journals, a 1937 entry fascinatingly records this transition in process. Here, Wescott describes a friend who offers anecdotes "of sailor-prostitutes who pretend to be doing for pay what they also evidently enjoy. The one who, having taken some active part in their intercourse or perhaps merely manifested some enthusiasm, begged Jack not to tell any of his colleagues, who would not respect him if they knew, etc. An odd and (I fancy) a new morality: commercialization of one's sex more respectable than the free gift of it." Glenway Wescott, *Continual Lessons: The Journals of Glenway Wescott, 1937–1955*, ed. Robert Phelps with Jerry Rosco (New York: Farrar, Straus, and Giroux, 1990), 9.

63. Michael Moon, *A Small Boy and Others: Imitation and Initiation in American Culture from Henry James to Andy Warhol* (Durham: Duke University Press, 1998), 121–23.

64. Wolves were also called "husbands" and "jockers" and punks were also called "lambs," "kids," "road kids," "preshuns," and "gonsils." Chauncey, 87, 89. Colin R. Johnson, *Just Queer Folks: Gender and Sexuality in Rural America* (Philadelphia: Temple University Press, 2013), 90. For an important history of the word "gunsel"/"gonsil" in Dashiell Hammett's *The Maltese Falcon* (1929), see Martin J. Northrop, "Booked: Sexuality and Taste in American Crime Fiction," PhD diss., Fordham University, 2015.

65. Chauncey, 88.

66. Eve Kosofsky Sedgwick, *Epistemology of the Closet* (Berkeley and Los Angeles: University of California Press, 1990), 47.

67. The metaphor of "living a double life or, wearing a mask and taking it off" which "gay" men used to describe their lives (the metaphor of the "closet" was not in circulation prior to the 1960s) further links homosexuality and situational homosexuality. Chauncey, 6. Craig M. Loftin argues that "Situational passing as heterosexual—that is, wearing the mask— . . . provided gay people with the necessary security that *allowed* them to consciously identify as homosexual and participate in a subaltern, camouflaged gay public sphere." Loftin's claim here suggests that homosexuality was situational too. Craig M. Loftin, *Masked Voices: Gay Men and Lesbians in Cold War America* (Albany: SUNY Press, 2012), 11, his emphasis. On the earliest known usage of the term "closet," see Benjamin Kahan, "Ray Johnson's Anti-Archive: Blackface, Sadomasochism, and the Racial and Sexual Imagination of Pop Art," *Angelaki* 23.1 (2018): 71. For more on the metaphor of the mask, see Brian Glavey, *The Wallflower Avant-Garde: Modernism, Sexuality, and Queer Ekphrasis* (Oxford: Oxford University Press, 2016), 109–12.

68. Ralph Werther *Autobiography of an Androgyne*, ed. Scott Herring (New Brunswick: Rutgers University Press, 2008), 20–21.

69. Chauncey refers to "[t]he central position of the fairy in the dominant cultural conception of homosexuality." Chauncey, 91.

70. Chauncey, 21.
71. I borrow the terms "universalizing" and "minoritizing" from Sedgwick, *Epistemology*, 1.
72. On false homosexuality, see Magnus Hirschfeld, *The Homosexuality of Men and Women*, trans. Michael A. Lombardi-Nash (Amherst, NY: Prometheus Books, 2000), 352. On spurious homosexuality, see Havelock Ellis, *Studies in the Psychology of Sex*, vol. 2 (Philadelphia: F. A. Davis Co., 1928–1931), 85, 86. On pseudo-homosexuality, see Iwan Bloch, *The Sexual Life of Our Time in Its Relations to Modern Civilization*, trans. M. Eden Paul (London: Rebman Limited, 1909), 426.
73. Browne, 11; Ford, 443–44. For a longer history of the conceptual entwinement of counterfeiting and homosexuality, see Will Fisher, "Queer Money," *ELH* 66.1 (1999): 1–23. On lying and homosexuality in Countee Cullen's work, see Jeremy Braddock, "The Poetics of Conjecture: Countee Cullen's Subversive Exemplarity," *Calloo* 25.4 (2002): 1253, 1261.
74. Lillian Hellman, *Conversations with Lillian Hellman*, ed. Jackson R. Bryer (Jackson: University Press of Mississippi, 1986), 25, reprinted from Harry Gilroy, "The Bigger the Lie," *New York Times*, December 14, 1952. The substitution of adultery (that Martha was sleeping with Karen's fiancé Joe) in Hellman's rewrite *These Three* (1936) might bear out Hellman's contention that the play is less about lesbianism than about a lie. See Patricia White, "Reading the Code(s)," in *Uninvited: Classical Hollywood Cinema and Lesbian Representability* (Bloomington: University of Indiana Press, 1999); and Robert J. Corber, *Cold War Femme: Lesbianism, National Identity, and Cold War Cinema* (Durham: Duke University Press, 2011).
75. The idea that homosexuality in the play is a lie is also a part of its performance history, as Ann Revere, who played Martha Dobie in the original 1934 production, states that Martha was not a lesbian: "She and the other girl were just good friends, in my mind, nothing more. Under the stress, she cracks and thinks she is [a lesbian]." Quoted in Lillian Faderman, *Odd Girls and Twilight Lovers: A History of Lesbian Life in Twentieth-Century America* (New York: Penguin, 1992), 104.
76. Diana Fuss, *Identification Papers* (New York and London: Routledge, 1995), 107–12. On same-sex institutions as sites for the production of homosexuality, see Kunzel, "Situating Sex," 259.
77. Lillian Hellman, *Four Plays by Lillian Hellman: "The Children's Hour," "Days to Come," "The Little Foxes," "Watch on the Rhine"* (New York: Modern Library, 1942), 53, her emphasis.
78. Estelle Freedman's excellent essay on the prison lesbian and interracial desire suggests that in the early twentieth-century situational homosexuality was a tool for buttressing racial and eugenic distinctions as well as sexual ones. "Assigning the male aggressor role to black women," criminologists eroticized and cemented racial difference, understanding race to provide a substitute for gender (Freedman, 144). Lillian Hellman's *The*

*Children's Hour* renders race as gender as this strain of criminology did, but also as sexual precocity. In the 1811 Scottish court case, *Miss Marianne Woods and Miss Jane Pirie against Dame Helen Cumming Gordon*, on which Hellman bases her play, Jane Cumming, the granddaughter of Dame Gordon, who accused Woods and Pirie of lesbianism, is illegitimate and born in India. For additional interpretations of the racial configuration of prison lesbianism, see Ruth M. Alexander, *The "Girl Problem": Female Sexual Delinquency in New York, 1900–1940* (Ithaca and London: Cornell University Press, 1995), 91–97, esp. 92; and Sarah Potter, "'Undesirable Relations': Same-Sex Relationships and the Meaning of Sexual Desire at a Women's Reformatory During the Progressive Era," *Feminist Studies* 30.2 (2004): 394–415. For the published transcripts of the case see *Miss Marianne Woods and Miss Jane Pirie against Dame Helen Cumming Gordon*, ed. Jonathan Ned Katz (New York: Arno Press, 1975). See also Lillian Faderman, *Scotch Verdict* (New York: Columbia University Press, 1994), and see Lillian Faderman, *Surpassing the Love of Men: Romantic Friendship and Love Between Women from the Renaissance to the Present* (New York: Perennial Edition, 2001), 147–56. Cumming's perversion, associated with the East, ultimately leads to Woods and Pirie's victory in the case. Hellman reincarnates Cumming into a bad seed named Mary, translating racialized identity into manipulative and aggressive behavior as well as sexual knowledge, suggesting a racial underpinning in the play's representation of situational homosexuality.

79. The imprisonment of the queer protagonist of the contemporaneous novel *Goldie* (1933) accords with this pattern of desire: "it is certain that the experiences as a prisoner . . . accelerated his descent and fostered his degeneracy." Kennilworth Bruce, *Goldie* (New York: William Godwin, 1933), 74.

80. Freedman, 150. Werther frequently describes his homosexuality and in particular his relation to fellatio as one of addiction. Werther, 25.

81. I use the term "closet" here in a metaphorical rather than a historical sense. The idea of the closet was not in circulation during this period and would not become a metaphor for "gay" life until much later.

82. My thinking about such middle terms is indebted to Valerie Traub's enumeration of and call for differentiation between "sexual inclination, tendency, preference, predisposition, orientation, consciousness, subjectivity, self-perception, and sub-culture." Valerie Traub, "The Past is a Foreign Country? The Times and Spaces of Islamicate Sexuality Studies," in *Islamicate Sexualities: Translations across Temporal Geographies of Desire*, ed. Kathryn Babayan and Asfaneh Najmabadi (Cambridge: Harvard University Press, 2008), 20. In a 1937 entry in *Continual Lessons*, Glenway Wescott describes a man as "of bisexual habit." This strikes me as embodying precisely this middle ground between acts and identities that now seems foreign to our dominant modes of understanding sexuality. Wescott, 11.

Judith Butler, *Bodies that Matter: On the Discursive Limits of "Sex"* (New York: Routledge, 1993), especially 1–23.

83. Howard Chudacoff, *The Age of the Bachelor: Creating an American Subculture* (Princeton: Princeton University Press, 1999), 115–20; and Fuss, *Identification Papers*, 107–12.

84. Margaret Otis's 1913 article about cross-sex love and desire at a women's reform school offers a sexological description of a version of the transformation model: "One case is on record of a girl, constantly involved in these love affairs with the colored, who afterwards, on leaving the institution, married a colored man. This, however, is unusual, for the girls rarely have anything to do with the colored race after leaving the school." Here, the nameless woman seems more invested in the cross racial erotics than her peers "constantly involved in these love affairs"; her unusual attachment suggests that the institution reroutes her desire in relation to race if not also in relation to biological sex. Margaret Otis, "A Perversion Not Commonly Noted," *Journal of Abnormal Psychology* 8.2 (June-July 1913): 113–16.

85. Sedgwick, *Epistemology*, 19.

86. Sedgwick, *Epistemology*, 20; Edward J. Kempf, *Psychopathology* (St. Louis: C. V. Mosby Company, 1921), 477, my emphasis.

87. Kempf, 478.

88. Hellman, *Four Plays*, 79, her emphasis.

89. Hellman, *Four Plays*, 79.

90. Boredom is frequently cited as an impetus for situational homosexuality. Charles Ford attempts to combat the practice "with tiring, interesting activities." Ford, 448.

91. Mikko Tuhkanen, "'Breeding (and) Reading': Lesbian Knowledge, Eugenic Discipline, and *The Children's Hour*," *MFS* 48.4 (2002): 1004.

92. Hellman, *Four Plays*, 52.

93. Hellman, *Four Plays*, 52. William Roughead, *Bad Companions* (New York: Duffield and Green, 1931), 123.

94. Martha Vicinus, "Lesbian History: All Theory and No Facts or All Facts and No Theory?" *Radical History Review* 60 (1994): 71.

95. Hellman, *Four Plays*, 38.

96. Hellman, *Four Plays*, 14. I have silently removed the italics from the stage direction here. The nervousness here might be read to suggest a predisposition towards lesbianism.

97. Hellman, *Four Plays*, 21–22.

98. Michel Foucault, *The History of Sexuality*, vol. 1, *An Introduction*, trans. Robert Hurley (New York: Vintage Books, 1990), 43.

99. Elizabeth Kennedy's case study of a lesbian, Julia, living in South Dakota in the 1920s and 1930s supplements my claim that situational homosexuality is more important to the history of lesbianism than the historiography now suggests. "Neither Julia nor any of [her] partners was

ever interested in making their relationships more serious. In fact, she does not call them relationships or affairs, but 'escapades,' indicating their frivolity. . . . Julia did not consider most of these women lesbians, despite their sexual predilections nor did they consider themselves as such." Elizabeth Lapovsky Kennedy, "'But We Would Never Talk about It': The Structures of Lesbian Discretion in South Dakota, 1928–1933," in *Inventing Lesbian Cultures in America*, ed. Ellen Lewin (Boston: Beacon Press, 1996), 27–28.

100. Mary McCarthy, "Verification," Supreme Court of the State of New York, Testimony, New York, New York, 18 October 1980. Lillian Hellman Papers, Harry Ransom Center, the University of Texas at Austin, Box 78, Folder 4.

101. See, for example, Robert M. Kaus, "The Plaintiff's Hour," *Harper's Magazine* 266.1594 (March 1983): 14–16, 18; and Norman Mailer, "An Appeal to Lillian Hellman and Mary McCarthy," *New York Times Book Review* (May 11, 1980): 3, 33. For the most thorough description and discussion of the case, see Alan Ackerman, *Just Words: Lillian Hellman, Mary McCarthy, and the Failure of Public Conversation in America* (New Haven: Yale University Press, 2011).

102. For example, Hellman expresses her frustration about the global character of the charge to Barbara Epstein: "There is nothing wrong with Mary McCarthy or anybody else calling me a liar as long as they designate where I have lied. . . . But nowhere in the television program did she make any designation of where I lied, and the only designations I have heard since the lawsuit began are really rather comic." Lillian Hellman to Barbara Epstein, November 18, 1980, Lillian Hellman Papers, Harry Ransom Center, the University of Texas at Austin, Box 78, Folder 5.

103. While much has been written on the truths and fabrications of Hellman's memoirs, Deborah Nelson's exploration of Mary McCarthy's theory of the fact stands out as offering an extremely rich context for understanding McCarthy's charge, even as she does not discuss the Hellman trial. Deborah Nelson, *Tough Enough: Arbus, Arendt, Didion, McCarthy, Sontag, Weil* (Chicago: University of Chicago Press, 2017), 72–95.

104. Carol Brightman, *Writing Dangerously: Mary McCarthy and Her World* (New York: Clarkson Potter Publishers, 1992), 102.

105. William Styron to Lillian Hellman, 2 April 1980, Lillian Hellman Papers, Harry Ransom Center, the University of Texas at Austin, Box 78, Folder 5.

106. For a fascinating reading of the HUAC proceedings and Hellman's role in them, see Joseph Litvak, *The Un-Americans: Jews, the Blacklist, and Stoolpigeon Culture* (Durham: Duke University Press, 2009).

107. See, for example, "Lillian versus Mary," *Washington Star* (March 23, 1980); and James Walcott, "What Unbecomes a Legend Most?" *Village Voice* (March 3, 1980): 51.

108. D. A. Miller, "Anal Rope," *Representations* 32 (1990): 116, his emphasis.
109. Following Guy Hocquenghem, who understands homosexuality as "first of all a criminal category," we can see the girls' school as "a projection of . . . phantasies of homosexuality on to the microcosmic society." Hocquenghem, 67.
110. Kaus, 14. These trials also summon the shade of Oscar Wilde.
111. Hellman, *Four Plays*, 69. Interestingly, and I think misguidedly, several states have found that an imputation of homosexuality is no longer defamatory, in effect making such a charge libel-proof. David Kluft, "What is More Defamatory? A False Accusation of Homophobia or Homosexuality?" September 3, 2014, http://www.trademarkandcopyrightlawblog .com/2014/09/whatismore/.
112. The 1961 film version (dir. William Wyler) featured a courtroom scene that was cut from the film's final print. In that scene, a judge finds Karen and Martha guilty of "having had sinful sexual knowledge of one another." On this scene, see Vito Russo, *The Celluloid Closet: Homosexuality in the Movies* (New York: Harper and Row, 1987), 139.
113. Lady Gaga's "Born This Way" (2011) provides a popular example of the hegemony of the congenital. Gaga's song is itself an homage to Valentino's "I Was Born This Way" (1975), which carries the spirit of gay liberation and contains the lyrics: "I'm happy, I'm carefree and I'm gay / Yes I'm gay / Tain't a fault 'tis a fact / I was born this way." Valentino's song has been covered many times since.
114. Jeffrey M. Jones, "Majority in the US Now Say Gays and Lesbians Born, Not Made," *Gallup*, http://www.gallup.com/poll/183332/majority-say -gays-lesbians-born-not-made.aspx. For a more sophisticated look at contemporary sexual attitudes, see Julie. R. Arseneau, Patrick R. Grzanka, Joseph R. Miles, and Ruth E. Fassinger, "Development and Initial Validation of the Sexual Orientation Beliefs Scale (SOBS)," *Journal of Counseling Psychology* 60.3 (2013): 407–20.
115. Suzanna Danuta Walters, *The Tolerance Trap: How God, Genes, and Good Intentions are Sabotaging Gay Equality* (New York: New York University Press, 2014), 84. John D'Emilio, "Born Gay?" in *The World Turned: Essays on Gay History, Politics, and Culture* (Durham: Duke University Press, 2002), 154.

CHAPTER TWO

1. I adapt the idea of the open body from Ed Cohen, *A Body Worth Defending: Immunity, Biopolitics, and the Apotheosis of the Modern Body* (Durham: Duke University Press, 2009), 7; and Justine Morrison, *The Politics of Anxiety in Nineteenth Century American Literature* (Cambridge: Cambridge University Press, 2011), 2, 16.
2. David M. Halperin, *How to Do the History of Homosexuality* (Chicago: University of Chicago Press, 2002), 103.
3. Cesare Lombroso, *The Man of Genius* (London: Walter Scott, 1891), v.

4. Havelock Ellis, *The Problem of Race-Regeneration* (New York: Moffat, Yard, and Company, 1911); Caleb Williams Saleeby, *The Methods of Race-Regeneration* (New York: Moffat, Yard, and Company, 1911); Bénédict Augustin Morel, *Traité des Dégénérescences* (Paris: J. B. Baillière, 1857); and Emil Kraepelin, "On the Question of Degeneration by Emil Kraepelin (1908)," *History of Psychiatry* 18.3 (2007): 399–404. On atavism, see *Atavistic Tendencies: The Culture of Science in American Modernity* (Minneapolis: University of Minnesota Press, 2008). Krafft-Ebing and other sexologists also famously propound ideas about sexual degeneration. See Ralph M. Leck, *Vita Sexualis: Karl Ulrichs and the Origins of Sexual Science* (Urbana: University of Illinois Press, 2016), 141–79.

5. George M. Beard, *Sexual Neurasthenia: Its Hygiene, Causes, Symptoms, Treatment* (New York: E. B. Treat, 1884), 106.

6. Sarah Grand, "The New Aspect of the Woman Question," *North American Review* 158.448 (1894): 274. On sex transformation, see also Benjamin Kahan, "Queer Modernism," in *A Handbook of Modernism Studies*, ed. Jean-Michel Rabaté (Wiley-Blackwell, May 2013), 355–56.

7. Joanne Meyerowitz, *How Sex Changed: A History of Transsexuality in the United States* (Cambridge: Harvard University Press, 2002), 5. On Carpenter, Hirschfeld, and Ulrichs, see George Chauncey, "From Sexual Inversion to Homosexuality: Medicine and the Changing Conceptualization of Female Deviance," *Salmagundi* 58/59 (1982–1983): 133.

8. Julian Gill-Peterson, "Implanting Plasticity into Sex and Trans/Gender," *Angelaki* 22.2 (2017): 51–52. See also Chandak Sengoopta, *The Most Secret Quintessence of Life: Sex, Glands, and Hormones, 1850–1950* (Chicago: University of Chicago Press, 2006).

9. Thomas Laqueur, *Making Sex: Body and Gender from the Greeks to Freud* (Boston: Harvard University Press, 1990); Greta LaFleur, *The Natural History of Sexuality in Early America* (Baltimore: Johns Hopkins University Press, 2018); Felicity Nussbaum, *Torrid Zones: Maternity, Sexuality, and Empire in Eighteenth-Century English Narratives* (Baltimore: Johns Hopkins University Press, 1995); Katy L. Chiles, *Transformable Race: Surprising Metamorphosis in the Literature of Early America* (Oxford: Oxford University Press, 2013); Andrew Curran, *Anatomy of Blackness* (Baltimore: Johns Hopkins University Press, 2011); Mary Floyd-Wilson, *English Ethnicity and Race in Early Modern Drama* (Cambridge: Cambridge University Press, 2003); and Roxann Wheeler, *The Complexion of Race: Categories of Difference in Eighteenth-Century British Culture* (Philadelphia: University of Pennsylvania Press, 2000). For a good introduction to humoral theory, see Noga Arikha, *Passions and Tempers: A History of the Humours* (New York: Ecco, 2007).

10. Susan Scott Parrish, *American Curiosity: Cultures of Natural History in the Colonial British Atlantic World* (Chapel Hill: The University of North Carolina Press, 2006), 79.

11. Wheeler, 23, 21–22.

12. For example, I think that Howard Chiang's assessment that sexology

"reinforce[s]" Laqueur's "two-sex model . . . by adhering to a binary op-
positional system for both sex and gender" simplifies the range of debate
and underestimates the continued prominence of the one-sex model (in
which men and women were not opposites or counterparts, but versions
of the same sex with different humoral compositions). Howard H. Chiang,
"Liberating Sex, Knowing Desire: *Scientia Sexualis* and Epistemic Turning Points in the History of Sexuality," *History of the Human Sciences* 23.5
(2010): 46.

13. Iwan Bloch, *Marquis de Sade's Anthropologia Sexualis of 600 Perversions, 120
    Days of Sodom; or, the School of Libertinage* (New York: Falstaff Press, 1934).
14. For a biographical account of Mann's same-sex desire, see Ronald Hay-
    man, *Thomas Mann: A Biography* (New York: Scribner, 1995).
15. While this chapter argues that Mann's *Death in Venice* is something like
    a death rattle of humoralism, humoralism actually extends even further
    into the twentieth century. Nicola Pende, for example, combines humoral-
    ism with endocrinology in *Constitutional Inadequacies: An Introduction to
    the Study of Abnormal Constitutions*, trans. Sante Naccarati (Philadelphia:
    Lea and Febiger, 1928). For more on Pende and his humoralism, see Fran-
    cesco Cassata, *Building the New Man: Eugenics, Racial Science, and Genetics
    in Twentieth-Century Italy*, trans. Erin O'Loughlin (Central European Uni-
    versity Press, 2011); and Marius Turda and Aaron Gillette, *Latin Eugenics in
    Comparative Perspective* (New York: Bloomsbury, 2014).
16. I agree with Jana Funke that "the relation between anthropological and
    sexological knowledge in the late nineteenth and early twentieth cen-
    tury . . . has not been explored in sufficient detail." Jana Funke, "Navigat-
    ing the Past: Sexuality, Race, and the Uses of the Primitive in Magnus
    Hirschfeld's *The World Journey of a Sexologist*," in *Sex, Knowledge, and the Re-
    ceptions of the Past*, ed. Kate Fisher and Rebecca Langlands (Oxford: Oxford
    University Press, 2015). See also Andrew P. Lyons and Harriet D. Lyons,
    *Irregular Connections: A History of Anthropology and Sexuality* (Lincoln:
    University of Nebraska Press, 2004); and *A Global History of Sexual Science*,
    ed. Veronika Fuechtner, Douglas E. Haynes, and Ryan M. Jones (Berkeley:
    University of California Press, 2018).
17. Bloch, 267. Felix Bryk echoes Bloch's position, contending "Woman
    everywhere remains woman, and man remains man, independent of
    color, of skin and race, white or black, yellow or copper red. . . ." Felix
    Bryk, *Voodoo-EROS*, trans. Mayne F. Sexton (New York: privately printed,
    1933), 16.
18. Bloch, 267.
19. Bloch, 266.
20. Iwan Bloch, *The Sexual Life of Our Time in Its Relations to Modern Civiliza-
    tion*, trans. M. Eden Paul (London: Rebman Limited, 1909), 456. Jay A.
    Gertzman has detailed the ways in which serious anthropological studies
    were sold as erotica. He describes how "anthropological" functions as a
    "code word" for "naked, libidinous natives and their curious customs." See

Jay A. Gertzman, *Bookleggers and Smuthounds: The Trade in Erotica, 1920–1940* (Philadelphia: University of Pennsylvania Press, 1999), 96. Similarly, Lisa Z. Sigel has described how the censorship of erotic postcards had different rules for white and nonwhite bodies: "Pubic hair, genitalia, and nipples could pass by the censors if the card portrayed a [']colonial['] or [']foreign['] subject. The censors even allowed images of naked men to pass if the subjects were 'natives.'" Lisa Z. Sigel, "Filth in the Wrong People's Hands: Postcards and the Expansion of Pornography in Britain and the Atlantic World, 1880–1914," *Journal of Social History* 33.4 (2000): 861. For more on the connection between anthropology and pornography, see Irvin C. Schick, *The Erotic Margin: Sexuality and Spatiality in Alterist Discourse* (New York: Verso, 1999), 77–103.

21. Havelock Ellis and John Addington Symonds, *Sexual Inversion: A Critical Edition*, ed. Ivan Crozier (New York: Palgrave, 2008), 112.

22. Iwan Bloch, *Anthropological Studies in the Strange Sexual Practices of All Races in All Ages*, trans. Keene Wallis (New York: Anthropological Press, 1933), 26.

23. Eugen Steinach, *Sex and Life: Forty Years of Biological and Medical Experiments* (New York: Viking Press, 1940), 113. In his *The Memoirs of a Sexologist*, Lenz similarly speaks of sexual development "in our latitudes," suggesting alternative sexual developments in other latitudes. Ludwig L. Lenz, *The Memoirs of a Sexologist: Discretion and Indiscretion* (New York: Cadillac Publishing Co, 1954), 128.

24. Auguste Forel, *The Sexual Question: A Scientific, Psychological, Hygienic, and Sociological Study* (Brooklyn, NY: Physicians and Surgeons Book Company, 1931), 189.

25. G. Frank Lydston posits that "The influence of climate upon sexual function has a powerful bearing not only on the negro race, but upon the Caucasian." In particular, he attributes the "frequency of rape by negroes" to the South's warm climate. Hunter McGuire and G. Frank Lydston, *Sexual Crimes Among the Southern Negroes, Scientifically Considered: An Open Correspondence Between Hunter McGuire and G. Frank Lydston* (Louisville, KY: Renz and Henry, 1893), 18, 17.

26. Charles de Montesquieu, *The Spirit of the Laws*, ed. Anne M. Cohler, Basia C. Miller, and Harold S. Stone (Cambridge: Cambridge University Press, 1989), 271. For more on Burton's relation to earlier climatic theories see Joanna de Groot, "Hybridizing Past, Present, and Future: Reflections on the 'Sexology' of R. F. Burton," in *Sex, Knowledge, and Receptions of the Past*, ed. Kate Fisher and Rebecca Langlands (Oxford: Oxford University Press, 2015), 151.

27. Robert Tobin, *Warm Brothers: Queer Theory and the Age of Goethe* (Philadelphia: University of Pennsylvania Press, 2000); and Robert Beachy, *Gay Berlin: Birthplace of a Modern Identity* (New York: Knopf, 2014), xi. The figure of the "warm brothers" that Tobin charts might suggest more generally

the relation between climate and sexuality over the *longue durée*. On warm brothers, see also Alice A. Kuzniar, "Introduction," in *Outing Goethe and His Age* (Palo Alto: Stanford University Press, 1996), 8–9.

28. Victor Segalen, *Essay on Exoticism: An Aesthetics of Diversity* (Durham: Duke University Press, 2002), 13.

29. Quoted in Iwan Bloch, *Anthropological and Ethnological Studies in the Strangest Sex Acts in Modes of Love of All Races Illustrated*, trans. Ernst Vogel (New York: Falstaff Press, 1935), 188.

30. James Joyce, *Ulysses*, ed. Hans Walter Gabler (New York: Vintage, 1986), 520.

31. Quoted in Robert Aldrich, *Colonialism and Homosexuality* (New York: Routledge, 2003), 322.

32. Nancy Mitford, *Love in a Cold Climate* (New York: Vintage, 2010), 27.

33. This chapter was the inspiration for my essay "Conjectures on the Sexual World-System" and I would suggest that it is possible to understand Burton as a theorist of the sexual world-system with the "wrong" principle of organization, one that took hold for about half a century. That is to say, Burton imagines an earlier sexual world-system organized by climate rather than by the homo/hetero binary. Benjamin Kahan, "Conjectures on the Sexual World-System," *GLQ* 23.3 (2017): 327–57. On climate over the *longue durée*, see Ferdinand Braudel, *The Mediterranean and the Mediterranean World in the Age of Philip II*, trans. Siân Reynolds (New York: Harper and Row, 1972).

34. On the relation between Lesbos and lesbianism, see David M. Halperin, *How to Do the History of Homosexuality* (Chicago: University of Chicago Press, 2002), 48–80. On buggering and Bulgaria, see Havelock Ellis, *Studies in the Psychology of Sex*, vol. 2 (Philadelphia: F. A. Davis Co., 1928–1931), 4; and Edward Carpenter, *Intermediate Types among Primitive Folk: A Study in Social Evolution* (London: George Allan & Co., 1914), 50. See also Kaier Curtin, *"We Can Always Call Them Bulgarians": The Emergence of Lesbian and Gay Men on the American Stage* (Boston: Alyson Publications, 1987). Pederasty as the "Greek Way" and Bohemia as connected to free love and homosexuality might provide other geographic examples. On the relation between Greece and pederasty, see K. J. Dover, *Greek Homosexuality* (Cambridge: Harvard University Press, 1989), 201n9. On Bohemia, see Chad Heap, *Slumming: Sexual and Racial Encounters in American Nightlife, 1885–1940* (Chicago: University of Chicago Press, 2009), 65.

35. Bloch, *Anthropological and Ethnological Studies*, 61. Todd Shepard notes the conceptual linkage of climate and sodomy in the Maghreb as late as 1960. Todd Shepard, "'Something Notably Erotic': Politics, 'Arab Men,' and Sexual Revolution in Post-decolonization France, 1962–1974," *Journal of Modern History* 84.1 (2012): 87.

36. Bloch, *Anthropological and Ethnological Studies*, 61.

37. Nussbaum, 95.

38. Richard F. Burton, "Terminal Essay," in *The Book of a Thousand Nights and a Night: A Plain and Literal Translation of the Arab Nights Entertainments*, trans. Richard F. Burton (London: Burton Club, 1886), vol. 10, 206–7.

39. On the relation between monogeny and polygeny, see Siobhan Somerville, *Queering the Color Line: Race and the Invention of Homosexuality in American Culture* (Durham: Duke University Press, 2000), 22–23.

40. M. F. Ashley Montagu, *Man's Most Dangerous Myth: The Fallacy of Race* (New York: Columbia University Press, 1942), 38. For more on race in the Sotadic Zone, see Anjali Arondekar, *For the Record: On Sexuality and the Colonial Archive in India* (Durham: Duke University Press, 2009), 45–47; and Neville Hoad, "Arrested Development or the Queerness of Savages: Resisting Evolutionary Narratives of Difference," *Postcolonial Studies* 3.2 (2000): 138–39.

41. I use the more familiar title *"The Arabian Nights"* rather than Burton's actual title *The Book of a Thousand Nights and a Night: A Plain and Literal Translation of the Arab Nights Entertainments* here.

42. Bloch, *Anthropological Studies*, v, 38.

43. Bloch, *Anthropological Studies*, 29. In 1920, Paul Kammerer and Eugen Steinach attempted to provide a biological basis for anthropological research about climate in their essay "Climate and Puberty." Conducting experiments on rats reared in high temperatures, the authors found that the "heat rats" experienced exaggerated development of sexual organs, earlier mating, and increased intensity of sex drive. The authors argued that, as Cheryl A. Logan phrases it, "racial differences were due to heat, to torrid tropical climates" and not to due to a genetic understanding of race. Cheryl A. Logan, *Hormones, Heredity, Race: Spectacular Failure in Interwar Vienna* (New Brunswick: Rutgers University Press, 2013), 68. These endo-crinological experiments offer another example of the historical hinge between the open (environmental) body and the closed (biological) body. I am grateful to Kadji Amin for this last point.

44. Bloch, *Anthropological Studies*, 30. For Bloch, the nakedness enabled by the hot weather also incites desire. Bloch, *Anthropological Studies*, 182.

45. Bloch, *Anthropological Studies*, 56.

46. Bloch, *Anthropological Studies*, 30.

47. Bloch, *Anthropological Studies*, 30. In the novel *Goldie* (1933), a jockey attri-butes his homosexuality to "the constant friction." A doctor tells him, "It will wear anything out, even a person's manhood." Kennilworth Bruce, *Goldie* (New York: William Godwin, 1933), 232.

48. Like Bloch's idea of sexuality rooted in an increasing need for variety, Forel similarly notes a "desire for change." Quoted in Michael Trask, *Class and Sexuality in American Literature and Social Thought* (Ithaca: Cornell University Press, 2003), 30.

49. This myth extends from at least the eighteenth century and may have earlier roots in the seventeenth century. See Marc Epprecht, *Heterosexual*

*Africa? The History of an Idea from the Age of Exploration to the Age of AIDS* (Athens: Ohio University Press, 2008), 43–44; and Luiz Mott, "Historical Roots of Homosexuality in the Lusophone Atlantic," in *Cultures of the Lusophone Black Atlantic*, ed. Nancy Priscilla Naro, Roger Sansi-Roca, and David H. Treece (New York: Palgrave, 2007), 75–76.

50. Bloch, *Anthropological Studies*, 32.
51. Bloch, *Anthropological Studies*, 32.
52. John Addington Symonds, *A Problem in Modern Ethics* (London: Forgotten Books, 2012), 80.
53. Symonds, 81.
54. John Aberth, *The Black Death: The Great Mortality of 1345–1350: A Brief History with Documents* (New York: Palgrave, 2005), 52.
55. Peter Baldwin, *Contagion and the State in Europe, 1830–1930* (Cambridge: Cambridge University Press, 1999), 3.
56. My reading builds here on Peta Mitchell's analysis of contagion in *Death in Venice*; see Peta Mitchell, *Contagious Metaphor* (London: Bloomsbury, 2012), 37–58. See also Carlo Cipolla, *Miasmas and Disease: Public Health and the Environment in the Pre-Industrial Age*, trans. Elizabeth Potter (New Haven: Yale University Press, 1992); and Jonathan Gil Harris, *Sick Economies: Drama, Mercantilism, and Disease in Shakespeare's England* (Philadelphia: University of Pennsylvania Press, 2004).
57. For a historical overview of the difficulties of germ theory's acceptance in the US context, see Nancy Tomes, *The Gospel of Germs: Men, Women, and the Microbe in American Life* (Cambridge: Harvard University Press, 1998).
58. Priscilla Wald, *Contagious: Cultures, Carriers, and the Outbreak Narrative* (Durham: Duke University Press, 2008), 2.
59. Wald, 2.
60. Thomas Mann, *Death in Venice and Other Tales*, trans. Joachim Neugroschel (New York: Penguin, 1999), 343. All other citations will be made in the text.
61. This contention finds additional support in Robert Tobin's reading of the relation between the words *Weltverkehr* and *Verkehr* in the passage where Aschenbach decides to travel. I mean this reading to encompass also the possibility that Aschenbach's secret is that of homosexuality. Robert Tobin, *Peripheral Desires: The German Discovery of Sex* (Philadelphia: University of Pennsylvania Press, 2015), 198.
62. My reading of this passage dovetails with Tobin's reading of the same passage. See Tobin, 202.
63. Burton, 248, 247, 246. On health and sexuality, see Vivian Pollack, "'Bringing help for the sick': Whitman and Prophetic Biography," in *Leaves of Grass: The Sesquicentennial Essays*, ed. Susan Belasco, Ed Folsom, and Kenneth M. Price (Lincoln: University of Nebraska Press, 2007), 244–65.

64. The only location where the geographies of Burton and Mann do not overlap substantially is in Burton's vision of the New World, which he emphasizes as being an "established racial institution" rather than being governed by the climatic logics that I am interested in here.

65. Quoting Sade approvingly, Bloch writes: "'The soft, effeminizing air' of Venice equally reflects the sexual pleasures of the Venetians." Bloch, *Marquis de Sade's Anthropologia Sexualis*, 269.

66. The scholarship on cholera is vast. For a popular account, see S. L. Kotar and J. E. Gessler, *Cholera: A Worldwide History* (New York: McFarland, 2014). For an account of cholera in Italy, see Frank M. Snowden, *Naples in the Time of Cholera, 1884–1911* (Cambridge: Cambridge University Press, 1995).

67. Frank Mort, *Dangerous Sexualities: Medico-Moral Politics in England Since 1830* (New York: Routledge, 1987), 12.

68. Mort, 12.

69. Mort, 12.

70. Bloch, *The Sexual Life of Our Time*, 475.

71. A character in *A Scarlet Pansy* (1932) understands disease to have caused his sexual abnormality: "I was brought up right, exactly as the doctors and psychologists specified. I was a he-man [sexually normal and virile] once. Yet look what happened. After having grip, complicated by pneumonia, and then meningitis, I was a different person; there was some inner change." Robert Scully, *A Scarlet Pansy*, ed. Robert J. Corber (New York: Fordham University Press, 2016), 166.

72. My thinking here is indebted to Michel Foucault, *The Birth of the Clinic: An Archaeology of Medical Perception*, trans. Alan Sheridan (New York: Vintage, 1994), 3.

73. Michel Foucault, *The History of Sexuality*, vol. 1, *An Introduction*, trans. Robert Hurley (New York: Vintage Books, 1990), 157.

74. The metaphoric criminality of "like a fugitive" further strengthens the ties between disease and homosexuality as homosexuality was associated with criminality since it was illegal under Paragraph 175.

75. Max Nordau, *Degeneration* (Lincoln: University of Nebraska, 1993).

76. On wanderlust, see Ian Hacking, *Mad Travelers: Reflections on the Reality of Transient Mental Illnesses* (Charlottesville: University of Virginia Press, 1998).

77. Charles Davenport, *The Feebly Inhibited; Nomadism, or the Wandering Impulse, with Special Reference to Heredity* (Washington, DC: Carnegie Institution of Washington, 1915), 26.

78. Davenport, 25.

79. On Mahler's relation to *Death in Venice*, see Hans Rudolf Vaget, "Film and Literature: The Case of 'Death in Venice': Luchino Visconti and Thomas Mann," *German Quarterly* 53.2 (1980): 165–66.

80. Davenport, 13. This association between licentious sexuality and va-

grancy dates, as Sarah Nicolazzo demonstrates, at least back to the eighteenth century. Sarah Nicolazzo, "Henry Fielding's *The Female Husband* and the Sexuality of Vagrancy," *Eighteenth Century* 55.4 (2014): 335–53.

81. P. R. Vessie, "The Wanderlust Impulse," *Medical Journal and Record* (July 2, 1924): 20.

82. Robert E. Park, Ernest W. Burgess, and Roderick Duncan McKenzie, *The City* (Chicago: University of Chicago Press, 1925), 158.

83. Tobin, 190.

84. Tobin, 194–95. In many respects, the sartorial features of this set resemble the costumes of gondoliers (and one of the men in the text possessing these characteristics is a gondolier). Gondoliers, as Ian Littlewood explains, "were the staple fare of tourists in search of sexual adventure." Ian Littlewood, *Sultry Climes: Travel and Sex Since the Grand Tour* (London: John Murray, 2001), 80.

85. Outside of the world of the text, cholera tends to be transmitted via contaminated water or food rather than from one person to another.

86. While this book is concerned with etiologies of sexuality, I also want to leave open the possibility that it might model a mode of etiological reading that is applicable to other objects (with disease and race furnishing two possibilities that I begin to explore in this chapter).

87. David M. Halperin, *One Hundred Years of Homosexuality and Other Essays on Greek Love* (New York: Routledge, 1990), 35. It might also suggest that Aschenbach's desire is infused with another minor perversion, "Pygmalionism," which is Havelock Ellis's term for "the sexual attraction of statues." Havelock Ellis, *Psychology of Sex: A Manual for Students* (New York: Emerson Books, 1937), 74. On this minor perversion, see Benjamin Kahan, "The First Sexology? Heinrich Kaan's *Psychopathia Sexualis* (1844)," in Heinrich Kaan, *Heinrich Kaan's "Psychopathia Sexualis" (1844)* (Ithaca: Cornell University Press, 2016), 23.

88. Halperin, *One Hundred Years*, 35.

89. Jeffrey Masten, *Queer Philologies: Sex, Language, and Affect in Shakespeare's Time* (Philadelphia: University of Pennsylvania Press, 2016), 172. In another passage from the story, Aschenbach is "deeply thrilled . . . that his interest and attention were not entirely unrequited": "What, for example, induced the beauty when he appeared on the beach in the morning, to stop using the boardwalk behind the cabins and to walk only in front, over the sand, past Aschenbach's domicile, sometimes so unnecessarily close to the writer, almost brushing his table, his chair, as the boy sauntered toward his family's cabana" (339).

90. See, for example, Stephen O. Murray and Will Roscoe, "Africa and African Homosexualities: An Introduction," in *Boy-Wives and Female Husbands: Studies of African Homosexualities*, ed. Stephen O. Murray and Will Roscoe (New York: St. Martin's Press, 1998), 6–9; and Sedgwick, *Epistemology*, 159n32.

91. Mann's text underlines the importance of Venice's history in inspiring Aschenbach's desire to visit the city, calling it "A city that's irresistible to a man of culture—both for its history and for its present-day appeal!" (302).
92. Halperin, *One Hundred Years*, 30.
93. Murray and Roscoe, 6–9. Chauncey has argued the "Western" system largely did not apply to working-class and African American men until the 1930s (before that they operated under a system more proximate to the Mediterranean model). George Chauncey, *Gay New York: Gender, Urban Culture, and the Making of the Gay Male World, 1890–1940* (New York: Basic Books, 1994), especially 65–98.
94. Halperin, *One Hundred Years*, ix. As Jana Funke, Margot Canaday, and Naomi Wood have each noted, the words pederasty and homosexuality were often used interchangeably. Funke writes: "pederastic (man-boy) and homoerotic (man-man) desires often appear to be conflated in the nineteenth century." Jana Funke, "'We Cannot be Greek Now': Age Difference, Corruption of Youth, and the Making of Sexual Inversion," *English Studies* 94.2 (2013): 140. Margot Canaday, *The Straight State: Sexuality and Citizenship in Twentieth-Century America* (Princeton: Princeton University Press, 2009), 20. Naomi Wood, "Creating the Sensual Child: Paterian Aesthetics, Pederasty, and Oscar Wilde's Fairy Tales," *Marvels and Tales* 16.2 (2002): 157. See also J. Z. Eglinton, *Greek Love* (New York: Oliver Layton Press, 1964).
95. Kadji Amin, *Disturbing Attachments: Gender, Modern Pederasty, and Queer History* (Durham: Duke University Press, 2017), 10. Eng-Ben Lim similarly notes that "critical discourse . . . eschew[s] any significant study of homoeroticism as it pertains to boys." Eng-Ben Lim, *Brown Boys and Rice Queens: Spellbinding Performance in the Asias* (New York: New York University Press, 2013), 4.
96. Amin, 28, 38. For differences between ancient and modern pederasty in Paris, see William A. Peniston, *Pederasts and Others: Urban Culture and Sexual Identity in Nineteenth-Century Paris* (Binghamton, NY: Harrington Park Press, 2004), 109–26. For an overview of the nosography of modern pederasty, see Diederick F. Janssen, "'Chronophilia': Entries of Erotic Age Preference into Descriptive Psychopathology" *Medical History* 59.4 (2015): 575–98.
97. Foucault, *History*, 57.
98. Foucault, *History*, 62.
99. Foucault, *History*, 63.
100. Foucault, *History*, 71. Bloch reverses this hierarchy, suggesting that *ars erotica* bespeaks preeminence in *psychopathia sexualis*: "Among the Aryan races the Aryans of India must be considered pre-eminent as refined practitioners of psychopathia sexualis, which they have reduced to a system. In addition to recognizing forty-eight *figurae Veneris* (different

postures in sexual intercourse), they practise every possible variety of sexual perversion." Here, Bloch seems to conflate the sixty-four positions of the *Kamasutra* with the forty-eight Japanese "hands" or sexual positions. Bloch, *The Sexual Life of Our Time*, 468–69, his emphasis.

101. Sanjay K. Gautam, *Foucault and the Kamasutra* (Chicago: University of Chicago Press, 2016), 25.
102. Gautam, 25.
103. Alain Grosrichard, *The Sultan's Court: European Fantasies of the East* (New York: Verso, 1998), 118–19.
104. Grosrichard, 17.
105. Laura Hanft Korobkin, *Criminal Conversations: Sentimentality and Nineteenth-Century Legal Stories of Adultery* (New York: Columbia University Press, 1998), 40.
106. Sharon Marcus, *Between Women: Friendship, Desire, and Marriage in Victorian England* (Princeton: Princeton University Press, 2007), 3.
107. Nayan Shah, *Stranger Intimacy: Contesting Race, Sexuality, and the Law in the North American West* (Berkeley: University of California Press, 2011), 132.
108. On the United States age of consent, see Carolyn Cocca, *Jailbait: The Politics of Statutory Rape Laws in the United States* (Albany: SUNY Press, 2004), 9–28; and Philip Jenkins, *Moral Panic: Changing Concepts of the Child Molester in Modern America* (New Haven: Yale University Press, 1998), 24–26. On England's age of consent, see Funke, 144–47. The age of consent was also raised for girls (from ten to twelve) in British India in 1891. See Mrinalini Sinha, *Colonial Masculinity: The "Manly Englishman" and the "Effeminate Bengali" in the Late Nineteenth Century* (Manchester: Manchester University Press, 1995), 138–72.
109. Eithne Luibhéid, *Entry Denied: Controlling Sexuality at the Border* (Minneapolis: University of Minnesota Press, 2002), 40.
110. Gayatri Spivak, *A Critique of Postcolonial Reason: Toward a History of the Vanishing Present* (Cambridge: Harvard University Press, 1999), 287.
111. Joseph Boone, *The Homoerotics of Orientalism* (New York: Columbia University Press, 2014), 54.
112. Foucault, *History*, 30.
113. Foucault, *History*, 104.
114. On sexuality's relation to power and particularly the eroticization of power, see Alan Sinfield, *Sexuality and Power* (New York: Columbia University Press, 2004).
115. William N. Eskridge, Jr., *Dishonorable Passions: Sodomy Laws in America, 1861–2003* (New York: Viking, 2008), 54–55.
116. Jenkins, 35.
117. Charles Gilbert Chaddock, "Sexual Crimes," in *A System of Legal Medicine*, vol. 2, ed. Allan McLane Hamilton and Lawrence Godkin (New York: E. B. Treat, 1894), 543.

118. W. Travis Gibb, "Indecent Assault upon Children," in *A System of Legal Medicine*, vol. 1, ed. Allan McLane Hamilton and Lawrence Godkin (New York: E. B. Treat, 1894), 650.

119. Funke, 140, 141.

120. Funke, 146. For more on how Symonds and other sexologists navigated age-differentiated male-male sex, see Emma Heaney, "The New Woman: Sexology, Literary Modernism, and the Trans Feminine Remainder," *Genre* 48.1 (2015): 10.

121. Jay Grossman, "'The Evangel-Poem of Comrades and of Love': Revising Whitman's Republicanism," *ATQ* 4.3 (1990): 201–18; Jay Grossman, "Epilogue: Whitman's Centennial and the State of Whitman Studies," in *Breaking Bounds: Whitman and American Cultural Studies*, ed. Betsy Erkkila and Jay Grossman (Oxford: Oxford University Press, 1996), 251–64; Betsy Erkkila, *Mixed Bloods and Other Crosses: Rethinking American Literature from the Revolution to the Culture Wars* (Philadelphia: University of Pennsylvania Press, 2005), 131–54; Kevin P. Murphy, *Political Manhood: Red Bloods, Mollycoddles, and the Politics of Progressive Era Reform* (New York: Columbia University Press, 2008), 104–24; Robert Caserio, "Queer Modernism," in *The Oxford Handbook of Modernisms*, ed. Peter Brooker, Andrzej Gąsiorek, Deborah Longworth, and Andrew Thacker (Oxford: Oxford University Press, 2010), 199–217; Masten, *Queer Philologies*, 130.

122. Caserio, 207. On the relation between homosexuality and egalitarianism, see Michael Bibler, *Cotton's Queer Relations: Same-Sex Intimacy and the Literature of the Southern Plantation, 1936–1968* (Charlottesville: University of Virginia Press, 2009), 5–10.

123. This idea of consenting adults as constructed against unconsenting children is evident as early as 1917 when the prominent sexologist and birth control advocate William J. Robinson writes: "We maintain that the relations between two adult persons are the concern of those two adults and of nobody else. No third person and certainly no State has any right whatever to interfere in the sex relations of two adults persons. It is only where minors are concerned, or where force is used or where children are the result that the State has a right to step in." William J. Robinson, "Our Sexual Misery: Some Informal Remarks," *American Journal of Urology and Sexology* (1917): 243.

124. Valerie Traub, "The Past is a Foreign Country? The Times and Spaces of Islamicate Sexuality Studies," in *Islamicate Sexualities: Translations across Temporal Geographies of Desire*, ed. Kathryn Babayan and Asfaneh Najmabadi (Cambridge: Harvard University Press, 2008), 12.

125. This universality helps to explain why many people find asexuality baffling. On asexuality, see Benjamin Kahan, *Celibacies: American Modernism and Sexual Life* (Durham: Duke University Press, 2013), 142–54.

CHAPTER THREE

1.  Ralph Werther, *Autobiography of an Androgyne*, ed. Scott Herring (New Brunswick: Rutgers University Press, 2008), 20–21.
2.  Ralph Werther, *The Female-Impersonators* (New York: Arno Press, 1975), 208, 210–11.
3.  Oscar Wilde and others, *Teleny, or The Reverse of the Medal*, ed. Amanda Caleb (Kansas City: Valancourt Books, 2010), 120, 123, 121.
4.  Robert Scully, *A Scarlet Pansy*, ed. Robert J. Corber (New York: Fordham University Press, 2016), 165, 124. Likewise, the novel *Goldie* (1933) attributes magic powers to the novel's fairie protagonist Goldie, noting his possession of a "telepathic quality peculiar to perverts." Kennilworth Bruce, *Goldie* (New York: William Godwin, 1933), 177. Bayard Taylor's "Twin-Love" (1871) similarly features a telepathic queer connection between twins. I am grateful to Chris Looby for bringing this story to my attention. Bayard Taylor, "Twin-Love," in *"The Man Who Thought Himself a Woman" and Other Queer Nineteenth-Century Short Stories*, ed. Christopher Looby (Philadelphia: University of Pennsylvania, 2017), 159–74.
5.  Donald Vining, *A Gay Diary, 1933–1946* (New York: Masquerade Books, 1996), 127.
6.  Quoted in Genny Beemyn, *A Queer Capital: A History of Gay Life in Washington, DC* (New York: Routledge, 2014), 27. This quip echoes Robert McAlmon's *Distinguished Air* (1925), which is subtitled "Grim Fairy Tales" and portrays queer culture.
7.  George Chauncey, *Gay New York: Gender, Urban Culture, and the Making of the Gay Male World, 1890–1940* (New York: Basic Books, 1994), 237.
8.  Edward Carpenter, *The Psychology of the Poet Shelley* (London: George Allen & Unwin, 1925), 58, 99, 58.
9.  Andrew Elfenbein, *Romantic Genius: The Prehistory of a Homosexual Role* (New York: Columbia University Press, 1999), 203.
10. Elfenbein, 203.
11. Carpenter, *Psychology*, 106.
12. Carpenter, *Psychology*, 38.
13. Carpenter, *Psychology*, 38, 39.
14. Carpenter, *Psychology*, 40, 39.
15. Edward Carpenter, *Days with Walt Whitman: With Some Notes on His Life and Work* (New York: Macmillan, 1906), 65.
16. This is a point made by Joy Dixon as she suggests that Carpenter's racialized thinking here is underpinned by the evolutionary anthropology of Edward Burnett Tylor. Joy Dixon, "'Out of your clinging kisses . . . I create a new world': Sexuality and Spirituality in the Work of Edward Carpenter," in *The Ashgate Research Companion to Nineteenth-Century Spiritualism and the Occult*, ed. Tatiana Kontou and Sarah Willburn (New York: Routledge, 2012), 153–55.

17. On the complex and contested authorship of the posthumous *Magia Sexualis* (1931), see John Patrick Deveney, *Paschal Beverly Randolph: A Nineteenth-Century Black American Spiritualist, Rosicrucian, and Sex Magician* (Albany: State University of New York Press, 1997), 226–28.

18. Alan Bray, *Homosexuality in Renaissance England* (New York: Columbia University Press, 1982), 19.

19. Pamela Thurschwell, *Literature, Technology, and Magical Thinking, 1880–1920* (Cambridge: Cambridge University Press, 2001), 34. The discourse of mesmerism (which is similar to hypnotism) is eroticized within *The Bostonians* (1886) as well: "He [Basil Ransom] grew more impatient . . . at [Selah] Tarrant's grotesque manipulations, which he resented as much as if he himself had felt their touch, and which seemed a dishonour to the passive maiden [Verena Tarrant]." This passage offers a homoerotics of the hypnotic (Basil imagining Selah's hands on him) as well as the veiled suggestion of an incestuous violation of Verena's sexual purity. Henry James, *The Bostonians*, ed. Pierre A. Walker (New York: Modern Library 2003), 57. For another important text connecting hypnotism and sexuality, see J. W. Carhart, *Norma Trist; or Pure Carbon: A Story of the Inversion of the Sexes* (Austin, TX: Eugene von Boeckmann, 1895).

20. Andreas Sommer, "Psychical Research and the Origins of American Psychology: Hugo Münsterberg, William James and Eusapia Palladino," *History of the Human Sciences* 25.2 (2012): 26; Heather Wolffram, *The Stepchildren of Science: Psychical Research and Parapsychology in Germany, c. 1870–1939* (Amsterdam: Rodopi, 2009). In his *Sexual Pathology*, Magnus Hirschfeld refers to the power of "fetish magic." Magnus Hirschfeld, *Sexual Pathology: A Study of Derangements of the Sexual Instinct*, trans. Jerome Gibbs (New York: Emerson Books, 1947), 85.

21. Jodie Medd, *Lesbian Scandal and the Culture of Modernism* (New York: Cambridge University Press, 2012), 76, 77. On the association between lesbianism and the occult, see Benjamin Kahan, *Celibacies: American Modernism and Sexual Life* (Durham: Duke University Press, 2013), 39.

22. As late as 1944, the poet Robert Duncan could ask if homosexuality were "supernatural?" Robert Duncan, "The Homosexual in Society," *Politics* 1.7 (August 1944): 210.

23. Dixon, "'Out of your clinging kisses,'" 147.

24. On mesmerism and animal magnetism, see Laurie Garrison, *Science, Sexuality, and Sensation Novels: Pleasures of the Senses* (New York: Palgrave, 2011). On telepathy, see Thurschwell. On elective affinity, see Michael P. Bibler, "Masculine Sentiment, Racial Fetishism, and Same-Sex Desire in Antebellum Southern Literature," in *The Oxford Handbook to the Literature of the US South*, ed. Barbara Ladd and Fred Hobson (New York: Oxford University Press, 2016), 138–60. On spiritualism, see Joy Dixon, *Divine Feminine: Theosophy and Feminism in England* (Baltimore: Johns Hopkins University Press, 2001); Joy Dixon, "Sexology and the Occult: Sexuality and Subjectivity in Theosophy's New Age," *Journal of the History of Sexual-*

*ity* 7.3 (1997): 409–33; and Alex Owen, *The Darkened Room: Women, Power, and Spiritualism in Late Nineteenth Century England* (Chicago: University of Chicago Press, 1989). On witchcraft, see Retha Warnicke, *The Rise and Fall of Anne Boleyn: Family Politics at the Court of Henry VIII* (Cambridge: Cambridge University Press, 1991); and Gaston Dubois-Desaulle, *Bestiality: An Historical, Medical, Legal, and Literary Study* (Boston: Panurge Press, 1933), 57–65. On shamanism, see Peter E. Firchow, "Private Faces in Public Places: Auden's *The Orators*," *PMLA* 92 (1977): 253–72; and Douglas Mao, "A Shaman in Common: Lewis, Auden, and the Queerness of Liberalism," in *Bad Modernisms*, ed. Douglas Mao and Rebecca L. Walkowitz (Durham: Duke University Press, 2006), 206–37.

25. Michel Foucault, *The History of Sexuality*, vol. 1, *An Introduction*, trans. Robert Hurley (New York: Vintage Books, 1990), 106.

26. Foucault, *History*, 106, 105, 106.

27. Foucault, *History*, 108. For a historical elaboration of this argument, see Brian Connolly, *Domestic Intimacies: Incest and the Liberal Subject in Nineteenth-Century America* (Philadelphia: University of Pennsylvania Press, 2014), especially 15–18.

28. Foucault, *History*, 109, 108–9.

29. Ludwig von Reizenstein, *The Mysteries of New Orleans*, trans. and ed. Steven Rowan (Baltimore: Johns Hopkins University Press, 2002), xiii, xvii.

30. Reizenstein, xx, xxii.

31. Reizenstein, 488, 413.

32. Benjamin Kahan, "The First Sexology? Heinrich Kaan's *Psychopathia Sexualis* (1844)," in Heinrich Kaan, *Heinrich Kaan's "Psychopathia Sexualis" (1844)* (Ithaca: Cornell University Press, 2016), 21–22.

33. Reizenstein, 148. Another reason that the *OED*'s definitions of lesbian and lesbianism are not very good is because they were actively suppressed, as Charlotte Brewer has detailed. Charlotte Brewer, *Treasure House of the Language: The Living OED* (New Haven: Yale University Press, 2007), 49–50, 205. For a historically later example of another text that combines lesbianism, magic, and botany, see Archibald Clavering Gunter, *A Florida Enchantment* (New York: Home Publishing Company, 1892).

34. Reizenstein, 486.

35. Reizenstein, 416.

36. Bibler, 149.

37. Reizenstein, 82.

38. Reizenstein, 82. A similar simultaneity occurs in Goethe's novel when Eduard and Ottilie embrace each other: "And they were in each other's arms. It was impossible to tell who had embraced the other first." Johann Wolfgang von Goethe, *Elective Affinities*, trans. Elizabeth Mayer and Louise Bogan (Chicago: Henry Regnery Company, 1963), 100.

39. Reizenstein, 18.

40. Reizenstein, 13.

41. Reizenstein, 148.

42. Reizenstein, 148.
43. Reizenstein, 304, his emphasis.
44. Reizenstein, 13, my emphasis.
45. Reizenstein, 462.
46. Magic and chemistry share a history in alchemy.
47. L. Edward Purcell, "Trilby and Trilby-Mania: The Beginning of the Best-seller System," *Journal of Popular Culture* 11.1 (1977): 65.
48. Purcell, 69–71.
49. Purcell, 74; Mary Titus, "Cather's Creative Women and Du Maurier's Cozy Men: 'The Song of the Lark' and 'Trilby,'" *Modern Language Studies* 24.2 (1994): 28; Frank Luther Mott, *Golden Multitudes: The Story of Best Sellers in the United States* (New York: Macmillan, 1947), 189.
50. George Du Maurier, *Trilby* (New York: Oxford, 1998), 15.
51. Purcell, 71, 74.
52. Du Maurier, 15.
53. Emma V. Miller and Simon J. James, "A Body Undressed for Text: *Trilby* in Parts," *Feminist Theory* 17.1 (2016): 99.
54. Mott, 189.
55. Sigmund Freud, *Three Essays on the Theory of Sexuality*, trans. James Strachey (New York: Basic Books, 2000), 19.
56. Du Maurier, 65, 53.
57. Du Maurier, 13, 12.
58. Du Maurier, 12–13.
59. Du Maurier, 13.
60. Du Maurier, 65.
61. For important exceptions, see Eve Kosofsky Sedgwick, *Touching Feeling* (Durham: Duke University Press, 2003), 17–21; and David M. Halperin, "What is Sex For?" *Critical Inquiry* 43.1 (2016): 1–31.
62. Freud, 15.
63. Arnold I. Davidson, *The Emergence of Sexuality: Historical Epistemology and the Formation of Concepts* (Cambridge: Harvard University Press, 2004), 82.
64. Freud, 2.
65. Freud, 19.
66. For more on sexuality that does not aspire to normative sexual acts, see Kahan, *Celibacies*, 5.
67. Du Maurier, 43.
68. Du Maurier, 47.
69. Du Maurier, 48.
70. Foucault, *History*, 44.
71. Du Maurier, 49.
72. Sander Gilman, *The Jew's Body* (New York: Routledge, 1991), 189.
73. Du Maurier, 52.
74. Owen, 218.
75. Du Maurier, 299.

76. Du Maurier, 299.
77. Du Maurier, 299.
78. Du Maurier, 299, 300.
79. An extremely similar scene appears in Paschal Beverly Randolph's novel *Ravalette* (1863): "The command was heard. It came forth, touched the girl's hand, and instantly she was thrown into a profound trance, where another touch revived her, not to wakeful consciousness. Instead of this, she rose . . . approached several musical instruments in succession and played upon them most exquisitely. The thing touched her head, and she made love in the most tender terms to three gentleman in succession, declaring to each in turn that he was her 'eternal affinity,' and had been so from the foundation of the world. . . . The scene continued for at least two hours, at the end of which time Mai dismissed the thing and restored the girl, who was totally oblivious to all that had occurred." Paschal Beverly Randolph, *Ravalette: The Rosicrucian's Story* (Quakertown, PA: Philosophical Publishing Company, 1939), 234–35.
80. Hugh Urban, *Magia Sexualis: Sex, Magic, and Liberation in Modern Western Esotericism* (Berkeley: University of California Press, 2006), 55.
81. Deveney, 1-2.
82. Quoted in Deveney, 319. Randolph uses the term "SEXUAL SCIENCE" in 1873 while Bloch's usage does not occur until 1907. For an interesting history of the term "*Sexualwissenschaf*," see Kirsten Leng, *Sexual Politics and Feminist Science: Women Sexologists in Germany, 1900–1933* (Ithaca: Cornell University Press and Cornell University Library, 2018), 17–19.
83. Deveney, 163.
84. Quoted in Deveney, 316.
85. Paschal Beverly Randolph, *Dealings with the Dead* (Utica, NY: Published by M. J. Randolph, 1861–62), 50. On the complex publication history of *Dealings with the Dead*, see Deveney, 349–50.
86. Randolph, *Dealings*, 223, his emphasis.
87. Paschal Beverly Randolph, *Eulis! The History of Love, its Wondrous Magic, Chemistry, Rules, Laws, Moods and Rationale; Being the Third Revelation of Soul and Sex* (Toledo, OH: Randolph Publishing Company, 1896), 81.
88. Randolph, *Ravalette*, 156, his emphasis.
89. Paschal Beverly Randolph, *The Unveiling, Or What I Think of Spiritualism* (Newburyport: William H. Huse and Co., 1860), 46, his emphasis.
90. Randolph, *Eulis!*, 123; Deveney, 5.
91. Deveney, 218. Randolph's work contests the historical periodization that Annamarie Jagose draws in *Orgasmology*. Annamarie Jagose, *Orgasmology* (Durham: Duke University Press, 2012), 40–77. For more on the historical periodization of orgasm, see Benjamin Kahan, "Unqueerness," *Feminist Formations* 28.2 (2016): 162–68.
92. Like Randolph, the sex magician Aleister Crowley puts limitless faith in will. The central precept of his most important text *The Book of the Law* (1904) asserts: "Do what thou wilt" and the concept of Thelema (from the

Greek word for will) is at the core of his beliefs. Aleister Crowley, *The Book of the Law* (Boston: Red Wheel, 1976), 9.

93. Foucault, *History*, 71.

94. Quoted in Deveney, 313–14.

95. Patrick D. Bowen, *A History of Conversion to Islam in the United States*, vol. 1, *White American Muslims before 1975* (Boston: Brill, 2015), 65. Elsewhere Randolph will also refer to his key teachings as "The True Oriental Secret" and the "great Oriental Secret." Quoted in Deveney, 348.

96. Quoted in Christine Ferguson, *Determined Spirits: Eugenics, Heredity and Racial Regeneration in Anglo-American Spiritualist Writing, 1848–1930* (Edinburgh: Edinburgh University Press, 2012), 125.

97. Ferguson, 125.

98. Deveney, 160.

99. Quoted in David M. Halperin, *How to Do the History of Homosexuality* (Chicago: University of Chicago Press, 2002), 127.

100. Karl Heinrich Ulrichs, *The Riddle of "Man-Manly" Love: The Pioneering Work on Male Homosexuality*, vol. 2, trans. Michael A. Lombardi-Nash (New York: Prometheus Books, 1994), 436.

101. See Vern L. Bullough, "Introduction," in Karl Heinrich Ulrichs, *The Riddle of "Man-Manly" Love: The Pioneering Work on Male Homosexuality*, vol. 1, trans. Michael A. Lombardi-Nash (New York: Prometheus Books, 1994), 22; and Hubert Kennedy, "Karl Heinrich Ulrichs: First Theorist of Homosexuality," in *Science and Homosexualities*, ed. Vernon Rosario (New York: Routledge, 1997), 26–45.

102. Paschal Beverly Randolph, *The Grand Secret; Or, Physical Love in Health and Disease* in *Rosicrucianism in America*, ed. J. Gordon Melton (New York: Garland Publishing, 1990), 19–20.

103. The ill-fated progeny of Eduard and Charlotte that Eduard calls "the fruit of double adultery" likewise bears resemblance and/or blood relation to all four of the central characters, suggesting his possession of two fathers and two mothers.

104. Halperin, *How to Do*, 129.

105. Quoted in Halperin, *How to Do*, 129, his emphasis.

106. Randolph, *Dealings*, 138.

107. Randolph, *Eulis!*, 33.

CHAPTER FOUR

1. John D'Emilio, "Capitalism and Gay Identity," in *The Lesbian and Gay Studies Reader*, ed. Henry Abelove, Michèlle Aina Barale, and David M. Halperin (New York: Routledge, 1993).

2. Henry Abelove, "Some Speculations on the History of Sexual Intercourse during the Long Eighteenth Century in England," in *Deep Gossip* (Minneapolis: University of Minnesota Press, 2005), 23, 26.

3. Abelove, 26. See also Kevin Floyd, *The Reification of Desire: Toward a Queer Marxism* (Minneapolis: University of Minnesota Press, 2009).

4. On the connection between norms, statistical thinking, and industrialism, see Lennard J. Davis, *Enforcing Normalcy: Disability, Deafness, and the Body* (New York: Verso, 1995), 26.

5. Jonathan Ned Katz, *The Invention of Heterosexuality* (Chicago: University of Chicago Press, 1995), 90. In his more recent work, Katz also outlines "entrepreneurs of desire"—"tavern and dancehall owners, movie and popular music producers, theatrical play producers, cosmetics and clothes manufacturers, advertising and marketing executives, and mainstream magazine, newspaper, and book publishers"—as an area for further inquiry into the "making of the modern hetero-homo system." Jonathan Ned Katz, "Envisioning the World We Make, Social-Historical Construction, A Model, A Manifesto," outhistory.com, accessed April 22, 2017.

6. My reading of Gramsci and Anderson is indebted to Thomas Yingling, *"Winesburg, Ohio* and the End of Collective Experience," in *New Essays on "Winesburg, Ohio,"* ed. John W. Crowley (New York: Cambridge University Press, 1990), 99–125.

7. This position is similar to that of John H. Ferres, who sees *Winesburg, Ohio* as "our most sensitive literary record of the human effects of the transition from an agrarian to an industrial-technological age in the American small town." John H. Ferres, "The Nostalgia of *Winesburg, Ohio,"* in *Winesburg, Ohio: Text and Criticism*, ed. John H. Ferres (New York: Penguin, 1996), 466.

8. Quoted in David Stouck, "Anderson's Expressionist Art," in *New Essays on "Winesburg, Ohio,"* ed. John W. Crowley (New York; Cambridge University Press, 1990), 40.

9. Sherwood Anderson, *Sherwood Anderson's Memoirs: A Critical Edition*, ed. Ray Lewis White (Chapel Hill: University of North Carolina Press, 1969), 289.

10. David Harvey, *The Condition of Postmodernity* (New York: Blackwell, 1989), 125–26.

11. Antonio Gramsci, *Selections from Prison Notebooks*, ed. and trans. Quintin Hoare and Geoffrey Nowell Smith (New York: International Publishers, 1971), 588.

12. Harvey, 126.

13. Douglas G. Brinkley, *Wheels for the World: Henry Ford, His Company, and a Century of Progress* (New York: Penguin, 2004), 275–81.

14. Gramsci, 601.

15. Sherwood Anderson, "The Future of Japanese and American Writing," in *Sherwood Anderson: The Writer at His Craft*, ed. Jack Salzman, David D. Anderson, and Kichinosuke Ohashi (Mamaroneck, NY: Paul P. Appel, 1979), 307, reprinted from *Jiji Shimpo [Current News]*, Japan, January 1928.

16. Sherwood Anderson, "New Orleans, the Double Dealer, and the Modern Movement in America," in *Sherwood Anderson: The Writer at His Craft*, 283, reprinted from *Double Dealer* 3 (March 1922), 119–26.

17. Michael Denning, *The Cultural Front: The Laboring of American Culture in the Twentieth Century* (New York: Verso, 2011), 28.

18. Jeffrey Nealon, *Foucault Beyond Foucault: Power and Its Intensifications since 1984* (Palo Alto: Stanford University Press, 2007), 60.

19. Shane Vogel, *The Scene of Harlem Cabaret: Race, Sexuality, Performance* (Chicago: University of Chicago, 2009), 104-31.

20. Sherwood Anderson, *The Modern Writer* (San Francisco: Lantern Press, 1925), 15.

21. Havelock Ellis similarly sees industrialization as having the effect of stipulating and specifying sexual difference and thus eradicating the sissy that Anderson sees in everyone. In *Man and Woman* (1894), Ellis writes that with the advent of "industrialism . . . more marked sexual differences in physical development seem (we cannot speak definitely) to have developed than are usually to be found in savage societies." Havelock Ellis, *Man and Woman: A Study of Human Secondary Sexual Characters* (New York: Walter Scott Publishing Company, 1904), 13.

22. This fear of mass-standardized Fordist sexuality is represented in an even more heightened form in Aldous Huxley's *Brave New World* (1932).

23. Sherwood Anderson, *Winesburg, Ohio: A Group of Tales of Ohio Small Town Life* (New York: Barnes and Noble, 2010), 38. All other citations to the text will be given parenthetically.

24. John D'Emilio and Estelle Freedman, *Intimate Matters: A History of Sexuality in America* (Chicago: University of Chicago Press, 2009), 176.

25. This association of free sexual expression and the country is echoed in Robert Scully's *A Scarlet Pansy* (1932) when a character named Teddy tries to seduce the protagonist Fay: "[Teddy] was anxious to get Fay out in the secluded romantic country where he could feel more free with her. In the city there was the ever-present crowd, at the theatre, at the restaurant, on the street, anywhere. Even the halls of their boarding house were constantly being invaded and there was no opportunity to caress at ease." Robert Scully, *A Scarlet Pansy*, ed. Robert J. Corber (New York: Fordham University Press, 2016), 69.

26. W. H. Auden, "Casino," in *Selected Poems*, ed. Edward Mendelson (New York: Vintage, 2007), 47. On the history and meaning of the hand in the late nineteenth and early twentieth centuries, see Jay Watson, *Reading for the Body: The Recalcitrant Materiality of Southern Fiction, 1893–1985* (Athens: University of Georgia, 2012), 31–86; and Abbie Garrington, *Haptic Modernism: Touch and the Tactile in Modernist Writing* (Edinburgh: Edinburgh University Press, 2013). On the sexuality of hands and touch, see Juana María Rodríguez, *Sexual Futures, Queer Gestures, and Other Latina Longings* (New York: New York University Press, 2014); and Elizabeth Freeman, *Time Binds: Queer Temporalities, Queer Histories* (Durham: Duke University Press, 2010), 95–135.

27. William Carlos Williams, *In the American Grain* (New York: New Directions, 2009), 177.

28. On *Contact*, see Natalia Cecire, "Experimentalism by Contact" *diacritics* 43.1 (2015): 6–35.

29. I am grateful to Michael Warner for bringing this poem to my attention.

30. On hands in Winesburg, see William M. Etter, "Speaking of Manhood in *Winesburg, Ohio*," in *Sherwood Anderson's Winesburg, Ohio*, ed. Precious McKenzie (Leiden: Brill Rodopi, 2016), 85; and Stouck, 41–42.

31. On eroticized celibacy, see Benjamin Kahan, *Celibacies: American Modernism and Sexual Life* (Durham: Duke University Press, 2013).

32. For a brief but important reading of "Hands," see Mark Whalan, *Race, Manhood, and Modernism in America: The Short Story Cycles of Sherwood Anderson and Jean Toomer* (Knoxville: University of Tennessee Press, 2007), 46–47.

33. Sherwood Anderson, *Letters of Sherwood Anderson*, ed. Howard Mumford Jones (Boston: Little, Brown, and Company, 1953), 410.

34. Aaron Ritzenberg, *The Sentimental Touch: The Language of Feeling in the Age of Managerialism* (Fordham University Press, 2013), 71; and Edwin Fussell, "*Winesburg, Ohio*, Art, and Isolation," in *Sherwood Anderson: A Collection of Critical Essays*, ed. Walter Bates Rideout (Upper Saddle River, NJ: Prentice-Hall, 1974), 45.

35. Eve Kosofsky Sedgwick, *Epistemology of the Closet* (Berkeley and Los Angeles: University of California Press, 1990), 35.

36. Louis-Ferdinand Céline's *Journey to the End of the Night* (1932) similarly depicts its protagonist Ferdinand attempting to articulate "an overwhelmingly vague desire" to a prostitute while working in Henry Ford's factory. Louis-Ferdinand Céline, *Journey to the End of the Night*, trans. John H. P. Marks (Boston: Little, Brown, and Company, 1934), 227.

37. Abelove, 26.

38. Michel Foucault, *The History of Sexuality*, vol. 1, *An Introduction*, trans. Robert Hurley (New York: Vintage Books, 1990), 44. Richard Cleminson and Francisco Vazquez García, *"Los Invsisibles": A History of Male Homosexuality in Spain, 1850–1939* (Cardiff: University of Wales Press, 2007), 44.

39. In a moment that might be read as cutting against the grain of my argument, Wing Biddlebaum's hands are described as "the piston rods of his machinery of expression" (4). I read this passage in conjunction with the description of Wing's hands as "fluttering pennants of promise" to suggest that while industrialism is inevitable for Anderson, its life-draining quality is not. That is, Wing's hands offer the possibility of an industrialism that could facilitate rather than annihilate expression.

40. Sherwood Anderson, "Introduction to Walt Whitman's *Leaves of Grass*," in *Sherwood Anderson: The Writer at His Craft*, ed. Jack Salzman, David D. Anderson, and Kichinosuke Ohashi (Mamaroneck, NY: Paul P. Appel, 1979), 19, 20, 21.

41. This passage echoes those "quite strong" people in "The Book of the Grotesque" who "snatched up a dozen" truths (xix).

42. The name "Webster" summons the standardization of the dictionary.

43. Sherwood Anderson, *Many Marriages* (New York: B. W. Huebsch, 1923), 10.

44. Anderson, *Many Marriages*, 12.
45. Edward Carpenter, *Civilization: Its Cause and Its Cure, and Other Essays* (London: Swan Sonnenschein and Co., 1891), 66–67.
46. George Chauncey, *Gay New York: Gender, Urban Culture, and the Making of the Gay Male World, 1890–1940* (New York: Basic Books, 1994), 14.
47. Simon Clarke, "The Crisis of Fordism and the Crisis of Capitalism," *Telos*, New York, 83 (Spring 1990), 71–98.
48. As D. A. Miller notes "perhaps the most salient index to male homosexuality, socially speaking, consists precisely in how a man looks at other men." D. A. Miller, "Anal Rope," *Representations* 32 (1990): 124. On homosexual panic in this story, see Eric Haralson, *Henry James and Queer Modernity* (Cambridge: Cambridge University Press, 2003), 11–13.
49. For an analysis of the imbrication of consumer and sexual desire in a roughly contemporaneous text, see Guy Davidson, "Ornamental Identity: Commodity Fetishism, Masculinity, and Sexuality in *The Golden Bowl*," *Henry James Review* 28 (2007): 26–42.
50. My understanding of the consolidating force of capital in the standardization of sexual object choice finds a complement in David K. Johnson's argument that gay consumerism was a "catalyst" for the formation of gay identity and the gay rights political movement in the 1950s and 1960s. David K. Johnson, "Physique Pioneers: The Politics of 1960s Gay Consumer Culture," *Journal of Social History* 43.4 (2010): 867–92.
51. My thinking here is indebted to Jeffrey Masten, *Queer Philologies: Sex, Language, and Affect in Shakespeare's Time* (Philadelphia: University of Pennsylvania Press, 2016).
52. Sedgwick, 8.
53. Some of the phrasing in this sentence is indebted to Lauren Berlant, "Starved," *South Atlantic Quarterly* 106.3 (2007): 435.

CHAPTER FIVE

1. Eve Kosofsky Sedgwick, *Touching Feeling: Affect, Pedagogy, Peformativity* (Durham: Duke University Press, 2003), 123.
2. Sedgwick, *Touching Feeling*, 123.
3. Sedgwick, *Touching Feeling*, 124.
4. Sedgwick, *Touching Feeling*, 124.
5. "Privilege of Unknowing" is collected in *Tendencies* (1993) as Eve Kosofsky Sedgwick, "Privilege of Unknowing: Diderot's *The Nun*," in *Tendencies* (Durham: Duke University Press, 1993), 23–51.
6. Stephen Kern, *A Cultural History of Causality: Science, Murder Novels, and Systems of Thought* (Princeton: Princeton University Press, 2004), 7.
7. David M. Halperin, *How to Do the History of Homosexuality* (Chicago: University of Chicago Press, 2002), 103.
8. For sexological texts that struggle with these questions of etiological prior-

ity, see Iwan Bloch, *Anthropological Studies in the Strange Sexual Practises of All Races in All Ages*, trans. Keene Wallis (New York: Anthropological Press, 1933); Benjamin Tarnowsky, *Anthropological, Legal, and Medical Studies on Pederasty in Europe* (New York: Falstaff Press, 1933); Auguste Forel, *The Sexual Question: A Scientific, Psychological, Hygienic, and Sociological Study* (Brooklyn, NY: Physicians and Surgeons Book Company, 1931); and Edward Prime-Stevenson, *The Intersexes: A Study of Similisexualism as a Problem in Social Life* (privately printed, 1908). Theo van der Meer also writes about this problem in an earlier period: "Despite the continuous warnings of its shepherds, so it was explained in 1730, the Dutch people had given in to hedonism. The trend had started with lesser sins, such as cardplaying and gambling, indulgence in food and drink and excessive dressing, and ended up with debauchery and finally sodomy. Sodomy was the result of the 'surpassing steps of sinfulness,' most authors agreed in 1830, which had affected the country's inhabitants. This explained the 'sudden' emergence of same-sex practices in the Republic." Theo van der Meer, "Sodomy and the Pursuit of a Third Sex," in *Third Sex, Third Gender: Beyond Sexual Dimorphism in Culture and History*, ed. Gilbert Herdt (New York: Zone Books, 1994), 182. Van der Meer further asserts that "It is obvious that an etiology in which homosexual behavior could be the result of cardplaying is not compatible with modern taxonomies of sexuality" (183). My position is, of course, exactly the opposite, that gambling and alcohol consumption are precisely the kinds of etiologies that might result in homosexuality in the modern/modernist period.

9. Sara Ahmed, *Willful Subjects* (Durham: Duke University Press, 2014), 78.
10. Benjamin Kahan, "The First Sexology? Heinrich Kaan's *Psychopathia Sexualis* (1844)," in *Heinrich Kaan's "Psychopathia Sexualis" (1844): A Classic Text in the History of Sexuality*, trans. Melissa Haynes (Ithaca: Cornell University Press, 2016), 19–23.
11. Annamarie Jagose, *Inconsequence: Lesbian Representation and the Logic of Sexual Sequence* (Ithaca: Cornell University Press, 2002), 24.
12. Jagose, 26.
13. Dana Seitler, *Atavistic Tendencies: The Culture of Science in American Modernity* (Minneapolis: University of Minnesota Press, 2008), 83, her emphasis.
14. Seitler, 83. Seitler also charts another kind of seriality in Ellis's work: the "grouping [of] similar-looking bodies together in a single photograph" to create "'semiotic clusters'" (90). These clusters suggest "the curiously additive and flexible nature of the perverse body and of the incoherence of its definitional fields" (91).
15. Eve Kosofsky Sedgwick, *Epistemology of the Closet* (Berkeley and Los Angeles: University of California Press, 1990), 31.
16. This sense of etiology without temporality rhymes with what Valerie Rohy, following Lacan, calls a "lost cause." By this she means an etiology that possesses a cause that is "opaque and inaccessible" and yet has

effects. Valerie Rohy, *Lost Causes: Narrative, Etiology, and Queer Theory* (Oxford: Oxford University Press, 2015), 70.

17. Eve Kosofsky Sedgwick, "Epidemics of the Will," in *Tendencies* (Durham: Duke University Press, 1993), 135.

18. Sedgwick, "Epidemics," 136. I borrow the term "sovereign" from Wai Chee Dimock, "Weak Theory: Henry James, Colm Tóibín, and W. B. Yeats," *Critical Inquiry* 39 (2013): 733.

19. There is a long history connecting alcohol and homosexuality. See, for example, Walt Whitman, "The Child's Champion," in *"The Man Who Thought Himself A Woman" and Other Queer Nineteenth-Century Short Stories*, ed. Christopher Looby (Philadelphia: University of Pennsylvania, 2017), 3–12. See also Michael Moon, *Disseminating Whitman: Revision and Corporeality in Leaves of Grass* (Cambridge: Harvard University Press, 1991), 26–58; and Michael Warner, "Whitman Drunk," in *Breaking Bounds: Whitman and American Cultural Studies*, ed. Betsy Erkkila and Jay Grossman (Oxford: Oxford University Press, 1996), 30–43.

20. Magnus Hirschfeld, *The Homosexuality of Men and Women*, trans. Michael A. Lombardi-Nash (Amherst, NY: Prometheus Books, 2000), 233.

21. Alcohol was also understood to facilitate interracial sex, helping to overcome the putatively more "natural" desire for intraracial sex. A 1920 article in the *Baltimore Afro-American* speculated, for example, that the reason "Chicago was known for race mixing" was because there were "[n]o Blue Laws in Chicago," which prohibited the sale of alcohol on Sundays. Quoted in Kevin Mumford, *Interzones: Black/White Sex Districts in Chicago and New York in the Early Twentieth Century* (New York: Columbia University Press, 1997), 30.

22. Bloch, *Anthropological Studies*, 137–38. In the Egyptian novel *Midaq Alley* (1966), one of the characters refers to homosexuality as "the other hashish." Naguib Mahfouz, *Midaq Alley* (New York: Anchor Books, 1992), 77.

23. Bloch also understands alcohol to be associated with prostitution and venereal disease. Iwan Bloch, *The Sexual Life of Our Time in Its Relations to Modern Civilization*, trans. M. Eden Paul (London: Rebman Limited, 1909), 293–97.

24. Pairing the idea that alcohol engenders homosexuality with Susan Lanser's provocative approach in *The Sexuality of History*, we might ask whether the temperance movement and Prohibition might be understood as attacks on homosexuality in addition to drinking and other kinds of vice. Such an enormous question would of course demand a great deal more research.

25. F. O. Matthiessen and Russell Cheney, *Rat and the Devil: Journal Letters of F. O. Matthiessen and Russell Cheney*, ed. Louis Hyde (Brooklyn, NY: Shoe String Press, 1978), 80, February 5, 1925.

26. Matthiessen and Cheney, 80.

27. Glenway Wescott's *Continual Lessons* describes a similar relationship be-

tween alcohol and homosexuality with respect to Wescott's lover Nelson in an entry from his 1941 journal: "Alcohol is a god, I wrote; and I remember how often I have let myself regard Nelson as, so to speak, godlike under its influence. But all spring it had a hopeless effect on our personal relationship, particularly because it is all connected and confused in Nelson's life with the difficulty of his sexual morals." Glenway Wescott, *Continual Lessons: The Journals of Glenway Wescott, 1937–1955*, ed. Robert Phelps with Jerry Rosco (New York: Farrar, Straus, and Giroux, 1990), 89.

28. This reading is profoundly indebted to Jay Grossman's work on Matthiessen, particularly his paper "F. O. Matthiessen (1902–1950), Anthropometry, and the Long Nineteenth Century," Invited lecture, Workshop in the History of Material Texts, University of Pennsylvania, March 31, 2014.

29. L. Pierce Clark, "Some Psychological Aspects of Alcoholism," *International Record of Medicine and General Practice Clinics* 109 (May 31, 1919): 931.

30. Clark, 931.

31. Clark, 931.

32. Simon Weijl, "Theoretical and Practical Aspects of Psychoanalytic Therapy of Problem Drinkers," *Quarterly Journal of Studies on Alcohol* 5.2 (1944): 202.

33. Ernest Hemingway, *A Moveable Feast: The Restored Edition* (New York: Scribner, 2009), 30.

34. This etiology continues to be available in later historical periods as well; Edmund White records a man telling him in his *States of Desire* (1980): "I think I drink because of my homosexuality." Edmund White, *States of Desire: Travels in Gay America* (New York: E. P. Dutton, 1980), 164.

35. I mean for these etiological sequences to be exemplary rather than exhaustive. Bénédict Augustin Morel's foundational *Treatise on the Degeneration of the Human Species* (1857), for example, understands alcohol to induce degeneration (associated with sexual deviance) across generations. Bénédict Augustin Morel, *Traité des Dégénérescences* (Paris: J. B. Baillière, 1857).

36. Because this desire is alloerotic it does not encounter the sequential trouble that volition does, and thus does not demand a weakened theory of etiology in the same way as the other sequential orderings.

37. Stephen Spender, "Introduction," in Malcolm Lowry, *Under the Volcano* (New York: Lippincott, 1971), xiii. Building on Jonathan Arac's reading of "the extended hysteron proteron" of the first chapter and what Jeffrey Masten calls that trope's "long associat[ion] with sodomy discourse," we might see the book as a whole as possessing a sodomitical structure. Jonathan Arac, "The Form of Carnival in *Under the Volcano*," *PMLA* 92.3 (1977): 481. Jeffrey Masten, *Queer Philologies: Sex, Language, and Affect in Shakespeare's Time* (Philadelphia: University of Pennsylvania Press, 2016), 237.

38. Malcolm Lowry, *Under the Volcano* (New York: Lippincott, 1971), 129. The name Quincey alludes to Thomas De Quincey and to his *Confessions of an*

*English Opium-Eater* (1821) in particular. On the relations between opium and queerness, see Nayan Shah, *Contagious Divides: Epidemics and Race in San Francisco's Chinatown* (Berkeley: University of California Press, 2001), 90–97.

39. Lowry, 131.
40. Lowry, 134.
41. Lowry, 134–35.
42. Lowry, 134.
43. William Blackstone, *Commentaries on the Laws of England, Book IV: Of Public Wrongs*, ed. Ruth Paley (Oxford: Oxford University Press, 2016), 143. Blackstone also refers to sodomy as of "deeper malignity" than rape even as he has already called rape an "abominable wickedness." Moreover he says sodomy may be "committed either with man or beast" (Blackstone, 142).
44. While this novel aligns alcohol and homosexuality most clearly, impotence also functions as an important etiology. This is also the case for Bloch and many other sexologists.
45. Douglas Day, *Malcolm Lowry: A Biography* (Oxford: Oxford University Press, 1984), 223.
46. Day, 178.
47. Day, 184, 195.
48. Lowry's now-lost novel *In Ballast to the White Sea* featured a protagonist guilty over a suicide and the suicide appears in much of Lowry's work. Malcolm Lowry, *Malcolm Lowry's "La Mordida": A Scholarly Edition*, ed. Patrick A. McCarthy (Athens: University of Georgia Press, 1996), 380 and 346. On *Ballast*, see Day, 123–25.
49. Day, 194. Pierre Loti's novel *My Brother Yves* (1883) furnishes a similar example of alcohol generating alloerotic attraction.
50. Jagose, 36.
51. Quoted in Blake Bailey, "Introduction," in Charles Jackson, *The Lost Weekend: A Novel* (New York: Vintage Books, 2013), xiii.
52. Jaime Harker, *Middlebrow Queer: Christopher Isherwood in America* (Minneapolis: University of Minnesota Press, 2013), 17.
53. Robert J. Corber, *Homosexuality in Cold War America: Resistance and the Crisis of Masculinity* (Durham: Duke University Press, 1997), 219n32.
54. On the relationship between homosexuality and genius, for example, see Andrew Elfenbein, *Romantic Genius: The Prehistory of a Homosexual Role* (New York: Columbia University Press, 1999). And on narcissism and homosexuality, see Michael Warner, "Homo-Narcissism; or, Heterosexuality," in *Engendering Men: The Question of Male Feminist Criticism*, ed. Joseph A. Boone and Michael Cadden (New York: Routledge, 1990), 190–206.
55. Scott Herring, *Queering the Underworld: Slumming, Literature, and the Undoing of Lesbian and Gay History* (Chicago: University of Chicago Press, 2007), 2–3.
56. Charles Jackson, *The Lost Weekend: A Novel* (New York: Vintage Books, 2013), 3, 42.

57. Jackson, 224–25. This passage has the structure of a riddle with many answers like the Hatter's riddle: "Why is a raven like a writing desk?" Lewis Carroll, *Alice in Wonderland*, ed. Donald J. Gray (New York: W. W. Norton and Company, 1992), 55. Thinking about alcoholism and sexuality in relation to the epistemology of the riddle (before the historical advent of the closet) promises to be a rich area for thinking about weak theory's simultaneous narratives. Sexuality as something that cannot be known, not a secret of the self, but something fundamentally mysterious—a riddle—is a frequent trope for describing homosexuality from its invention in the nineteenth century and throughout much of the twentieth century. See, for example, Karl Heinrich Ulrichs, *The Riddle of "MAN-MANLY" Love: The Pioneering Work on Male Homosexuality*, trans. Michael A. Lombardi-Nash (Buffalo, NY: Prometheus Books, 1994); Bloch, *The Sexual Life of Our Time*, 487; Rebecca Patterson, *The Riddle of Emily Dickinson* (Cambridge: Houghton Mifflin, 1951); Edward Hubler, ed., *The Riddle of Shakespeare's Sonnets* (New York: Basic Books, 1962); Kennilworth Bruce, *Goldie* (New York: William Godwin, 1933), 91; and Ralph Werther (Earl Lind), *The Riddle of the Underworld* (unpublished, 1921), http://outhistory.org/exhibits/show/earl -lind/manuscript.
58. This passage from *The Lost Weekend* also offers an unstable ordering with an identity-based explanation ("a drunk") surprisingly preceding an act-based explanation ("you drank").
59. Michel Foucault, *Abnormal: Lectures at the Collège De France, 1974–1975*, trans. Graham Burchell (New York: Picador, 2003), 282.
60. The nineteenth-century Parisian police ledger entitled "Pederasts and Others" that "included male prostitutes, vagrants, thieves, as well as men who sought the company and sexual favors of other men" offers an example of decompartmentalization. William A. Peniston, *Pederasts and Others: Urban Culture and Sexual Identity in Nineteenth-Century Paris* (Binghamton, NY: Harrington Park Press, 2004), 2
61. I borrow the word "domain" here from Peter Coviello, *Tomorrow's Parties: Sex and the Untimely in Nineteenth Century America* (New York: New York University Press, 2013), 4.
62. Foucault, *History*, 44.
63. On the intersection between attempts to cure alcohol and homosexuality, see Annamarie Jagose, *Orgasmology* (Durham: Duke University Press, 2012), 117–19.
64. On assemblage, see Jasbir K. Puar, *Terrorist Assemblages: Homonationalism in Queer Times* (Durham: Duke University Press, 2007); and Alexander G. Weheliye, *Habeas Viscus: Racializing Assemblages, Biopolitics, and Black Feminist Theories of the Human* (Durham: Duke University Press, 2014).
65. Iwan Bloch, *Anthropological and Ethnological Studies in the Strangest Sex Acts in Modes of Love of All Races Illustrated* (New York: Falstaff Press, 1935), 207.
66. Bloch, *Anthropological and Ethnological Studies*, 208, 207.
67. Bloch, *Anthropological and Ethnological Studies*, 207.

68. Eve Kosofsky Sedgwick, *Epistemology of the Closet* (Berkeley and Los Angeles: University of California Press, 1990), 47.
69. Guy Hocquenghem, *Homosexual Desire* (Durham: Duke University Press, 1993), 109.
70. Auguste Forel, *The Sexual Question: A Scientific, Psychological, Hygienic, and Sociological Study* (Brooklyn, NY: Physicians and Surgeons Book Company, 1931), 217. Similarly, Freud argues in his *Three Essays on the Theory of Sexuality* (1905) that "It is not easy to estimate the relative efficacy of the constitutional and accidental factors [on sexual development] . . . It should, however, on no account be forgotten that the relation between the two is a co-operative and not a mutually exclusive one. The constitutional factor must await experiences before it can make itself felt; the accidental factor must have a constitutional basis in order to come into operation." Freud's insistence on the cooperative relation between acquired ("accidental") and congenital ("constitutional") factors domesticates the unsettling power of these accidental factors by locating them in the body. Sigmund Freud, *Three Essays on the Theory of Sexuality*, trans. James Strachey (New York: Basic Books, 2000), 105.

### AFTER SEDGWICK

1. These questions are indebted to Paul Saint-Amour, "Counterfactual," presented at the Modernist Studies Association conference, November 2015; and Elizabeth Freeman, "Still After" in *After Sex? On Writing since Queer Theory*, ed. Janet Halley and Andrew Parker (Durham: Duke University Press, 2011), 495–500. On the erotic pursuit of Sedgwick, see Jonathan A. Allen, "Falling in Love with Eve Kosofsky Sedgwick," *Mosaic* 48.1 (2015): 1–16. On being after Sedgwick, see Jason Edwards, *Eve Kosofsky Sedgwick* (New York: Routledge, 2009), 136–37.
2. Eve Kosofsky Sedgwick, *Epistemology of the Closet* (Berkeley and Los Angeles: University of California Press, 1990), 27.
3. This sentence is indebted to some of the brilliant thinking in Jeffrey Masten, "Material Cavendish: Paper, Performance, 'Sociable Virginity,'" *MLQ* 65.1 (2004): 58.
4. Jonathan Goldberg, "On the Eve of the Future," *Criticism* 52.2 (2010): 283–91.
5. Valerie Traub, "The Present Future of Lesbian Historiography," in *A Companion to Lesbian, Gay, Bisexual, Transgender, and Queer Studies*, ed. George Haggerty and Molly McGarry (Oxford: Blackwell, 2007), 135.
6. Peter Coviello, *Tomorrow's Parties: Sex and the Untimely in Nineteenth-Century America* (New York University Press, 2013), 4.
7. Eve Kosofsky Sedgwick, *Between Men: English Literature and Male Homosocial Desire* (New York: Columbia University Press, 1985), 1.
8. Sedgwick, *Between Men*, 172, 173, 174.
9. Sedgwick, *Between Men*, 49, 207.

10. Sedgwick, *Between Men*, 88–89.
11. See also Matt Houlbrook, *Queer London: Perils and Pleasures in the Sexual Metropolis, 1918–1957* (Chicago: University of Chicago Press, 2005), 149, 178–80.
12. Sedgwick, *Between Men*, 27; and Eve Kosofsky Sedgwick, "How to Bring Your Kids Up Gay: The War on Effeminate Boys," in *Tendencies* (Durham: Duke University Press, 1993), 154–64. For an excellent account of Sedgwick's career, see Heather Love, "The Performative and the Peri-," *Women's Review of Books* 21.6 (2004): 12–13.
13. In my essay, "Conjectures on The Sexual World-System," I also interrogate Sedgwick's first axiom: "People are different from each other" (Sedgwick, *Epistemology*, 22). Benjamin Kahan, "Conjectures on the Sexual World-System," *GLQ* 23.3 (2017): 327–57.
14. Sedgwick, *Epistemology*, 91.
15. Sedgwick, *Epistemology*, 49, 92.
16. For a different account of this impasse, see Howard H. Chiang, "Liberating Sex, Knowing Desire: *Scientia Sexualis* and Epistemic Turning Points in the History of Sexuality," *History of the Human Sciences* 23.5 (2010): 42–69.
17. Randolph Trumbach, *Sex and the Gender Revolution*, vol. 1, *Heterosexuality and the Third Gender in Enlightenment London* (Chicago: University of Chicago Press, 1998), 19. Dominic Janes similarly charts a narrative that approaches transhistorical continuity, imagining a protocloset ("a sodomitical closet") existing since at least the eighteenth century. Dominic Janes, *Picturing the Closet: Male Secrecy and Homosexual Visibility in Britain* (Oxford: Oxford University Press, 2015), 12.
18. Several of the sentences in this paragraph are borrowed from Benjamin Kahan, "What is Sexual Modernity?" *Modernism/modernity Print Plus* 1.3 (2016), https://modernismmodernity.org/forums/what-sexual-modernity.
19. Randolph Trumbach, "London's Sodomites: Homosexual Behavior and Western Culture in the 18th Century," *Journal of Social History* 11.1 (1977): 15.
20. Alan Bray, *Homosexuality in Renaissance England* (New York: Columbia University Press, 1996), 85.
21. Bray, 84.
22. Theo van der Meer, "Sodomy and Its Discontents: Discourse, Desire, and the Rise of a Same-Sex Proto-Something in the Early Modern Dutch Republic," *Historical Reflections / Réflexions Historiques*, 33.1 (2007): 55. For more on the Dutch subcultural organization, see Theo van der Meer, "Sodomy and the Pursuit of a Third Sex in the Early Modern Period," in *Third Sex, Third Gender: Beyond Sexual Dimorphism in Culture and History*, ed. Gilbert Herdt (New York: Zone Books, 1994), 148–58. Arend H. Huussen Jr. also describes a Dutch homosexual subculture: "There were special meeting places in the open air and indoors; and homosexuals used peculiar mimicry, specific signs, love names, and a network of friends and

contacts." Arend H. Huussen, Jr., "Sodomy in the Dutch Republic During the Eighteenth Century," in *Hidden From History: Reclaiming the Gay and Lesbian Past*, ed. Martin Bauml Duberman, Martha Vicinus, and George Chauncey (New York: Penguin, 1989), 147.

23. Michel Rey, "Parisian Homosexuals Create a Lifestyle, 1700–1750: The Police Archives," in *'Tis Nature's Fault: Unauthorized Sexuality during the Enlightenment*, ed. Robert Purks Maccubbin (Cambridge: Cambridge University Press, 1988), 186.

24. Stephen Shapiro, "Of Mollies: Class and Same-Sex Sexualities in the Eighteenth Century," in *In a Queer Place: Sexuality and Belonging in British and European Contexts*, ed. Kate Chedgzoy, Emma Francis, and Murray Pratt (London: Ashgate, 2002), 158.

25. The contemporaneous cases of Germany and the United States make for interesting comparison. In a discussion of eighteenth-century Germany, Robert Tobin writes: "Currently, the documentation for the existence of German sodomitical subcultures similar to the ones in England and Holland is lacking." Robert Tobin, *Warm Brothers: Queer Theory and the Age of Goethe* (Philadelphia: University of Pennsylvania Press, 2000), 8. While Tobin suggests that it is possible that German cities had not yet achieved the population density necessary to sustain such a subculture, he retains the possibility of their existence. In particular he draws attention to changes in family structure and cites a tantalizing German quotation from 1789 from a man whose sexual drive "was oriented exclusively toward men": "In a larger city, which I do not want to mention by name, an entire society of these misattuned lovers is supposed to have come together, which draws ever more into their fraternity, in order to find more nourishment for their lusts" (Tobin, *Warm Brothers*, 13–14). Tobin points out that while the unnamed city may have been outside Germany, such ideas were becoming increasingly available within Germany. Similarly, Clare A. Lyons suggests that while documentation of such subcultures does not exist in eighteenth-century Philadelphia, she thinks their existence is likely, "given the nature of . . . transatlantic commerce and culture." Clare A. Lyons, "Mapping an Atlantic Sexual Culture: Homoeroticism in Eighteenth-Century Philadelphia," *William and Mary Quarterly* 60.1 (2003): 141. Moreover, she is certain that "Philadelphians . . . were well informed about the eighteenth-century European homoerotic social types" at the time (Lyons, 149). Other American historians, like Richard Godbeer, disagree; he contends that Philadelphia "had no equivalent of the 'molly houses' . . . or the homoerotic subculture that London and other major European cities offered." Richard Godbeer, *Sexual Revolution in Early America* (Baltimore: Johns Hopkins Press, 2002), 407n6. Like Godbeer, I am skeptical of Lyons's claim since the only two individuals that she can find as possible mollies seem to be more recognizable as persons engaging in what she calls "cross-dressing" or "transvestite"

practices (Lyons, 125, 119). Moreover, she does not substantiate her claim that readers in Philadelphia received, absorbed, or comprehended the representations and reports of mollies as such.

26. Bray, 89, 91. Faramerz Dabhoiwala's account of the failure of a 1650 Act "for suppressing the detestable sins of incest, adultery, and fornication" to provide an adequate legal framework to convict offenders of these sins (a failure that was felt with especial acuteness around 1700) and the general sense that "London was inadequately policed" until 1740 might suggest that the molly crackdowns are part of a reactionary sexual panic (47, 53, 64). See Faramerz Dabhoiwala, *The Origins of Sex: A History of the First Sexual Revolution* (New York: Penguin, 2012), 37–77.

27. For more on the English molly see Mary McIntosh, "The Homosexual Role," *Social Problems* 16.2 (1968): 182–92; Rictor Norton, *Mother Clap's Molly House: The Gay Subculture in England, 1700–1830* (London: Gay Men's Press, 1992); G. S. Rousseau, "The Pursuit of Homosexuality in the Eighteenth Century: 'Utterly Confused Category' and/or Rich Repository?" in *'Tis Nature's Fault: Unauthorized Sexuality during the Enlightenment*, ed. Robert Purks Maccubbin (Cambridge: Cambridge University Press, 1988), 132–68; Alan Bray and Michel Rey, "The Body of the Friend," in Alan Bray, *The Friend* (Chicago: University of Chicago Press, 2003), 140–76.

28. Bryant T. Ragan, Jr., "The Enlightenment Confronts Homosexuality," in *Homosexuality in Modern France*, ed. Jeffrey Merrick and Bryant T. Ragan Jr. (Oxford: Oxford University Press, 1996), 13. For more on homosexuality in early eighteenth-century France, see Jeffrey Merrick, "Sodomitical Inclinations in Early Eighteenth-Century Paris," *Eighteenth-Century Studies* 30.3 (1997): 289–95; Jeffrey Merrick, "Sodomitical Scandals and Subcultures in the 1720s," *Men and Masculinities* 1.4 (1999): 365–84; Michel Rey, "Police and Sodomy in Eighteenth Century Paris: From Sin to Disorder," in *The Pursuit of Sodomy: Male Homosexuality in Renaissance and Enlightenment Europe*, ed. Kent Gerard and Gert Hekma (New York: Haworth Press, 1989), 129–46.

29. Van der Meer, "Sodomy and Its Discontents," 45.

30. Theo van der Meer, "Sodom's Seed in the Netherlands: The Emergence of Homosexuality in the Early Modern Period," *Journal of Homosexuality* 34.1 (1997): 1. Van der Meer's "Sodomy and Its Discontents," 46, puts the number of deaths at a hundred. See also van der Meer, "Sodomy and the Pursuit of a Third Sex in the Early Modern Period," 139.

31. Bray, *Homosexuality*, 92.

32. Alan Bray, *The Friend* (Chicago: University of Chicago Press, 2003), 212. See also Michel Foucault, "Sex, Power, and the Politics of Identity," in *Ethics: Subjectivity and Truth*, ed. Paul Rabinow (New York: New Press, 1997), 171; and Philippe Ariès, "Thoughts on the History of Homosexuality," in *Western Sexuality: Practice and Precept in Past and Present Times* (Oxford: Basil Blackwell, 1985), 69.

33. David M. Halperin, *How to Do the History of Homosexuality* (Chicago: University of Chicago Press, 2002), 192n53, 128.

34. Michael Warner, *Publics and Counterpublics* (New York: Zone Books, 2002), 112.

35. Van der Meer, "Sodomy and Its Discontents," 45.

36. Van der Meer, "Sodomy and Its Discontents," 45.

37. Hal Gladfelder, "In Search of Lost Texts: Thomas Cannon's *Ancient and Modern Pederasty Investigated and Exemplify'd*," *Eighteenth-Century Life* 31.1 (2007): 35. For Cannon's text, see Thomas Cannon, "The Indictment of John Purser, Containing Thomas Cannon's *Ancient and Modern Pederasty Investigated and Exemplify'd*," ed. Hal Gladfelder, *Eighteenth-Century Life* 31.1 (2007): 39–61. Jeremy Bentham's "On Paederasty" (1785) is the most famous early defense of sodomy.

38. John White, *The First Century of Scandalous, Malignant Priests* (London: Printed by George Miller, dwelling in the Black-Friars, 1643). Bray, *Homosexuality*, 43, 66–67, 69–70, 126–27n27.

39. In its description of Wilson, White's pamphlet also describes buggery as a "usuall frequenter of Ale-houses and a great drinker," tantalizingly evoking the possibility of early configurations of molly houses. White, 2. For more on White, see Iwan [Ivan] Bloch, *Sexual Life in England: Past and Present* (London: Oracle, 1996), 393–94.

40. White, 2.

41. Bray, *Renaissance*, 66.

42. Halperin, *How to Do*, 42.

43. Oldbaileyonline.org, accessed September 13, 2016. Rictor Norton, *Georgian Underworld* (2003), chap. 16, rictornorton.co.uk. See also Tonya Cassidy, "People, Place, Performance: Theoretically Revisiting Mother Clap's Molly House," in *Queer People: Negotiations and Expressions of Homosexuality, 1700–1800*, ed. Chris Mounsey and Caroline Gonda (Lewisburg, PA: Bucknell University Press, 2007), 99–113.

44. Oldbaileyonline.org, accessed September 13, 2016.

45. For information on and English language excerpts of *Der Eigene*, see Harry Oosterhuis, *Homosexuality and Male Bonding in Pre-Nazi Germany*, trans. Hubert Kennedy (New York: Harrington Park Press, 1991). Michael Bibler, "Possessive Intimacy" (unpublished manuscript). The word "enjoy" signifies in relation to both sexuality and property. See Jeffrey Masten, *Queer Philologies: Sex, Language, and Affect in Shakespeare's Time* (Philadelphia: University of Pennsylvania Press, 2016), 104–5.

46. Oldbaileyonline.org, accessed September 13, 2016.

47. Henry Abelove, "Some Speculations on the History of Sexual Intercourse during the Long Eighteenth Century in England," in Henry Abelove, *Deep Gossip* (Minneapolis: University of Minnesota Press, 2003), 23.

48. Abelove, 26. On sexuality and modernity, see Benjamin Kahan, "What is Sexual Modernity?" *Modernism/modernity Print Plus* 1.3 (2016), https://modernismmodernity.org/forums/what-sexual-modernity.

49. Abelove, 27.
50. For an important discussion of aim, see David M. Halperin's "What is Sex For?" *Critical Inquiry* 43.1 (2016): 1–31.
51. Van der Meer, "Sodomy and the Pursuit of a Third Sex," 201, 200. See also Huusen, 146.
52. Van der Meer, "Sodomy and the Pursuit of a Third Sex," 200. King James I similarly finds Biblical precedent, saying in reference to George Villiers, then Earl of Buckingham, that "Jesus had done the same as he was doing . . . for Christ had his John and he had his George," in reference to St. John the Apostle. Quoted in Dabhoiwala, 129. For more on the reception of David and Jonathan and Jesus and John, see Dabhoiwala, 134–35.
53. Van der Meer, "Sodomy and the Pursuit of a Third Sex," 201.
54. Raymond Williams, *Marxism and Literature* (Oxford: Oxford University Press, 2009), 132. My contention here contradicts Robert Beachy's claim that homosexuality "as an immutable characteristic" is a German invention of the late nineteenth century. Beachy, "The German Invention of Homosexuality," *Journal of Modern History* 82.4 (201): 806.
55. Arnold I. Davidson, *The Emergence of Sexuality: Historical Epistemology and the Formation of Concepts* (Cambridge: Harvard University Press, 2004), 32.
56. Halperin, *How to Do*, 42, his emphasis.
57. Kim M. Phillips and Barry Reay, *Sex Before Sexuality: A Premodern History* (Cambridge: Polity, 2008), 82.
58. Valerie Traub, *The Renaissance of Lesbianism in Early Modern England* (Cambridge: Cambridge University Press, 2002), 197, her emphasis.
59. Annamarie Jagose, *Orgasmology* (Durham: Duke University Press, 2012), 49.
60. George Chauncey, *Gay New York: Gender, Urban Culture, and the Making of the Gay Male World, 1890–1940* (New York: Basic Books, 1994); and Peter Coviello, "Plural: Mormon Polygamy and the Biopolitics of Secularism," *History of the Present: A Journal of Critical History* 7.2 (2017): 219–41. H. G. Cocks's work provides a model from an earlier period; see *Visions of Sodom: Religion, Homoerotic Desire, and the End of the World in England, c. 1550–1850* (Chicago: University of Chicago Press, 2017).
61. Richard von Krafft-Ebing, *Psychopathia Sexualis: With Especial Reference to the Antipathic Sexual Instinct*, trans. Franklin S. Klaf (New York: Stein and Day, 1965), 369.
62. Havelock Ellis and John Addington Symonds, *Sexual Inversion: A Critical Edition*, ed. Ivan Crozier (New York: Palgrave, 2008), 192.
63. Stephen Orgel, *Impersonations: The Performance of Gender in Shakespeare's England* (Cambridge: Cambridge University Press, 1996), 1.
64. Iwan Bloch, *The Sexual Life of Our Time in Its Relations to Modern Civilization*, trans. M. Eden Paul (London: Rebman Limited, 1909), 508, 509.
65. Quoted in Robert Beachy, *Gay Berlin: Birthplace of a Modern Identity* (New York: Knopf, 2014), 103. On Brand, see also Oosterhuis and Andrew Hewitt, *Political Inversions: Homosexuality, Fascism, and the Modernist Imaginary* (Stanford: Stanford University Press, 1996).

66. Magnus Hirschfeld, *The Homosexuality of Men and Women*, trans. Michael A. Lombardi-Nash (Amherst, NY: Prometheus Books, 2000), 733.

67. Hirschfeld, 335, 777, 777. I say the majority here is encompassed in these two categories because Hirschfeld sees the remaining 10 percent of homosexuals to be attracted to either very young people ("paedophiles") or very old ones ("gerontophiles"). It is also worth noting that Hirschfeld coins the term ephebophiles earlier in his *Nature of Love* (1906) and that this taxonomy represents a shift to account for what he understands as the increasing prominence of ephebophiles and androphiles. Ulrichs shares a similar taxonomy around age of object choice. See Jana Funke, "'We cannot be Greek Now': Age Difference, Corruption of Youth, and the Making of Sexual Inversion," *English Studies* 94.2 (2013): 145.

68. On the United States age of consent, see Carolyn Cocca, *Jailbait: The Politics of Statutory Rape Laws in the United States* (Albany: SUNY Press, 2004), 9–28. On England's age of consent, see Funke, 144–47.

69. Paula S. Fass, *Kidnapped: Child Abduction in America* (Oxford: Oxford University Press, 1997).

70. Ann Laura Stoler, *Race and the Education of Desire: Foucault's History of Sexuality and the Colonial Order of Things* (Durham: Duke University Press, 1995), 12.

71. Marlon B. Ross, *Manning the Race: Reforming Black Men in the Jim Crow Era* (New York: New York University Press, 2004), 2.

72. Siobhan Somerville, *Queering the Color Line: Race and the Invention of Homosexuality in American Culture* (Durham: Duke University Press, 2000), 3.

73. Somerville, 35.

74. Marc Epprecht, *Heterosexual Africa? The History of an Idea from the Age of Exploration to the Age of AIDS* (Athens: Ohio University Press, 2008), 35.

75. Cheryl Harris, "Whiteness as Property," *Harvard Law Review* 106.8 (1993): 1714.

76. Madoka Kishi, "The Erotics of Race Suicide: The Making of Whiteness and the Death Drive in the Progressive Era, 1880–1920," PhD diss., Louisiana State University, 2015.

77. Ross, 10, 11, 11, 11.

78. Quoted in Margot Canaday, *The Straight State: Sexuality and Citizenship in Twentieth-Century America* (Princeton: Princeton University Press, 2009), 31.

79. Marlon B. Ross, "Beyond the Closet as Raceless Paradigm," in *Black Queer Studies: A Critical Anthology*, ed. E. Patrick Johnson and Mae G. Henderson (Durham: Duke University Press, 2005), 167.

80. Ross, "Beyond," 168. Kevin Mumford further underlines this connection between homosexuality and racialization when he notes that *Strange Brother* (1931) and several other novels with queer themes were placed "in the so-called colored section" of rental libraries. Kevin Mumford, *Interzones: Black/White Sex Districts in Chicago and New York in the Early Twentieth Century* (New York: Columbia University Press, 1997), 74.

81. On sexological discourse about native sexuality, see Mark Rifkin, *When Did Indians Become Straight? Kinship, the History of Sexuality, and Native Sovereignty* (Oxford: Oxford University Press, 2011), 32–38 and 175–76; and Jennifer Terry, *An American Obsession: Science, Medicine, and Homosexuality in Modern Society* (Chicago: University of Chicago Press, 1999), 87.

82. Canaday, 28. On germ theory and the Page Act, see Eithne Luibhéid, *Entry Denied: Controlling Sexuality at the Border* (Minneapolis: Minnesota University Press, 2002), 37. For the ways in which Chinese bodies were cast as menacing disease agents in the US imaginary, see Nayan Shah, *Contagious Divides: Epidemics and Race in San Francisco's Chinatown* (Berkeley: University of California Press, 2001).

83. The other provision barred immigrants who had committed "crimes of moral turpitude" (which invariably included sodomy). Because "moral turpitude" required a conviction and thus a higher burden of proof, it was seldom used without operating in conjunction with the "likely to become a public charge" clause.

84. Canaday, 41.

85. Canaday, 41. The relationship between class and sexuality was also multidirectional and reversible—vagrancy could lead to perversion just as perversion could lead to vagrancy. Along these lines, Canaday describes a case where even though an immigration official describes finding "no direct proof . . . of sodomy or other unnatural crimes in . . . the Mint Hotel," vagrancy functions as evidence enough of sodomy for deportation (quoted in Canaday, 41). Here, we see the languages of class and race having not just "mutual effects," as Somerville describes them, but of constructing and stipulating sex as they are stipulated by sex (Somerville, 3).

86. Seth Koven, *Slumming: Sexual and Social Politics in Victorian London* (Princeton: Princeton University Press, 2004), 4.

87. Michael Trask, *Class and Sexuality in American Literature and Social Thought* (Ithaca: Cornell University Press, 2003), 1.

88. This sentence is indebted to Scott Herring's review of *Slumming* in *American Historical Review* 115.1 (2010): 242–43. The scholarship on late nineteenth- and early twentieth-century slumming is vast; see, for example, Lewis A. Erenberg, *Steppin' Out: New York Nightlife and the Transformation of American Culture, 1890–1930* (Chicago: University of Chicago Press, 1981); Seth Koven, *Slumming: Sexual and Social Politics in Victorian London* (Princeton: Princeton University Press, 2004); Scott Herring, *Queering the Underworld: Slumming, Literature, and the Undoing of Lesbian and Gay Literature* (Chicago: University of Chicago Press, 2007); Robert Dowling, *Slumming in New York: From the Waterfront to Mythic Harlem* (Urbana: University of Illinois Press, 2007); Chad Heap, *Slumming: Sexual and Racial Encounters in American Nightlife, 1885–1940* (Chicago: University of Chicago Press, 2009); and J. Chris Westgate, *Staging the Slums, Slumming the Stage: Class, Poverty, Ethnicity, and Sexuality in American Theatre, 1890–1916* (New York: Palgrave, 2014).

89. Heap, 5.
90. Heap, 5.
91. Heap, 156.
92. Heap, 241, 249.
93. Heap, 250.
94. Sedgwick, *Epistemology*, 31.
95. Sedgwick, *Epistemology*, 31.
96. Chauncey, 14.
97. Rictor Norton, *Myth of the Modern Homosexual: Queer History and the Search for Cultural Unity* (London: Cassell, 1998), 75. As examples of this slowness, Norton argues that the term "homosexual" only gains traction with the Eulenburg scandal and does not appear in American newspapers until 1914. He also records that the writer J. R. Ackerley had not heard the terms "homo or hetero" in 1918, contending that the importance of medical terminology is overstated. Norton, *Myth*, 76. Norton provides a useful corrective, but also overstates his case.
98. Alfred C. Kinsey, Wardell B. Pomeroy, and Clyde E. Martin, *Sexual Behavior in the Human Male* (Bloomington: Indiana University Press, 1975), 615–16.
99. Quoted in Jonathan Ned Katz, *The Invention of Heterosexuality* (Chicago: University of Chicago Press, 1995), 99. For important work on Vidal's sexuality, see Guy Davidson, "Embarrassment in 1968: Gore Vidal's Sexuality in the Public Sphere," *Mosaic* 48.1 (2015): 147–64.
100. Barry Reay, *New York Hustlers: Masculinity and Sex in Modern America* (Manchester: Manchester University Press, 2010), 234–35.
101. For a related attempt at describing the emergence of heterosexuality, see Jonathan Ned Katz, "Envisioning the World We Make, Social-Historical Construction, A Model, A Manifesto," outhistory.com, accessed March 23, 2016.
102. George Chauncey, "From Sexual Inversion to Homosexuality: Medicine and the Changing Conceptualization of Female Deviance," *Salmagundi* 58/59 (1982–1983): 124.
103. Valerie Traub, "The Present Future of Lesbian Historiography," in *A Companion to Lesbian, Gay, Bisexual, Transgender, and Queer Studies*, ed. George Haggerty and Molly McGarry (Oxford: Blackwell, 2007), 125. I follow Sharon Marcus in seeing a "particular indifference of Victorians to a homo/hetero divide for women" and understand a similar indifference to be operative in the US context. Sharon Marcus, *Between Women: Friendship, Desire, and Marriage in Victorian England* (Princeton: Princeton University Press, 2007), 13.
104. Judith Bennett, "Confronting Continuity," *Journal of Women's History* 9.3 (1997): 88, 83, her emphasis.
105. Theresa Braunschneider, *Our Coquettes: Capacious Desire in the Eighteenth Century* (Charlottesville: University of Virginia Press, 2009), 8–11.

NOTES TO PAGES 132-134

106. As I mentioned earlier, Westphal's article actually appeared in 1869; see Halperin, *One Hundred*, 155n2.
107. Michel Foucault, *Abnormal: Lectures at the Collège De France, 1974–1975*, trans. Graham Burchell (New York: Picador, 2003), 280. Chauncey, "From Sexual Inversion," 114–46, especially 143.
108. Sedgwick, *Between Men*, 21.
109. Arnold I. Davidson, *The Emergence of Sexuality: Historical Epistemology and the Formation of Concepts* (Cambridge: Harvard University Press, 2004), 15, his emphasis. The importance of reproduction to sexuality is evident in Havelock Ellis's contention that "the question of sex—with the racial questions that rest on it—stands before the coming generations as the chief problem for solution." The reason that racial questions rest on sexual ones is that race is reproduced through reproductive sex (which Ellis's reference to "the coming generations" underlines). Ellis and Symonds, 91. See also Lindon Barrett, *Conditions of the Present: Selected Essays*, ed. Janet Neary (Durham: Duke University Press, 2018), 197.
110. Davidson, 15.
111. Tim Hitchcock's meditations on "a coherent history of sexuality in eighteenth-century England" has influenced my thinking here. Tim Hitchcock, "The Reformulation of Sexual Knowledge in Eighteenth-Century England," *Signs* (2012): 823. See also Traub, *Thinking Sex*, 150–52.
112. Sigmund Freud, *Three Essays on the Theory of Sexuality*, trans. James Strachey (New York: Basic Books, 2000), 15. Krafft-Ebing's category of "paraesthesia of sexual feeling," for example, does not distinguish between aim and object. Richard von Krafft-Ebing, *Psychopathia Sexualis: With Especial Reference to the Antipathic Sexual Instinct*, trans. Franklin S. Klaf (New York: Stein and Day, 1965), 52.
113. Eve Kosofsky Sedgwick, "Jane Austen and the Masturbating Girl," *Critical Inquiry* 17 (1991): 826.
114. Sedgwick, "Jane Austen," 826.
115. I am grateful to Gayle Rubin for helping me with this point. Foucault argues that if the imagination uncouples the sexual instinct from reproduction, then pleasure itself secures this decoupling and "becomes a psychiatric object" (beginning around 1849 with Claude-François Michéa's study of Sergeant Betrand's desecration of graves). Foucault, *Abnormal*, 286–87.
116. Foucault, *Abnormal*, 278. Heinrich Kaan, *Heinrich Kaan's "Psychopathia Sexualis": A Classic Text in the History of Sexuality (1844)*, ed. Benjamin Kahan, trans. Melissa Haynes (Ithaca: Cornell University Press, 2016), 82.
117. Kaan, 82.
118. I have adapted these paragraphs from Benjamin Kahan, "The First Sexology? Heinrich Kaan's *Psychopathia Sexualis* (1844)," in Heinrich Kaan, *Heinrich Kaan's "Psychopathia Sexualis" (1844)* (Ithaca: Cornell University Press, 2016), 14–15.

119. We might note, for example, just how ungendered Kaan's perversions are, focused on things like statues and corpses. But even Kaan's version of "Lesbian love" occurs "either between men or between women" suggesting that gender has not yet taken on its diacritical importance for object choice. This will occur in its encounter with inversion and phrenology. Kaan, 79.

120. Michael Lynch, "'Here is Adhesiveness': From Friendship to Homosexuality," *Victorian Studies* 29.1 (1985): 70.

121. Lynch, 91.

122. Davidson, 32. My argument builds on Molly McGarry's intriguing and unelaborated claim that phrenology was "a sort of first draft of sexology." Molly McGarry, *Ghosts of Futures Past: Spiritualism and the Cultural Politics of Nineteenth-Century America* (Berkeley: University of California Press, 2008), 168.

123. Foucault, *History*, 154. It is possible that Foucault may have meant 1887, the year that Alfred Binet coins the term "fetishism." See Alfred Binet, "Du fétichisme dans l'amour," *Revue Philosophique* 24 (1887): 143–67.

124. Norman Domeier, *The Eulenburg Affair: A Cultural History of Politics in the German Empire*, trans. Deborah Lucas Schneider (Rochester, NY: Boydell and Brewer, 2015).

125. Iwan Bloch, *The Sexual Life of Our Time in Its Relations to Modern Civilization*, trans. M. Eden Paul (London: Rebman Limited, 1909), 466–67, 471.

126. On Money, see Lisa Downing, Iain Morland, and Nikki Sullivan, *Fuckology: Critical Essays on John Money's Diagnostic Concepts* (Chicago: University of Chicago Press, 2015).

127. Canaday, 52, 216.

128. Canaday, 216.

129. Robert O. Brennan and David T. Durack, "Gay Compromise Syndrome," *Lancet* 381.8259 (1981): 1338–39; and Lawrence K. Altman, "New Homosexual Disorder Worries Health Officials," *New York Times*, May 11, 1982.

130. Google Ngram Viewer, accessed January 29, 2017.

131. For an overview of some of the conceptual problems and limitations of the Google Ngram Viewer, see Eitan Adam Pechenick, Christopher M. Danforth, and Peter Sheridan Dodds, "Characterizing the Google Book Corpus: Strong Limits to Inferences of Socio-Cultural and Linguistic Evolution," *PLOS: ONE*, October 7, 2015. A similar *n*-gram mapping suggests that "sexual preference" with its focus on choice fares far less well ("sexual orientation" is used between five and almost eight times as much as "sexual preference"). Google Ngram Viewer, accessed January 29, 2017.

132. Sedgwick, *Epistemology*, 47.

133. Coviello, 4.

134. Halperin, 107.

135. Bibler, "Possessive Intimacy"; Reay, *New York Hustlers*; and Benjamin Kahan, *Celibacies: American Modernism and Sexual Life* (Durham: Duke University Press, 2013).

# Bibliography

Abelove, Henry. "Some Speculations on the History of Sexual Intercourse during the Long Eighteenth Century in England." In *Deep Gossip*, 21–28. Minneapolis: University of Minnesota Press, 2005.

Aberth, John. *The Black Death: The Great Mortality of 1345-1350: A Brief History with Documents*. New York: Palgrave, 2005.

Ackerman, Alan. *Just Words: Lillian Hellman, Mary McCarthy, and the Failure of Public Conversation in America*. New Haven: Yale University Press, 2011.

Ahmed, Sara. *Willful Subjects*. Durham: Duke University Press, 2014.

Aldrich, Robert. *Colonialism and Homosexuality*. New York: Routledge, 2003.

Alexander, Ruth M. *The "Girl Problem": Female Sexual Delinquency in New York, 1900–1940*. Ithaca and London: Cornell University Press, 1995.

Allen, Jonathan A. "Falling in Love with Eve Kosofsky Sedgwick." *Mosaic* 48.1 (2015): 1–16.

Altman, Lawrence K. "New Homosexual Disorder Worries Health Officials." *New York Times*, May 11, 1982.

Amin, Kadji. *Disturbing Attachments: Gender, Modern Pederasty, and Queer History*. Durham: Duke University Press, 2017.

Anderson, Sherwood. "The Future of Japanese and American Writing" In *Sherwood Anderson: The Writer at His Craft*, edited by Jack Salzman, David D. Anderson, and Kichinosuke Ohashi, 305–9. Mamaroneck, NY: Paul P. Appel, 1979. Reprinted from *The Jiji Shimpo* [*Current News*], Japan, January 1928.

———. "Introduction to Walt Whitman's *Leaves of Grass*." In *Sherwood Anderson: The Writer at His Craft*, edited by Jack

Salzman, David D. Anderson, and Kichinosuke Ohashi, 19–21. Mamaroneck, NY: Paul P. Appel, 1979.

———. *Letters of Sherwood Anderson*. Edited by Howard Mumford Jones. Boston: Little, Brown, and Company, 1953.

———. *Many Marriages*. New York: B. W. Huebsch, 1923.

———. *The Modern Writer*. San Francisco: Lantern Press, 1925.

———. "New Orleans, The Double Dealer, and the Modern Movement in America." In *Sherwood Anderson: The Writer at His Craft*, edited by Jack Salzman, David D. Anderson, and Kichinosuke Ohashi, 281–92. Mamaroneck, NY: Paul P. Appel, 1979. Reprinted from *Double Dealer* 3 (March 1922), 119–26.

———. *Sherwood Anderson's Memoirs: A Critical Edition*. Edited by Ray Lewis White. Chapel Hill: University of North Carolina Press, 1969.

———. *Winesburg, Ohio: A Group of Tales of Ohio Small Town Life*. New York: Barnes and Noble, 2010.

Anonymous. "Lillian versus Mary." *Washington Star*, March 23, 1980.

Arac, Jonathan. "The Form of Carnival in *Under the Volcano*." *PMLA* 92.3 (1977): 481–89.

Ariès, Philippe. "Thoughts on the History of Homosexuality." In *Western Sexuality: Practice and Precept in Past and Present Times*, 62–75. Oxford: Basil Blackwell, 1985.

Arikha, Noga. *Passions and Tempers: A History of the Humours*. New York: Ecco, 2007.

Arondekar, Anjali. *For the Record: On Sexuality and the Colonial Archive in India*. Durham: Duke University Press, 2009.

Arseneau, Julie. R., Patrick R. Grzanka, Joseph R. Miles, and Ruth E. Fassinger. "Development and Initial Validation of the Sexual Orientation Beliefs Scale (SOBS)." *Journal of Counseling Psychology* 60.3 (2013): 407–20.

Auden, W. H. "Casino." In *Selected Poems*, edited by Edward Mendelson, 47–48. New York: Vintage, 2007.

Bailey, Blake. "Introduction." In Charles Jackson, *The Lost Weekend: A Novel*, xiii–xx. New York: Vintage Books, 2013.

Baldwin, Peter. *Contagion and the State in Europe, 1830–1930*. Cambridge: Cambridge University Press, 1999.

Barnes, Djuna. *Ladies Almanack: showing their Signs and their tides; their Moons and their Changes; the seasons as it is with them; their Eclipses and their Equinoxes; as well as a full Record of diurnal and nocturnal Distempers*. New York: New York University Press, 1992.

Barrett, Lindon. *Conditions of the Present: Selected Essays*. Edited by Janet Neary. Durham: Duke University Press, 2018.

Bauer, Heike. *English Literary Sexology: Translations of Inversion, 1860–1930*. New York: Palgrave, 2009.

———. "Literary Sexualities." In *The Cambridge Companion to the Body in Literature*, edited by David Hilman and Ulrika Maude, 101–15. Cambridge: Cambridge University Press, 2015.

Beachy, Robert. *Gay Berlin: Birthplace of a Modern Identity*. New York: Knopf, 2014.

———. "The German Invention of Homosexuality." *Journal of Modern History* 82.4 (2010): 801–38.

Beam, Lura. *Bequest from a Life: A Biography of Louise Stevens Bryant*. Baltimore: Waverly Press, 1963.

Beard, George M. *Sexual Neurasthenia: Its Hygiene, Causes, Symptoms, Treatment*. New York: E. B. Treat, 1884.

Bech, Henning. *When Men Meet: Homosexuality and Modernity*. Chicago: University of Chicago Press, 1997.

Beemyn, Genny. *A Queer Capital: A History of Gay Life in Washington, DC*. New York: Routledge, 2014.

Bennett, Judith. "Confronting Continuity." *Journal of Women's History* 9.3 (1997): 73–94.

Benstock, Shari. *Women of the Left Bank: Paris, 1900–1940*. Austin: University of Texas Press, 1987.

Ben-Zvi, Linda. *Susan Glaspell: Her Life and Times*. Oxford: Oxford University Press, 2007.

Berlant, Lauren. "On Citizenship and Optimism." Interviewed by David K. Seitz. *Society and Space*, March 22, 2013. http://societyandspace.org/2013/03/22/on-citizenship-and-optimism/.

———. "Starved." *South Atlantic Quarterly* 106.3 (2007): 433–44.

Berryman, Mildred Papers. Library Special Collections, Charles E. Young Research Library, University of California, Los Angeles. UCLA MSS 2170. Box 1, Folder 4.

Bersani, Leo. *Homos*. Cambridge: Harvard University Press, 1995.

Bibler, Michael. *Cotton's Queer Relations: Same-Sex Intimacy and the Literature of the Southern Plantation, 1936–1968*. Charlottesville: University of Virginia Press, 2009.

———. "Masculine Sentiment, Racial Fetishism, and Same-Sex Desire in Antebellum Southern Literature." In *The Oxford Handbook to the Literature of the US South*, edited by Barbara Ladd and Fred Hobson, 138–60. New York: Oxford University Press, 2016.

———. "Possessive Intimacy." Unpublished manuscript.

Binet, Alfred. "Du fétichisme dans l'amour." *Revue Philosophique* 24 (1887): 143–67.

Black, Cheryl. *The Women of Provincetown, 1915–1922*. Tuscaloosa: University of Alabama Press, 2002.

Blackstone, William. *Commentaries on the Laws of England, Book IV: Of Public Wrongs*. Edited by Ruth Paley. Oxford: Oxford University Press, 2016.

Bloch, Iwan [Ivan]. *Anthropological and Ethnological Studies in the Strangest Sex Acts in Modes of Love of All Races Illustrated*. Translated by Ernst Vogel. New York: Falstaff Press, 1935.

———. *Anthropological Studies in the Strange Sexual Practises of All Races in All Ages*. Translated by Keene Wallis. New York: Anthropological Press, 1933.

———. *Marquis de Sade: The Man and His Age*. Translated by James Bruce. Magnolia Books, 2013.

———. *Marquis de Sade's Anthropologia Sexualis of 600 Perversions, 120 Days of Sodom; or, the School of Libertinage*. Translated by Richard Sabatier. New York: Falstaff Press, 1934.

———. *Sexual Life in England: Past and Present*. Translated by William H. Forstern. Hertfordshire, UK: Oracle, 1996.

———. *The Sexual Life of Our Time in Its Relations to Modern Civilization*. Translated by M. Eden Paul. London: Rebman Limited, 1909.

Bogard, Travis, and Jackson R. Bryer, eds. *The Provincetown Players and the Playwrights' Theatre, 1915–1922*. Jefferson, NC: McFarland, 2004.

Bongiorno, Frank. *The Sex Lives of Australians: A History*. Collingwood, Australia: Black Inc., 2012.

Boone, Joseph. *The Homoerotics of Orientalism*. New York: Columbia University Press, 2014.

Bowen, Patrick D. *A History of Conversion to Islam in the United States*. Vol. 1., *White American Muslims before 1975*. Boston: Brill, 2015.

Braddock, Jeremy. "The Poetics of Conjecture: Countee Cullen's Subversive Exemplarity." *Calloo* 25.4 (2002): 1250–71.

Braudel, Ferdinand. *The Mediterranean and the Mediterranean World in the Age of Philip II*. Translated by Siân Reynolds. New York: Harper and Row, 1972.

Braunschneider, Theresa. *Our Coquettes: Capacious Desire in the Eighteenth Century*. Charlottesville: University of Virginia Press, 2009.

Bray, Alan. *The Friend*. Chicago: University of Chicago Press, 2003.

———. *Homosexuality in Renaissance England*. New York: Columbia University Press, 1982.

Bray, Alan, and Michel Rey. "The Body of the Friend." In Alan Bray, *The Friend*, 140–76. Chicago: University of Chicago Press, 2003.

Brennan, Robert O., and David T. Durack. "Gay Compromise Syndrome." *Lancet* 381.8259 (1981): 1338–39.

Brewer, Charlotte. *Treasure House of the Language: The Living OED*. New Haven: Yale University Press, 2007.

Brightman, Carol. *Writing Dangerously: Mary McCarthy and Her World*. New York: Clarkson Potter Publishers, 1992.

Brinkley, Douglas G. *Wheels for the World: Henry Ford, His Company, and a Century of Progress*. New York: Penguin, 2004.

Bristow, Joseph. *Sexuality*. New York: Routledge, 1997.

Browne, Stella. *The Sexual Variety and Variability Among Women and Their Bearing Upon Social Reconstruction*. London: C. W. Beaumont, 1915.

Bruce, Kennilworth. *Goldie*. New York: William Godwin, 1933.

Bryk, Felix. *Voodoo-EROS*. Translated by Mayne F. Sexton. New York: privately printed, 1933.

Bullough, Vern L. "Introduction." In Karl Heinrich Ulrichs, *The Riddle of "Man-Manly" Love: The Pioneering Work on Male Homosexuality, Volume 1*, trans. Michael A. Lombardi-Nash, 21–27. New York: Prometheus Books, 1994.

Bunzl, Matti. "Sexual Modernity as Subject and Object." *Modernism/modernity* 9.1 (2002): 165–75.

Burgess, Ernest Watson Papers. The University of Chicago Library. Box 128 Folder 7.

Burton, Richard F. "Terminal Essay." In vol. 10 of *The Book of a Thousand Nights and a Night: A Plain and Literal Translation of the Arab Nights Entertainments*, trans. Richard F. Burton, 63–302. London: Burton Club, 1886.

Butler, Judith. *Bodies that Matter: On the Discursive Limits of "Sex."* New York: Routledge, 1993.

Canaday, Margot. *The Straight State: Sexuality and Citizenship in Twentieth-Century America*. Princeton: Princeton University Press, 2009.

Cannon, Thomas. "The Indictment of John Purser, Containing Thomas Cannon's *Ancient and Modern Pederasty Investigated and Exemplify'd*." Edited by Hal Gladfelder. *Eighteenth-Century Life* 31.1 (2007): 39–61.

Carhart, J. W. *Norma Trist; or Pure Carbon: A Story of the Inversion of the Sexes*. Austin, TX: Eugene von Boeckmann, 1895.

Carpenter, Edward. *Civilization: Its Cause and Its Cure, and Other Essays*. London: Swan Sonnenschein and Co, 1891.

———. *Days with Walt Whitman: With Some Notes on His Life and Work*. New York: Macmillan, 1906.

———. *Homogenic Love and Its Place in a Free Society*. London: Redundancy Press, 1980.

———. *The Intermediate Sex: A Study of Some Transitional Types of Men and Women*. New York: Mitchell Kennerley, 1931.

———. *Intermediate Types among Primitive Folk: A Study in Social Evolution*. London: George Allan & Co., 1914.

———. *The Psychology of the Poet Shelley*. London: George Allen & Unwin, 1925.

———. *Towards Democracy: Complete Edition in Four Parts*. London: George Allen and Unwin Limited, 1918.

Carroll, Lewis. *Alice in Wonderland*. Edited by Donald J. Gray. New York: W. W. Norton and Company, 1992.

Carter, Julian B. *The Heart of Whiteness: Normal Sexuality and Race in America, 1880-1940*. Durham: Duke University Press, 2007.

Caselli, Daniela. *Improper Modernism: Djuna Barnes's Bewildering Corpus*. Burlington, VT: Ashgate, 2009.

———. "Literary and Sexual Experimentalism in the Interwar Years." In *The Cambridge Companion to American Gay and Lesbian Literature*, edited by Scott Herring, 103–21. Cambridge: Cambridge University Press, 2015.

Casper, Johann Ludwig. "Ueber Nothzucht und Päderastie und deren Ermittelung Seitens des Gerichtsarztes." *Vierteljahrsschrift für gerichtliche und öffentliche Medicin* 1 (1852): 21–78.

Cassata, Francesco. *Building the New Man: Eugenics, Racial Science, and Genetics in Twentieth-Century Italy*. Translated by Erin O'Loughlin. Budapest: Central European University Press, 2011.

Caserio, Robert. "Queer Modernism." In *The Oxford Handbook of Modernisms*, edited by Peter Brooker, Andrzej Gąsiorek, Deborah Longworth, and Andrew Thacker, 199–217. Oxford: Oxford University Press, 2010.

Cassidy, Tonya. "People, Place, Performance: Theoretically Revisiting Mother Clap's Molly House." In *Queer People: Negotiations and Expressions of Homosexuality, 1700–1800*, edited by Chris Mounsey and Caroline Gonda, 99–113. Lewisburg, PA: Bucknell University Press, 2007.

Cecire, Natalia. "Experimentalism by Contact." *diacritics* 43.1 (2015): 6–35.

Céline, Louis-Ferdinand. *Journey to the End of the Night*. Translated by John H. P. Marks. Boston: Little, Brown, and Company, 1934.

Chaddock, Charles Gilbert. "Sexual Crimes." In *A System of Legal Medicine*, vol. 2, edited by Allan McLane Hamilton and Lawrence Godkin, 525–72. New York: E. B. Treat, 1894.

Chauncey, George. "From Sexual Inversion to Homosexuality: Medicine and the Changing Conceptualization of Female Deviance." *Salmagundi* 58/59 (1982–1983): 114–46.

———. *Gay New York: Gender, Urban Culture, and the Making of the Gay Male World, 1890–1940*. New York: Basic Books, 1994.

Chiang, Howard H. "Historicizing the Emergence of Sexual Freedom: The Medical Knowledge of Psychiatry and the Scientific Power of Sexology, 1880–1920." *Journal of the North Carolina Association of Historians* 16 (2008): 35–76.

———. "Liberating Sex, Knowing Desire: *Scientia Sexualis* and Epistemic Turning Points in the History of Sexuality." *History of the Human Sciences* 23.5 (2010): 42–69.

Chidley, William James. *The Answer: A Philosophical Essay*. Sydney, Australia: A. J. Tomalin, 1912.

Chiles, Katy L. *Transformable Race: Surprising Metamorphosis in the Literature of Early America*. Oxford: Oxford University Press, 2013.

Chudacoff, Howard. *The Age of the Bachelor: Creating an American Subculture*. Princeton: Princeton University Press, 1999.

Cipolla, Carlo. *Miasmas and Disease: Public Health and the Environment in the Pre-Industrial Age*. Translated by Elizabeth Potter. New Haven: Yale University Press, 1992.

Clark, L. Pierce. "Some Psychological Aspects of Alcoholism." *International Record of Medicine and General Practice Clinics* 109 (May 31, 1919): 930–33.

Clarke, Simon. "The Crisis of Fordism and the Crisis of Capitalism." *Telos*, New York, 83 (Spring 1990): 71–98.

Cleminson, Richard, and Francisco Vazquez García. *"Los Invsisibles": A History of Male Homosexuality in Spain, 1850–1939*. Cardiff: University of Wales Press, 2007.

Cocca, Carolyn. *Jailbait: The Politics of Statutory Rape Laws in the United States*. Albany: SUNY Press, 2004.

Cocks, H. G. *Visions of Sodom: Religion, Homoerotic Desire, and the End of the World in England, c. 1550–1850*. Chicago: University of Chicago Press, 2017.

Cohen, Ed. *A Body Worth Defending: Immunity, Biopolitics, and the Apotheosis of the Modern Body.* Durham: Duke University Press, 2009.

Connolly, Brian. *Domestic Intimacies: Incest and the Liberal Subject in Nineteenth-Century America.* Philadelphia: Penn Press, 2014.

Corber, Robert J. *Cold War Femme: Lesbianism, National Identity, and Cold War Cinema.* Durham: Duke University Press, 2011.

———. *Homosexuality in Cold War America: Resistance and the Crisis of Masculinity.* Durham: Duke University Press, 1997.

Coviello, Peter. "Plural: Mormon Polygamy and the Biopolitics of Secularism." *History of the Present: A Journal of Critical History* 7.2 (2017): 219–41.

———. *Tomorrow's Parties: Sex and the Untimely in Nineteenth-Century America.* New York: New York University Press, 2013.

Crowley, Aleister. *The Book of the Law.* Boston: Red Wheel, 1976.

Crozier, Ivan. "Nineteenth-Century British Psychiatric Writing About Homosexuality before Havelock Ellis: The Missing Story." *Journal of the History of Medicine and Allied Sciences* 63.1 (2008): 65–102.

Crozier, Ivan, and Heike Bauer. "Sexology, Historiography, Citation, Embodiment: A Review and (Frank) Exchange." *History of the Human Sciences,* June 27, 2017. http://www.histhum.com/?p=367.

Cryle, Peter, and Elizabeth Stephens. *Normality: A Critical Genealogy.* Chicago: University of Chicago Press, 2000.

Curran, Andrew. *Anatomy of Blackness.* Baltimore: Johns Hopkins University Press, 2011.

Curtin, Kaier. *"We Can Always Call Them Bulgarians": The Emergence of Lesbian and Gay Men on the American Stage.* Boston: Alyson Publications, 1987.

Dabhoiwala, Faramerz. *The Origins of Sex: A History of the First Sexual Revolution.* New York: Penguin, 2012.

Daniel, Drew. "'Why Be Something That You're Not?': Punk Performance and the Epistemology of Queer Minstrelsy." *Social Text* 31.3 (2013): 13–34.

Davenport, Charles. *The Feebly Inhibited; Nomadism, or the Wandering Impulse, with Special Reference to Heredity.* Washington, DC: Carnegie Institution of Washington, 1915.

Davidson, Arnold I. *The Emergence of Sexuality: Historical Epistemology and the Formation of Concepts.* Cambridge: Harvard University Press, 2004.

Davidson, Guy. "Embarrassment in 1968: Gore Vidal's Sexuality in the Public Sphere." *Mosaic* 48.1 (2015): 147–64.

———. "Ornamental Identity: Commodity Fetishism, Masculinity, and Sexuality in *The Golden Bowl.*" *Henry James Review* 28 (2007): 26–42.

Davis, Lennard J. *Enforcing Normalcy: Disability, Deafness, and the Body.* New York: Verso, 1995.

Day, Douglas. *Malcolm Lowry: A Biography.* Oxford: Oxford University Press, 1984.

De Groot, Joanna. "Hybridizing Past, Present, and Future: Reflections on the 'Sexology' of R. F. Burton." In *Sex, Knowledge, and Receptions of the Past,* edited by Kate Fisher and Rebecca Langlands, 135–59. Oxford: Oxford University Press, 2015.

D'Emilio, John. "Born Gay?" In *The World Turned: Essays on Gay History, Politics, and Culture*, 154–64. Durham: Duke University Press, 2002.

———. "Capitalism and Gay Identity." In *The Lesbian and Gay Studies Reader*, edited by Henry Abelove, Michèlle Aina Barale, and David M. Halperin, 467–76. New York: Routledge, 1993.

D'Emilio, John, and Estelle Freedman. *Intimate Matters: A History of Sexuality in America*. Chicago: University of Chicago Press, 2009.

Denning, Michael. *The Cultural Front: The Laboring of American Culture in the Twentieth Century*. New York: Verso, 2011.

DePastino, Todd. *Citizen Hobo*. Chicago: University of Chicago Press, 2003.

Deutsch, Helen, and Stella Hanau. *The Provincetown: A Story of the Theatre*. New York: Farar and Rinehart, 1931.

Deveney, John Patrick. *Paschal Beverly Randolph: A Nineteenth-Century Black American Spiritualist, Rosicrucian, and Sex Magician*. Albany: State University of New York Press, 1997.

Dickinson, Robert Latou, and Lura Beam. *A Thousand Marriages: A Medical Study of Sex-Adjustment*. Baltimore: The Williams and Wilkins Company, 1931.

Dickinson, Thomas H. *Winter Bound: A Play in Three Acts and Nine Scenes*. Library of Congress, unpublished manuscript, PS3507.I3537 W5 (Rare Bk Coll).

Dimock, Wai Chee. "Weak Theory: Henry James, Colm Tóibín, and W. B. Yeats." *Critical Inquiry* 39 (2013): 732–53.

Dixon, Joy. *Divine Feminine: Theosophy and Feminism in England*. Baltimore: Johns Hopkins University Press, 2001.

———. "'Out of your clinging kisses . . . I create a new world': Sexuality and Spirituality in the Work of Edward Carpenter." In *The Ashgate Research Companion to Nineteenth-Century Spiritualism and the Occult*, edited by Tatiana Kontou and Sarah Willburn, 143–63. New York: Routledge, 2012.

———. "Sexology and the Occult: Sexuality and Subjectivity in Theosophy's New Age." *Journal of the History of Sexuality* 7.3 (1997): 409–33.

Doan, Laura. *Disturbing Practices: History, Sexuality, and Women's Experience of Modern War*. Chicago: University of Chicago Press, 2013.

———. *Fashioning Sapphism: The Origins of a Modern English Lesbian Culture*. New York: Columbia University Press, 2001.

———. "Marie Stopes's Wonderful Rhythm Charts: Normalizing the Natural." *Journal of the History of Ideas* 78.4 (2017): 595–620.

———. "'The Outcast of One Age is the Hero of Another': Radclyffe Hall, Edward Carpenter, and the Intermediate Sex." In *Palatable Poison: Critical Perspectives on The Well of Loneliness*, edited by Laura Doan and Jay Prosser, 162–78. New York: Columbia University Press, 2001.

Domeier, Norman. *The Eulenburg Affair: A Cultural History of Politics in the German Empire*. Translated by Deborah Lucas Schneider. Rochester, NY: Boydell and Brewer, 2015.

Dover, K. J. *Greek Homosexuality*. Cambridge: Harvard University Press, 1989.

Dowling, Robert. *Slumming in New York: From the Waterfront to Mythic Harlem.* Urbana: University of Illinois Press, 2007.

Downing, Lisa, Iain Morland, and Nikki Sullivan. *Fuckology: Critical Essays on John Money's Diagnostic Concepts.* Chicago: University of Chicago Press, 2015.

Dubois-Desaulle, Gaston. *Bestiality: An Historical, Medical, Legal, and Literary Study.* Boston: Panurge Press, 1933.

Duggan, Lisa. "Queering the State." *Social Text* 39 (1994): 1–14.

Du Maurier, George. *Trilby.* New York: Oxford, 1998.

Duncan, Robert. "The Homosexual in Society." *Politics* 1.7 (August 1944): 209–11.

Edelman, Lee. "Unnamed: Eve's *Epistemology.*" *Criticism* 52.2 (2010): 185–90.

Edwards, Jason. *Eve Kosofsky Sedgwick.* New York: Routledge, 2009.

Eglinton, J. Z. *Greek Love.* New York: Oliver Layton Press, 1964.

Elfenbein, Andrew. *Romantic Genius: The Prehistory of a Homosexual Role.* New York: Columbia University Press, 1999.

Ellis, Havelock. *Man and Woman: A Study of Human Secondary Sexual Characters.* New York: The Walter Scott Publishing Company, 1904.

———. *The Problem of Race-Regeneration.* New York: Moffat, Yard, and Company, 1911.

———. *Psychology of Sex: A Manual for Students.* New York: Emerson Books, 1937.

———. *Studies in the Psychology of Sex*, vol. 2. Philadelphia: F. A. Davis Company, 1921.

Ellis, Havelock, and John Addington Symonds. *Sexual Inversion: A Critical Edition.* Edited by Ivan Crozier. New York: Palgrave, 2008.

Epprecht, Marc. *Heterosexual Africa? The History of an Idea from the Age of Exploration to the Age of AIDS.* Athens: Ohio University Press, 2008.

Erenberg, Lewis A. *Steppin' Out: New York Nightlife and the Transformation of American Culture, 1890–1930.* Chicago: University of Chicago Press, 1981.

Erkkila, Betsy. *Mixed Bloods and Other Crosses: Rethinking American Literature from the Revolution to the Culture Wars.* Philadelphia: University of Pennsylvania Press, 2005.

Erzen, Tanya. *Straight to Jesus: Sexual and Christian Conversions in the Ex-Gay Movement.* Berkeley: University of California Press, 2006.

Escoffier, Jeffrey. "Gay-for-Pay: Straight Men and the Making of Gay Pornography." *Qualitative Sociology* 26.4 (2003): 531–55.

Eskridge, William N., Jr. *Dishonorable Passions: Sodomy Laws in America, 1861–2003.* New York: Viking, 2008.

Etter, William M. "Speaking of Manhood in *Winesburg, Ohio.*" In *Sherwood Anderson's Winesburg, Ohio*, edited by Precious McKenzie, 77–106. Leiden: Brill Rodopi, 2016.

Faderman, Lillian. "Lesbian Chic: Experimentation and Repression in the 1920s." In *The Gender and Consumer Culture Reader*, edited by Jennifer Scanlon, 153–65. New York: New York University Press, 2000.

———. *Odd Girls and Twilight Lovers: A History of Lesbian Life in Twentieth-Century America.* New York: Penguin, 1992.

———. *Scotch Verdict.* New York: Columbia University Press, 1994.

———. *Surpassing the Love of Men: Romantic Friendship and Love Between Women from the Renaissance to the Present.* New York: Perennial Edition, 2001.

Fass, Paula S. *Kidnapped: Child Abduction in America.* Oxford: Oxford University Press, 1997.

Féray, Jean-Claude, and Manfred Herzer. "Homosexual Studies and Politics in the 19th Century: Karl Maria Kertbeny." Translated by Glen W. Peppel. *Journal of Homosexuality* 19.1 (1990): 23–47.

Ferguson, Christine. *Determined Spirits: Eugenics, Heredity and Racial Regeneration in Anglo-American Spiritualist Writing, 1848–1930.* Edinburgh: Edinburgh University Press, 2012.

Ferguson, Roderick A. *Aberrations in Black: Toward a Queer of Color Critique.* Minneapolis: University of Minnesota Press, 2004.

———. *The Reorder of Things: The University and Its Pedagogies of Minority Difference.* Minneapolis: University of Minnesota Press, 2012.

Ferres, John H. "The Nostalgia of *Winesburg, Ohio.*" In *Winesburg, Ohio: Text and Criticism*, edited by John H. Ferres, 466–73. New York: Penguin, 1996.

Field, Andrew. *Djuna: The Life and Times of Djuna Barnes.* New York: G. P. Putnam's Sons, 1983.

Firchow, Peter E. "Private Faces in Public Places: Auden's *The Orators.*" *PMLA* 92 (1977): 253–72.

Fisher, Kate, and Jana Funke. "British Sexual Science Beyond the Medical: Cross-Disciplinary, Cross-Historical, and Cross-Cultural Translations." In *Sexology and Translation: Cultural and Scientific Encounters Across the Modern World*, edited by Heike Bauer, 95–114. Philadelphia: Temple University Press, 2015.

Fisher, Will. "Queer Money." *ELH* 66.1 (1999): 1–23.

———. "The Sexual Politics of Victorian Historiographical Writing about the 'Renaissance.'" *GLQ* 14.1 (2008): 41–67.

Floyd, Kevin. *The Reification of Desire: Toward a Queer Marxism.* Minneapolis: University of Minnesota Press, 2009.

Floyd-Wilson, Mary. *English Ethnicity and Race in Early Modern Drama.* Cambridge: Cambridge University Press, 2003.

Flynt, Josiah. "Homosexuality among Tramps." In Havelock Ellis and John Addington Symonds, *Sexual Inversion: A Critical Edition*, edited by Ivan Crozier, 296–300. New York: Palgrave, 2008.

Foote, Stephanie. "Afterword: Ann Aldrich and Lesbian Writing in the Fifties." In Ann Aldrich, *We Walk Alone*, edited by Marijane Meaker, 157–83. New York: First Feminist Press, 2006.

Forberg, Friedrich Karl. *Manual of Classical Erotology.* New York: Grove Press, 1966.

Ford, Charles A. "Homosexual Practices of Institutionalized Females." *Journal of Abnormal Psychology* 23.4 (1929): 442–48.

Forel, Auguste. *The Sexual Question: A Scientific, Psychological, Hygienic, and Sociological Study.* Brooklyn, NY: Physicians and Surgeons Book Company, 1931.

Forster, E. M. *Maurice: A Novel*. New York: W. W. Norton & Company, 1993.

Foucault, Michel. *Abnormal: Lectures at the Collège De France, 1974–1975*. Edited by Valerio Marchetti and Antonella Salomoni. New York: Picador, 2003.

———. *The Birth of the Clinic: An Archaeology of Medical Perception*. Translated by Alan Sheridan. New York: Vintage, 1994.

———. *The History of Sexuality*, vol. I, *An Introduction*. Translated by Robert Hurley. New York: Vintage Books, 1990.

———. "Nietzsche, Genealogy, History." In *The Foucault Reader*, edited by Paul Rabinow, 76–100. New York: Pantheon Books, 1984.

———. "Sex, Power, and the Politics of Identity." In *Ethics: Subjectivity and Truth*, edited by Paul Rabinow, 163–74. New York: New Press, 1997.

Fowler, O. S. *The Practical Phrenologist*. Boston: O. S. Fowler, 1869.

Freccero, Carla. "Undoing the Histories of Homosexuality." In *Queer/Early/ Modern*, 31–50. Durham: Duke University Press, 2006.

Freedman, Estelle B. "The Prison Lesbian: Race, Class, and the Construction of the Aggressive Female Homosexual, 1915–1965." In *Feminism, Sexuality, and Politics*, 141–58. Chapel Hill: University of North Carolina Press, 2006.

Freeman, Elizabeth. "Packing History, Count(er)ing Generations." *New Literary History* 31.4 (2000): 727–44.

———. "Still After." In *After Sex? On Writing since Queer Theory*, edited by Janet Halley and Andrew Parker, 495–500. Durham: Duke University Press, 2011.

———. *Time Binds: Queer Temporalities, Queer Histories*. Durham: Duke University Press, 2010.

———. *The Wedding Complex: Forms of Belonging in Modern American Culture*. Durham: Duke University Press, 2002.

Freud, Sigmund. *Three Essays on the Theory of Sexuality*. Translated by James Strachey. New York: Basic Books, 2000.

Fuechtner, Veronika, Douglas E. Haynes, and Ryan M. Jones, eds. *A Global History of Sexual Science*. Berkeley: University of California Press, 2018.

Funke, Jana. "'Navigating the Past': Sexuality, Race, and the Uses of the Primitive in Magnus Hirschfeld's *The World Journey of a Sexologist*." In *Sex, Knowledge, and the Receptions of the Past*, edited by Kate Fisher and Rebecca Langlands, 111–34. Oxford: Oxford University Press, 2015.

———. "'We Cannot Be Greek Now': Age Difference, Corruption of Youth and the Making of Sexual Inversion." *English Studies* 94.2 (2013): 139–53.

Fuss, Diana. "Freud's Fallen Women: Identification, Desire, and 'A Case of Homosexuality in a Woman.'" In *Fear of a Queer Planet: Queer Politics and Social Theory*, edited by Michael Warner, 42–68. Minneapolis: University of Minnesota Press, 1993.

———. *Identification Papers*. New York and London: Routledge, 1995.

Fussell, Edwin. "*Winesburg, Ohio*, Art and Isolation." In *Sherwood Anderson: A Collection of Critical Essays*, edited by Walter Bates Rideout, 39–48. Upper Saddle River, NJ: Prentice-Hall, 1974.

Gainor, Ellen J. *Susan Glaspell in Context: American Theatre, Culture, and Politics, 1915–1948*. Ann Arbor: University of Michigan Press, 2004.

Garrington, Abbie. *Haptic Modernism: Touch and the Tactile in Modernist Writing.* Edinburgh: Edinburgh University Press, 2013.

Garrison, Laurie. *Science, Sexuality, and Sensation Novels: Pleasures of the Senses.* New York: Palgrave, 2011.

Gautam, Sanjay K. *Foucault and the Kamasutra.* Chicago: University of Chicago Press, 2016.

Gertzman, Jay A. *Bookleggers and Smuthounds: The Trade in Erotica, 1920–1940.* Philadelphia: University of Pennsylvania Press, 1999.

Gibb, W. Travis. "Indecent Assault upon Children." In *A System of Legal Medicine*, vol. 1, edited by Allan McLane Hamilton and Lawrence Godkin, 649–57. New York: E. B. Treat, 1894.

Gide, André. *Corydon.* Translated by Richard Howard. New York: Open Road, 2015.

Gill-Peterson, Julian. "Implanting Plasticity into Sex and Trans/Gender," *Angelaki* 22.2 (2017): 47–60.

Gilman, Sander L. *The Jew's Body.* New York: Routledge, 1991.

Gladfelder, Hal. "In Search of Lost Texts: Thomas Cannon's *Ancient and Modern Pederasty Investigated and Exemplify'd.*" *Eighteenth-Century Life* 31.1 (2007): 22–38.

Glavey, Brian. *The Wallflower Avant-Garde: Modernism, Sexuality, and Queer Ekphrasis.* Oxford: Oxford University Press, 2016.

Godbeer, Richard. *Sexual Revolution in Early America.* Baltimore: Johns Hopkins Press, 2002.

Goethe, Johann Wolfgang von. *Elective Affinities.* Translated by Elizabeth Mayer and Louise Bogan. Chicago: Henry Regnery Company, 1963.

Goldberg, Jonathan. "On the Eve of the Future." *Criticism* 52.2 (2010): 283–91.

Golston, Michael. *Race and Rhythm in Modernist Poetry and Science.* New York: Columbia University Press, 2008.

Gould, George M. *A Dictionary of New Medical Terms.* London: Bailliere, Tindall, and Cox, 1905.

Gramsci, Antonio. *Selections from Prison Notebooks.* Edited and translated by Quintin Hoare and Geoffrey Nowell Smith. New York: International Publishers, 1971.

Grand, Sarah. "The New Aspect of the Woman Question." *North American Review* 158.448 (1894): 270–76.

Green, Martin. *Children of the Sun.* London: Constable, 1977.

Grosrichard, Alain. *The Sultan's Court: European Fantasies of the East.* New York: Verso, 1998.

Grossman, Jay. "Epilogue: Whitman's Centennial and the State of Whitman Studies." In *Breaking Bounds: Whitman and American Cultural Studies*, edited by Betsy Erkkila and Jay Grossman, 251–64. Oxford: Oxford University Press, 1996.

———. "'The Evangel-Poem of Comrades and of Love': Revising Whitman's Republicanism." *ATQ* 4.3 (1990): 201–18.

———. "F. O. Matthiessen (1902–1950), Anthropometry, and the Long Nineteenth Century." Invited lecture presented at the Workshop in the History of Material Texts, University of Pennsylvania, March 31, 2014.

Gunter, Archibald Clavering. *A Florida Enchantment.* New York: Home Publishing Company, 1892.

Hacking, Ian. *Mad Travelers: Reflections on the Reality of Transient Mental Illnesses.* Charlottesville: University of Virginia Press, 1998.

———. "Making Up People." In *Historical Ontology*, 99–114. Cambridge: Harvard University Press, 2002.

———. *The Social Construction of What?.* Cambridge: Harvard University Press, 1999.

Haeberle, Erwin J. "The Jewish Contribution to the Development of Sexology." *Journal of Sex Research* 18.4 (1982): 305–23.

Halberstam, Judith (Jack). *Female Masculinity.* Durham: Duke University Press, 1998.

Halley, Janet E. "The Politics of the Closet: Towards Equal Protection for Gay, Lesbian, and Bisexual Identity." *UCLA Law Review* 36 (1989): 915–76.

———. "Sexual Orientation and the Politics of Biology: A Critique of the Argument from Immutability." *Stanford Law Review* 46.3 (1994): 503–68.

Halperin, David M. *How to Be Gay.* Cambridge: Harvard University Press, 2012.

———. *How to Do the History of Homosexuality.* Chicago: University of Chicago Press, 2002.

———. *One Hundred Years of Homosexuality and Other Essays on Greek Love.* New York: Routledge, 1990.

———. *Saint Foucault.* Oxford: Oxford University Press, 1995.

———. "What is Sex For?" *Critical Inquiry* 43.1 (2016): 1–31.

Haralson, Eric. *Henry James and Queer Modernity.* Cambridge: Cambridge University Press, 2003.

Hardie, Melissa Jane. "Post-Structuralism: Originators and Heirs." In *The Cambridge Companion to American Gay and Lesbian Literature*, edited by Scott Herring, 206–23. Cambridge: Cambridge University Press, 2015.

Harker, Jaime. *Middlebrow Queer: Christopher Isherwood in America.* Minneapolis: University of Minnesota Press, 2013.

Harris, Cheryl. "Whiteness as Property." *Harvard Law Review* 106.8 (1993): 1707–91.

Harris, Jonathan Gil. *Sick Economies: Drama, Mercantilism, and Disease in Shakespeare's England.* Philadelphia: University of Pennsylvania Press, 2004.

Hartman, Saidiya V. *Scenes of Subjection: Terror, Slavery, and Self-Making in Nineteenth-Century America.* Oxford: Oxford University Press, 1997.

Harvey, David. *The Condition of Postmodernity.* New York: Blackwell, 1989.

Hayman, Ronald. *Thomas Mann: A Biography.* New York: Scribner, 1995.

Heaney, Emma. "The New Woman: Sexology, Literary Modernism, and the Trans Feminine Remainder." *Genre* 48.1 (2015): 1–33.

Heap, Chad. "The City as Sexual Laboratory: The Queer Heritage of the Chicago School." *Qualitative Sociology* 26.4 (2003): 457–87.

————. *Slumming*. Chicago: University of Chicago Press, 2009.

Hellman, Lillian. *Conversations with Lillian Hellman*. Edited by Jackson R. Bryer. Jackson: University Press of Mississippi, 1986.

————. *Four Plays by Lillian Hellman: "The Children's Hour," "Days to Come," "The Little Foxes," "Watch on the Rhine."* New York: Modern Library, 1942.

Hellman, Lillian, to Barbara Epstein. November 18, 1980, Lillian Hellman Papers, Harry Ransom Center, The University of Texas at Austin, Box 78. Folder 5.

Hemingway, Ernest. *A Moveable Feast: The Restored Edition*. New York: Scribner, 2009.

Henry, George W. *Sex Variants: A Study of Homosexual Patterns*. New York: Paul B. Hoeber, 1948.

Herring, Scott. "Catherian Friendship; Or, How Not to Do the History of Homosexuality." *Modern Fiction Studies* 52.1 (2006): 66–91.

————. *The Hoarders: Material Deviance in Modern American Culture*. Chicago: University of Chicago Press, 2014.

————. *Queering the Underworld: Slumming, Literature, and the Undoing of Lesbian and Gay History*. Chicago: University of Chicago Press, 2007.

————. Review of *Slumming: Sexual and Racial Encounters in American Nightlife, 1885–1940*, by Chad Heap. *American Historical Review* 115.1 (2010): 242–43.

Hewitt, Andrew. *Political Inversions: Homosexuality, Fascism, and the Modernist Imaginary*. Stanford: Stanford University Press, 1996.

Hirschfeld, Magnus. *The Homosexuality of Men and Women*. Translated by Michael A. Lombardi-Nash. Amherst, NY: Prometheus Books, 2000.

————. *Sexual Pathology: A Study of Derangements of the Sexual Instinct*. Translated by Jerome Gibbs. New York: Emerson Books, 1947.

Hirth, Georg. *Entropie der Keimsysteme und erbliche Entlastung*. Munich: G. Hirth's Verlag, 1900.

Hitchcock, Tim. "The Reformulation of Sexual Knowledge in Eighteenth-Century England." *Signs* (2012): 823–32.

Hoad, Neville. "Arrested Development or the Queerness of Savages: Resisting Evolutionary Narratives of Difference." *Postcolonial Studies* 3.2 (2000): 133–58.

Hocquenghem, Guy. *Homosexual Desire*. Translated by Daniella Dangoor. Durham: Duke University Press, 1993.

Houlbrook, Matt. *Queer London: Perils and Pleasures in the Sexual Metropolis, 1918–1957*. Chicago: University of Chicago Press, 2005.

Hubler, Edward, ed. *The Riddle of Shakespeare's Sonnets*. New York: Basic Books, 1962.

Hughes, Charles H. "Homo Sexual Complexion Perverts in St. Louis." *Alienist and Neurologist* 28.4 (1907): 487–88.

————. "An Organization of Colored Erotopaths." In *Gay American History: Lesbians and Gay Men in the USA*, edited by Jonathan Ned Katz, 42–43. New York: Crowell, 1976.

Huussen, Arend H., Jr. "Sodomy in the Dutch Republic During the Eighteenth Century." In *Hidden from History: Reclaiming the Gay and Lesbian Past*, edited by Martin Bauml Duberman, Martha Vicinus, and George Chauncey, 141–52. New York: Penguin, 1989.

Jackson, Charles. *The Lost Weekend: A Novel*. New York: Vintage Books, 2013.

Jagose, Annamarie. *Inconsequence: Lesbian Representation and the Logic of Sexual Sequence*. Ithaca: Cornell University Press, 2002.

———. *Orgasmology*. Durham: Duke University Press, 2012.

James, Henry. *The Bostonians*. Edited by Pierre A. Walker. New York: Modern Library, 2003.

Janes, Dominic. *Picturing the Closet: Male Secrecy and Homosexual Visibility in Britain*. Oxford: Oxford University Press, 2015.

Janssen, Diederick F. "'Chronophilia': Entries of Erotic Age Preference into Descriptive Psychopathology." *Medical History* 59.4 (2015): 575–98.

Jenkins, Philip. *Moral Panic: Changing Concepts of the Child Molester in Modern America*. New Haven: Yale University Press, 1998.

Jewett, Sarah Orne. *The Country of Pointed Firs and Other Stories*. New York: Signet Classics, 2009.

Johnson, Colin R. *Just Queer Folks: Gender and Sexuality in Rural America*. Philadelphia: Temple University Press, 2013.

Johnson, David K. "Physique Pioneers: The Politics of 1960s Gay Consumer Culture." *Journal of Social History* 43.4 (2010): 867–92.

Johnstone, A. W. "The Relation of Menstruation to Other Reproductive Functions." *American Journal of Obstetrics* 32 (1895): 33–48.

Jones, Jeffrey M. "Majority in the US Now Say Gays and Lesbians Born, Not Made." *Gallup*, http://www.gallup.com/poll/183332/majority-say-gays-lesbians-born-not-made.aspx.

Jouve, Emeline. *Susan Glaspell's Poetics and Politics of Rebellion*. Iowa City: University of Iowa Press, 2017.

Joyce, James. *Ulysses*. Edited by Hans Walter Gabler. New York: Vintage, 1986.

Kaan, Heinrich. *Heinrich Kaan's "Psychopathia Sexualis" (1844): A Classic Text in the History of Sexuality*. Translated by Melissa Haynes. Edited by Benjamin Kahan. Ithaca: Cornell University Press, 2016.

Kahan, Benjamin. *Celibacies: American Modernism and Sexual Life*. Durham: Duke University Press, 2013.

———. "Conjectures on the Sexual World-System." *GLQ* 23.3 (2017): 327–57.

———. "The First Sexology? Heinrich Kaan's *Psychopathia Sexualis* (1844)." In Heinrich Kaan, *Heinrich Kaan's "Psychopathia Sexualis" (1844): A Classic Text in the History of Sexuality*, 1–23. Translated by Melissa Haynes. Edited by Benjamin Kahan. Ithaca: Cornell University Press, 2016.

———. "Queer Modernism." In *A Handbook of Modernism Studies*, edited by Jean-Michel Rabaté, 343–58. Malden, MA: Wiley-Blackwell, 2013.

———. "Ray Johnson's Anti-Archive: Blackface, Sadomasochism, and the Racial and Sexual Imagination of Pop Art." *Angelaki* 23.1 (2018): 61–84.

———. "Unqueerness." *Feminist Formations* 28.2 (2016): 162–68.

————. "What is Sexual Modernity?" *Modernism/modernity Print Plus* 1.3 (2016). https://modernismmodernity.org/forums/what-sexual-modernity.

Katz, Jonathan Ned. "Envisioning the World We Make, Social-Historical Construction, A Model, A Manifesto." Published February 2, 2016. http://outhistory.org/exhibits/show/katz-writing-work/katz-vision-intro.

————. *Gay American History: Lesbians and Gay Men in the USA*. New York: Crowell, 1976.

————. *The Invention of Heterosexuality*. New York: Dutton, 1995.

————, ed. *Miss Marianne Woods and Miss Jane Pirie against Dame Helen Cumming Gordon*. New York: Arno Press, 1975.

Kaus, Robert M. "The Plaintiff's Hour." *Harper's Magazine* 266.1594 (March 1983): 14–16, 18.

Kaylor, Michael Matthew. *Secreted Desires: The Major Uranians: Hopkins, Pater, and Wilde*. Brno, CZ: Masaryk University Press, 2006.

Kempf, Edward J. *Psychopathology*. St. Louis: C. V. Mosby Company, 1921.

Kennedy, Elizabeth Lapovsky. "'But we would never talk about it': The Structures of Lesbian Discretion in South Dakota, 1928–1933." In *Inventing Lesbian Cultures in America*, edited by Ellen Lewin, 15–39. Boston: Beacon Press, 1996.

Kennedy, Hubert. "Karl Heinrich Ulrichs: First Theorist of Homosexuality." In *Science and Homosexualities*, edited by Vernon Rosario, 26–45. New York: Routledge, 1997.

————. *Karl Heinrich Ulrichs: Pioneer of the Modern Gay Movement*. San Francisco: Peremptory Publications, 2002.

Kent, Kathryn R. *Making Girls into Women: American Women's Writing and the Rise of Lesbian Identity*. Durham: Duke University Press, 2003.

Kern, Stephen. *A Cultural History of Causality: Science, Murder Novels, and Systems of Thought*. Princeton: Princeton University Press, 2004.

Kimmel, Michael. *Manhood in America: A Cultural History*. Oxford: Oxford University Press, 2012.

King, Thomas A. *The Gendering of Men: 1600–1750*, vols 1 and 2. Madison: University of Wisconsin, 2004, 2008.

Kinsey, Alfred C., Wardell B. Pomeroy, and Clyde E. Martin. *Sexual Behavior in the Human Male*. Bloomington: Indiana University Press, 1975.

Kishi, Madoka. "The Erotics of Race Suicide: The Making of Whiteness and the Death Drive in the Progressive Era, 1880–1920." PhD diss, Louisiana State University, 2015.

Kluft, David. "What is More Defamatory? A False Accusation of Homophobia or Homosexuality?" September 3, 2014. http://www.trademarkand copyrightlawblog.com/2014/09/whatismore/.

Korobkin, Laura Hanft. *Criminal Conversations: Sentimentality and Nineteenth-Century Legal Stories of Adultery*. New York: Columbia University Press, 1998.

Kotar, S. L., and J. E. Gessler. *Cholera: A Worldwide History*. New York: McFarland, 2014.

Koven, Seth. *Slumming: Sexual and Social Politics in Victorian London*. Princeton: Princeton University Press, 2004.

Kraepelin, Emil. "On the Question of Degeneration by Emil Kraepelin (1908)." *History of Psychiatry* 18.3 (2007): 399–404.

Krafft-Ebing, Richard von. *Psychopathia Sexualis: With Especial Reference to the Antipathic Sexual Instinct*. Translated by Franklin S. Klaf. New York: Stein and Day, 1965.

Kunzel, Regina. *Criminal Intimacy: Prison and the Uneven History of Modern American Sexuality*. Chicago: University of Chicago Press, 2008.

———. "Situating Sex." *GLQ* 8.3 (2002): 253–70.

Kuzniar, Alice A. "Introduction." In *Outing Goethe and His Age*, 1–32. Palo Alto: Stanford University Press, 1996.

Ladenson, Elisabeth. "Colette for Export Only." *Yale French Studies* 90 (1996): 25–46.

LaFleur, Greta. *The Natural History of Sexuality in Early America*. Baltimore: Johns Hopkins University Press, 2018.

Lanser, Susan S. "1928: Sapphic Modernity and the Sexuality of History." In "What is Sexual Modernity," edited by Benjamin Kahan. Special issue, *Modernism/modernity Print-Plus* 1.3, October 25, 2016. https://modernism modernity.org/forums/posts/1928-sapphic-modernity-and-sexuality -history.

———. *The Sexuality of History: Modernity and the Sapphic, 1565–1830*. Chicago: University of Chicago Press, 2014.

Laqueur, Thomas. *Making Sex: Body and Gender from the Greeks to Freud*. Boston: Harvard University Press, 1990.

Latour, Bruno. *We Have Never Been Modern*. Translated by Catherine Potter. Cambridge: Harvard University Press, 1993.

Leck, Ralph M. *Vita Sexualis: Karl Ulrichs and the Origins of Sexual Science*. Urbana: University of Illinois Press, 2016.

Leng, Kirsten. *Sexual Politics and Feminist Science: Women Sexologists in Germany, 1900–1933*. Ithaca: Cornell University Press and Cornell University Library, 2018.

Lenz, Ludwig L. *The Memoirs of a Sexologist: Discretion and Indiscretion*. New York: Cadillac Publishing Co., 1954.

Lichtenstein, Perry M. "The 'Fairy' and the Lady Lover." *Medical Review of Reviews* 21 (1921): 369–74.

Littlewood, Ian. *Sultry Climes: Travel and Sex Since the Grand Tour*. London: John Murray, 2001.

Lim, Eng-Ben. *Brown Boys and Rice Queens: Spellbinding Performance in the Asias*. New York: New York University Press, 2013.

Litvak, Joseph. *The Un-Americans: Jews, the Blacklist, and Stoolpigeon Culture*. Durham: Duke University Press, 2009.

Lochrie, Karma. *Heterosyncrasies: Female Sexuality When Normal Wasn't*. Minneapolis: University of Minnesota Press, 2005.

Loftin, Craig M. *Masked Voices: Gay Men and Lesbians in Cold War America*. Albany: SUNY Press, 2012.

Logan, Cheryl A. *Hormones, Heredity, Race: Spectacular Failure in Interwar Vienna*. New Brunswick: Rutgers University Press, 2013.

Lombroso, Cesare. *The Man of Genius*. London: Walter Scott, 1891.

Looby, Christopher. "The Literariness of Sexuality: Or, How to Do the (Literary) History of (American) Sexuality." *American Literary History* 25.4 (2013): 841–54.

———. "Marmoreanism." Paper presented at the MLA Convention, Philadelphia, January 6, 2017.

———. "Strange Sensations: Sex and Aesthetics in 'The Counterpane.'" In *Melville and Aesthetics*, edited by Geoffrey Sanborn and Samuel Otter, 65–84. New York: Palgrave, 2011.

Love, Heather. *Feeling Backward: Loss and the Politics of Queer History*. Cambridge: Harvard University Press, 2009.

———. "Made for TV." In "Virtual Roundtable on *Orange is the New Black*." *Public Books*, May 15, 2014. http://www.publicbooks.org/virtual-roundtable -on-orange-is-the-new-black/.

———. "The Performative and the Peri-." *Women's Review of Books* 21.6 (2004): 12–13.

Lowry, Malcolm. *Malcolm Lowry's "La Mordida": A Scholarly Edition*, edited by Patrick A. McCarthy. Athens: University of Georgia Press, 1996.

———. *Under the Volcano*. New York: Lippincott, 1971.

Luibhéid, Eithne. *Entry Denied: Controlling Sexuality at the Border*. Minneapolis: University of Minnesota Press, 2002.

Lynch, Michael. "'Here is Adhesiveness': From Friendship to Homosexuality." *Victorian Studies* 29.1 (1985): 67–96.

Lyons, Andrew P., and Harriet D. Lyons. *Irregular Connections: A History of Anthropology and Sexuality*. Lincoln: University of Nebraska Press, 2004.

Lyons, Clare A. "Mapping an Atlantic Sexual Culture: Homoeroticism in Eighteenth-Century Philadelphia." *William and Mary Quarterly* 60.1 (2003): 119–54.

Macnish, Robert. "Adhesiveness." *Lancet* 2 (6 August 1836): 633.

Mahfouz, Naguib. *Midaq Alley*. New York: Anchor Books, 1992.

Mailer, Norman. "An Appeal to Lillian Hellman and Mary McCarthy." *New York Times Book Review* (May 11, 1980): 3, 33.

Mann, Thomas. *Death in Venice and Other Tales*. Translated by Joachim Neugroschel. New York: Penguin, 1999.

Mao, Douglas. *Fateful Beauty: Aesthetic Environments, Juvenile Development, and Literature, 1860–1960*. Princeton: Princeton University Press, 2008.

———. "A Shaman in Common: Lewis, Auden, and the Queerness of Liberalism." In *Bad Modernisms*, edited by Douglas Mao and Rebecca L. Walkowitz, 206–37. Durham: Duke University Press, 2006.

Marcus, Sharon. *Between Women: Friendship, Desire, and Marriage in Victorian England*. Princeton: Princeton University Press, 2007.

Massaro, Toni M. "Gay Rights, Thick and Thin." *Stanford Law Review* 49.1 (1996): 45–110.

Masten, Jeffrey. "Material Cavendish: Paper, Performance, 'Sociable Virginity.'" *MLQ* 65.1 (2004): 49–68.

———. "More or Less Queer." In *Shakesqueer: A Queer Companion to the Complete Works of Shakespeare*, edited by Madhavi Menon, 309–18. Durham: Duke University Press, 2011.

———. *Queer Philologies: Sex, Language, and Affect in Shakespeare's Time*. Philadelphia: University of Pennsylvania Press, 2016.

Matthiessen, F. O., and Russell Cheney. *Rat and the Devil: Journal Letters of F. O. Matthiessen and Russell Cheney*. Brooklyn: Shoe String Press, 1978.

Mbembe, Achille. "Necropolitics." Translated by Libby Meintjes. *Public Culture* 15.1 (2003): 11–40.

McCarthy, Mary. "Verification." Supreme Court of the State of New York. Testimony. New York, NY. 18 October 1980. Lillian Hellman Papers, Harry Ransom Center, The University of Texas at Austin, Box 78, Folder 4.

McGarry, Molly. *Ghosts of Futures Past: Spiritualism and the Cultural Politics of Nineteenth-Century America*. Berkeley: University of California Press, 2008.

McGuire, Hunter, and G. Frank Lydston, *Sexual Crimes Among the Southern Negroes, Scientifically Considered: An Open Correspondence Between Hunter McGuire and G. Frank Lydston*. Louisville, KY: Renz and Henry, 1893.

McIntosh, Mary. "The Homosexual Role." *Social Problems* 16.2 (1968): 182–92.

Medd, Jodie. *Lesbian Scandal and the Culture of Modernism*. New York: Cambridge University Press, 2012.

Merrick, Jeffrey. "Sodomitical Inclinations in Early Eighteenth-Century Paris." *Eighteenth-Century Studies* 30.3 (1997) 289–95.

———. "Sodomitical Scandals and Subcultures in the 1720s." *Men and Masculinities* 1.4 (1999): 365–84.

Meyerowitz, Joanne. *How Sex Changed: A History of Transsexuality in the United States*. Cambridge: Harvard University Press, 2002.

Miller, D. A. "Anal Rope." *Representations* 32 (1990): 114–33.

———. *Place for Us (Essay on the Broadway Musical)*. Cambridge: Harvard University Press, 1998.

Miller, Emma V., and Simon J. James. "A Body Undressed for Text: *Trilby* in Parts." *Feminist Theory* 17.1 (2016): 83–105.

Mitchell, Peta. *Contagious Metaphor*. London: Bloomsbury, 2012.

Mitford, Nancy. *Love in a Cold Climate*. New York: Vintage, 2010.

Moll, Albert. *Perversions of the Sex Instinct: A Study of Sexual Inversion*. Translated by Maurice Popkin. Newark: Julian Press, 1931.

Montagu, M. F. Ashley. *Man's Most Dangerous Myth: The Fallacy of Race*. New York: Columbia University Press, 1942.

Montesquieu, Charles de. *The Spirit of the Laws*. Edited by Anne M. Cohler, Basia C. Miller, and Harold S. Stone. Cambridge: Cambridge University Press, 1989.

Moon, Michael. *Disseminating Whitman: Revision and Corporeality in Leaves of Grass.* Cambridge: Harvard University Press, 1991.

———. *A Small Boy and Others: Imitation and Initiation in American Culture from Henry James to Andy Warhol.* Durham: Duke University Press, 1998.

Moon, Michael, and Eve Kosofsky Sedgwick. "Divinity: A Dossier, A Performance Piece, A Little-Understood Emotion." In *Tendencies*, 215–51. Durham: Duke University Press, 1993.

Moore, Alison M. *Sexual Myths of Modernity: Sadism, Masochism, and Historical Teleology.* Lantham, MD: Lexington Books, 2016.

Morel, Bénédict Augustin. *Traité des Dégénérescences.* Paris: J. B. Baillière, 1857.

Morrison, Justine. *The Politics of Anxiety in Nineteenth Century American Literature.* Cambridge: Cambridge University Press, 2011.

Mort, Frank. *Dangerous Sexualities: Medico-Moral Politics in England Since 1830.* New York: Routledge, 1987.

Mott, Frank Luther. *Golden Multitudes: The Story of Best Sellers in the United States.* New York: Macmillan, 1947.

Mott, Luiz. "Historical Roots of Homosexuality in the Lusophone Atlantic." In *Cultures of the Lusophone Black Atlantic*, edited by Nancy Priscilla Naro, Roger Sansi-Roca, and David H. Treece, 75–95. New York: Palgrave, 2007.

Mumford, Kevin. *Interzones: Black/White Sex Districts in Chicago and New York in the Early Twentieth Century.* New York: Columbia University Press, 1997.

Murphy, Brenda. *The Provincetown Players and the Culture of Modernity.* Cambridge: Cambridge University Press, 2005.

Murphy, Kevin P. *Political Manhood: Red Bloods, Mollycoddles, and the Politics of Progressive Era Reform.* New York: Columbia University Press, 2008.

Murphy, Timothy. *Gay Science: The Ethics of Sexual Orientation Research.* New York: Columbia University Press, 1997.

Murray, Stephen O., and Will Roscoe. "Africa and African Homosexualities: An Introduction." In *Boy-Wives and Female Husbands: Studies of African Homosexualities*, edited by Stephen O. Murray and Will Roscoe, 1–20. New York: St. Martin's Press, 1998.

Musser, Amber. "The Literary Symptom: Krafft-Ebing and the Invention of Masochism." In *Mediated Deviance and Social Otherness: Interrogating Influential Representations*, edited by Kylo-Patrick Hart, 286–94. Newcastle, UK: Cambridge Scholars Publishing, 2007.

Naiman, Eric. *Sex in Public: The Incarnation of Early Soviet Ideology.* Princeton: Princeton University Press, 1997.

Nealon, Jeffrey. *Foucault Beyond Foucault: Power and Its Intensifications since 1984.* Palo Alto: Stanford University Press, 2007.

Nelson, Deborah. *Tough Enough: Arbus, Arendt, Didion, McCarthy, Sontag, Weil.* Chicago: University of Chicago Press, 2017.

Nelson, Maggie. *The Argonauts.* Minneapolis: Graywolf Press, 2015.

Nicolazzo, Sarah. "Henry Fielding's *The Female Husband* and the Sexuality of Vagrancy." *Eighteenth Century: Theory and Interpretation* 55.4 (2014): 335–53.

Nordau, Max. *Degeneration.* Lincoln: University of Nebraska, 1993.

Northrop, Martin J. "Booked: Sexuality and Taste in American Crime Fiction." PhD diss., Fordham University, 2015.

Norton, Rictor. *Georgian Underworld.* 2003. http://rictornorton.co.uk/gu00.htm.

———. *Mother Clap's Molly House: The Gay Subculture in England, 1700–1830.* London: Gay Men's Press, 1992.

———. *Myth of the Modern Homosexual: Queer History and the Search for Cultural Unity.* London: Cassell, 1998.

Nussbaum, Felicity. *Torrid Zones: Maternity, Sexuality, and Empire in Eighteenth-Century English Narratives.* Baltimore: Johns Hopkins University Press, 1995.

Oosterhuis, Harry. *Homosexuality and Male Bonding in Pre-Nazi Germany.* Trans. Hubert Kennedy. New York: Harrington Park Press, 1991.

———. *Stepchildren of Nature: Krafft-Ebing, Psychiatry, and the Making of Sexual Identity.* Chicago: University of Chicago Press, 2000.

Orgel, Stephen. *Impersonations: The Performance of Gender in Shakespeare's England.* Cambridge: Cambridge University Press, 1996.

Orwell, George. *Down and Out in Paris and London.* New York: Harcourt Brace Javanovich, 1961.

Otis, Margaret. "A Perversion Not Commonly Noted." *Journal of Abnormal Psychology* 8.2 (June-July 1913): 113–16.

Owen, Alex. *The Darkened Room: Women, Power, and Spiritualism in Late Nineteenth Century England.* Chicago: University of Chicago Press, 1989.

Oziebio, Barbara. *Susan Glaspell: A Critical Biography.* Chapel Hill: University of North Carolina Press, 2000.

Park, Robert E., Ernest W. Burgess, and Roderick Duncan McKenzie. *The City.* Chicago: University of Chicago Press, 1925.

Parrish, Susan Scott. *American Curiosity: Cultures of Natural History in the Colonial British Atlantic World.* Chapel Hill: University of North Carolina Press, 2006.

Patterson, Rebecca. *The Riddle of Emily Dickinson.* Cambridge: Houghton Mifflin, 1951.

Pease, Donald E. "New Americanists: Revisionist Interventions into the Canon." *Boundary 2* 17.1 (1990): 1–37.

Pechenick, Eitan Adam, Christopher M. Danforth, and Peter Sheridan Dodds. "Characterizing the Google Book Corpus: Strong Limits to Inferences of Socio-Cultural and Linguistic Evolution." *PLOS ONE*, October 7, 2015. http://journals.plos.org/plosone/article?id=10.1371/journal.pone.0137041.

Pende, Nicola. *Constitutional Inadequacies: An Introduction to the Study of Abnormal Constitutions.* Translated by Sante Naccarati. Philadelphia: Lea and Febiger, 1928.

Peniston, William A. *Pederasts and Others: Urban Culture and Sexual Identity in Nineteenth-Century Paris.* Binghamton, NY: Harrington Park Press, 2004.

Peppis, Paul. *Sciences of Modernism: Ethnography, Sexology, and Psychology.* Cambridge: Cambridge University Press, 2014.

Phillips, Kim M., and Barry Reay. *Sex Before Sexuality: A Premodern History.* Cambridge: Polity, 2008.

Pollack, Vivian. "'Bringing Help for the Sick': Whitman and Prophetic Biography." In *Leaves of Grass: The Sesquicentennial Essays*, edited by Susan Belasco, Ed Folsom, and Kenneth M. Price, 244–65. Lincoln: University of Nebraska Press, 2007.

Posner, Richard A. *Sex and Reason.* Cambridge: Harvard University Press, 1992.

Potter, Sarah. "'Undesirable Relations': Same-Sex Relationships and the Meaning of Sexual Desire at a Women's Reformatory During the Progressive Era." *Feminist Studies* 30.2 (2004): 394–415.

Prime-Stevenson, Edward. *The Intersexes: A Study of Similisexualism as a Problem in Social Life*: privately printed, 1908.

Prosser, Jay. *Second Skins: The Body Narratives of Transsexuality.* New York: Columbia University Press, 1998.

Puar, Jasbir K. *Terrorist Assemblages: Homonationalism in Queer Times.* Durham: Duke University Press, 2007.

Purcell, L. Edward. "Trilby and Trilby-Mania: The Beginning of the Bestseller System." *Journal of Popular Culture* 11.1 (1977): 62–76.

Raffalovich, Marc-André. *Uranism and Unisexuality: A Study of Different Manifestations of the Sexual Instinct.* New York: Palgrave, 2016.

Ragan, Bryant T., Jr. "The Enlightenment Confronts Homosexuality." In *Homosexuality in Modern France*, edited by Jeffrey Merrick and Bryant T. Ragan, Jr., 8–29. Oxford: Oxford University Press, 1996.

Randolph, Paschal Beverly. *The Ansairetic Mystery: A New Revelation Concerning Sex!.* In *Paschal Beverly Randolph: A Nineteenth-Century Black American Spiritualist, Rosicrucian, and Sex Magician*, 311–26. Albany: State University of New York Press, 1997.

———. *Dealings with the Dead.* Utica, NY: Published by M. J. Randolph, 1861–62.

———. *Eulis! The History of Love, its Wondrous Magic, Chemistry, Rules, Laws, Moods and Rationale; Being the Third Revelation of Soul and Sex.* Toledo, OH: Randolph Publishing Company, 1896.

———. *The Grand Secret; Or, Physical Love in Health and Disease.* In *Rosicrucianism in America*, edited by J. Gordon Melton, 1–87. New York: Garland Publishing, 1990.

———. *Ravalette: The Rosicrucian's Story.* Quakertown, PA: Philosophical Publishing Company, 1939.

———. *The Unveiling, Or What I think of Spiritualism.* Newburyport: William H. Huse and Co., 1860.

Reay, Barry. *New York Hustlers: Masculinity and Sex in Modern America.* Manchester: Manchester University Press, 2010.

Reid-Pharr, Robert F. *Archives of Flesh: African America, Spain, and Post-Humanist Critique.* New York: New York University Press, 2016.

Reizenstein, Ludwig von. *The Mysteries of New Orleans.* Translated and edited by Steven Rowan. Baltimore: Johns Hopkins University Press, 2002.

Rey, Michel. "Parisian Homosexuals Create a Lifestyle, 1700–1750: The Police Archives." In *'Tis Nature's Fault: Unauthorized Sexuality during the Enlightenment*, edited by Robert Purks Maccubbin, 179–91. Cambridge: Cambridge University Press, 1988.

———. "Police and Sodomy in Eighteenth Century Paris: From Sin to Disorder." In *The Pursuit of Sodomy: Male Homosexuality in Renaissance and Enlightenment Europe*, edited by Kent Gerard and Gert Hekma, 129–46. New York: Haworth Press, 1989.

Rich, Adrienne. "Compulsory Heterosexuality and Lesbian Existence." *Signs* 5.4 (1980): 631–60.

Rifkin, Mark. *When Did Indians Become Straight? Kinship, the History of Sexuality, and Native Sovereignty*. Oxford: Oxford University Press, 2011.

Ritzenberg, Aaron. *The Sentimental Touch: The Language of Feeling in the Age of Managerialism*. New York: Fordham University Press, 2013.

Rivers, W. C. *Walt Whitman's Anomaly*. London: George Allen & Company, 1913.

Robinson, William J. "Our Sexual Misery: Some Informal Remarks." *American Journal of Urology and Sexology* (1917): 241–55.

Rodríguez, Juana María. *Sexual Futures, Queer Gestures, and Other Latina Longings*. New York: New York University Press, 2014.

Rohy, Valerie. *Lost Causes: Narrative, Etiology, and Queer Theory*. Oxford: Oxford University Press, 2015.

Rosario, Vernon A. "Homosexual Bio-Histories: Genetic Nostalgias, and the Quest for Paternity." In *Science and Homosexualities*, edited by Vernon A. Rosario. New York: Routledge, 1997.

Ross, Marlon B. "Beyond the Closet as Raceless Paradigm." In *Black Queer Studies: A Critical Anthology*, edited by E. Patrick Johnson and Mae G. Henderson, 161–89. Durham: Duke University Press, 2005.

———. *Manning the Race: Reforming Black Men in the Jim Crow Era*. New York: NYU Press, 2004.

Roughead, William. *Bad Companions*. New York: Duffield and Green, 1931.

Rousseau, G. S. "The Pursuit of Homosexuality in the Eighteenth Century: 'Utterly Confused Category' and/or Rich Repository?" In *'Tis Nature's Fault: Unauthorized Sexuality during the Enlightenment*, edited by Robert Purks Maccubbin, 132–68. Cambridge: Cambridge University Press, 1988.

Rubin, Gayle. "Geologies of Queer Studies: It's Déjà Vu All Over Again." In *Deviations: A Gayle Rubin Reader*, 347–56. Durham: Duke University Press, 2011.

Russo, Vito. *The Celluloid Closet: Homosexuality in the Movies*. New York: Harper and Row, 1987.

Saint-Amour, Paul. "Counterfactual." Paper presented at the Modernist Studies Association conference, November 2015.

Saleeby, Caleb Williams. *The Methods of Race-Regeneration*. New York: Moffat, Yard, and Company, 1911.

Sarlos, Robert Karoly. *Jig Cook and the Provincetown Players: Theatre in Ferment*. Amherst: University of Massachussets Press, 1982.

Schaffner, Anna Katharina. "Fiction as Evidence: On the Uses of Literature in Nineteenth-Century Sexological Discourse." *Comparative Literature Studies* 48.2 (2011): 165–99.

Schick, Irvin C. *The Erotic Margin: Sexuality and Spatiality in Alterist Discourse.* New York: Verso, 1999.

Schuller, Kyla. *The Biopolitics of Feeling: Race, Sex, and Impressibility in the Nineteenth Century United States.* Durham: Duke University Press, 2017.

Scully, Robert. *A Scarlet Pansy.* Edited by Robert J. Corber. New York: Fordham University Press, 2016.

Sedgwick, Eve Kosofsky. *Between Men: English Literature and Male Homosocial Desire.* New York: Columbia University Press, 1985.

———. "Epidemics of the Will." In *Tendencies*, 130–42. Durham: Duke University Press, 1993.

———. *Epistemology of the Closet.* Berkeley and Los Angeles: University of California Press, 1990.

———. "How to Bring Your Kids Up Gay: The War on Effeminate Boys." In *Tendencies*, 154–64. Durham: Duke University Press, 1993.

———. "Jane Austen and the Masturbating Girl." *Critical Inquiry* 17 (1991): 818–37.

———. "Privilege of Unknowing: Diderot's *The Nun*." In *Tendencies*, 23–51. Durham: Duke University Press, 1993.

———. *Touching Feeling.* Durham: Duke University Press, 2003.

See, Sam. "The Comedy of Nature: Darwinian Feminism in Virginia Woolf's Between the Acts." *Modernism/modernity* 17.3 (2010): 639–67.

Segalen, Victor. *Essay on Exoticism: An Aesthetics of Diversity.* Durham: Duke University Press, 2002.

Seitler, Dana. *Atavistic Tendencies: The Culture of Science in American Modernity.* Minneapolis: University of Minnesota Press, 2008.

———. "Queer Physiognomies, or How Many Ways Can We Do the History of Sexuality?" *Criticism* 46.1 (2004): 71–102.

Sengoopta, Chandak. *The Most Secret Quintessence of Life: Sex, Glands, and Hormones, 1850–1950.* Chicago: University of Chicago Press, 2006.

Shah, Nayan. *Contagious Divides: Epidemics and Race in San Francisco's Chinatown.* Berkeley: University of California Press, 2001.

———. *Stranger Intimacy: Contesting Race, Sexuality, and the Law in the North American West.* Berkeley: University of California Press, 2011.

Shapiro, Stephen. "Of Mollies: Class and Same-Sex Sexualities in the Eighteenth Century." In *In a Queer Place: Sexuality and Belonging in British and European Contexts*, edited by Kate Chedgzoy, Emma Francis, and Murray Pratt, 155–76. London: Ashgate, 2002.

Shepard, Todd. "'Something Notably Erotic': Politics, 'Arab Men,' and Sexual Revolution in Post-decolonization France, 1962–1974." *Journal of Modern History* 84.1 (2012): 80–115.

Sigel, Lisa Z. "Filth in the Wrong People's Hands: Postcards and the Expansion of Pornography in Britain and the Atlantic World, 1880–1914." *Journal of Social History* 33.4 (2000): 859–85.

Sinfield, Alan. *Out on Stage: Lesbian and Gay Theatre in the Twentieth Century.* New Haven: Yale University Press, 1999.

———. *Sexuality and Power.* New York: Columbia University Press, 2004.

Sinha, Mrinalini. *Colonial Masculinity: The "Manly Englishman" and the "Effeminate Bengali" in the Late Nineteenth Century.* Manchester: Manchester University Press, 1995.

Smith, Alison. "Other New Plays." *World* (November 18th, 1929): 15.

Snowden, Frank M. *Naples in the Time of Cholera, 1884–1911.* Cambridge: Cambridge University Press, 1995.

Somerville, Siobhan. *Queering the Color Line: Race and the Invention of Homosexuality in American Culture.* Durham: Duke University Press, 2000.

Sommer, Andreas. "Psychical Research and the Origins of American Psychology: Hugo Münsterberg, William James, and Eusapia Palladino." *History of the Human Sciences* 25.2 (2012): 23–44.

Spender, Stephen. "Introduction." In Malcolm Lowry, *Under the Volcano*, xi–xxx. New York: Lippincott, 1971.

Spillers, Hortense J. "Mama's Baby, Papa's Maybe: An American Grammar Book." *Diacritics* 17.2 (1987): 64–81.

Spivak, Gayatri. *A Critique of Postcolonial Reason: Toward a History of the Vanishing Present.* Cambridge: Harvard University Press, 1999.

Stein, Melissa N. *Measuring Manhood: Race and the Science of Masculinity, 1830–1934.* Minneapolis: University of Minnesota Press, 2015.

Steinach, Eugen. *Sex and Life: Forty Years of Biological and Medical Experiments.* New York: Viking Press, 1940.

Stoler, Ann Laura. *Race and the Education of Desire: Foucault's "History of Sexuality" and the Colonial Order of Things.* Durham: Duke University Press, 1995.

Stopes, Marie Carmichael. *Married Love: A New Contribution to the Solution of Sex Difficulties.* London: A. C. Fifield, 1919.

Stouck, David. "Anderson's Expressionist Art." In *New Essays on "Winesburg, Ohio,"* edited by John W. Crowley, 27–51. New York: Cambridge University Press, 1990.

Styron, William, to Lillian Hellman. 2 April 1980. Lillian Hellman Papers, Harry Ransom Center, The University of Texas at Austin, Box 78, Folder 5.

Sutton, Katie. "Sexological Cases and the Prehistory of Transgender Identity Politics in Interwar Germany." In *Case Studies and the Dissemination of Knowledge*, edited by Joy Damousi, Birgit Lang, and Katie Sutton, 85–103. New York: Routledge, 2015.

Symonds, John Addington. *A Problem in Modern Ethics.* London: Forgotten Books, 2012.

Tamley, B. S. "Female Exhibitionism: A Psychosexual Study." *American Journal of Urology and Sexology* (1917): 212–22.

Tardieu, Ambroise Auguste. *Étude medico-légale sur les attentats aux mœurs*. Paris: J.-B. Baillière, 1857.

Tarnowsky, Benjamin. *Anthropological, Legal, and Medical Studies on Pederasty in Europe*. New York: Falstaff Press, 1933.

Taylor, Bayard. "Twin-Love." In *"The Man Who Thought Himself a Woman" and Other Queer Nineteenth-Century Short Stories*, edited by Christopher Looby, 159–74. Philadelphia: University of Pennsylvania Press, 2017.

Terry, Jennifer. *An American Obsession: Science, Medicine, and Homosexuality in Modern Society*. Chicago: University of Chicago Press, 1999.

Thomas, Kendall. "Beyond the Privacy Principle." *Columbia Law Review* 92.6 (1992): 1431–516.

Thurschwell, Pamela. *Literature, Technology, and Magical Thinking, 1880–1920*. Cambridge: Cambridge University Press, 2001.

Titus, Mary. "Cather's Creative Women and Du Maurier's Cozy Men: 'The Song of the Lark' and 'Trilby.'" *Modern Language Studies* 24.2 (1994): 27–37.

Tobin, Robert. *Peripheral Desires: The German Discovery of Sex*. Philadelphia: University of Pennsylvania Press, 2015.

———. *Warm Brothers: Queer Theory and the Age of Goethe*. Philadelphia: University of Pennsylvania Press, 2000.

Tomes, Nancy. *The Gospel of Germs: Men, Women, and the Microbe in American Life*. Cambridge: Harvard University Press, 1998.

Trask, Michael. *Cruising Modernism: Class and Sexuality in American Literature and Social Thought*. Ithaca: Cornell University Press, 2003.

Traub, Valerie. "The Past is a Foreign Country? The Times and Spaces of Islamicate Sexuality Studies." In *Islamicate Sexualities: Translations across Temporal Geographies of Desire*, edited by Kathryn Babayan and Asfaneh Najmabadi, 1–40. Cambridge: Harvard University Press, 2008.

———. "The Present Future of Lesbian Historiography." In *A Companion to Lesbian, Gay, Bisexual, Transgender, and Queer Studies*, edited by George Haggerty and Molly McGarry, 124–45. Oxford: Blackwell, 2007.

———. *The Renaissance of Lesbianism in Early Modern England*. Cambridge: Cambridge University Press, 2002.

———. *Thinking Sex with the Early Moderns*. Philadelphia: University of Pennsylvania Press, 2015.

Trumbach, Randolph. "London's Sodomites: Homosexual Behavior and Western Culture in the 18th Century." *Journal of Social History* 11.1 (1977): 1–33.

———. *Sex and the Gender Revolution*. Vol. 1, *Heterosexuality and the Third Gender in Enlightenment London*. Chicago: University of Chicago Press, 1998.

Tuhkanen, Mikko. "Breeding (and) Reading: Lesbian Knowledge, Eugenic Discipline, and *The Children's Hour*." *MFS* 48.4 (2002): 1001–40.

Turda, Marius, and Aaron Gillette. *Latin Eugenics in Comparative Perspective*. New York: Bloomsbury, 2014.

Ulrichs, Karl Heinrich. *The Riddle of "Man-Manly" Love: The Pioneering Work on Male Homosexuality*. Translated by Michael A. Lombardi-Nash. Buffalo: Prometheus Books, 1994.

Urban, Hugh. *Magia Sexualis: Sex, Magic, and Liberation in Modern Western Esotericism*. Berkeley: University of California Press, 2006.

Vaget, Hans Rudolf. "Film and Literature: The Case of 'Death in Venice': Luchino Visconti and Thomas Mann." *German Quarterly* 53.2 (1980): 159–75.

Van der Meer, Theo. "Sodom's Seed in the Netherlands: The Emergence of Homosexuality in the Early Modern Period." *Journal of Homosexuality* 34.1 (1997): 1–16.

———. "Sodomy and Its Discontents: Discourse, Desire, and the Rise of a Same-Sex Proto-Something in the Early Modern Dutch Republic." *Historical Reflections / Réflexions Historiques* 33.1 (2007): 41–67.

———. "Sodomy and the Pursuit of a Third Sex." In *Third Sex, Third Gender: Beyond Sexual Dimorphism in Culture and History*, edited by Gilbert Herdt, 137–212. New York: Zone Books, 1994.

Vessie, P. R. "The Wanderlust Impulse." *Medical Journal and Record* (July 2, 1924): 19–22.

Vicinus, Martha. "Lesbian History: All Theory and No Facts or All Facts and No Theory?" *Radical History Review* 60 (1994): 57–75.

Vining, Donald. *A Gay Diary, 1933–1946*. New York: Masquerade Books, 1996.

Vogel, Shane. *The Scene of Harlem Cabaret: Race, Sexuality, Performance*. Chicago: University of Chicago Press, 2009.

Wahlert, Lance. "The Burden of Poofs: Criminal Pathology, Clinical Scrutiny, and Homosexual Etiology in Queer Cinema." *Journal of Medical Humanities* 34.2 (2013): 149–75.

Walcott, James. "What Unbecomes a Legend Most?" *Village Voice* (March 3, 1980): 51.

Wald, Priscilla. *Contagious: Cultures, Carriers, and the Outbreak Narrative*. Durham: Duke University Press, 2008.

Walters, Suzanna Danuta. *The Tolerance Trap: How God, Genes, and Good Intentions are Sabotaging Gay Equality*. New York: New York University Press, 2014.

Ward, Jane. *Not Gay: Sex Between Straight White Men*. New York: New York University Press, 2015.

Wardley, Lynn. *Lamarck's Daughters: Fiction, Feminism, and the Power of Life*. Unpublished manuscript.

Warner, Michael. "Homo-Narcissism; or, Heterosexuality." In *Engendering Men: The Question of Male Feminist Criticism*, edited by Joseph A. Boone and Michael Cadden, 190–206. New York: Routledge, 1990.

———. "Irving's Posterity." *ELH* 67.3 (2000): 773–99.

———. *Publics and Counterpublics*. New York: Zone Books, 2002.

———. *The Trouble with Normal: Sex, Politics, and the Ethics of Queer Life*. Cambridge: Harvard University Press, 2000.

———. "Whitman Drunk." In *Breaking Bounds: Whitman and American Cultural Studies*, edited by Betsy Erkkila and Jay Grossman, 30–43. Oxford: Oxford University Press, 1996.

Warnicke, Retha. *The Rise and Fall of Anne Boleyn: Family Politics at the Court of Henry VIII.* Cambridge: Cambridge University Press, 1991.

Waters, Chris. "Sexology." In *Palgrave Advances in the Modern History of Sexuality,* edited by H. G. Cocks and Matt Houlbrook, 41–63. New York: Palgrave, 2006.

Watson, Jay. *Reading for the Body: The Recalcitrant Materiality of Southern Fiction, 1893–1985.* Athens: University of Georgia Press, 2012.

Weheliye, Alexander G. *Habeas Viscus: Racializing Assemblages, Biopolitics, and Black Feminist Theories of the Human.* Durham: Duke University Press, 2014.

Weijl, Simon. "Theoretical and Practical Aspects of Psychoanalytic Therapy of Problem Drinkers." *Quarterly Journal of Studies on Alcohol* 5.2 (1944): 200–11.

Wescott, Glenway. *Continual Lessons: The Journals of Glenway Wescott, 1937–1955.* Edited by Robert Phelps with Jerry Rosco. New York: Farrar, Straus, and Giroux, 1990.

Westphal, Carl. "Die conträre Sexualempfindung, Symptom eines neuropathischen (psychopathischen) Zustandes." *Archiv für Psychiatrie und Nerven krankheiten* 2 (1870): 73–108.

Werther, Ralph. *Autobiography of an Androgyne.* Edited by Scott Herring. New Brunswick: Rutgers University Press, 2008.

———. *The Female-Impersonators.* New York: Arno Press, 1975.

———. "The Riddle of the Underworld." http://outhistory.org/exhibits/show/earl-lind/manuscript.

Westgate, J. Chris. *Staging the Slums, Slumming the Stage: Class, Poverty, Ethnicity, and Sexuality in American Theatre, 1890–1916.* New York: Palgrave, 2014.

Whalan, Mark. *Race, Manhood, and Modernism in America: The Short Story Cycles of Sherwood Anderson and Jean Toomer.* Knoxville: University of Tennessee Press, 2007.

Wheeler, Roxann. *The Complexion of Race: Categories of Difference in Eighteenth-Century British Culture.* Philadelphia: University of Pennsylvania Press, 2000.

White, Edmund. *States of Desire: Travels in Gay America.* New York: E. P. Dutton, 1980.

White, John. *The First Century of Scandalous, Malignant Priests.* London: Printed by George Miller, dwelling in the Black-Friars, 1643.

White, Patricia. "Reading the Code(s)." In *Uninvited: Classical Hollywood Cinema and Lesbian Representability.* Bloomington: University of Indiana Press, 1999.

Whitman, Walt. "The Child's Champion." In *"The Man Who Thought Himself A Woman" and Other Queer Nineteenth-Century Short Stories,* edited by Christopher Looby, 3–12. Philadelphia: University of Pennsylvania Press, 2017.

Wilde, Oscar, and others [attributed]. *Teleny, or The Reverse of the Medal.* Edited by Amanda Caleb. Kansas City: Valancourt Books, 2010.

Williams, Raymond. *Marxism and Literature.* Oxford: Oxford University Press, 2009.

Williams, William Carlos. *In the American Grain.* New York: New Directions, 2009.

Wilson, Elizabeth A. *Psychosomatic: Feminism and the Neurological Body.* Durham: Duke University Press, 2004.

Wittig, Monique. *The Straight Mind and Other Essays.* Boston: Beacon Press, 1992.

Wolffram, Heather. *The Stepchildren of Science: Psychical Research and Parapsychology in Germany, c. 1870–1930.* Amsterdam: Rodopi, 2009.

Wood, Naomi. "Creating the Sensual Child: Paterian Aesthetics, Pederasty, and Oscar Wilde's Fairy Tales." *Marvels and Tales* 16.2 (2002): 156–70.

Wooden, Wayne S., and Jay Parker. *Men Behind Bars: Sexual Exploitation in Prison.* New York and London: Plenum Press, 1982.

Yingling, Thomas. "*Winesburg, Ohio* and the End of Collective Experience." In *New Essays on "Winesburg, Ohio.,"* edited by John W. Crowley, 99–125. New York: Cambridge University Press, 1990.

# Index

Abelove, Henry, 6, 24, 85–86, 122, 132–33
acquired sexuality, 4, 7, 13, 14, 15, 17, 103, 114, 131; becomes situational sexuality, 38
Adhesiveness, 13, 134–35
age: and the body, 45, 47, 58; and sexuality, 58–59, 64, 125–26
Ahmed, Sara, 102
AIDS, 100, 136, 146n53
Aiken, Conrad, 109
aim, sexual, 56, 122–23; Freud on, 75–77, 93, 132–33; supplanted by sexual object, 133
alcohol, 11, 87; encourages sexual perversion, 105; and homosexuality, 1, 24, 25, 102–14, 190n24, 191n27; and interracial sex, 190n21; and will, 106–7
alliance. *See* elective affinity
Amin, Kadji, 60
Anderson, Sherwood, *Winesburg, Ohio*, 24, 86–90; on land hunger, 94–96; objects and desire in, 96–99; sexuality of hands in, 90–92, 93
*anthropologia sexualis*, 21, 23, 49–51, 59, 60; as universalizing, 47, 59, 64, 135
Arac, Jonathan, 191n37
*ars erotica*, 49, 51, 60–61, 63, 80–81, 176n100; definition, 60
Asch, Sholem, 27, 155n5
Auden, W. H., 48, 90

Barnes, Djuna, 3, 25, 140n11, 141n14; *Ladies Almanack*, 17, 27, 32
Barney, Natalie Clifford, 27
Beachy, Robert, 14
Beam, Lura, 32–33
Beard, George, 46
Bech, Henning, 160n47
Bennet, Judith, 131
Bergler, Edmund, 24
Berlant, Lauren, 3
Bibler, Michael, 71, 121, 137
Blackstone, William, 109
Bloch, Iwan, 23, 24, 65, 79, 147n59; on alcohol and homosexuality, 105–6; on *anthropologia sexualis*, 47, 135; on *ars erotica*, 176n100; on causes of homosexuality, 1–2, 3, 19, 48, 54; on decompartmentalized sexuality, 113–14; on homosexuality and disease, 54; on pederasty, 125; on tropics and sexuality, 49, 50–52
body: and age, 45, 47, 58; co-opted by sexuality, 15, 45, 101; female, 29, 45; germ theory of, 23, 47, 58, 81; humoral theory of, 22–23, 46–47, 53–55, 57, 58; mis-sexed, 82–83; ownership of, 121, 123; permeable, 45, 46; perverse, 13, 189n14; phrenology's use of, 135; produces sexual identity, 15, 40; solidified, 45, 47; stability of, 45, 47, 58

Boone, Joseph, 24, 63, 118
botany, sexualized, 70–71, 102
Bourdet, Edouard, 27
Bowen, Elizabeth, 27
Brand, Adolph, 125
Braunschneider, Theresa, 131
Bray, Alan, 24, 68, 118, 119–20, 121
Browne, Stella, 24, 34
buggery: as bestiality, 121. *See also* sodomy
Burton, Richard, 22, 49, 59, 171n33; on the New World, 174n64; on Sotadic Zone, 22, 49–52, 53, 62, 127
Butler, Judith, 12, 39, 121, 141n16
Byron, Lord, 67

Canaday, Margot, 25, 35, 36, 118, 128, 129, 136, 176n94
Cannon, Thomas, 120
Carpenter, Edward: anti-industrialization, 96; *The Intermediate Sex*, 19, 46; racialized thinking of, 179n16; on Shelley, 67; *Towards Democracy*, 19; on Whitman, 68
Caserio, Robert, 64
Caspar, Johann Ludwig, 54
Cavafy, C. P., 90
celibacy, 21, 91, 101, 106, 137, 148n78
censorship, 18, 170n20
Chaddock, Charles Gilbert, 64
Chauncey, George, 25, 36, 124, 128, 129, 176n93; on masculinity, 11–12; on object choice, 96–97, 118, 131, 132; on situational homosexuality, 33–34, 37, 159n42
Cheney, Russell, 106–7
Chiang, Howard, 19, 139n1, 168n12
Chidley, William James, 29
*Children's Hour, The. See* Hellman, Lillian
Chinese immigrants, 62, 128
Clark, Leon Pierce, 107
Clarke, Simon, 97
class: and sexuality, 11–12, 25, 36, 37, 97, 116–17, 118, 128–30, 135
climate, 1, 23, 61, 64; and biology, 172n43; definition, 46–47; language of, 25; and sexuality, 22–23, 25, 47–49, 52–54, 170n23, 170n25, 171n33, 171n35
Cocteau, Jean, 108
Colette, *The Pure and the Impure*, 27
Comstock, Anthony, 18

congenital sexuality, 4, 17, 130; becomes orthodoxy, 22, 44, 45, 135–37; congenital vs. acquired debate, 4, 14–19, 22, 27, 37–38, 44, 113, 114–15, 145n51; early expressions of, 123; and object choice, 102, 130; seen as authentic, 38, 40; slower to be applied to lesbianism, 37, 41; strategic deployment of, 64; temporal stability of, 15, 21, 33; underpins modern sexual identity, 124; value claims of, 22
consent, distinguishes Western from Oriental sexualities, 59–60, 62; implicated in sexual identity, 58; legal age of, 61–62, 63, 64, 126, 178n123; in marriage, 61
Corber, Robert J., 111
coverture, 61, 82
Coviello, Peter, 5, 8, 10, 14, 25, 118, 124, 137
cross-dressing, 1, 70, 72, 101–2, 196n25
Crowley, Aleister, 20, 183n92
Crozier, Ivan, 19

Daniel, Drew, 143n39
Davenport, Charles, 55, 56
Davidson, Arnold, 24, 76, 118, 124, 132–33, 135, 140n6, 145n46
Davidson, Guy, 188n49, 202n99
Day, Douglas, 109
de Beauvoir, Simone, 31
decompartmentalization, 113
degeneration, 14, 15, 45, 55, 147n59
Delarue-Mardrus, Lucie, 27
D'Emilio, John, 15, 23, 44, 85, 90
dendrophilia, 8, 62
Denning, Michael, 88
*Der Eigene*, 19–20, 121, 125, 198n45
desire, 12, 22, 23, 39, 59, 98–99, 125; aim-based, 75–78; and alcohol, 104–5, 107–9, 111; alloerotic, 108, 109; consumer, 24, 90, 97–98, 188n50; cyclic, 27–29, 28–29, 32; forges sexual subjectivity, 58, 70, 73; heterosexual, 27, 29, 33; immutable, 58; lesbian, 3, 30–32; linked to climate, 49, 51, 53; mimetic, 72, 93, 116, 132; object-focused, 3, 26, 102; objectless, 69, 74, 75, 92; same-sex, 13, 37, 59, 82, 117, 135; sodomitic, 120; standardized by modernity, 90, 93, 98–99; untidy complexity of, 25

religious censure, 2; sequencing practices of, 24, 103, 110; on tropics, 50–51; vernacular, 2–3, 20

sexuality: and age, 45, 47, 52, 57, 58, 125–26; aim-based, 23, 69, 75, 76, 77, 78, 121, 132; vs. alliance, 69, 71, 73–74; alloerotic, 13, 108, 109, 134; of children, 38, 63–64, 178n123; and class, 11–12, 25, 36, 37, 97, 116–17, 118, 128–30, 135; and climate, 22–23, 25, 47–49, 50–54, 170n23, 170n25, 171n33; congenital vs. acquired, 4, 7, 9, 10, 13, 14, 18, 22, 27, 37, 44, 113, 114, 116, 130, 135, 137; definition, 3; and gender, 129, 130, 135; invention of, 3, 11, 24, 52, 118, 123–24; laws regulating, 18, 22, 62–64, 126, 128, 136, 177n108, 178n123; and magic, 23, 66–69, 74; models of, 12, 34, 59, 61–63, 106, 176n93; and modernity, 3, 8, 16, 29, 117; and the normal, 140n4; object-based, 12, 58, 86, 87, 96–97, 98, 129, 132; pleasure vs. truth in, 60–61; as property in the person, 121; and race, 25, 51, 62, 126, 135, 163n78, 165n84, 170n20; seasonal, 30; and sequence, 24, 102–10, 114, 134; and will, 23, 56, 79–80, 102, 104, 106–7. *See also* acquired sexuality; congenital sexuality; desire; homosexuality; inversion; lesbianism; object choice; queerness; sexual orientation; situational homosexuality

sexuality studies, 3, 4, 7, 21, 34, 66, 68, 76, 79, 85, 100, 113, 117, 147, 159n42

sexual orientation, 4, 9, 14, 24, 99, 102, 117, 135, 136

Shah, Nayan, 61–62

Shapiro, Stephen, 119

Shelley, Percy Bysshe, 67

Shepard, Todd, 171n35

Sigel, Lisa Z., 170n20

situational homosexuality, 22, 25, 30, 33; definition, 26; deprivation model of, 28, 34, 36, 37, 38, 40, 44, 104; discounted, 159n42; disinhibition model of, 104; eclipsed in late twentieth century, 44, 58; panic model of, 28, 39–40, 41, 42, 44; and sexual identity, 33, 35; stabilizes homo/hetero binary, 35, 38, 43–44; transformation model of, 28, 39, 40, 44, 106; transmuted from

acquired homosexuality, 27; among working class, 130

slavery, 23, 61, 71, 80

slumming, 128–29

Snead, W. F., 21

sodomy, 16, 37, 68, 105, 109, 119, 123, 189n8; and climate, 171n35; defended, 120–22, 123; entrapment and persecution of, 119–21, 128; heterosexual, 130; jokes about, 108; and literary form, 191n37; as proto-homosexual, 120; vagrancy and, 35

Somerville, Siobhan, 25, 118, 126, 201n85

Sommer, Andreas, 68

Spender, Stephen, 42, 108

Spillers, Hortense J., 5

Spivak, Gayatri, 62

Starling, Ernest, 46

statues: sex with, 8, 62, 132, 203n119. *See also* pygmalionism

Stein, Gertrude, 107

Steinach, Eugen, 48

Stoler, Ann Laura, 126

Stopes, Marie: *Married Love*, 20, 28; on modernity, 28

Styron, William, 42–43

Suber, Margareta, 20

subjectivity, 14, 21–22, 23, 75–76; sexual, 69, 73–75, 80, 114, 121, 124

Symonds, John Addington, 19, 20, 48, 59, 60, 64; on causes of homosexuality, 51–52

Tamassia, Arrigo, 82

Tarnowsky, Benjamin, 1

Terry, Jennifer, 14–15

theory, weak, 10, 94, 100, 102, 114; definition, 101

Thurschwell, Pamela, 68

Tobin, Robert, 48, 57, 170n27, 173n61

trade, 25, 33, 37, 130, 159n44; definition, 36

Trask, Michael, 25, 118, 128, 129

Traub, Valerie, 11, 64, 116, 131, 143n33, 164n82

Trumbach, Randolph, 24, 118, 119, 123

Tuhkanen, Mikko, 40

Ulrichs, Karl Heinrich, 16, 46, 82, 132

Urban, Hugh, 79

www.ingramcontent.com/pod-product-compliance
Lightning Source LLC
Chambersburg PA
CBHW032128020426
42334CB00016B/1079